EXCITING STORIES OF MY PERSONAL BRUSHES WITH GREATNESS:

Memoirs of Another Time (1922 to 1956)

Stories of an incredible Anglo/American family who lived in a golden era; of relations with Royalty, Heads of State, Celebrities, Heroes and Heroines, Scoundrels and Scandals; the most destructive war in the history of the world and untold historic events

Charles Austin Sherman III

authorHOUSE®

AuthorHouse™
1663 Liberty Drive
Bloomington, IN 47403
www.authorhouse.com
Phone: 1-800-839-8640

First published by AuthorHouse   3/9/2011

ISBN: 978-1-4567-4198-3 (e)
ISBN: 978-1-4567-4199-0 (sc)

Printed in the United States of America

Contents

The Roaring Twenties   1
A Flight to Remember   9
A Lesson for Life   13
A Career Change   15
An Invitation   19
Wedding of the Year   23
Welcome to Wookitipi   27
6 Connaught Street   33
Johnny Dodge: Politician, Financier, Adventurer   37
St. Peter's Court: Private Boarding School   43
A Royal Wedding   45
Mother's Coming Out Day   49
Vignettes from St. Peter's Court: 1930 to 1934   53
The Birds and the Bees   59
Johnny Dodge: Man of Mystery   61
A Question of Sensitivity   65
Roger: Super Dog   71
Two Half Brothers   75
Friends, in Eton and the Hereafter   77
Ernest and Wallis Simpson   91
Europe, Full of Surprises: Paris, 1936   109
Vienna   115
Munich   117
Berchtesgaden   119
An Extraordinary Conversation   127
Venice   131
Switzerland   137
The Musketeers   141
Farewell to Eton   153
The Phony War, 1939 to 1940   159
The Real War, at Home and Abroad   163

Several Escapes, Including the Great One   169
The Conspiracy, 1944   175
On the School Front   199
To Sea   205
The S.S. Benedict   209
On the Edge, 1942   225
Changing Places   231
Paris Liberated   245
A Matter of Life and Death   265
Karlsruhe   273
Home Again, at Last   283
Into the Movie World   287
The Russian Berlin   299
Brazil   323
Politics   337
Vignettes from New York   341
Evita Perón   351
The Great Event and After   359
The New World   369

The Roaring Twenties

It was the age of the flapper, the Charleston, and the Black Bottom dances. The age of youthful liberation, of breaking the rules and making new ones. An age that saw the arrival of the radio, the automobile, and the airplane; not to mention the telephone, women smoking, and shortened bathing suits for the ladies, which actually showed legs naked – how shocking!

It was the time for champagne and roses, wild excesses, and never-ending discoveries. It was the age of Prohibition, speakeasies, and Al Capone, and it saw the most talented, glamorous, and sophisticated Broadway of all time.

It was only four years after the end of the War to End all Wars. Those who had survived the First World War were in the mood to celebrate the miracle of still being alive. And celebrate they did.

As for me, I burst upon this world feet first, much to my beloved mother's discomfort. It was April 30, 1922. After my birth, I resided in my mother and father's apartment, high above Central Park and the busy environs of Manhattan.

My original nanny was from the East End of London, and my mother was somewhat surprised that her baby's first words were spoken with a strong cockney accent. A new and proper-speaking English nanny was quickly acquired, and, as my vocabulary increased, my East End accent disappeared into the mist of time.

As I slowly began to appreciate my situation, involving a nanny whom I liked very much and parents of whom I saw very little, I came to particularly enjoy being taken in my perambulator to Central Park, where Nanny would talk to the other nannies and I would enjoy looking at the clouds

1

and the birds and the charming environment of the park. But my favorite place to visit, particularly as I grew out of babyhood into childhood, was my grandfather's summer home at Oyster Bay, Long Island.

At the end of every May we would leave our New York apartment and set up house in a large and gracious-looking building that had been built by my grandfather after the original ancestral home had gone up in flames. It was surrounded by acres of lawn and trees leading down to the beach.

I loved Oyster Bay. The staff built me a treehouse and anchored it between the large branches of a big oak tree. If it was a pleasant day, I had lunch in my treehouse, delivered by one of the staff in a basket attached to a rope with a hook on the end. I pulled my sandwich and apple and glass of milk up to my tiny veranda – a flat part of the limb supporting my house – and ate it contentedly, master of all I surveyed. Pure heaven.

The Colgate Hoyt family lived on one side of our house. I don't remember who lived on the other side. Almost every weekend, there were huge parties of different kinds: tennis parties, and croquet parties, swimming and picnic parties, luncheon and dinner parties, and once in a while even children's parties.

All of our neighbors seemed to know each other, so whoever was giving the party for that day expected to include the neighbors and their weekend guests. My favorite parties were the ones on Saturday night that began after dinner around ten o'clock. The night festivities would always end with fireworks, which would keep me awake anyway, so even I was allowed to stay up.

What I liked most was an enormous wood and dead brush bonfire that had been laboriously erected by the staff of whichever host's part of the beach was being used. There was great competition during the summer between the staffs of the various homes, and a thousand-dollar award to the winner at the end of the season – and this was when a thousand dollars was a thousand dollars.

The bonfire would be twenty feet high and almost as wide, and it made a wonderful rumbling noise, spewing sparks into the night, while we young folk danced fiercely around the bonfire, imagining ourselves as American Indians performing a wild war dance. There was also quite a bit of skinny-dipping going on, with lots of splashing and shrieks of laughter, all very innocent.

In time, grandfather's home was sold. Today it seems like a lovely dream from another world, our summer days so full of joy and contentment in our own little Eden, surrounded by good friends: our neighbors, as well as grandfather's staff of employees who took care of the house grounds, a second family indeed, of whom we were all very fond and proud.

I was christened Charles Austin Sherman III. However, my mother started calling me Peterkins, for reasons known only to her, and by the time I had reached the terrible twosome years, my name had developed into Peter, which it has remained to this day.

My family's roots are Anglo-Saxon on both sides, my father's ancestry having been traced back to the late thirteen hundreds. There is still a Sherman Manor House in Dedham, near Colchester, in England, whence the Shermans first migrated to America in the late sixteen hundreds. The last I heard, it was a private girls' school.

Roger Sherman, my great-great-great-great-grandfather, became Governor of Connecticut, Mayor of New Haven for life, and Treasurer of Yale. I am the only member of my family who didn't go to Yale, because after I finished my secondary education at Eton College in England, I went off to war, as did most of my contemporaries. By the time I returned to England, I was simply not interested in further formal education.

Roger Sherman was a valued partner of Thomas Jefferson, who once said of him, "Without my good friend Roger Sherman, we would not have a Declaration of Independence." Sherman worked closely with Jefferson and Benjamin Franklin to draft that document. Even as British forces were killing those unsympathetic to the crown, Jefferson entrusted Sherman to lobby others at the Continental Convention to support independence. Despite all of Sherman's efforts, the vote was close. But as we know, it passed with a desperate push from Jefferson's "good friend."

As a Connecticut congressman in 1789, Sherman crafted the only working draft of the Bill of Rights known to exist today. He later served on future President James Madison's committee that created the Constitution's first ten amendments, the Bill of Rights. Sherman died in 1793 on the Senate floor. He was seventy-two.

Incidentally, Roger Sherman was the only man who signed all four of the founding documents of the United States: the Continental Association, 1774; the Declaration of Independence, 1776; the Articles of Confederation, 1777; and the Federal Constitution, 1787.

If you ever get to the Rotunda in Washington, D.C., you will see, unless they have been moved somewhere else, two tall statues on pedestals, one on either side of the main room, facing toward one another. One is of Thomas Jefferson; the other is of Roger Sherman. When I looked up at my distinguished ancestor, sculpted with a grim expression on his rugged face – for those were very grim times, with many of the signers coming to a pitiful end – I wept. I was so proud of him for what he had stood for. For the first time in my life, I realized the nature of the heritage from which I was descended. I was forty-two years old at that time.

My paternal great-great-grandfather, on my mother's side, was General William Thomas Ward of Virginia. I am also the great-grandson of Todd R. Caldwell, my mother's maternal grandfather, who was thrice elected Governor of North Carolina, a gentleman held in high esteem by many North Carolinians to this day.

My mother's marriage to my father caused quite a stir in both North and South, she being descended from the earliest settlers in the state of North Carolina, and he being from the equally highly regarded Sherman clan, among the oldest and most esteemed families in the state of New York. The social worlds in both the North and the South were enchanted with the marital amalgamation and hoped it would prove successful.

Friends who knew them at the time, both before and during the marriage, said it was like something out of a Scott Fitzgerald novel.

My parents were introduced at a costume ball at the Astor Hotel, by Dad's best friend, and from then on, it seemed to be a trip to the moon. My father, a recent Yale graduate who had served as an ambulance driver during the First World War, was a fine-looking man, blessed with an inordinate amount of charm. My mother was a great beauty, the number-one debutante of the year in Charlotte, and had charisma and charm galore. Her friends said they loved to be around her because they felt so good and upbeat while in her presence. My dad was twenty-one and my mother eighteen. Unfortunately, both she and my father were incredibly innocent and immature in spite of their veneer of sophistication. Within a few weeks of meeting, and without telling anybody, they got married in a church, with only a couple of women workers mopping the floor to act as witnesses.

According to my mother, many years later, their honeymoon night was something of a farce, since neither of them had been told about the birds and the bees. Obviously, they must have finally worked it out, or I wouldn't be here.

My mother and father became a couple in New York society. Cholly Knickerbocker, the nation's omnipotent judge and reporter of New York's social crème-de-la-crème and café society, whose daily columns in the New York *Post* were carried in newspapers all over America, took a particular interest in these two celebrities and continually wrote them up.

But there was a serpent in Eden. After a little over two years, the bubbles finally went out of the champagne. It took a while, and in the meantime they lived a very glamorous life with an equally glamorous and self-centered group of people, some brilliant and very successful due to their own talents, others just going along for the ride. Among the latter were my mother and father. They had no special goals, too much money, perhaps, and too much time on their hands. Adding to my parents' personal situation was another equally traumatic experience in the making: serious cracks were beginning to appear in the Sherman business empire.

My grandfather, whom I loved more than I did my father, was a dear, sweet, good man, a poet and adventurer perhaps, but not a businessman. He was, and had been for many years, the head of the Sherman business, with a junior partner who had handled the business side for him with considerable success. But the partner had died eighteen months before, and now the Sherman business, which had been the major distributor of cotton on the Eastern Seaboard for generations, was being subverted by newly discovered substitutes.

Adding to this calamity, my dear grandfather was losing enormous sums of money on investments of dubious reward. One such venture involved renting a large ship with captain and crew, with machinery brought aboard that had been designed and specially built at great expense under grandfather's direction. The purpose? To filter gold from the sea. Naturally, no gold was found. The captain remained permanently drunk. The crew complained in a strange language of being seasick and remained below deck most of the time. The ship's timetable was extended again and again in the desperate search for the unaccommodating gold, and the ship itself almost sank during a ghastly storm. But enough of that debacle. I won't tell you any more: You've got the gist.

As the bloom leaves the rose, so did my parents' passion for glitter and celebrity. Worse still, their relationship with each other was breaking down. I don't doubt that there was blame on both sides, but Dad's extreme extravagances and his lack of responsibility toward his wife and son were a big part of it, leading to the eventual breakup.

On the other side of the coin was a passionate, undated love letter that Dad inadvertently found in a box, on my mother's dresser, written to her by his best friend, the one who had introduced him to her. He refused to believe of her protestations that the letter referred to a brief and very innocent relationship before she ever met my father, demanding to know why she had kept it unless the affair was still going on. Nothing my mother said would appease him.

Years later Mother told me her side of the story: She did have a teenage crush on Dad's friend, but it happened months before she met my father and it had already gone the way of other teenage crushes. But she had been touched by the friend's letter and had put it in the bottom drawer of the box that rested on her dresser. Time is a great healer, and she had soon returned to her exuberant teenage lifestyle, the relationship erased from her mind as was the letter, though they remained friends until Dad claimed her for his own.

She regretted not having burned the letter, but she felt that her marriage was on the rocks even before her husband discovered it. Dad never spoke to his best friend again.

Though the Sherman business was falling apart, it was doing so honorably, with every bank and company to which it might be owing money being fully repaid down to the last cent. In order to accomplish this, Grandfather sold the Oyster Bay house, as well as his house in town, and went deeply into his reserves. It was a sickening end to a great dynasty, but inevitable.

Of course, all of this financial downgrading and adapting to a lesser standard of living took a few years, and other members of the family not directly involved with the business provided any funds needed to ensure that Grandfather and Grandmother lived comfortably for the rest of their lives.

My parents' marriage had come to a sad but amicable end. Dad was now on his own, and he decided to try his luck in California, where I was later told he married another lady, said to be the love of his life. I hope she was. She died from cancer not long into their marriage. I never saw my father again.

But what about Mother and me? She, completely untutored for the workplace, was suddenly faced with the biggest challenge of her young life – finding a job.

Mother had never realized just how popular and beloved she was until her life with my father crumbled. She was not just a beautiful lady. People have told me that on first meeting her they were dazzled by the loveliness of her personality, her warmth, and her intuitive talent for asking all the right questions.

Her behavior, even in her teens, was never studied, always sincere, always natural. She loved to laugh, and her laughter was infectious.

Wherever she went, she drew people to her, both men and women, and it wasn't long before the group was having the time of their lives. This charismatic power endured over her entire lifetime, helping to ease the path for many great projects that she instigated and achieved in her life, some of them against enormous odds, as you will read later.

Looking back on it now, I realize what a prize she must have been, even though she was entering the work force in her early twenties, utterly unprepared to earn her own living. But despite her lack of training, modeling agencies, advertising companies, beauty companies, and cigarette companies all vied for her signature on a contract.

However, Mother couldn't make up her mind, mainly because none of the offers really appealed to her.

Fortunately for her and me, a good friend of grandfather's, Emil Pfizer, head of Pfizer Pharmecuticals, stepped into the picture when he realized the situation. Having been a frequent guest at grandfather's country home, and elder statesman to my mother these past summers that she had resided at Oyster Bay, Emil arranged with my grandfather that he would become an unofficial surrogate father to my mother and her son, Peter. Emil kept us in Dad's apartment, and added a governess for me, a lady whom I got to love very quickly, for she became the best governess that any boy could every have. She was to be my governess and teacher and good friend from four years old to six and a half. Her name was Miss Milligan.

Emil Pfizer was an unassuming looking man, belying his kindness and astute mind, and he treated my mother as he would treat his most gorgeous orchid, in awe and with much respect. He was enchanted by her and very kind to me, and I became quite fond of him. For her part, mother was grateful to have Emil in her life, and I think she genuinely enjoyed his friendship. Indeed, he added a good sum of money for Miss Milligan and me to see and experience more of the country. "Travel is the best education," he would say, and so travel we did, leaving New York in some different direction for at least a couple of months, two or three times a year. For me, it was three years of pure heaven, and it matured me a bit beyond my age group. But I was still a child, with childlike fantasies. For example, at six years old, I still believed in Santa Claus.

A Flight to Remember

I'm not sure exactly, but I believe it was sometime in the spring of 1928, while she was visiting Mexico City with Emil Pfizer, that Mother met Ann Morrow, the daughter of the American ambassador to Mexico.

On being advised that Emil Pfizer was in town on a visit with my mother, the ambassador immediately extended an invitation to the two of them for dinner at the embassy.

In case you are wondering, I can tell you that, whenever they stayed at a hotel together, their suites were always on separate floors. Emil, a bachelor, was impeccably correct, a careful guardian of my mother's reputation.

Sometime before their arrival, Charles Lindbergh had recently become the first man to fly the Atlantic Ocean solo in his single-engine plane, the *Spirit of St. Louis*. This feat made him a world-class hero of fantastic stature. He had, in fact, been invited by the Mexican government to be honored by the Mexican people.

According to Mother, who never failed to get to the bottom of rumors, whether true or false, she was able to confirm what she had heard in New York: that Charles Lindbergh, during his tremendous reception from the Mexican government and people, had managed to fall in love with the American ambassador's daughter, Ann Morrow. He was indeed courting her, though mostly from a considerable distance, since all the world wanted to see the incredible all-American hero, thus keeping him on the go as an ambassador of goodwill for the United States.

Apparently, Lindbergh had already taught Ann the rudiments of flying, and she had followed his advice to practice her flying skills every day that weather would allow. She had already gotten her pilot's license by the time Mother and Emil met her.

9

Ann was about to return to America with her father, who had business at the State Department in a couple of weeks. Since she had discovered that Mother had a small son who had never been in an airplane, she proposed that, when she left Washington for New York ahead of her father, she would fly Miss Milligan and me with her from Roosevelt Field, the very airport from which her future husband had taken off in the *Spirit of St. Louis* to fly the Atlantic. Wow!

Among Mother's many lucky beaus had been a president and owner of a bank, who would have preferred flying to banking but found it wasn't as lucrative; nonetheless, he kept his own plane on his own landing strip on his country estate outside Charlotte, North Carolina. He and Mother had spent many a weekend flying to various destinations in that state, where his friends and their wives welcomed them on their own landing strips or at nearby airfields. There they would lunch and spend the afternoon golfing, playing tennis, or fishing in a nearby stream, followed by tea served in the proper English manner, before winging back to Charlotte.

Mother loved flying, but she told me that she felt she might prove to be a distraction for me if she went along; instead, this was to be my day to enjoy flying with Ann Morrow, and she was glad for me to have such an opportunity. So a week later, Emil, Mother, Miss Milligan and I were chauffeured out to Roosevelt Field, an airport on Long Island, where Ann Morrow received us warmly and took my governess and me to the plane. It was a small, enclosed passenger plane, with one engine, if I remember correctly; the engine, which had already been started, was making, to my youthful ears, one heck of a noise. I was excited but also fearful, when I realized that I was about to be taken up into the sky by this thundering, shaking machine.

Miss Milligan took my hand and tried to seat me next to the window, but I didn't want to look out and I sat in the inside seat, a very scared little boy. The airplane began to make even more noise as the engine increased in speed and the plane raced down the runway. That was enough for me! I jumped out of my seat and lay in a fetal position on the floor, where I felt a bit safer in spite of the vibration from the metal floor.

Finally, the plane's engine calmed down, and we seemed to have reached the altitude we were supposed to reach. Gingerly, I got up from the floor and, after regaining a little bit of confidence, I asked Miss Milligan if I could sit by the window. She gave up her seat to me, and I was met by the most exciting sight I had ever seen. We were approaching nothing less than Niagara Falls, still in the distance, bathed by the morning sun, a great mist shrouding the upper level of the falls.

I was suddenly aware that Miss Milligan had moved out of her seat, and Ann Morrow had taken it; she lifted me up so that I was standing on the seat and getting an even better view then before. I got very agitated when I suddenly thought there was no one at the controls of the plane, but she assured me that she had brought along a copilot, and then began to describe what we were seeing beneath us. She held me tight so that I wouldn't fall, and she had such a nice voice, a soft voice, but easily heard despite the noise, so I felt very relaxed and comfortable with her. I was fascinated by the Falls, and the fact that on one side of the Falls was America and on the other Canada, each being so alike, and yet so different, as I found out in later years.

t was a great experience for a little boy, particularly flying with the future Mrs. Lindbergh herself, whom I thought was a wonderful lady and who opened my young eyes to the magic of flight.

A Lesson for Life

Some months later, Miss Milligan and I were in Atlantic City, at a hotel on the boardwalk, with the beach and the water right across the road. I had a green visor to keep the sun out of my eyes, a bright red bucket, and a wooden spade. Each morning the beach and the water were my playground. Paradise! After my nap in the afternoon, we would go to see some attraction that Miss Milligan thought might interest her charge. Most of them I enjoyed. My favorite was a very big, manmade, but real-looking wooden elephant. You climbed a ladder and found yourself inside the elephant and able to peer out through the two portholes that represented its eyes as seen from outside. I don't know why, but this wooden elephant, named Lucy, fascinated me, and it was always at the top of my list of places to go.

Once day Miss Milligan told me she was taking me to Woolworth's, one of the hundreds of that company's stores across the country at the time. I don't remember what she bought after we arrived at the store, but it seemed to be taking her quite a while to make up her mind, so I started investigating another part of the store. Something bright and colorful attracted my attention. It was the ribbon counter, where ribbons of every color of the rainbow were displayed. I was dazzled, and, without giving it a thought, stuffed a bunch of the ribbons in the pockets of my shorts for further perusal at our hotel.

At this stage of my life, the word or idea of stealing was not in my vocabulary. They were beautiful ribbons, and I just wanted to admire them in private. Later, I could take them back to Woolworth's and return them to the ribbon counter. The next morning after breakfast, Miss Milligan decided to do the laundry and, of course, she found the ribbons in the pockets of my shorts. With an expression of disbelief rather than thunder, she explained to me that you must never take something from a store without paying for it, and that I may very well have gotten the employee who was responsible for the ribbon section fired for stealing when the management discovered the ribbons missing.

I was shocked that I might have put the saleslady in such a bad position with the management, and immediately asked what I could do to resolve the situation.

Without a word, Miss Milligan took my hand and returned me to the store, ribbons and all. I was led to the manager's office, where, subdued and teary-eyed, I apologized for taking the ribbons without paying for them and begged the manager not to fire the ribbon counter employee. The manager agreed, and after Miss Milligan had paid for the ribbons, he took us to the milk bar, where he gave us each a chocolate ice cream cone. I never, ever stole anything again – not even a hotel towel.

A wonderful three years passed for me and Miss Milligan, who had become my tutor, and a very good one she was, opening my mind to the wonders of mathematics and reading and writing, the latter two subjects to which I became addicted.

In the course of our travels, we came upon an incredible variety of people and places and the energy to be found in great and growing cities. Meeting people from every walk of life on our two or three trips a year out of New York matured me beyond my years and gave me the confidence of experience and an easy relationship with adults, whom I found much more interesting than children, anyway.

A Career Change

I n the meantime, my mother, who had done very well at the dress
shop, was beginning to become bored with being a saleslady, however
successful and well paid. It was time for her to find another challenge.
The year was 1926. She cogitated for a while on her next step, using Emil
Pfizer as her sounding board and practical counselor for each new idea.
But one career Emil had never considered was the one my mother chose:
to become an actress and conquer Broadway.

I think the best way to describe what happened next is to quote
verbatim from the New York correspondent's article in the newspaper, the
Asheville *Citizen*, in North Carolina.

"A North Carolina Society girl is the latest addition to the long list of
stage workers to have come from the South. She is Minerva Sherman, who
has been selected as the understudy for Miss Violet Heming, the star of
William Harlbut's latest success 'Chivalry.' The great grand-daughter of a
Governor of North Carolina, coming from and married into two illustrious
families, Miss Sherman is making her first professional appearance here
in New York.

"Miss Sherman is actually Minerva Arrington Sherman of Charlotte,
North Carolina, and New York. She is the wife of Charles Austin Sherman
of New York City, scion of a noted family here. Miss Sherman was Minerva
Arrington of Charlotte, and she has made numerous appearances throughout
North Carolina in various little theatre and amateur productions. Last
summer she was a featured performer in a special pageant in Asheville,
NC. Miss Sherman, as she is known professionally, is the great grand-
daughter of Todd R. Caldwell of North Carolina and of General William
Thomas Ward of Kentucky. She came to New York as the young and pretty

bride of Charles Austin Sherman of Yale '21, son of Charles A. Sherman, a governor of the exclusive Union Club here. Only last year, two portraits of the southern belle, each by a noted artist, were hung in Reinhardt's and the Anderson Galleries, and were viewed by New York's social set with interest.

"The young woman, however, was dissatisfied with the monotony of social activities and followed her natural longing to take up stage work. Without playing upon her social position, she visited a Broadway producer and convinced him she would work hard if just given a job in 'a stage crowd' without a line to speak. She was taken on, and when trials came to see who would understudy Miss Heming, the dramatic star, Miss Sherman was elected as the most promising.

"Society, which feted the young matron a year or so ago, had no inkling that the pretty young lady had gone into stage work, until the story became known a few days ago."

What the reporter didn't know was that my mother was estranged from my father. Neither did he know of her dress shop experience.

In spite of the fact that mother had no opportunity to take over the star's role, she did participate in the crowd scenes, and the stage and lighting directors ensured that she was well lighted. The society that she had tired of descended on the theater in huge numbers, just to catch a glimpse of their "darling Minerva." The producers and backers took note and, when *Chivalry* finally closed, she won a real speaking role as the second lead in the play *Sweet William*. What is perhaps more important is that doors opened for her into the intoxicating world of the theater, where the creative people who were the backbone of everything that was performed on the Broadway stage became her friends and admirers, as indeed Mother become theirs. Particularly intrigued by composers, she developed a special relationship with George Gershwin. I must have been about four years old when Mother told me one evening, with considerable awe, that she had just returned from having tea at Gershwin's apartment. After tea, the composer informed her and five other guests that they had been invited there to listen to his latest composition, which until that moment had been heard only by his brother, Ira; they were then to give him their honest reactions.

From the first notes to the grand finale, everyone in the room was transfixed … exalted … numbed. At the end, there was complete silence. Mother told me she was the first to finally energize herself. She got up from her chair and went over to Gershwin, still sitting at the piano, put her arms around him, kissed him, and, with tears streaming down her face, told him how overwhelmed she had been by the driving excitement and fantastic rhythm of the piece. "It was so new, and strange, and so beautiful!" she exclaimed.

Gershwin took a linen handkerchief out of his pocket and dabbed away her tears, then thanked her with a hug and a kiss. The composition was *Rhapsody in Blue*. As we know, it became a classic.

So did one other composition become a classic, although not nearly so grand as *Rhapsody in Blue*. This was "Dinah," a song written for and about my mother and dedicated to her. Published in 1925, its lyrics were by Sam Lewis and Joe Young, with the music by Harry Akst. My favorite rendition is that of the late Dinah Shore. Bing Crosby also made a solo recording of the song and later recorded it as a duet with Shore.

My mother's name at that time was still Minerva A. Sherman, and more than one composer who had come under her spell was inspired to write a song about her. Aware that using Minerva Sherman as their name for the southern belle in this song about the South would not have been acceptable, they did a neat little trick.

The names Minerva and Diana both referred to goddesses of ancient times, so they took the name Diana and "southernized" it into "Dinah." For Sherman they substituted the proud name of Lee, aware that that certainly would not offend anyone, and thus was born the song "Dinah." Here are a few lines to jog your memory:

> *Dinah, is there anyone finer,*
> *In the state of Carolina?*
> *If there is and you know her,*
> *Show her to me.*
> *Dinah, with her Dixie eyes*
> *blazing,*
> *How I'd like to sit and gaze in-*
> *to the eyes of Dinah Lee.*
>
> *Every night*
> *why do I shake with fright,*
> *Because my Dinah might*
> *change her mind about me?*
> *Got to tell you about Dinah,*
> *If she went to China,*
> *I would hop an ocean liner,*
> *Just to be with Dinah Lee.*

The composers also wrote a song called "Roses, Red Roses, Remind Me of You" and dedicated it to my mother. The idea came from the fact that an anonymous admirer of my mother sent her a big bunch of long-stemmed red roses every performance night. Even though neither of the plays Mother performed in was a musical, the composers had seen her in the first week after *Chivalry* opened and had been won over by her presence on the stage. So, instead of writing a song for her, they wrote two songs about her. The first one, "Dinah," became a classic; the second one died stillborn.

Among the many theatrical personages riding the crest of the wave at that time was Eddie Cantor, whom Mother met when he was performing in *Whoopee* on Broadway. She said he was very pleasant and rather gallant, but had a reputation for being a skinflint with a dollar. She also met Marilyn Miller, who was anything but cheap, and whom she admired enormously.

Al Jolson, on the other hand, she couldn't stand. "He thought he was the only person in the room," she said. "If you didn't gush over him and his talent, he would turn his back on you and walk away." Jimmy Durante, of the schnozzola, she thought was one of the sweetest men she had ever known.

For the jazz musicians, this was a great time, with a speakeasy on almost every corner serving bathtub gin and offering great jazz music, under the protection of the so-called guardians of the law. Everybody looked the other way, for everyone was doing it and almost everyone was guilty. It was Prohibition on the outside, the Roaring Twenties on the inside. Life was for the living. Oh, what fun it must have been!

An Invitation

Sometime in the summer of 1928, when I was in my sixth year, Mother received an invitation from Fred Dalziel, a New York friend and former beau of hers, to spend a weekend at his Palm Beach estate in Florida. It would be a house party, and the thought of leaving New York, which had been under almost constant rain for weeks, was unbearably tempting; moreover, her most recent play, *Sweet William*, had finally closed, and a new play had not yet been offered to her. This combination of circumstances convinced her that an invitation to sunny Florida, with a beach and emerald water just beyond the back door, could not be refused.

She took the train, arriving on the appointed Friday, and rang Fred Dalziel's front door. It was around five in the afternoon. It was a perfect day – sunny and with a light breeze that would grow stronger as the day wore on. She had brought her bathing suit, and since the rest of the guests were playing tennis, golfing, or shopping, she decided to go for a swim. After having her bag unpacked by one of Fred's maids, she put on her bathing suit, wrapped her bath towel around her, and headed down to the beach.

Being a good swimmer, she was soon drawn from tanning on the beach into the salty spray of the Atlantic Ocean. The tide was high and she happily paddled quickly away from the shore. After about twenty minutes of alternatively swimming and floating on her back, she decided to take a leisurely swim back to shore, where she could see someone wearing a bathing suit coming out of the large glass-enclosed veranda of her host's house.

The wind was picking up by now and blowing the waves higher. Mother started swimming back, but, after five minutes or so, she realized that not only had she not proceeded any closer to land, but she was actually being drawn farther out. Believing in her own strength and swimming ability, she energized herself to her maximum speed, but the wind was blowing the waves higher and higher and she soon lost sight of land altogether. Finding herself still being drawn out to sea, and beginning to feel extremely tired, she panicked and let out a rebel yell, and another, and another. Nobody answered. She wondered what had happened to the man she had seen, coming out of her host's house, and she also wondered if she was being carried way out to sea, never to be heard from again.

Feeling weaker and weaker, she tried a couple more rebel yells that blew away in the wind, which was now creating white caps on the waves. Feeling terribly alone, she realized she was drowning. As her strength was finally exhausted, she let herself slip below the waves.

The person my mother had seen coming out of Fred Dalziel's home was a magnificent-looking man, six feet three inches tall, with an athlete's figure and a splendid, heroic face. This was Colonel John Bigelow Dodge, an American by birth and education, a naturalized British subject, and a major hero of the First World War. During that war he had become the youngest colonel in the British Army, at the age of twenty-five, which wasn't bad for a former American citizen. He had fought in the battles of Gallipoli; swum the Hellespont; and become a good friend of Winston Churchill. His final battles had been fought in France, and he had won two medals for gallantry, the Distinguished Service Order and the Distinguished Service Cross.

At this particular moment in his life, he was desperately swimming toward what he hoped was the right direction of a yell for help from a panicked female. He had only heard her once, since he always swam with his head underwater, coming up only for a two-second gulp of air before ducking below the surface again.

Reaching the general area from which he thought he had heard the anguished yell, he kicked down against the water and rose up a few inches above the top of the waves. Nothing. In a final attempt to locate his quarry, he swam underwater and dove head first into my mother.

Mother didn't remember the blow, but it galvanized her into a feeble, semiconscious awareness of her situation, and with her rescuer's help, they reached the surface, where he turned her on her back and took her a good half mile parallel to the land until the undertow weakened enough to bring her up onto the beach.

Afterward, my mother called him her guardian angel. He called her his favorite mermaid.

Six weeks later they were married. It became known on both sides of the Atlantic as the marriage of the year. It was 1928. It would last some thirty-three more very good years.

Wedding of the Year

I attended my mother's wedding to Johnny Dodge, without actually knowing Johnny Dodge. He had not spoken to me since my mother had presented me to him. He had patted me on the head, as one might a stray dog, but failed to find words to express any communication with me. I felt hurt by his apparent coldness, although, looking back on it, I can see that marrying my mother was one thing, but having to take on the responsibility of a six-year-old child was a little bit more than he had bargained for. However, being a gentleman, he had had to accept me. At that time he reminded me a little bit of my father, who I always felt had regretted my presence in his life.

Even at my early age, I could see that Johnny Dodge was very highly regarded among his peers, and that anyone and everyone who entered his circle of friends and acquaintances felt especially honored to know him.

For my part, my cosseted and carefree life with Miss Milligan had come to an abrupt end. As I stood on the deck of the French Line's ocean liner, the *Île de France*, looking through the deck's railing down to the dock where my beloved governess was standing, some distance apart from my mother and Johnny's friends who had come to see them off, I was not a happy boy. All of them had come aboard and gone to the bon voyage party in my mother's and Johnny's cabin for a brief visit before the ship's horns had blasted, summoning them to return to the dock.

During their party in the cabin, I had stayed on deck with Miss Milligan, both of us too heartbroken to speak, hugging each other with tears streaming down our faces. It was the first real crisis in my life, something that had happened so suddenly that I could barely catch my breath, with only Miss Milligan to love me and encourage me about my future.

Now she was back there, down on the dock, appearing so tiny from this distance, waving her tear-drenched handkerchief and looking so alone.

I was grateful to Emil Pfizer, who Mother told me had given Miss Milligan a bountiful sum for all she had done, taking care of me and educating me. In addition, Emil had found her a new position in another household with a single child, whose family he knew well and could vouch for, after she had enjoyed a month's paid vacation.

The *Île de France* was finally disconnected from the dock; the ropes were thrown from the dock back to the ship's sailors to curl and stow aboard; the anchor rose; and slowly the tugs pulled the great ship out of the harbor and into the gray Atlantic.

My impressions of the ship were good. I had my own cabin, and almost immediately discovered that I was pretty much expected to take care of myself. This worked out fine for me, as the cabin stewards, recognizing that I was being left to my own devices, set up communications with the crew responsible for operating the social and entertaining part of the ship, with the result that I saw just about every part of the vessel, including the vast engine room, spotlessly clean, the engineering officers watching over large instruments, measuring various components of these earsplittingly loud enormous pounding engines that were driving the equally large propellers.

I also attended the horse racing in the morning (ship's version) and visited the bridge, where I exchanged greetings with the captain of the ship, who on the last day of the voyage presented me with a miniature metal model of the good ship *Île de France*, which sits in a place of honor on my work table to this day.

I had lunch with Mother and Johnny, who was bravely trying to find common ground with me but with little success, until Mother would bail us out with some crazy story or piece of gossip that would get us both to laughing. After lunch I could always go to a matinee in the movie theater, while Mother and Johnny played bridge with friends onboard. They did see a movie with me once.

Dinner was served to me in my cabin, so that my parents would not have to worry about me and could be left to enjoy the parties that were given before dinner, one of which was held in my mother's and Johnny's cabin. In order not to offend anyone, my mother told me, they generally had to attend two or three parties before dinner.

Of course, everybody dressed for dinner in those days. Twice I hid behind a pillar at the top of the stairs leading down to the elegantly decorated dining room, where the ladies wore their beautiful evening gowns and brilliant jewelry, and the men looked so splendid, most of them in tail coat and white tie.

The second and last time I was watching the glamorous scene from the top of the stairs, the dessert was being served, and the dance band struck up. I saw Mother and Johnny rise from their table and join the many other dancers already on the floor. They were a dazzling pair, Johnny with such a dominant presence, such a wonderful strong face, carrying himself like an emperor, and my gorgeous mother happier than she had ever been, in the arms of this gallant husband whom she was to adore for the rest of their lives. Everyone seemed to be looking at them, and many stopped dancing to admire them and give them more room. I was so proud of them.

When we had first come aboard ship, Johnny had suggested to me that I have my breakfast in the dining room. I never did. I was too shy and embarrassed to eat alone, the only child in that large room full of adults, some with children, but not one child alone. Even though I may have behaved beyond my years, I was still only six, and I had suddenly been deprived of an accustomed and vital part of my life – Miss Milligan. She was not there anymore to give me confidence or say, "You can do it." So on the first morning after the ship was at sea, I asked the cabin steward what time Mother and Johnny had requested breakfast. "Nine-thirty." At ten I presented myself at their cabin, much larger than mine, and was received with some surprise and a welcoming kiss from Mother. Johnny, to my amazement, asked me if I was hungry; when I said I was, he handed me a plate with some scrambled eggs and a buttered croissant, for which I was very grateful. Mother gave me a puzzled look and poured me a glass of milk from the silver pitcher. Johnny said, "My word, this young man's got a good appetite. When did you have breakfast?" "Early," I replied. "I should think so," said Johnny. "Well, Peter, you are welcome to stop off here for your second breakfast any day." And that's exactly what I did.

Ahead was a new chapter in the lives of all three of us. Southampton was coming into view, and the curtain was going up for my mother and me on an amazing new world of wealth and sophistication, unique personalities and people with great power, practically all of them friendly and warm and eager to help us adapt to our new surroundings. But wait: There is a dark cloud hanging over this picture – the Honourable Mrs. Lionel Guest, Johnny Dodge's mother.

Welcome to Wookitipi

Our first stop upon reaching London was a delightful house at 6 Connaught Street, in an elegant part of the city, a wedding gift from Lionel and Flora Guest, Johnny's mother and stepfather. Not a bad way to start a marriage.

Flora and Lionel Guest had their townhouse on Connaught Square, in the next block. At least they were not living right next door. It didn't really matter at the moment, for we had time only to have our trunks and bags unpacked by the staff of five, who had been vetted and hired by Flora before our arrival, and then repacked for the weekend. Johnny suggested that I address her as Aunt Flora.

By four in the afternoon, we were on the train to Ferring, a small seaside town on the coast of Sussex, located between Worthing and Angmering, where the Lionel Guests resided in their country home, named Wookitipi, the centerpiece of a sixty-acre gentleman's farm. To give you some background on Flora Guest I must present a brief biography of her recent exploits in the marital game.

Born and educated in America, she had married Charles Stuart Dodge, a gentleman of good pedigree and a member of the Union Club in New York, where my grandfather was the Governor. She had two children by Charles Dodge, and then divorced him for reasons of which I have no idea. Apparently he took financial care of their son and daughter, up to her maarriage to Lionel Guest.

When Johnny finished his education at McGill University in Montreal, Canada, Flora, who had great dreams of crashing London society and marrying nothing less than a Duke – though an Earl wouldn't be too bad

– gathered up her goods and chattel and her children, Johnny and Lucy, and crossed the ocean to England, her expectations high.

Unfortunately for Flora, none of the Dukes or Earls or other lonely peers favored this reasonably handsome if gushing woman, and she finally had to settle for an "Honourable Mrs.," the younger son's limiting distinction; the hated "Mrs." would remain.

Poor Flora. If she had been a Duchess or even a Lady, she would have been in seventh heaven, her whole attitude improved, instead of being married to an Honourable Mr. and serving out her youth into middle-age bulk, her looks fading and her companion of a husband to be coddled and cared for until the end of time. Only her beloved child, Johnny Dodge, saved her sanity, and now he had gone and married an American woman, of all people – she having carefully forgotten that she had been an American before her marriage to Lionel and still had her American passport.

But Flora was nothing if not determined. She had decided that her hold on her son was irrevocable, and she was going to use her power, by fair or unfair means, to break up this marriage or die in the effort. After all, he had known Minerva for only six weeks! She would smash this relationship in no time.

One thing to her credit, at least in her eyes, was that she had married into a distinguished triumvirate – the Guests, the Churchills, and the Marlboroughs – all being related to one another, in some way, over many generations. In addition, the Guests had a considerable fortune, and that included Lionel Guest. He was a nice gentleman but was completely under the thumb of Flora, who treated him as if she were his nanny and he her child. He was sickly and remained so, until he died of tuberculosis some years after we arrived in England.

Lionel's limousine, driven by the chauffeur Fisk, met us at the train station and drove us and our weekend baggage back to Wookitipi, a rambling but pleasant enough building, set between the road and the farm. In the latter area, chickens of every species – including beautiful Chinese chickens – pecked around the grounds, and a herd of Jersey milk cows roamed the fields, along with goats, a bull, and sundry other breeds. One poor man, named Palmer, seemed to be in charge of the whole farm; he was very pleasant to me and fast became my friend. And boy did I need a friend!

Aunt Flora, who received us in her drawing room, was a large, heavyset woman with hooded eyes and a patronizing attitude, whose presence in that room scared me even before she spoke. She embraced Johnny first, offering a quick peck on the cheek to my mother – and to me not even a shake of the hand. Then she turned to my mother and said, "What a nice-looking son you have! But of course we will have to buy him some better clothes. English boys would make fun of him in those clothes." Even Johnny looked puzzled by his mother's observation, for there had been quite a few English boys on the boat, and we were all dressed in similar outfits.

"Poor Lionel has a fever, so I am letting him rest this afternoon," she continued. "I hope he will be able to join us for dinner tonight. In the meantime, we will have some tea, and then Rose will show you to your rooms and help you unpack and be down for dinner by seven."

Aunt Flora had four Pekinese dogs that she doted on and fed constantly, while being served tea by Rose. The dogs were yapping unmercifully and forever clawing at our legs and trying to jump into our laps, so there was little time for eating or conversation.

During all this commotion, Aunt Flora laughed heartily, egging the dogs on to leap ever higher, telling them how "wonderful, precious, adorable, and so very intelligent" they were.

Later, seeing Mother's demolished stockings, I remembered that the dogs always jumped up at Aunt Flora's side, never on her legs. Well-trained, diabolical dogs!

Dinner was not much better than tea, except that the dogs were quartered in another part of the house in order to provide a tranquil atmosphere for "dear Lionel." He turned out to be soft-spoken and fascinated with astronomy, of which he was very knowledgeable, according to other astronomers who quoted him in learned magazines dedicated to the study of the stars.

Uncle Lionel was slim and pale, with good thick hair gone white at an early age. He looked and acted frail, but his passion for astronomy gave him the opportunity to cut the bond with his overbearing wife for at least two or three hours on a clear night, since he was the proud owner of a really large telescope housed in a big, round building about twenty yards from the house. The telescope and its housing were equipped to revolve at a set speed to coincide with that of the star being studied, and I was allowed to stand at the eyepiece looking up to the heavens, as Uncle Lionel explained the history and geography of each star he was observing.

As soon as Aunt Flora realized that Uncle Lionel and I enjoyed each other, she stopped my visits to the telescope. I was "too tiring for dear Lionel"; I "sapped his strength." Uncle Lionel didn't say a word.

The next morning the cock woke me up at about six; once awake, I dressed in my shirt and shorts. It was still summer, and I went out to see what, if anything, was happening on the farm.

Palmer was there, herding the chickens back to the chicken coops, so I asked him if I could help him by shepherding them from the other side. "Sure," he said. "That'll be a great help." So I did so, with Palmer on one side and me on the other. We had almost reached the chicken huts, when Flora Guest appeared in bathrobe and slippers, waving her hands violently in the air, screaming, "Stop, stop, Peter, stop, stop, I say!" I obeyed her immediately, horrified and uncertain as to why she was so upset.

Charging up to me, she raised her hand and then thought better of it, turning on poor Palmer, who was standing with a shell-shocked expression on his face, wringing his hands in contrition.

"How dare you? Don't you ever let me see this wretched boy helping you with your work again. He's probably scared the chickens half to death. As it is, I doubt if we will have any eggs today."

Poor Palmer was looking as afraid as I was feeling. He had taken off his cap and was apologizing all over the place, his body bent in supplication. I was appalled that he was forced to grovel before this tyrant of a woman and me.

Aunt Flora had called me a wretched boy. These were not comforting words for a six-year-old on the first morning of his life in a new and unknown country.

I didn't tell my mother about this incident, partly because I knew she was already under quite a strain, and partly because Aunt Flora didn't choose to tell her either. I could feel that Mother was somewhat on edge and apprehensive, and, when we got a moment together on the last day of an interminably long weekend, I asked her how she had enjoyed the weekend. "Enjoy?" she cried. "Enjoy! This whole visit has been a nightmare. Between Flora's efforts to undermine our marriage with all of her criticisms of my clothes, my hair, my Southern drawl, and my bridge playing, not to mention those damned dogs from hell, I'm about ready for the crazy house!"

Worst of all, Johnny did not stand up for his wife. In his defense he told Mother that he was an only son (though he did have a sister, Lucy, about whom you will hear more later). Furthermore, neither he nor his mother had anticipated his marriage. After all, he was thirty-five years old, considerably older than the few friends he had who had survived the First World War, and who had joyfully and quickly fallen into the arms of matrimony and fatherhood. They had left him to a life of adventure and, later, finance, and to little thought of becoming betrothed – until he met my mother.

"Wouldn't it be best just to give my mother time to get to know you better? I know she would soon come around to seeing what a wonderful wife I have," seemed to be Johnny's plan. What could my mother say?

Those miserable days at Wookitipi finally came to an end, and even Johnny seemed to lighten up when the train left the station. Halfway to London he got up to exercise his legs in the train's corridor. I took the opportunity to ask Mother what Wookitipi meant. "It's Chinese," she replied. "Personally, I think it's the name of some ghastly form of Chinese torture!" Little did we know.

6 Connaught Street

Our house on Connaught Street was a delight. The five people who made up the staff soon became my friends, addressing me as Master Peter, all but one being Irish, full of fun, and friendly without being familiar. They were good workers and crazy about my mother. Bertha, our cook, the German lady, was at first rather reticent, but was soon won over by Mother's warmth and knowledge of food and menus. Though a loner, Bertha was a superb chef, not caring if she was preparing a meal for two or twenty-two. With the help of Kitty, she always managed to ensure that the food arrived on the table hot by way of a dumbwaiter, which carried the food from the basement kitchen to the dining room on the first floor.

Besides the kitchen, there was a large area taking up most of the basement beyond it, which was dedicated to the servants' rest periods and days off. There were the staff's dining room table and chairs next to the kitchen, and then comfortable armchairs and footstools, a large sofa, a Ping-Pong table, a card table and chairs, a radio and a gramophone with records, all at the other end.

The staff each got half a day off during the week, plus all day Sunday. Bertha got only Sunday off, which suited her just fine, for she was a true workaholic; if she wasn't in my mother's quarters planning that day's luncheon and dinner menus or preparing a meal for the staff, who ate the same food as we did, she would become quite depressed. Even on her free Sundays, she would cook breakfast for us and the staff, and when we came back from church we would find our beds made up and our breakfast dishes removed, the dining room once again spotless.

For dinner that night, Bertha would have prepared cold cuts, asparagus

33

to be dipped in a delicious thick yellow sauce, potato salad with bacon bits and onions, and for dessert my favorite of all English desserts, trifle. All would be laid out on the sideboard, from which we could help ourselves.

Bertha limited herself to two pastimes on her so-called day off. If the weather was in a good mood, she would walk to Hyde Park, a sandwich and a thermos of iced coffee in her bag; there she would rent a folding chair and watch the world go by. At five o'clock, one of the regimental bands proffered for the people's entertainment would arrive in the bandstand and strike up a grand marching tune, thereby providing Bertha with a one-hour concert, from which she would return home, sunburned and radiant. If it was raining, or looked like rain, she would choose a movie from the daily newspaper and take a bus to the cinema and back. You could always tell what kind of movie she had seen. If it was romantic, she returned with a soft, contented look on her face. If it was a tragic or dramatic movie, with a sad story, with red eyes and puffy face. If it was a comedy she enjoyed, with bursts of wild laughter, followed by a transparently false hacking cough, engineered to cover up her joyful mirth. We loved to hear her laugh, wild or not. Otherwise, she never laughed and rarely smiled.

Molly, Kitty's older sister, was my mother's personal maid, and she was responsible for the other staff, the number of which later rose to seven. Bertha was master of herself.

In the days before and after the First and Second World Wars, staff were referred to as servants, which was not considered a derogatory term at all. On the contrary, the servants were happy and proud to be in a good house with good employers, where they were housed and fed and became a vital part of their employer's family. Their uniforms, as well as their doctors', dentists', and hospital visits or stays, were all paid by their employers, as were their two-week vacations every year, plus train or bus fare in addition to their weekly salaries. When they retired, those who had been with the family for some years were assured of a set amount of money every month plus their stipend from the government. At least in those days, the British gentleman would give as much loyalty to his staff as they would give to him, which created one heck of a good bonding.

Our house soon settled into a quiet, cheerful rhythm. Once a week, a Mr. Bruce, who owned a stable not too far away, would come down our street, trotting on a beautiful black horse, a chestnut pony following on the end of a lead. Johnny Dodge had arranged these outings for me, without my asking. I was thrilled.

Since the chestnut pony was also called Chestnut, I had no trouble remembering his name.With a soft mouth and an easy temperament, he was a joy to ride, even though I had to learn the English saddle.

Mr. Bruce, on his magnificent horse, aptly named Beauty, and I on my Chestnut, would reach Hyde Park through back streets and alleys, the better to make speed, arriving at Rotten Row, where the soft, well raked track gave the animal hooves a firm traction. With a grunt from Mr. Bruce, we were off at full gallop, the wind in our faces and my pony's exuberance matching my own, creating a spiritual kinship between us and a sense of utter freedom in our souls.

Meanwhile, back at the house, new and strange things were happening. I will quote directly from a clipping from the *Daily Express* at the time:

"Number 6, Connaught Street, the John B. Dodge's house, is being decorated in a most unusual and charming way under the direction of Mrs. Dodge and Mrs. Gordon Ives, Lady Ridley's clever and artistic daughter, who is, by the way, Lord Wimborne's niece, as Lady Ridley is his sister. There is not one conventionally shaped room in the house, as all have a slanting wall or odd corner chopped off somewhere. Even the entrance hall is not straight, but bends a little. The dining room and serving room behind are painted a soft primrose yellow with ceilings of duck's egg blue. The doors are Venetian red. At the top of the stairs is a square landing with walls of the same primrose yellow, on which Mrs. Ives is painting life-sized hollyhocks, growing out of red pots, and which is to be an aviary. The window opens onto a courtyard, which is being transformed by the view of a cottage, surrounded by hollyhocks, and with the sea as a background, that is being painted thereon. The drawing room and library are painted yellow, and the bedroom and dressing-room above in a soft salmon pink, with jade green furniture. All this sounds a trifle gaudy, but it is not. The effect is most charming and cheerful, like Mrs. Dodge herself."

Johnny Dodge: Politician, Financier, Adventurer

After Johnny Dodge returned from the First World War, he had made a beeline to Flora and Lionel Guest's homes in London and Ferring. He spent most of his time in the country house, being coddled and made over by his mother, who fed him plenty of milk and cream from her Jersey cows, eggs from her chickens, and vegetables, including American corn, grown on the farm. Flora did her best to make her son relax and be comfortable, but her aggressive and possessive attitude apparently was too much even for him at this time, when he was still shell-shocked and, frankly, demoralized by the unbelievable carnage he had witnessed and the friends he had lost through five hellish years of war.

To give Flora credit, she could come to his aid rather dramatically. When Johnny was shot in the hand, his right hand, during the battle at Gallipoli, Flora was informed that the doctors would have to remove his hand. She somehow rushed to the hospital where he had been taken and talked her way into stopping the operation and bringing him home for convalescence. While recovering, he took long walks in the country. Within a month, he returned to service, his right hand still intact but no longer useful; from then on he shook hands with his left hand.

Lionel Guest, a gentle and good man, whose surprisingly successful good works and financial investments designed to benefit the poor in the Mile End of London had amazed many of his contemporaries, realized that Johnny, now finally home from the war, needed a cause toward which he could direct his energy and talents. What Lionel had started, Johnny could build upon. Lionel's initiative had been squelched by his subordination to his wife's possessive ways and constant cries of feigned alarm, but he could at least pass the torch to his stepson, and possibly maneuver him into eventually running for political office, perhaps even a seat in Parliament.

Lionel had set the bait, and Johnny took it with relish. He had always been a supporter of the underdogs and the less privileged. The men under his command during the war had worshipped him for his courage, his compassion, and his leadership. He constantly led his troops into battle, even though, with his formidable height and build, he was a conspicuous target for the enemy. But only once had he been wounded. His troops, who were in awe of him, suffered far fewer casualties than others.

Believe it or not, one of the first things he did when he came back from the war, sometime before Lionel even broached the subject of Mile End, was to record his political party registration as a Socialist, something that stunned his family and friends. However, this carried him into the Mile End stage of his life with a large plus mark, for there were not many Conservatives in that district. It also gave him a greater feeling of camaraderie with the underprivileged majority of his potential constituency, especially with those who were returning from the war.

Johnny even rented a house in Mile End, so that he could be more readily available to his future constituents. Having taken over Lionel's responsibilities, he was determined to prove himself even more dedicated to the betterment of job opportunities and health care, his two most passionate causes, along with demanding that a due respect and appreciation be given to the returning veterans.

Now he had to gain the people of Mile End's confidence and approval. For the first year, therefore, he strode the streets of the area, generally in the evenings and almost all day on the weekends, introducing himself, speaking to groups in the streets, in pubs, and coming out of church and cinemas, and even individuals, plying all of them with questions about their needs, their ambitions, their hopes. Mostly, they needed jobs.

With some help from Lionel, and more help from his mother, he spoke at every possible meeting, whether the British Legion or the Garbage Union. The citizenry had invented imaginary titles for Johnny and his mother. Johnny's title was Mile End John, and his mother's, The Duchess of Mile End. Whoopee! At last!

His relentless pursuit of the inhabitants of Mile End, and his many contributions to their welfare, including a brand new Club House for their enjoyment provided by contributions from some of his wealthier friends, finally secured Johnny's election to the London County Council, a first and very important step in his political career. It also elevated him to becoming a personage rather than a person, and fodder for the local and regional media.

In 1921, three years after entering politics in the East End of London and starting work in the City (about which, more later), Johnny got a call from a very secret branch of the British Government, followed by an interview that explained the mission he was being asked to pursue. After being given a "cover" for his absence from his place of work and his Mile End responsibilities, and having received permission from his somewhat bemused partners for a phony sabbatical, he joyfully set off for Moscow. His mission was to go to Russia in the guise of a businessman intent on opening an import/export business with the Russian government.

Lenin, though sick, was still in command; with the aid of a British Cabinet Minister's letter of introduction, Johnny was warmly received by Lenin himself and given assurances that his mission would not be compromised by the Communist Party. He was also provided with a letter signed by Lenin that would protect his freedom to pursue his objectives within the boundaries of Red Russia. Johnny's real purpose was to learn as much as he could about the power struggle going on in the back rooms of the Kremlin, where the prize would be the crowning of the next leader of the Soviet Union,

on the death of Lenin. In addition, Johnny was able to send back to London accounts of an amazing number of Russia's secrets, as overheard by his interpreter, a Russian mole in the pay of the British, and the good offices of General Leon Trotsky, a brilliant communist who was maneuvering for the top spot. The General had been impressed by Johnny's audacity and negotiating skills, and helped him open doors that he would not have known about, assuring Johnny of reaching his goal.

Once the pact had been signed for importing and exporting goods between the two countries, proving to the Kremlin that Johnny Dodge was, as they thought, a genuine businessman, he was able to send back ever more valuable information to London. Much of this was also, as London had requested, forwarded to the top brass of the White Russian Army, which was still in command of a large area of Russia.

All of this spying and subterfuge took time and enormous risk, and Johnny and his poor mole worked endlessly under the glare of the State Police, who couldn't understand why this foreigner and his interpreter had been given so much leeway to operate within the very Kremlin walls and even in the private offices of the men running the country.

But it all came to a sudden end with the death of Lenin. Trotsky fled to Mexico after being ousted by Stalin, and was later murdered in his Mexican home on Stalin's orders.

Johnny was arrested and jailed three times, once for more than a month. Finally, with no visible reason to keep him any longer, his captors released him and he returned to London. He had tried to bring his mole, and by now good friend, back with him, but the mole had a family and responsibilities and preferred to remain in Russia. It was a bad call. He was shot within a week of Johnny's departure, and his family was shipped off to Siberia.

Fortunately for Johnny's image with the Russian hierarchy, Stalin cancelled the bogus import-export pact before it could be implemented, denouncing it as a fabrication of the British to facilitate their spying on the Russian government. How right he was!

Upon his return to England, Johnny, who had become completely disenchanted with the so-called communist experiment, immediately changed his political party registration from Socialist to Conservative. He also took off on a well-deserved three-month vacation, part of it on his friend Samuel Courtauld's yacht, where he renewed his prewar friendship with another guest aboard the yacht, Winston Churchill.

Being back with Johnny for a few weeks of peaceful isolation made Winston realize what a fine and honorable friend he had; the trip cemented their friendship for life. Even though Winston was out of office for many years, he made Johnny a point man for him. The friendship gave Johnny an open line to Winston whenever he secured some information that could be of value to his friend, or when he needed to see him privately. It was to be an exciting and eventful relationship.

In tandem with Johnny's benevolent and political career was his business career, also suggested by the kindly Lionel Guest. Lionel traded in the Market in the City with the stockbrokerage firm of Nathan & Roselli, a small but exceedingly successful company, whose partners were all Jews, with the exception of the manager, who was a pure Anglo-Saxon and a Bible-spouting Christian. The Jewish partners and the Christian manager had lunch together every working day in their own office dining room, with the manager, Mr. Crouch, in the place of honor at the head of the table. He would always say a prayer for their food and their souls, to which they would all give a solemn amen before putting fork to plate.

It was an amicable arrangement, as everyone at the table was exceedingly smart in the business. One of them even played the violin in the Stock

Exchange Symphony Orchestra, which performed once or twice a year, under a guest conductor, and which always won a positive acclamation from the newspapers' music critics.

But the firm, Nathan & Roselli, had one very important piece missing. In spite of the fact that they had some very impressive Jewish and non-Jewish customers, including Lionel, they did not have anyone of distinction who could represent them by having an immediate carte blanche entrée to the clubs, banks, businesses, high society, etc., of the city. Lionel had gone down there for an appointment with the partners, where he made a very good argument on behalf of Johnny, so good, in fact, that the partners took less than ten minutes to approve his request. The fact that the Guest ménage did a great deal of business with the firm no doubt helped, but it was up to Johnny to prove himself, which would mean starting from scratch in the main office with all of the other clerks from whom he would have to learn the business within one year. He would then be accepted into a position of trust as an ambassador between the firm and the gilded clients, a position that would become Johnny's beat. Johnny, though not particularly inspired by the idea, was tempted by the challenge and accepted the offer. Within the year he was accepted into partnership. His first visit was to the fathers – each the president of a chain of banks – of two of his war buddies. Both fathers had been versed by their sons on who Johnny Dodge was, in case they didn't know. One of them did; one of them didn't. It didn't matter. Johnny returned to the office that afternoon toting two enormous orders, which charged the partners with such joy that they broke open a bottle of their best champagne to celebrate the occasion. Even Mr. Crouch, who didn't drink, celebrated with a ginger beer. Johnny's learning and wonderful coaching by the partners had paid off, and, as Johnny's confidence grew, so did his value to the company and, finally and inevitably, his financial reward. Of course all of this came about long before he careened into my mother below the surface of the Atlantic Ocean off the sands of Palm Beach.

St. Peter's Court: Private Boarding School

s for me, I had heard my mother and Johnny talking about the necessity of my going to a proper school, now that Miss Milligan was no longer able to tutor me.

A proper school in England for a family of our social level was a private boarding school, generally miles away from home. Not having ever been to a boarding school, I did not know whether I would like it or not, but I did know I would miss our new home, and Mother, and even Johnny, who, though unable to communicate with a six-year-old, had given that six-year-old the joy of Chestnut and Rotten Row, for which I would forever be in his debt.

Finally, my mother gave me the news that I had been entered into a private preparatory school in Broadstairs, Kent, where the term began in ten days. Clothes had to be bought, including an Eton Bumfreezer for Sundays, and a tuck-box – a wooden box, three feet long by two feet wide – with a real lock and key to safeguard its contents, usually candies and books and preserves and stuff. I would have that box with me through St. Peter's Court and Eton College.

The train journey to Broadstairs turned out to be quite fun, and when we arrived at the Broadstairs station, we found buses drawn up for seventy-two pupils to be taken to the number-one private prepartory boarding school in all of England. Even the royal family had sent two of their sons to St. Peter's Court long before I went to school there. They were the Duke of Gloucester and the Duke of Kent, two of the four living sons of King George V and Queen Mary, to whom my mother was presented at Court in Buckingham Palace in the early thirties. The Prince of Wales, who was to play a unique role in our lives, had been privately tutored in the Palace, as was the Duke of York, who succeeded to the throne when Edward, Prince of Wales and then King, abdicated.

A Royal Wedding

One day in 1933, when I was eleven years old, we heard that it had been announced in the Court Circular that the Duke of Kent, who had been educated at St. Peter's Court, was betrothed to Marina, Princess of Greece and Denmark. What was even more exciting was that our headmaster and his ever-popular wife, Midge, had been invited to the wedding, and we could celebrate the event by having a day free from class.

On the day of the wedding, the Reverend Mr. Ridgeway and Mrs. Ridgeway entered the school dining room while we were all having breakfast, dressed in their "go to the royal wedding" outfits. She was wearing a purple gown, dressed up with a beautiful pearl necklace at her neck and a diamond bracelet on her wrist. He was wearing what I would surmise was a courtier's costume, black knee breeches with white stockings and shiny black buckled shoes, a white ruffled shirt, and a silver-colored tail coat. They looked so happy, and we were all so happy for them, and proud that they had been invited to this grand occasion. It was almost like being there ourselves. They left immediately afterward, in order to be in London on time for the wedding.

Flash forward a couple of years to when I was a new boy at Eton. I was standing on the pavement in front of the Corner House at the end of the Long Walk, my residence for the four years I was there. I was watching the cars returning to London from the nearby Ascot Races, and in particular the bobby who was directing the traffic. He had the High Street traffic stopped to let six green buses come through from a side street onto the road to London, when he suddenly realized, as did I, that the dark blue Rolls-Royce waiting at the head of the line for the buses to go through was being driven by none other than the Duke of Kent himself, with the Princess Marina at his side. In a second, the bobby's arm signals changed, the last two buses screeched to a sudden halt, and the Duke's car rolled regally forward, the Duke smiling his thanks to the policeman.

They were a fabulous-looking couple, the Duke exceedingly handsome, his wife quite gorgeous, wearing a wide-brimmed hat, a type of hat that would become a very elegant part of her wardrobe for the rest of her life. For me, it was a magic moment.

Sadly, the Duke was killed in an airplane accident during the war in 1942 at the age of forty. His bereaved wife never married again, but after the war she did return to a more normal existence, enjoying the company of creative people in both the theater and the arts.

Even in the world of charitable events, there are people who try to turn the purpose of the event to their own personal advantage. This had happened to the Princess, after the war, when she was the patron of a certain well-considered charity. The manager of the charity acquired some severe gambling debts, and, not knowing any other way out, took to stealing from the charity's account. Someone close to the Princess, who knew my mother and was aware that she had sat on the board of many charitable events, as well as presiding over the English Speaking Union's American and Australian Forces Leave Program for the entire war without accepting a penny for her services, asked for her help.

Mother, of course, accepted the challenge and in complete secrecy resolved what could have been a serious fiasco.

Some time later, Mother decided to put together one of her spectacular dinner parties that almost always were made up of fascinating people from all walks of life. Because the ambiance was so comfortable and the food and wine so good, and Mother and Johnny such great hosts, the subjects' repartee could sometimes become brilliant, and the evenings always turned out to be a smashing success. I, too, was invited to these occasions, by this time being in my mid-twenties, and I can assure you that I rarely missed one.

Mother had never considered having royalty for a dinner party, suspecting that it would put something of a chill on the evening, but this time she decided to invite the Princess Marina, whom she had found to be absolutely delightful, and who had immediately accepted the invitation, asking if she could bring a friend. "Of course," said Mother. The friend turned out to be the sophisticated genius who had written the world's smoothest plays and most wonderful music and songs to go with them,

46

Noel Coward. Not only did he add enormously to the dinner party, but after dinner we all trooped up the stairs to the music room, where the Steinway grand piano awaited the master's touch. Everyone stayed on until the early hours of the morning, enraptured with his extraordinary talent.

Mother's Coming Out Day

Somewhat to my mother's surprise, Flora Guest graciously offered to sponsor her by introducing her into Mayfair society. The more Mother thought about it, the more suspicious of her mother-in-law's intentions she became. Land mines would definitely be placed in her path, she decided, and she could depend only upon her own Southern astuteness to defuse them before they could harm or, no doubt in Flora's mind, destroy her.

There was no way that Mother could refuse Flora's offer, so she resigned herself to a coming battle of wits, certain that Flora was intent on administering the *coup de grâce* at the earliest possible moment. Nothing happened for three weeks, and the suspense was beginning to get to her, when the phone rang at 6 Connaught Street. Molly answered it and informed Mother that Mrs. Guest wished to speak to her. Mother told me later that she flinched, feeling the blood ooze out of her, then pulled herself together and took the phone.

"Hello, Flora."

"Hello, Minerva. Are you all right?"

"Oh, yes, thank you. And you?"

"Fine, fine. On Tuesday of next week there is a dinner at the Mayflower Hotel for the Blind Servicemen and the Greater London Fund for the Blind. Johnny can't go, because that same night he has to be at the club that he and his friends have donated to Johnny's constituency in Mile End, for its transference to the control of the British Legion. Don't worry, Minerva, it's mostly women who go to these affairs. The Queen of Spain will be there, and lots of other dignitaries, and you'll be able to make your entrance upon British society and also support a good cause. I've bought the tickets. Write me a check for fifty pounds, and I'll give you your ticket on the way to the hotel. Any questions?"

"Yes, Flora. What's the dress code?"

"Oh, an evening gown, of course, and your jewels. Nothing pretentious, you understand? I shall come up by car with the chauffeur Fisk on Tuesday morning, so we don't have to be dependent on taxis. Lionel rarely uses the car anyway. I'll call you as soon as I get in."

"Sounds great. Thank you for making the effort. I know this is putting you out quite a bit."

"Nonsense, Minerva. It'll be fun. See you on Tuesday. 'Bye."

"Goodbye, Flora, and thank you again."

According to Molly, Mother put down the phone and danced a little jig. Then she stopped, wanting desperately to believe. Reluctantly, but with a mortified expression, she said, "Oh, Molly, she's good, she's very, very good!"

Poor Mother. For one brief moment she had desperately wanted to believe Flora –it would have been so wonderful – but her intuitive sensibility told her that Flora was Flora, and she had better watch herself, whether dealing with a seemingly kind and gracious Flora or a mean and horrible Flora.

Molly, Mother's personal maid, friend, and chief of staff, was my private informant of all the goings on at our house while I was absent at St. Peter's Court. Mother had approved of this arrangement, for she trusted Molly completely and knew that she could be depended upon to be discreet when necessary.

Fortunately for Molly, Mother, and me, Molly had been gifted with a photographic memory, and what she remembered was what she truly saw and heard. Without this gift of hers, I would not have been as cognizant of the many dramas being played out within the walls of 6 Connaught Street, and Molly would not have been as good a staff leader as she was.

Later, when we moved to a considerably larger house on Lower Berkely Street and the staff jumped from seven to ten, it was necessary to put a majordomo in charge. At this point, Molly happily relinquished her managerial position for full-time attention to Mother.

But today was Mother's Coming Out Day, and there was excitement and nervous anticipation throughout the house. Even though Johnny was not going to be able to attend the function, he was very upbeat and affectionate with his wife, and had gone with her to a famous dress designer's salon to pick out a dress for this splendid occasion. It was in a

soft pink shade, a color that suited Mother particularly well, and was styled
to show off her figure above the waist to its best, her lovely shoulders free
of bondage, her firm breasts pressed against the pliant material. Her legs,
which men have told me were to die for, long and beautifully shaped, were
hidden, but in silhouette, the skirt was spread, as if begging for a waltz,
and was delineated by a sprinkling of tiny silk roses, a stronger pink than
her gown.

According to the society gossip and society magazines that came out
after the "Perfect Dinner," Mother and her gown were a colossal success, my
favorite headline being, "American Bride Wins Mayfair's Heart." Moreover,
Flora Guest was on her best behavior, introducing Mother to more titled
ladies and gentlemen than Mother could have imagined gathered into one
room, almost all of whom immediately wanted to take her under their
wing and introduce her to their friends. The name "Minerva," followed
by "Johnny Dodge's wife," could be heard echoing in the wake of Flora
and Mother's parade.

Mother, of course, was thrilled with all the adulation, particularly
when the Queen of Spain requested that she be brought forward and
presented to her. I was told that Mother managed a pretty good curtsy,
remembered from her débutante days.

Among the personages whom Mother met that night, all underlined
by Flora in the program listing the activities for the evening and the names
of all the ticket holders, were the Countess of Oxford, Sir John and Lady
Lavery, Baron Emile and Baroness d'Erlanger, the Marquis of Carisbrook,
the Duke and Duchess of Lacera, Mr. and Mrs. Courtauld (the same
Mr. Courtauld on whose yacht Johnny had had the wonderful reunion
with Winston Churchill), the Marchioness of Londonderry, Viscount
Castleneagh, the Spanish Ambassador and the Marquise de Merry del
Val, the Master of Sempill, the Countess of How, the Dowager Lady
Gelentanar, and Sir Ernest and Lady Oppenheimer. Mother was afraid
that so much attention was being paid to her that Flora would be jealous,
but if Flora was jealous she certainly wasn't showing it and seemed to be
hugely enjoying herself and her protégée's success.

Johnny was already home when Mother and Flora returned to 6
Connaught Street, where Flora insisted on coming in and regaling Johnny
with the incredible first-night success of his beautiful wife. Johnny, slightly
bewildered by his mother's sudden change of attitude, took my mother in
his arms and kissed her lovingly. "I'm so proud of you," he said, and choked
up. Mother took his hand and Flora's and led them back down the stairs

to the dining room, where a cold buffet was set on the sideboard, the table laid, all owing to Bertha, who had stayed up so that she could turn on the flame under the turtle soup and the coffee urn when Mother and Flora returned. As it turned out, they had never touched the food proffered at the dinner, because they were too busy circulating around the hotel's ballroom. Molly was also in attendance, waiting to put Mother's clothes away and draw her bath, much desired after such an exhausting evening, and, most important of all, to hear Mother's version of her coming out.

As Mother said when she bade Flora good night, "It truly has been a night to remember, Flora. I thank you with all my heart."

Two days after Mother's spectacular success, the invitations started coming in, the majority from the ladies, for tea, but also from many of Johnny's friends who had not attended the event but had read about it in the society pages in their newspapers and magazines. They, too, sent invitations for dinner, anxious to meet Johnny's wife, already a celebrity in her own right.

This was all like champagne for Mother's ego, and built her confidence up to the point where she decided that, whatever Flora did or didn't do, she would be respectful of her,but never again intimidated by her. I wish I could have felt the same way: I was scared of her into my twenties.

Looking back on Flora's unexpectedly good behavior, I suspect that she had originally imagined that she could dominate and isolate Mother from those attending the dinner to whom she wished to present Mother. She was convinced that her own forceful personality would overwhelm Mother's simply by her familiarity with those guests to whom she was presenting her daughter-in-law.

Flora, like her son Johnny, was unquestionably a presence, but star quality she did not have, nor did she have the beauty or overwhelming charm that Mother so naturally exuded, captivating without effort those who came within her circle. When Flora, who was no fool, realized that Mother was making an enormous impression on all those distinguished acquaintances to whom she was presented, she changed direction, deeming it would be to her advantage as the "presenter" to have her daughter-in-law succeed, since it would reflect not only to her credit but also to her beloved son's credit, for having made such a great choice of wife.

Hence Flora's amazing turnaround. Whether temporary or permanent, it made for a glorious and long-remembered evening for Mother, and was one of the rare moments when I felt some measure of gratitude to my aunt.

Vignettes from St. Peter's Court:
1930 to 1934

Charles Ridgeway

It was supposed that Charles Ridgeway, the son of the headmaster and his wife, probably in his late thirties or early forties, was being groomed to eventually take over the position of headmaster. He had a square body and a round face; bereft of charm and personality, he was nonetheless a pleasant enough man. Unlike his wonderful father and mother, he did not seem comfortable with either children or grownups, and much to his parents' regret had never taken a lady out alone. Also, he appeared to be friendless. I never saw him in anybody's company except the staff or visiting parents, and he seemed to have no particular favorite among them.

Charles had a private study on the dormitory floor, where the butler would bring him a glass of sherry every evening at about six, which I suspected was the high point of his day. When excited or upset, he had the dreadful habit of scratching his bottom with considerable vigor, which was not very much appreciated by the boys' parents or the boys themselves, for that matter.

At my first half term, when we boys were being visited by our parents, my mother arrived uninformed of Charles Ridgeway's grossly unbecoming habit. Who should be the first to greet her but the man himself? Obviously, he was excited and nonplussed, for his first reaction was to attack his bottom with alarming force. Mother, of course, was at first astonished, not quite sure whether to avert her eyes or even remove herself from the scene, but Charles was trying to welcome her as a new parent, and she feared doing anything that might cause him to be even more abrasive to his derrière.

Poor Mother: In spite of all her efforts to master herself, she was suddenly consumed with the giggles, which only caused Charles to scratch ever more aggressively and Mother to burst into hysterical laughter. Since Mother's laughter was very catching, the unfortunate parents who were standing with their sons nearby and were well aware of Charles's proclivity, were suddenly bereft of all control and joined in the general jubilation.

I, of course, was torn between utter embarrassment and the exhaustion that comes from desperately trying to control the uncontrollable. To make matters worse, Charles, whose expression had at first been pained, then, apparently not deducing the reason for the hysteria around him, decided to join in the merriment, which only drove the general hilarity to falling-down madness. Amazingly, when Mother finally regained enough composure to actually speak to Charles, he greeted her with these words: "I seem to have missed the point, but there is nothing like a good laugh, is there?"

Mother agreed and, taking his arm, walked him back into the school building and up into his study, which I had shown her when she first arrived and she was inspecting my dormitory. I stayed behind, too unnerved to follow her into some other unexpected situation. My body feeling weak from laughing, I went in search of my friend Oscar Busch.

Some forty minutes later, Mother returned, looking pleased and happy. She had known from me that Charles liked sherry, and she had taken him back to his study, where she sat him down so that he could not scratch himself anymore and they each had a glass of sherry together (even though Mother hated sherry). Charles had brought out a bottle he kept hidden for special occasions. Actually, everybody in the school knew where it was hidden, but all were honor bound not to go near it. According to Mother, they had a pleasant and stilted conversation, but she did tell him a funny joke, which brought a genuine laugh from him, leaving Charles, she felt, reasonably assuaged.

Later, he told me that I was very lucky to have such a wonderful mother. I agreed.

Mr. Linford

Mr. Linford's class was the first class I took. I sat in the second row of desks and had a beautiful window view of the playing fields, which, though pleasing to the eye, was somewhat distracting to my concentration, which was never good to begin with. I must admit that, scholasticaly, I was not at all a good student, doing well only in writing (though I was a terrible speller – and still am). I enjoyed writing my first poem at four years old, and my first short story at six.

My real problem was one that was not understood in those days, but that dogged me to some degree all my life, even though it is today reasonably easy to cure. It's called Attention Deficit Disorder. Hence, I must confess that, except for writing, I was an abominable burden on my teachers, and how I got into Eton I will never know, particularly since I was placed not in the bottom class at Eton, but in the one above the bottom class. The Reverend Mr. Ridgeway, when he received my entrance results from the school, went around the school all day with a glazed expression in his eyes.

I couldn't blame him. If ever there should have been a failure at passing the exams, it would have been I, and here I had come out smelling like a rose.

Whoopee for me!

But to get back to Mr. Linford. He, too, was a bit of a loner, and with an odd sense of humor. In his first class of the term, our Latin class, he would have us reciting amo, amas, amat, etc., etc. And also eram, eras, erat, and when we got to "erat" he would leap up onto the chair behind his desk and scream, "A rat, a rat, where's the rat?" The new boys, including me, all jumped up on the benches behind our desks, while the second-term boys guffawed patronizingly from their seats. It was fun, and it was ridiculous, but in some way it gave us a valuable connection with this schoolmaster, who spent his holidays cruising the oceans until the next term. Knowing the pathetic salaries of teachers in those days, I can only assume that he was endowed with a supplemental income from somewhere else.

Actually, one summer holiday he came to our home for a month to tutor me. On his arrival, Mother welcomed him and asked how he felt. "Constipated," he replied, and was escorted to his room by one of the staff.

Mother never asked after his health again.

Mr. Thorn

Mr. Thorn was very tall and angular, and a born bachelor. During the winter terms, particularly when watching a football match against another prep school, he would always have a droplet hanging precariously at the end of his nose. All the boys and even some of the masters, both from our school and the competing schools, would be fascinated by that droplet.

Sometimes, when it was especially cold and the sun was shining down, it would take on the colors of the rainbow and become a shimmering work of art. But what kept our attention, and our hope, was that the droplet would fall from his nose. Amazingly, it never happened.

Mr. Thorn was the first and only schoolmaster at our school to own a car, a small, very streamlined and smart-looking Ford. It cost him one hundred pounds, brand new. In those days, that was about five hundred dollars. I got to ride in it on a few occasions and was thrilled.

Mr. Thorn was in his late sixties, never having married. He appeared hearty, but uncomfortable with parents. One day he told the Reverend Mr. Ridgeway that he was engaged to be married. Unbelievable, but true: Ridgeway was delighted. When he asked who the lucky lady was, he was almost jolted out of his skin when told the answer, she being a charming woman of considerable wealth, socially and charitably in the upper crust of the Broadstairs elite.

Nine months from the day of their wedding, a baby boy was born, and Mr. Thorn, who had moved out of his quarters at St. Peter's Court into his bride's palatial home, became a stern but joyful father. Some people can really surprise you, can't they?

Madame LeBrun

I am inclined to believe that Madame LeBrun, our French teacher, was the saving grace that helped me, knowingly or unknowingly, to pass my exams into Eton. I knew that she favored me a little bit, but all teachers are inclined to have their favorites, even though they would probably swear on a stack of bibles that they didn't.

It was near the very end of the last term of my last year at St. Peter's Court, and this nice roly-poly lady was handing out to her students large single sheets of paper, which contained eight long paragraphs from a French novel, in French. It filled one whole single-spaced page, and we were supposed to translate it into English. This sounded reasonably easy, but very little was easy for me at school, and I inwardly groaned as I set to the task.

At the end of class, she collected all our papers, and said that she would return them, corrected, at the next French class. A few days later, we returned to Madame LeBrun's classroom and were given back our corrected papers, my results falling in the middle of the class. I was so pleased with myself for not having ended up in my usual place at or near the bottom that I made a point of reading her corrected version over and over again to myself, not so much for remembering the story, but to applaud my middle-level victory.

Next came the real thing: the examination that would surely eliminate me from any chance of going to Eton. Two weeks later, the seven students, including me, sat in a classroom alone, except for an examiner from another local school to ensure fairness, who told us the rules of taking the exam and then sat in stony silence at the master's desk while the clock ticked on to the appointed hour. Our examination papers were each in a separate sealed envelope, which we were forbidden to open until the clock struck the hour.

There were eight minutes to go. Nobody was allowed to speak, so we just sat, our inner core turning to ice, the suspense breaking into dampness on our foreheads. It was the longest eight minutes I can ever remember.

Finally, the examiner gave the signal to go, and the examination began. At first I sat numbed, recognizing nothing that made an iota of sense, and I wondered if I should escape to the bathroom and drown myself in the toilet.

But somewhere in the first hour I saw some things that I could answer. And then I discovered that the largest part of the exam was taken up by the challenge to translate that selfsame lesson that Madame LeBrun had given us and corrected. I couldn't believe my luck, for I had burnt that piece into my brain out of pure egotism, being so full of myself for not having ended up at the bottom of the pile. Here it was two weeks later, and I could translate it again with the greatest of ease.

When the examination results were announced, and I had surprised everybody, including myself, by passing into a class at Eton higher than the bottom class, I knew it had to have something to do with my perfect translation of that French piece that Madame LeBrun had given us just two weeks before. The examination papers had not even arrived at St. Peter's Court until after Madame LeBrun had returned our corrected papers, so I am ninety-nine percent sure that there was no way she could have seen the examination papers ahead of time, since on arrival through the post they were immediately put in the the Reverend Mr. Ridgeway's safe until examination day.

Was it an incredible stroke of luck that Madame LeBrun had given us that test just two weeks before the exams, or was there another answer? I believe in luck, and that's exactly what it was. I hope.

The Birds and the Bees

Almost all young boys, I believe, upon laying their eyes upon some particular young lady, have felt the sudden longing, that unexpected warmth, that momentarily knocks them off balance. I certainly did, more than once, and my reaction was so innocent: to write a poem about her, to put her on a pedestal beyond my reach, the subject of my desire to be revered and shared with no one, not even my best friend.

My upbringing had been so protected by nannies and Miss Milligan, continuing on at St. Peter's Court, that if there was a big bad world out there, I knew little about it. But the honest-to-God truth is that the twenties, thirties, and forties (war and all) were far more civilized, far better mannered – in all classes – and far more honest than the world today. In those days a man's word was his bond, and you didn't break that bond without being stigmatized for the rest of your life. Today, anything goes.

But now to get back to the topic of this chapter, the Birds and the Bees. On the last day of term, those boys who were leaving to go on to Eton, Harrow, Winchester, etc., and who had passed their examinations – all seven of us had, even I – were invited to the headmaster's study for what purpose we were not told. My good friends Patrick Plunket, Henry C., and Oskar Busch were leaving at the same time, the first two coming on to Eton with me, while Oscar, much to my chagrin, was leaving to go to Harrow. I am glad to say that we continued to stay with each other on holidays, usually for a couple of weeks.

The Reverend Mr. Ridgeway, who had been talking to Mrs. Ridgeway when we arrived, welcomed us warmly and seated us, while Mrs. Ridgeway made a hasty retreat. All of us boys were twelve to twelve and a half years old.

Let me make a final preface, which if you are young today you will not believe, but it is a fact that I had never heard the word "sex," as in SEX, mentioned in my life. Neither had any of the other boys in the room except one who had been brought up on a farm, and he connected its usage only to the reproductive practices of this or that animal.

I felt sorry for Mr. Ridgeway, for he was such a good man, and even he seemed embarrassed during his lecture on sex and how we were conceived, with the aid of two drawings, both excruciatingly intimate and in your face. I was appalled, numbed and frankly a little queasy. If this was what sex was all about, I wanted no part of it.

Seven silent boys exited the room, our faces funereal. Needing fresh air, we walked outside and sat glumly on some chairs on the patio off the parking area. Finally, Oscar, God bless him, started to giggle and soon had us all in uncontrollable laughter, a mad and marvelous release from the oppressive weirdness of our beloved headmaster's presentation.

As a final note on this subject, let me mention that my very best friend at Eton, Gavin Colville, when we were about fifteen, told me on his return from the summer holidays how much he had enjoyed the Disney movie, *Snow White and the Seven Dwarfs*. He also told me in absolute seriousness that he had fallen completely in love with Snow White and that he would one day seek his very own Snow White, for only someone as pure and lovely as she would be his wife.

Sadly, Gavin's RAF bomber was shot down over Germany early in the Second World War, and he did not survive. I loved him very much and valued his friendship above all others, and only hope that he finally found his Snow White in heaven.

Johnny Dodge: Man of Mystery

J ohnny Dodge had two major advantages: the wonderful support he received from the firm's partners, and the surprisingly subtle and creative advice of Mr. Crouch, the manager. Now, in the mid-thirties, he was making an indelible mark for himself, not only in the City, but in other European capitals and the United States.

Of course it didn't hurt him that his mother, though not landing a Duke or an Earl, had married into the Guest family, to the wealthy Honourable Lionel Guest, son of the late Lord Wimborne and cousin of the Duke of Marlborough, who also had an American wife himself, one Consuela Vanderbilt.

Besides his adventures in Russia, Johnny had visited Siberia, Mongolia, China, Burma, India, Persia (Iran), Turkey, the Caucasus, and Australia; in addition, he had, of course, grown up in the United States and Canada, where he had attended McGill University in Montreal. He was, at thirty-six, a very well-traveled and well-versed man in the ways of humankind. And did he have charisma!

He was also a secretive man. Mother, many years into their marriage and still madly in love with him, told me that Johnny lived in three distinct worlds. The first two were with his wife and family and friends and in the high-stepping, rarefied, and fascinating world of the chosen few, those commanding great power in banking, industry, commerce, government, and diplomacy. Johnny had an amazing gift for cultivating these titans of their chosen fields, using one fine contact to lead him to another and another, often across oceans and countries; when these extraordinary men visited our London home, they could never say enough good things about Johnny, and Mother and Flora purred happily, for once in harmony.

As Johnny's influence spread, so did his prophetic observations on the growing military power of the three most dangerous dictators of the time, Stalin, Hitler, and Mussolini. Many of his opinions were naturally in step with those of Winston Churchill, who was desperately trying to galvanize the country, and in particular Prime Ministers Baldwin and later Chamberlain, to do something about the enormous gap in military preparedness between the democracies – including the isolationist United States – and the dictatorships, particularly Hitler's Nazi Germany.

Speaking of dictators leads me to one of the only times that Mother actually shared a brief insight into the third, secretive part of Johnny's life, the one her husband seemed to relish the most.

It was in the fifties, and they were having a quiet dinner at home, when Johnny asked her if she would like to visit Yugoslavia with him for a few days. Thinking that he had been attracted by the propaganda blitz issuing from the Yugoslavian Tourist Bureau, touting the beauty and pleasures to be found in that country with vivid photographs on posters catching your eye on every bus and Underground train in London in recent weeks, she gave a joyful assent, quickly putting Molly to work choosing and packing her clothes for the trip.

They left by plane, seated in aisle seats across from each another, Johnny needing more leg room that the average passenger and Mother preferring not to disturb the other passengers seated with her if she decided to exercise her legs, as prescribed by their doctor, who was years ahead of his time.

Johnny had given Mother some color brochures and repeated that, even though this would be a somewhat unusual kind of a holiday, and he had a mission of considerable importance to perform, she was to take it all in stride. Indeed, knowing Mother's upbeat attitude, he felt that she might even enjoy it.

After landing at the airport, they were escorted off the plane first and greeted at the bottom of the stairs by an English-speaking police officer. Their luggage having been rushed through Customs unopened, they were then led to a long black Russian-made car, whose driver soon chauffeured them through the twilight up a winding road to the top of a medium-sized mountain. There stood a castle, with a water-filled moat and the drawbridge down. They entered a large courtyard.

During the ride from the airport, Johnny told Mother about Marshall Tito, the President of Yugoslavia, and what a great leader he had been during the Second World War. His guerrilla army had fought in the mountains and the forests against the Germans, finally chasing them out altogether, and bringing the many independent states of Yugoslavia into one united country with himself as President. He was a Communist and a dictator, though more of a benevolent dictator like Getulio Vargas, who had led Brazil for over twenty years.

Tito was not only a very brave and brilliant leader of his country, he was also prickly when he felt that someone was trying to take advantage of him. When he decided that Stalin, the most powerful Communist in the world, was trying to use him, he cut off all communication with the Russian government. He would have no trade with Stalin from that day on, for which he enjoyed Stalin's exasperated and angry respect.

After being escorted to very luxurious quarters in the guest wing of the castle by an Oxford-educated aide to the President, Johnny and Mother were given an hour to rest, bathe, and dress again, before the same aide would return to escort them to dinner. His name was Hans, and by the time their trip was over he was completely under their spell and actually teary-eyed at their leaving.

The evening went splendidly. First, Tito greeted Johnny with a big hug, and then pinned him with Yugoslavia's highest military medal of honor for his bravery during the First and Second World Wars. After that, he presented his wife to Johnny and my mother, who had already received a kiss on the hand from the President.

Mother said Mrs. Tito was attractive in a heavy-boned way, and with the help of Hans, who had joined them at the table, the evening developed into a very pleasant one, though it focused on the war. Afterward, Johnny told Mother he thought Tito was more knowledgeable of the English language than he gave out, but that he seemed agreeable enough.

The plan for the next two or three days was for Johnny and Tito to meet and discuss Johnny's mission, while Mrs. Tito and Mother would spend the days driving around the countryside in one of Tito's chauffeured cars, having their lunches in one of the many colorful inns dotting their route. It was beautiful countryside, just as the posters in the Underground had said, and the weather was perfect.

Mother and Mrs. Tito took to each other immediately. Although neither of them could speak much of the other's language, they made up for it with hand motions, considerable arm waving, and facial manipulations that often ended in hysterical laughter. Mother was greatly relieved that Mrs. Tito had the same sense of humor that she had, for otherwise it could have been a deadly situation that not even Mother could have saved.

Years later, Tito divorced his wife. As far as I know, he never married again.

On their return to London, Johnny reported on his trip to the Foreign Office, where, he eventually admitted to Mother, the purpose and implementation of this mission had been hatched. Naturally, he had been glad to report that his mission had been successful.

Never a word about Johnny's mission got into the press. To this day, I have no idea what the true purpose of his trip was. This was the secret side of Johnny's life, and having given him her word, Mother never questioned him about it, though she did say, rather sadly, I thought, that it was better to have half of Johnny than no Johnny at all. He was her man, the only man she ever really adored.

A week later he took her for a ten-day vacation on the French Riviera. Ooh la la!

A Question of Sensitivity

In the second year of Johnny's marriage to my mother, his firm decided that, with a beautiful wife and hostess who could share the entertaining with him, Johnny needed a country residence to welcome his gilt-edged clients during the English summer, hopefully the safest time of the year weather-wise.

Johnny already had a sixty-six-foot sailing yacht with diesel engine, docked nearby in Worthing and recently re-christened *Minerva*, another whammy-blow to Flora, and one-up for Mother. By all accounts, Johnny was a wonderful sailor, enjoying entertaining his clients with trips around the coast and sometimes across the water to the French Riviera, a favorite watering hole of his.

His crew was a complete family of four, the Captain's surname being Frankenstein, though he was known as Captain Frank for short. His wife, Stella, was a surprisingly good cook. His son, Hotspier, twenty-one years old, was later to go into the Navy during the Second World War and get blown up on HMS *Hood*; in the meantime, he was extraordinarily good at fixing just about anything that went wrong, and in addition was a genius at handling the sails. So was his sister, Pamela, eighteen, though her main jobs were to serve the meals, keep the cabins clean, and change and make up the beds. The whole family was versatile, and though I rarely went aboard the vessel, I never heard a cross word between any of them.

The reason I seldom went aboard the *Minerva* was that just looking at the yacht, beautiful though it was, made me feel seasick. I even got sick in the car, if it was a long trip. When I reached eleven, it all went away, thank goodness.

Incidentally, it was about this time that the Royal Yacht Squadron, the most prestigious yacht club in the world, invited Johnny to become a member. He accepted, and moved his yacht and crew to Cowes.

Our country house was located in Ferring, at least ten minutes by car from Wookitipi. Johnny immediately named it Florida, in memory of the state that gave him the woman he loved above all others. This was a double whammy-blow to Flora, who bit her tongue and bided her time until Lionel should die, now sooner rather than later, while she planned her revenge.

The house had been a mini hotel but looked more like a squire's home, boasting eight very comfortable bedrooms and baths, a large drawing room with marble fireplace, a beautiful dining room, and a small but efficient bar. It sat slap in the middle of eight acres of well-tended lawn and flower beds, with oak trees circling the estate against a stone wall, eight feet high, broken only at the entrance by two heavily barred gates, electrically operated. The driveway led in a circular route to the house's front entrance and followed around to a parking area in the back, where the staff lived in an wing extended from the house. The roof was thatched, something I had never seen before but was to see many times again; it looked quaint at first, and yet it belonged.

The only two sporting pastimes that I really excelled in were tennis and horseback riding; my shelves weighed down with silver cups and trays from both singles and doubles tennis matches. This is not to forget the joy of hunting the fox, though I sometimes, particularly when we couldn't find our quarry, got an eerie feeling that the fox was following us.

Every year, when the hunting season started in the fall, Molly and I would leave London to spend two days and nights at Florida, in order for me to have a day of hunting with the Crowley and Horsham pack. The Master of the Hunt was Mr. Cubit, a stern and cold man as far as I was concerned, but I'm sure a good Master anyway.

There's really nothing in the world quite like the experience of fox hunting in England. The sport is banned today, I'm sorry to say.

I hunted with three packs, three of them, before and after the Second World War Before the war were the Crowley and Horsham and the Blackmoor-Vale packs; before and after the war I hunted with my spinster step-aunt, Aura Guest, whom I adored, and her pack, the Guest pack.

Never married, Aunt Aura lived in a charming weathered house in Somerset, with a cook, a butler, and a very well-educated French overseer. The last had put her feet to the fire by placing her in a cottage on the estate for six years in the late twenties and early thirties, during which time practically all the staff were placed in positions with other employers, the main building was closed down and locked up, and the Frenchman, whose first name was Guy (I can't remember his last name), put into motion a complete recuperation plan for the financial survival of her estate. In those six years he had gotten it financially stable and productive, after which the big house could be reopened and Aunt Aura returned to her mansion. Believe it or not, she could then also be Master and ride to hounds again with her very own pack, the Guest pack, which I believe shared part of the area belonging to the Blackmoor-Vale pack.

When Aunt Aura was in her sixties, she acted like she was still in her forties. She was tone deaf (didn't follow music at all), but in all other ways she was a bubbling lady. Why she never married I cannot imagine, but in her own way she lived a good life, close to nature, close to her beloved animals: whether horses or dogs or wild beasties of the night, she loved them all.

Furthermore, when she was in the sidesaddle, her horse Archibald pressing on the reins, as thrilled and eager to go as she was, and the hounds suddenly bursting into voice with the scent of the fox to drive them, and the thrilling sound of the bugle sending the riders over hill and dale, ditches, fences, water, and whatever – all that was pure heaven to Aunt Aura. She was of that generation, now long gone. I'm glad for them: they had it all, and died knowing nothing better and nothing worse.

For my part, while with the pack of the Crowley and Horsham hunt and keeping a respectful distance from the others, I discovered that a new and younger member of the hunt could earn three distinct prizes. Your chances of actually getting a fox are probably one in three to one in five, but the jumping of fences and wide ditches and the excitement of the hounds in full chase all made up for a day when no fox was caught. As to the prizes, I won my first when I was nine: it was the "pad," the paw of the fox, and upon presenting it to me, the Master of the Hunt Mr. Cubit spread the bloody paw across my face, with undue relish, I thought. I immediately reinterpreted this such that I became an American Indian putting on his war paint, and I swore an oath that I wouldn't take it off until the end of the week. And I didn't, in spite of the fact that Mother refused to let me go downtown (to the village, really) for Kit Kats and other chocolate nourishment – indeed, refused to let me off the premises until I removed it. It was a deadlock. I think we were both kind of glad when it was over.

This was the only time Mother was in Ferring for the hunt, so she never saw me returning triumphantly with the brush (tail) or the mask (face). The pad was elevated by a silver ring on one end; the brush, also. The mask, stuffed and fixed to a board, had an inscription underneath noting my name, the name of the hunt, and the day I was awarded it.

One day, when I was eleven years old and had already attended three hunts that season, I got the idea to ask Molly if she would like to come to the hunt with me. She was thrilled, so I made arrangements to reserve two rather than one seat on the bus that picked me up among the others who were going to Miss Marshall's Riding Stables, where most of us kept our ponies.

My pony was Sarah, an ebony-colored mount that could fly over any obstruction in its way, and when I say fly, I mean fly! She was the fastest pony I ever rode, but she also had a mind of her own, and if she decided she didn't want to go where you wanted to go, you didn't go. I had a love/hate relationship with her, but when she was in good humor, she was the best.

I had warned Molly that she would have an hour's walk from Miss Marshall's stables to the rendezvous on the downs (small hills) where we would join the Crowley and Horsham Pack. She said she didn't care; in fact, when we started off, she kept up with Sarah with no apparent effort at all. When we made it onto the downs and finally the hunt came into view, Molly's face was flushed with the chill air and the exertion from the walk; she looked so pretty in one of Mother's pass-me-downs, and I was so happy for her. And then I saw a groom up on his piebald horse and beckoned him over. He and I had become friends, even though he was in his late twenties and I was only eleven. He stirred his horse into a short canter and drew up with a big smile, more for Molly than for me. I said, rather grandly, I thought, "Molly, this is my good friend Harry Bossam, who has taught me a lot about hunting." Harry jumped off his horse and stretched out his hand to Molly, whereupon I said, "And this is Molly, my mother's maid." I looked at Molly, and in that moment I knew I had said something terrible: her face that one moment had been so happy and expectant, at the next was so clearly hurt, so lost, so without words.

Suddenly the hounds got the scent, the bugle blew, and the hunt began. Harry Bossam, God bless him, took her hand in his and said, "I'm sorry, Miss Molly, but I must go. I hope I may see you again one day." And he got back on his horse, bowed to Molly, and cantered off to join the hunt.

Molly stood, looking at nothing, seeing nothing, and all because an eleven-year-old jerk named Peter Sherman had failed his mother's constant admonishment "to always treat royalty as you would your maid, and your maid as you would royalty."

I got down from Sarah and burst into tears, and Molly, already crying, put her arms around me as I did her, and we held each other close until we had no more tears left.

Why in the world did I have to add "my mother's maid"? I didn't introduce Harry Bossam as "a groom." I am truly sorry that Molly had to suffer that insensitive and utterly unnecessary addition to my introduction. While writing this, I have relived every minute and every word of it. I have long since accepted Molly's forgiveness through blinding tears, and I feel so much better for it. Molly could forgive me, but I never could forgive myself – until now. I'm sorry you had to go through this with me, but it's been good for me to have you along. Thank you very much.

Roger: Super Dog

Roger was a Cairn, a small, shaggy, short-legged terrier. We got him as a pup, and from the very beginning we knew he was different from all other dogs. For one thing, even when he was little he had a commanding presence; when he was being walked, in the tiny gated park in the middle of Connaught Square, the other dogs would move out of his way as if majesty were passing. Even the big dogs respected him, and should one or two get perilously close, he would bark. It was more of a chirp when he was young, but the chirp and Roger's superman charge after his disrespectful neighbors set his antagonists in hurried retreat.

Roger was a character and a loner, which he remained almost to the end of his days. He neither demanded friends nor had any friends, because he was not a neighborly dog, and yet our family and friends were all in awe of him. We wondered sometimes if he really was a dog, or rather some ancient spirit that had inexplicably ended up in a dog's body. Maybe a Mandarin, perhaps the imperial Manchu, a member of the Tartar people forming the last Chinese imperial dynasty? Whatever: He was one unique dog, and the best part was that he was no trouble at all, living and ruling his own kingdom, which consisted of all the staff, the family, and everyone who came and entered the house.

Roger would go up to a stranger and, from a few inches off the floor, stare up at him or her right in the eye, utterly still, until the stranger could bear it no longer and either moved on or started making doggy talk and leaning down to pet him. Moving on was the thing to do. Petting was just not done. After all, have you ever tried to pet a King? Roger, who possessed the speed of Superman, would suddenly move his head up as if someone had come in behind his tormentor, who would immediately turn to see who was there. No one was there! When the visitor turned back, Roger would have vanished. Nobody knew how, and the visitor would be left bending down to pet the air. Usually, the visitor would then draw him or herself up, look around the room with considerable alarm, and leave with an expression of absolute disbelief, too embarrassed to tell anyone about it. Who would believe it anyway?

It was during the summer, a time of long weekends, with many guest and tennis tournaments. We had four tennis courts at the far end of the estate, a gift from Lionel and Flora, with a clubhouse attached, and on weekends, particularly, they were fully occupied most of the day. There was also a private path that took exactly one minute to traverse to reach the beach – a pebble beach, I am sorry to say, but one can get used to almost anything, and anyway there were miles of sand and rock to explore when the tide went out, often, it seemed, for at least half a mile.

There was always something new to discover, and I still carried a small metal spade and bucket for bringing back unusual seashells and sea life that caught my curiosity. When the tide was in, I paddled my "foldboat" merrily over the waves for whole mornings on end, captain of my fate.

For some days Mother and I had been observing Roger, who had become more and more lethargic. He was now in his ninth year. He had taken to lying in one place for hours on end, and the staff had started bringing his food to him rather than expecting him to go to the same dish in the same place in the butler's pantry, as had been his custom during the previous years of his life. Having decided that Roger needed a doctor, we drove to Worthing (there being no vet in Ferring), where we had made an appointment with a vet on the recommendation of a friend.

The veterinarian put Roger on the table in his surgery room, and after twenty minutes of feeling him and listening to him through his stethoscope, Roger behaving perfectly, he gave us his findings. Roger had a massive tumor that should have killed him some time ago and would kill him very shortly. Alas, only when the tumor started impinging painfully on Roger's little body was it discovered, almost inevitably too late.

It was at that moment when Mother and I realized what an important role in our lives this little fellow had played, and how much pride we had taken in his imperial behavior and superior isolation from the rest of the world. His very stoicism in the face of great pain had not broken his spirit or his courage, and certainly not his character. What a dog! What a king!

We told the vet we would bring Roger back at ten a.m. the next morning. On the drive back, Roger allowed me to hold him on my lap, and, as Mother drove us through the entrance gates, I marveled that in the three or four years that we had so far lived at Florida, during the summer, Roger had guarded his preserve so faithfully that not one single dog in all that time had poked even one black nose through the gates, let alone trodden upon the sacred grounds that were reserved for his pleasure alone.

The next morning, a good half an hour earlier than she was supposed to wake me, Molly came rushing into my bedroom in a state of high excitement, exclaiming, "Master Peter, Master Peter, look out the window! Come and look out quick!" Sleepy, but curious as to what had provoked such excitement in Molly at this early time of day, I lurched out of bed, while she rushed off to wake my parents to the spectacle. Spectacle was, indeed, the only word for it. There was Roger, looking half his age, leading a pack of twenty-three dogs, all neighbors' dogs, around his estate with yelps and barks of joy coming from his newfound friends, all their tails wagging furiously, even Roger's, God love him.

As soon as they passed out of sight, I ran to Johnny and Mother's suite, where I found them standing at the window, staring open-mouthed at the fantastic parade going by, holding hands, both of them teary-eyed. So was I. It was a sight I will never forget. I think that, somewhere in Roger's Mandarin mind, he knew his hours were numbered and felt the best gift he could give to those poor neighborhood creatures who had been eagerly seeking his permission to enter the gates for so many years would be a guided tour by the master himself.

Roger must have finally ushered them out, for after breakfast there was no sign of his guests, and Roger was enjoying his favorite meal, one usually reserved for Sundays, but a treat on this fatal day. It was warm porridge, with brown sugar and rich cream on top, a dish that I had incorporated into the house breakfast menu after gorging myself on it during the cold winter mornings when it was served at breakfast at St. Peter's Court.

One day Roger had been sitting at my feet as I was eating this breakfast, and had started making funny noises in his throat. I ordered a duplicate to be prepared for Roger. He ate every bit of it! An unusual breakfast for an unusual dog.

Roger was not fond of cars, but he lay quietly in my lap until we reached the vet's office in Worthing. The vet asked if we were ready. We said yes, and I placed Roger on the surgery table, so white and sterile-looking, and Mother and I each kissed Roger, fearing that to hug him would cause him pain. The vet shot the injection into him. Roger didn't complain. In fact, he started wagging his tail and licking our tear-stained faces, as if saying goodbye, and then he just keeled over and was gone.

We didn't say a word going home. What was there left to say?

We had a burial service for him the next morning, just the family and the guests staying over. He was laid to rest beneath the branches of his favorite oak tree, with his own little tombstone. There wasn't a dry eye in the house.

Two Half Brothers

I have two half brothers, both being the sons of Mother and Johnny Dodge. The first, David John Bigelow Dodge, was born when I was nine years old, and the second, Tony Lionel Arrington Bigelow Dodge, when I was twelve years old. David had a very impressive christening, and I will quote from the London *Times* of that day:

Distinguished Godfathers
"Few children have three such well-known godfathers as David, the son of Colonel John B. Dodge and Mrs. Dodge, who was christened yesterday at St. John's Church, Southwick-Crescent, London. His godfathers are the Honourable Sir Harry Stoner, a Groom-in-Waiting to the King; the Honourable Piers Legh, Equerry to the Prince of Wales; and the Honourable Lionel Guest. Colonel Dodge is the son of the Honourable Mrs. Lionel Guest.

"Lord Desborough, Lady Lily Fitzgerald, the Dowager Marchioness of Blandford, the Honourable Mrs. Piers Legh, and the Honourable Mrs. Lionel Guest were present at the ceremony."

Tony Dodge couldn't remember where he was christened, but his godfathers were General Lord Bernard Freyburg and Victor Cazelot, both prominent in their day.

I was devoted to both my brothers, and we had some wonderful times together once we all became adults.

Friends, in Eton and the Hereafter

I n my day, 1934–1937, Eton College, a village at the foot of Windsor, separated from the larger town by a small bridge, contained approximately eleven hundred Etonians split up into houses of about fifty students each, plus housemaster and family.

My house was called the Corner House, situated at the end of the Long Walk, and its resident housemaster was Mr. B.G. Whitfield. Like my previous headmaster at St. Peter's Court, he appeared born to take charge and play a significant role in our development during our formative years.

Mr. Whitfield was low-key and easy to talk to; he had a rather high-pitched voice as a result of being gassed by the enemy in the trenches during the First World War. Nice-looking, of medium height, wonderful with "his boys," he had a wife and son whom we rarely if ever saw, since his family flat was in a separate part of the Corner House, with a separate entrance.

Each of us boys had his own room, with maid service. The contents consisted of a folding bed, a fireplace, one window, a wardrobe for absolutely everything, a table and two chairs on which to study for the next day's class and to have high tea served in the afternoon, a cupboard on the wall for jams and easily preserved foods, plus room for one's tuck-box. Frankly, it was something of a squeeze, but it was mine, all mine.

What made my situation even better was that Gavin Colville, whose father, I was told, had made a fortune in steel and bore the grand title of High Sheriff, and I had become good friends from the second day after we met, and remained so for the rest of Gavin's life. This was the period when a young man's friendships were honed, and I must take a moment to emphasize the wonder and satisfaction I enjoyed during this time, and how lucky I was to have such a coterie of friends, not only at Eton, but also at Ferring and in London.

At Eton, as I have already mentioned, besides Gavin Colville, there were two of my friends from St. Peter's Court, Patrick Plunket and Henry C., who had come on to Eton at the same time with me. Both Henry and Patrick survived the war – a rare outcome.

All of us visited each other during those lazy summer holidays, and it was one round of complete and utter idleness, except for doing whatever we wanted to do. We also bonded by going to whoever's home we felt like. Sometimes there would be four of us, all staying at one friend's house. But it was always easy on the parents of our friends, because they all had plenty of staff to run their houses and grounds, as I did; thus, if there were many of us gathered at one family home, we would have a cricket match with the staff, at which time they would almost invariably beat us, and staff and guests would be honored by our hosts personally serving glasses of iced lemonade and smoked salmon sandwiches (no crust, of course), or, if we were especially lucky, caviar sandwiches. It was all very democratic and great fun.

I was a good wicket keeper, but a terrible batsman, and, though I made the first cricket team at St. Peter's Court, Eton's first team was way beyond me. I must confess, nevertheless, that I hungered, deep down, to be on the Eton team against Harrow at Lords, and dreamed of smashing the ball all over the field to tumultuous applause and a gigantic win over our traditional opponent.

In addition, at Ferring, I had two good friends, Rollo and Richard Spencer, both of whom were brilliant at just about everything they did. At school they were always winning top honors, both scholastically and athletically. Rollo was three years older than Richard and I, so it was with Richard that I did the most, including bicycle and boating adventures and just about everything in between.

One day we were shooting our air guns (pellets) at targets; finally tiring of this pursuit, we challenged each other to a shooting match, each of us from behind a barrel, each barrel being about fifty feet from the other. The purpose was to try to hit each other, which in hindsight seems pretty silly, since neither of us had any intention of letting one person see any part of the other person. After complete silence for a few minutes, Richard started baiting me with imaginative slurs on my character that he hoped would rattle me into showing some defiance and perhaps exposing some part of my person. My remaining mute and invisible drove him to fire off his gun at my barrel. I remained silent.

When he stopped firing, I chanced a quick look and realized that he was reloading his gun, because he had inadvertently allowed a small portion of his derrière to appear from behind the barrel. I aimed and fired, whereupon Richard let out a loud yell and leaped almost six feet into the air. It was such a funny sight that I couldn't contain my laughter, while poor Richard ran around his barrel yelling, "Ouch! Ouch! Ouch!" I was doubled up with merriment. I finally got him to stop and let us look at the damage, which was fortunately negligible, though it obviously stung like the devil.

We maintained our friendship until he and his brother, Rollo, volunteered for war service, Rollo into the Army and Richard into the RAF. Rollo was killed at Dunkirk during the evacuation, and Richard four months later in an unarmed RAF plane on a training flight for student pilots, when an enemy fighter plane came out of the sun with guns blazing and blew him and his plane to pieces.

What a waste that was: both brothers gone, their mother and Rollo's fiancée bereft of their cherished company for the rest of their lives. "War is hell," indeed, as a very distant relative of mine declared during the American Civil War.

Peter Carr, who with his younger brother and family lived a minute's bike ride from our Ferring home, was always entertaining and great fun to be with. For one thing, he played the xylophone like a master, and when in the mood he would provide us with a concert. Also, he had an incredibly pliable face that he could scrunch into the weirdest expressions; since I never could decide whether he was doing it on purpose or whether it was a habit of which he was unaware, I was hard-pressed to contain myself, feeling that he deserved applause, but not daring to clap.

Peter was a delightful friend, but after the war, which he survived, I am happy to report, I never saw him again, though my mother told me that he had married. When she had congratulated him upon his firstborn, he looked at her with a pained expression and said, "But I don't understand how it happened!" That was Peter.

When Lord Lothian, Great Britain's very popular ambassador to the United States during a major part of the Second World War, died in office, his title passed to his closest male relative, my friend Peter Carr, making him the present Lord Lothian.

Another friend of mine, Peter Steele (I seem to attract Peters, don't I?), whom I met through his sister, Ann, became a very good friend. When war came, he joined the RAF; on his leaves he would come to London and stay at Claridge's, from where we would go out on the town together with our ladies of the moment and have a great time.

On one leave, he wanted to be just with me, and during the evening he got rather drunk, a condition I had never seen him in before. He confessed that he was running somewhat scared: All the members of his squadron had been alerted and given an extra long leave, because their commander had told them that they were shortly going on a bombing mission that would be very dangerous, with many fatalities. If it was successful, it would be a stunning blow to the enemy and could possibly shorten the war.

Before the war, at this time of the year – that is, winter – certain eligible ladies of society were honored by being presented at Court to the King and Queen; my mother was one of those, presented in 1931, along with a friend of hers, Wallis Warfield Simpson, to the best of my recollection. The beautiful white gowns, feathered crowns, and elegant fans were no longer a part of this occasion, discontinued for the duration of the war, but each year there was still a presentation for the débutantes at Grosvenor House. This was a splendid hotel where I used to take my girlfriends to dinner downstairs, where we would dance to Sidney Lipton's band until the wee hours of the morning.

For this particular débutante presentation party, I had been invited to sit with Pamela Tate and her family. I think Pam was the first lady I ever had a crush on. Her parents had had a house not far from ours at Ferring. Pam's father was Mr. Tate of Tate and Lyle Sugar, and one of the nicest men I have ever known.

I knew that Ann Steele, Peter's sister, was being presented this particular year, and, sure enough, when I entered the ballroom, I saw her and her parents seated on the other side of the room. After a proper time with Pam and my hosts, I excused myself and went across to greet them.

Mr. Steele graciously stood up when he saw me coming. After I had kissed Ann and her mother, I was invited to sit down. First telling Ann how beautiful she looked on this, her coming out day, and complimenting her mother on her dress, I asked if Peter would be coming for his sister's presentation. There was utter silence for about fifteen seconds, and then I said, "Oh, no!," as I remembered Peter's words from our last visit together. "I'm sorry," said Mr. Steele. "You didn't see his obituary in the *Times*?" I had to confess that I didn't take the *Times* (fine paper though it was; at that time in my life I was more attracted to the *Express* or the *Daily Mirror*).

Naturally, I was shocked by the steady trickle of deaths in battle of my closest friends, and wondered if by the end of the war I would be friendless, or even perhaps if I might have joined my friends on the other side.

Incidentally, Ann was a very attractive young lady who had a natural gift for playing the piano and strong leanings toward becoming a concert pianist. After I returned from the war and put my energy into furthering my career, I never saw the Steele family again, and I have often wondered whether she pursued such a career or whether marriage and children set her on another path.

Before leaving my account of the Steeles, I would like to tell you an extraordinary tale. Peter Steele had a much younger brother, who, because he was sickly, had a governess to take care of him and teach him reading, writing, and arithmetic. His governess was homely, but a very nice lady, and we enjoyed each other. I had observed on one visit with Peter and Ann that the governess received a letter about twice a week from someone with very good penmanship, and one day I asked her who her friend was who wrote so elegantly. She flushed crimson, and her hand went to her mouth, as if to stop any flow of words.

Finally, over two or three days of digging, she told me his name and where he lived, but never would she tell me how or where or when she met him. I was pleased as I could be for her, while flabbergasted, to say the least, that the gentleman in question had the acumen to realize what a fine woman he was getting. The gentleman turned out to be the father of my friend Gavin, Mr. Colville! Within a few months they were married, and she became the mistress of his estate. She and Gavin got along as well as I had with her. The newlyweds were blissfully happy together, she softening him and bringing him more out of his shell, and she, released from the bonds of servitude, full of enthusiasm and love and newfound freedom.

With their first anniversary fast approaching, Mr. Colville arranged for a suite at the Dorchester, in London, and tickets to two plays in the West End, along with three dinner parties for her to meet his London friends. His wife, being a smart lady anyway, and secure in his love and her position, was as happy as anyone could be. She decided to go ahead of him by car, so that she could order some clothes and a gift for him, and her husband would follow two days later by train, since he, like most men, detested shopping.

Mrs. Colville embraced her husband lovingly; the chauffeur opened the car door; and with much waving of arms they drove down the driveway and out the gates onto the highway. Two hours later, their car was a flaming wreck, smashed into by a heavy-duty truck driven by an unlicensed driver, who died along with Mrs. Colville and the chauffeur.

In the icy winters at Eton, Gavin and I came back in the late afternoons from playing football or rugby or fives or squash to a delicious high tea. We had eggs, bacon (rashers), or sausages (bangers), and toast, or crumpets with Devonshire clotted cream and strawberry or cherry jam, all nicely prepared by the floor maid and served on our own plates and saucers.

Gavin Colville was a nice, slim boy, in character a true English oak, absolutely reliable in his words and actions, idealistic almost to a fault, and a true friend, come what may. The boys could have tea in the afternoon in their own rooms or in another boy's room. Because my room was a tiny bit larger than Gavin's, we had tea together daily in my room for three and a half years.

On visits during the holidays to Gavin's father's house, a typical country estate with a long winding driveway to the massive entrance, I was reminded of that endlessly winding driveway up to the house in the book *Rebecca*, by Daphne DuMaurier, so well depicted in the ensuing film. Mr. Colville was formal in manner and smoked a pipe constantly, starting after breakfast when he would take the London *Times* into the guest bathroom on the ground floor and remain there until he had read it from cover to cover. People passing the bathroom door would know he was in there because of the smoke from his pipe that would seep silently out from under the door. A newly engaged servant, on seeing the smoke, went on a mad charge through the house yelling "Fire!" -- finally drawing a somewhat embarrassed Mr. Colville out to see what all the noise was about.

Gavin's father was a good host. He liked entertaining his neighbors and Gavin's friends. Since I was there usually some time in the summer, and there was a large swimming pool on the lawn in front of the house, I spent many a blissful time before lunch or dinner with Gavin, playing one-on-one water polo, or just plain cooling off after a long hot day. Yes, we had a few such, even in England!

To close out on Gavin's father, the loss of his wife, the former governess, kept him woman-shy for some years. Later on he met and married the much younger daughter of the Honourable Mr. and Mrs. Piers Legh – Piers Legh being Equerry to the Prince of Wales and godfather to my half brother David Bigelow Dodge. As far as I know, Mr. and Mrs. Colville lived happily ever after.

Eton imprinted on my mind a list of do's and don'ts that have stood me in good stead ever since. It was done so subtly – by example, by a look, by an action, by a book, by a lecture, by a speech, by a talk, by a master, by my housemaster, by a boy, by the Provost. It didn't matter how, you just knew that your mind was developing in ways that stretched your vision and your way of seeing things and people and dealing with situations that would never have occurred to you without the visionary mantra that would be laid upon you for the rest of your life, courtesy of your time at Eton College.

But for now, I am fifteen years old, it is 1936, two and a half years have passed since I entered Eton, my youthful friendships remain comfortable and secure, and Mother and Johnny are taking me on a six-week car trip through France, Germany, Austria, Italy, Hungary, and Switzerland. "Half" (term) ends in a week, and a few days after that we'll be on our way. How could life be any better than this? It couldn't!

But some men, like Winston Churchill and Johnny Dodge, knew better. They spoke privately and publicly of their fears for the future of the free world if we did not start immediately arming ourselves in time to confront a military complex presently of overwhelming strength and capability, waiting and eager for Adolf Hitler's command to spring into action.

England, however, remained complacent, with Blackshirts (a pathetic imitation of Germany's Brownshirts) marching to the beat of war drums through placid English towns, their leader exchanging platitudes with his leader, Hitler, and a powerful group of British Society freaks grandstanding with fulsome praise for this madman's Germany, even to the point of suggesting an alliance.

When Joachim von Ribbentrop, Hitler's new ambassador to the Court of St. James, presented his credentials to King George V, he outraged the Court by giving the Nazi salute, his right arm straight out in front of him. In spite of this gesture, a Nazi-influenced bunch of numskulls took Ribbentrop under their wing and paraded him through some of the great homes of England as if he were a demigod.

These were treasonable times, though no one would admit to it. There were a surprising number of people at the top of the tree who were so afraid, or so captivated, or so bewitched by Hitler that they were not above selling their county to the dictator if it would secure their position for the future. They did not know that Hitler's promises were made to be broken.

I, all innocent and eager for the taste of foreign lands, knew none of this. Not yet.

In my first year at Eton I had the opportunity of witnessing King George V's Jubilee Celebration Parade, with Mother and Johnny, from the Honourable Piers Legh's chambers in St. James Palace, London. It was a gorgeous day for the King and Queen Mary, both so long on the throne and so admired by their subjects. He looked like a king should look, and had always been an example of how a king should behave. His wife complemented him perfectly, a regal lady with a fine posture who looked taller than she was because of the imposingly high hats she favored.

The first royal members we saw, on that day, were my favorites, the Duke and Duchess of Kent (formerly the Princess Marina), coming out of the palace beneath our window onto the parade route, the Duke more handsome than any movie star and his wife gorgeous beyond words. The Duke was in uniform, the Princess in a dress that I have forgotten, but wearing an Ascot kind of a hat with a big floppy rim to it, such as I had once seen on her head when she and the Duke were returning to London from the Ascot Races through Eton's main street. Then she was in an enclosed car; now she was in an open vehicle that showed her off better to the populace. Unfortunately, a breeze blowing all that day forced her into the uncomfortable situation of having to hold on to her hat or take it off. The last I saw of her she was bravely holding it on and smiling beautifully to the adoring crowds. I felt for her.

It was a splendid day to be alive in England's green and pleasant land, and, although an American, on this day I felt British and acted British and spoke British. All my friends were British, and for that day and not a few others I was British, too, not forgetting that my ancestors had originated in England before moving to America back in the third quarter of the sixteen hundreds. But Roger Sherman's blood coursed through my veins as well, as did Todd Caldwell's, and, as far as I was concerned, it was as blue as any of the British bluebloods' blue blood!

Pims No. 1 was served around noon, followed by a picnic lunch at one p.m. of cold chicken and potato salad and hard boiled eggs and other picnic food, ending with a trifle, to this day my favorite of all desserts. In the meantime we watched a pageant passing beneath our window never to be seen again, as it included people from all the countries of the British Empire. My vote for the best went to the Hindu Gurkha regiment from Nepal, as I was a great fan of Rudyard Kipling's tales of glory, many of which emphasized the incredible bravery and professionalism of these soldiers in battle. It was an exhilarating spectacle. All those watching the parade yelled their patriotic throats dry with excitement and a sentimental devotion to their sovereign, while we in the Honourable Piers Legh's chambers were equally enthused, if slightly more subdued in expressing our patriotic fervor.

India, the Dominions, so many satellite countries and islands, not to mention the Europeans: All were represented in their incredibly varied and colorful uniforms, marching impeccably to their national music. The Australians and Canadians were particularly popular with the crowds, as was the Queen of Togo, a rather large black lady with a big smile and a gigantic umbrella held over her head to protect her from the rain or sun, waving joyfully to the crowds, who returned her greetings with an enormous ovation.

Of course, the greatest ovation of all was reserved for the King and Queen, with Johnny and Piers Legh and Mother and me and the rest of the gathering cheering their majesties with a roar such as to rattle the glasses together on the dining-room sideboard. Our enthusiasm even provoked the royal couple to look up in our direction and give a brief but definite wave to all of us.

What a day! At the age of thirteen, what a lucky boy was I!

In the same year that we celebrated his Jubilee, the King died. It was completely unexpected. He had seemed so well during his Jubilee festivities, but some months later he developed a cold, which progressed into pneumonia, and his condition quickly deteriorated. The King's doctor started to provide a daily news brief for the news media on his condition, and, as he slowly slipped away, upped it to twice a day.

A very good friend of ours, Bernard Richatson-Hatt, the head of Reuters News Agency at the time, invited us to come by his office the night the King's death was anticipated, when B, as his friends all called him, expected to be the first to receive word of the King's passing. He would then distribute the news with suitable background and funeral arrangements to all of his media clients and agents around the world. Reuters was the major news agency in Great Britain, and B had made absolutely sure, he hoped, that Reuters would be number one with the sad story.

The Reuters headquarters offices were big, with desks and typewriters and secretaries and managers all covering other news events while waiting for the big story to break. We waited at B's desk until one in the morning, by which time there was nothing left to do but go home. Mother and I had already dozed off in our wooden office chairs, while Johnny and B talked man talk, oblivious to the late hour.

The next night the King died, and the world heard it first from Reuters, care of B. Richatson-Hatt. The British Empire went into mourning, and I returned to the new half at Eton, where I met with Gavin and Patrick and Henry, and discovered that all Eton students would be able to witness the final leg of George V's funeral parade ending in the courtyard before the Royal Chapel at Windsor Castle. There we three would manage to have the best view of the royal houses of Europe and more distant kingdoms gathered together, plus innumerable heads of state from every corner of the globe.

What an honor this was! It was also apparently a tradition going back some centuries to our founder, Henry VI, who established Eton College in 1440, the same year he founded King's College, Cambridge. Being in the habit of leaving his London Palace for Windsor Castle in the summer, and needing suitable educational opportunities for both the children of his court and the children of his domestic staff, he democratically lumped them together in newly built buildings just over the bridge, where Eton begins.

A long and warm relationship between the sovereign and Eton continues even to this day. In fact, I can remember Gavin and a boy from another house being invited to tea at Windsor Castle with the Princesses Elizabeth and Margaret. Gavin afterward told me that he and the other boy were both tongue-tied at first, but ended up having a good time. Princess Margaret, he reported, was full of mischief, while Princess Elizabeth, more restrained, nonetheless smiled a lot and obviously enjoyed her sister's playfulness. Gavin added that their parents, King George VI and Queen Elizabeth, came in at the end of the tea party to meet the princesses' guests, and it was abundantly clear to him that this was a warm and very loving family.

In my day, the Provost of Eton was Lord Cecil, descendant of a family that has served the Kings and Queens of England through many reigns, being accorded many responsibilities on behalf of the reigning monarch, along with many honors and rewards. The Biltmore Forest, which has strong connections to the Cecil family, is an enormous house, still fully furnished, located on a grand estate in Asheville, North Carolina; it is well worth a visit if you are in the area.

On the day of the funeral, Gavin and I were among the first to arrive across the courtyard facing the entrance to the Royal Chapel at Windsor

Castle; we were glad we had made the effort, because it also provided us with a perfect view of the funeral parade, considerably smaller than that which had been witnessed by the Londoners, because of the logistics of the last lap between the railway station and Windsor Castle. It was still a grand and solemn occasion, featuring the distant sound of the mourning drums, the beat slow; the steady snap of the soldiers' boots; and the clip-clop of those beautiful horses.

When they finally came into view, I realized what a marvelous spot we had commandeered for ourselves, for the most important and prestigious people in the parade were all at the front and would have to stop where we could see them and the coffin, a mere thirty feet away. It was the first and last time that any of us would see the heads of almost all the world's nations in one place at one time, standing so close to us while the coffin was being carried into the Royal Chapel, all performed in a solemn and oppressive silence. I suspect that most of us boys felt a tug at our hearts and not a few shed a tear or two.

Just a few feet behind the late King's hearse stood Mother and Johnny's friend Edward, the Prince of Wales – now, upon his father's death, the new King of England. In my view, he looked tired and irritable, which after so much sadness and so much walking was more than understandable. In addition to all the foreign royalty, just behind Edward were the British Royal Dukes – Gloucester, Kent, York, and Norfolk – the last being the Parade Marshall, responsible for all such royal occasions, which he always orchestrated superbly.

It was a scene I can visualize to this day. For just a few minutes, there in that courtyard, time seemed to stand still and take a deep breath, commemorating the past and the glory of the Empire, along with the high regard in which the monarchy was held, and the serenity of a world at peace. It was the beginning of the end of an epoch, but with so little time left. So little time.

When I returned from the war, one of the first people to invite me to lunch was B. Richatson-Hatt, no longer the head of Reuters, but Director of Public Relations for the Bank of England. I was very much impressed by his new position and title, since I had decided to make public relations my own career, as a natural continuation of my diplomatic experience in Paris and Brussels with the SHAEF Diplomatic Missions. Having only recently returned to London, I had not yet applied for a position, though it was very much on my mind.

B took me to Simpson's for lunch, where he asked me all about my war experiences. I finally reminded him of the time that we had come to his office at Reuters and waited for news of the King's passing, giving up by one in the morning and going home to bed. He had told us at the time, when we left his office that night, that he would not go to sleep until he got the call from Buckingham Palace.

Exactly when he received the call I do not remember, but for the British media, B said it was perfect timing for the next morning's newspapers. Because of the long lag between British and American time, it would serve America's morning papers almost as well.

But this time B told me a story of the night the king died that shows not even a beloved monarch can be immune to murder. B swore me to secrecy, and I had to promise not to tell this story until after his death. I promised. At this point, he has been dead for many years. As far as I can remember, the story goes like this.

Someone on the staff at Reuters knew the two nurses in attendance on King George during his final days, one his day nurse and the other his night nurse. An arrangement had been negotiated with both of them that whoever was on duty at the time of death would describe to the Reuters staff member immediately by phone the final moments of the King's passing, including who was in the room at the time. The doctor would precede her with the news and exact time of death.

As it happened, the Queen had retired shortly before, as had the Prince of Wales and the Duke of York. There remained only the doctor and the nurse, the doctor fatigued from lack of sleep and distraught from the enormous pressure being put on him by the ever more demanding news media from all over the world (some even offering him hefty compensation if they were given the news and details first).

As time wore on, the King's breathing remained shallow but regular, while the doctor became more and more agitated, until the nurse suggested that he sit down and rest himself and maybe sleep. She would wake him if there was a change in his royal patient's condition. This kindly suggestion had the opposite effect to what she expected, as the doctor exploded in a ranting outburst of self-pity over the pressures he was under, even to the point of turning on the King and yelling at him, "Die, damn you, die!"

The nurse was stunned. She could only watch, as the doctor brought out from his inside coat pocket a long, thin case, from which he drew a syringe. Almost throwing it at the nurse, he demanded that she inject its contents into the King's arm. The nurse refused. After screaming obscenities at her, the doctor grabbed the needle and plunged it into the King's arm himself. Within seconds, the King's heart stopped.

The doctor finally sat down and burst into tears. The nurse grabbed the phone and alerted Reuters of the King's demise, and the time of same, but without a word of the doctor's behavior or the true reason for the King's death.

B. Richatson-Hatt got his scoop, and the nurse, terrified of the consequences and the perilous situation she was in, sealed her lips, telling only her future husband, the Reuters staff employee who had originally made the connection with her. He repeated it to a curious Inspector from Scotland Yard only after his wife's early death. The Inspector sat on it for a while before finally deciding to pass it on up to the Chief.

The Chief had him to his office, where he berated him for believing such a cock and bull story. He ordered him to put it out of his mind immediately and never speak of it again, to anyone. The Inspector called the husband back and told him to forget it. Angered and frustrated, the husband finally took the story to his boss, B. Richatson-Hatt, from whom I heard it.

The powers that be did a good job of keeping the dirty secret under wraps through two royal reigns. And now, who cares?

Time marches on.

Ernest and Wallis Simpson

Mother first met Wallis Warfield Simpson in 1930, when they both came out of the Hungaria Restaurant at two-thirty in the afternoon and found that a heavy rainstorm was eliminating their chances for a taxi. Being intelligent people not chained by English reserve, they introduced themselves to each other; when they discovered that they were both going in the same general direction, they joined forces and soon commandeered a taxi in which they exchanged phone numbers, each having found the other attractive and stimulating and American. Moreover, both were married to Englishmen.

That evening, Mother told Johnny about her meeting with Wallis Simpson, and Johnny, seeing how pleased Mother was about her new acquaintance, suggested inviting Wallis and her husband to their next dinner party. The invitation was sent, and accepted.

Dinner at our house was run on time. You were invited for seven o'clock, with cocktails and finger hors d'oeuvres, generally smoked salmon and caviar. Dinner itself would begin at eight p.m., when we would go from the drawing room on the second floor down to the dining room on the first floor. Mother even used incense for her dinner parties, though never in the dining room; its use caught on, and soon everyone was trying to outdo each other's incense, one lady spraying her house with Chanel No. 5 perfume, with gagging results.

The dining room seated twenty guests, with Johnny at one end of the table and Mother at the other. Dinner was under the baton of our genius majordomo, Charles, who was responsible for running the entire house and staff and was in his element at dinner parties, making absolutely sure that everything was handled so smoothly that the guests were barely aware of the domestics' presence.

Wallis was a fascinating woman, slim, a dressmaker's dream, not beautiful, but with a strong face, a long nose, great eyes that held you fixed while in conversation, and a mind that could dazzle. Ernest was dark-haired, with a military bearing; he wore a moustache on his handsome face, was soft spoken, and, like his wife, was always impeccably groomed. His father, a British subject, had lived in America for many years, finally creating a firm of shipping brokers in New York. Both Wallis and Ernest had been married before. After they obtained their divorces, Ernest, who had fallen for Wallis almost from the moment he met her, proposed; after some hesitation on her part, they were married and set up house in a flat in Bryanston Square near Marble Arch, London. Ernest was now working in the London office of the family firm.

Mother and Wallis became close friends. Wallis and Ernest were grateful to Mother and Johnny for their continued hospitality and friendship, and for launching Wallis into that sophisticated world that she now dreamed of conquering.

Once Mother had made the original connections for her through a series of dinner parties at our and other people's homes, Wallis was finally ready to dip her toe in the water. She sent out her first invitations to four couples, Johnny and Mother included, plus the host and hostess.

The Simpson flat was elegant, as well Mother knew, for Wallis had rarely made decorating decisions without consulting Mother. Obviously, Wallis had been greatly impressed with our uniquely designed and decorated house at 6 Connaught Street. Although her dining room was small, thanks to Mother and Wallis and the interior decorator it became chic as well as intimate, providing a sophisticated setting for a medium-sized group of guests.

Wallis was like a sponge, taking advantage of every invitation to other people's homes in order to pick out something that could possibly be used in the future, perhaps in another flat or even in a house. She was a very clever lady, having had a good education including college, but had been handicapped in her first marriage by her husband having been an alcoholic who physically abused her, severely restricting any efforts she might have made toward normal social entertaining. Having been publicly humiliated in her first marriage, she had enjoyed few intimate friends most of her life, except perhaps for Herman and Kitty Rogers, whom she had met in Peking, China, in the mid-twenties (she called it her Year of the Lotus), and who became among her most loyal friends in the glamorous but difficult years ahead.

Wallis's father died within months of her birth, leaving her mother genteelly penniless. This caused a brief crisis, but her father's brother, who was a much better provider, came to the rescue. So did Bessie Merryweather, Wallis's aunt and confidante, who played a considerable role during Wallis's formative years, supplying financial assistance and a warm friendship, which was to last until Bessie Merryweather's death. Wallis's mother finally married again, and the comfortably-off second husband provided the means for Wallis to attend a private college and earn her diploma.

Out in the real world, Wallis also had the aid of her Aunt Bessie. She finally met Ernest Simpson, who loved her dearly and was the only one who behaved honorably, though his heart was broken, in what was to become a very undignified situation. The perpetrator of the indignity – Edward, Prince of Wales – was described prophetically on the occasion of his christening in July of 1894 by the first Labour Member of Parliament, Kier Hardie, as follows:

"From his childhood onward," he declared, "this boy will be surrounded by sycophants and flatterers by the score, and will be taught to believe himself as of a superior creation. A line will be drawn between him and the people he is to be called upon some day to reign over. In due course, following the precedent which has already been set, he will be sent on a tour round the world, and probably rumors of a morganatic alliance will follow, and the end of it all will be the country will be called upon to pay the bill."

How true; how true.

But for now, all is calm. Wallis is giving elegant dinner parties, as is Mother; and Edward has just been granted the use of Fort Belvedere by his father, the King. Regarding the dinner parties, a friend who had been to both Mother's and Wallis's on more than one occasion, declared that "the difference between Minerva's and Wallis's is that Minerva's dinners are relaxed and generally joyful, whereas at Wallis's you feel 'on stage,' and if you don't perform well, you may not be invited back." Also, though both were superb hosts, Mother was not as intense as Wallis and had a much better sense of humor.

Not long before Mother's presentation to Court, Johnny had attended a levee at Buckingham Palace along with the husbands or fathers of most of the ladies being presented shortly thereafter, including Ernest Simpson. This was an all-male affair, King George V receiving each gentleman as his name and title was announced. Johnny said the levee was social rather than ceremonial, with drinks and a chance to connect with old friends and new.

In spite of my being only nine years old at this time (1930–1931), I was becoming a little more mature than my peers of the same age or even some considerably older, mainly because I spent my vacations almost entirely among adults, to whom I was always more attracted than my own age group. I also loved gossip. Most men feign distaste for gossip, but it is really to protect their male image, since gossip is considered a female pastime. Believe you me, we males are equally fascinated with gossip, and today I constantly hear the question, "What's the gossip?" from my male friends, whether single, married, or divorced.

Early on in this chapter I referred to Wallis as being a sponge. I was a gossip sponge, but under Johnny and Mother's tutelage I learned the difference between good old gossip and something received confidentially, almost always meaning "not for public consumption."

Before Mother would tell about her presentation at Court, she shared some gossip that really surprised me. Of course, it was about Wallis. As Wallis explained it to Mother, she had become acquainted with a brother-in-law of Consuelo Thaw, sister of the Viscountess Thelma Furness, when she was living at Coronado Beach, California, in 1918. The connection was pretty slim, but her letter to the Viscountess, mistress to Edward, Prince of Wales, since 1928, had led to an invitation to Wallis and Ernest to spend the weekend of January 10 and 11, 1931, at Burrough Court, Milton Mowbray, Leicestershire, the country estate of Lady Furness.

They went, but quickly regretted it, as everyone seemed to know everyone else and the Simpsons knew no one. Moreover, the main topic of conversation was hunting, of which they were both ignorant. In addition, Wallis had a bad cold. On the second day, at lunch, Wallis was seated next to the Prince of Wales; having been told that royalty must be allowed to lead any conversation, she spent the entire lunch nursing her cold and scared to death of saying something that would breach the boundaries laid down by this ridiculous restriction on normal conversation. Soon enough, the Simpsons returned to London, Wallis putting the weekend out of her mind as a complete waste of time.

On June 10 of that same year, Mother and Wallis, with husbands in attendance, were presented to King George V and Queen Mary. Mother and Johnny then went to a party given by Lady Emerald Cunard (of the shipping line), while Wallis and Ernest went to a party thrown by the Prince of Wales's mistress, that is, Lady Furness, where Wallis again met the Prince, this time impressing him enough that he later that night delivered the Simpsons to their home in his car. By the time 1931 was over, the Prince of Wales and the Simpsons had been with each other on five social occasions, the last at Mrs. Thew's birthday party on December 17. Soon after that, the Prince accepted their first invitation to him to dine at their flat in Bryanston Square.

To return to my beloved mother, the photographs of her presentation at Court were absolutely stunning, Mother looking radiantly beautiful in an elegant white gown with white gloves drawn up over her elbows. She also wore a diamond tiara, a gift from Johnny, from which rose white-plumed feathers, and a perfectly gorgeous necklace of pearls with earrings to match, a gift from Emil Pfizer. The latter continued to be a family friend, coming every two or three years to London, always with word from my precious governess Miss Milligan, whose letters I treasure to this day.

Emil would come in the summer and stay at the Savoy Hotel, with his suite on the Embankment side of the hotel, affording a view of the River Thames and the boats of many sizes going by. The great French artist Claude Monet had stayed some weeks at the Savoy many years before, with the same view as Emil; the artist had painted the constantly changing light on the Thames and surroundings, each canvas a treasure, today drawing immense crowds to museums wherever they are displayed.

Emil would always spend one weekend at Florida in Ferring, and we loved to have him, for he had been a true friend to Mother and me and we were both very fond of him. In due course, Emil became a client of Johnny's, though Mother told me that Johnny had instructed his office never on any account to send Emil Pfizer a bill for his services, as Johnny appreciated Emil's honorable and generous care of Mother and me in previous years.

John Bigelow Dodge was the genuine article: a true gentleman, in every circumstance.

Lady Thelma Furness, the mistress of Edward, Prince of Wales, since 1928, must have been incredibly sure of that relationship, or else she was tiring of it. For whatever reason, and despite her obvious awareness of the Prince's growing interest in and attraction to Wallis, she seems to have encouraged the relationship.

Lady Thelma sailed for America on January 25, 1934, on a month-long visit to see friends and no doubt to be lionized, we Americans being so fascinated with titled personages, even when they are rude, boorish, arrogant, and unappreciative. Of course, the nice ones are very, very nice!

The day before her departure, she had called Wallis and said, "I'm afraid the Prince is going to be lonely, Wallis: won't you look after him?"

Wallis naturally took full advantage of the opportunity to cement her relationship with her besotted Prince, even while writing from Fort Belvedere to her Aunt Bessie Merryweather: "You did give me a lecture and I quite agree with all you say regarding HRH, and if Ernest raises any objections to the situation I shall give up the Prince at once. So far things are going beautifully, and the three of us are always together. Don't pay any attention to gossip."

Lady Furness returned on March 22, her name vaguely linked by the press with that of the Aga Khan's eldest son, Prince Aly Khan; but it was enough to encourage the transition of Prince Edward's affections completely and finally to Wallis Simpson. If there was any doubts as to the couple's relationship, they were dispelled during the Prince's August and September holiday that year, when Wallis, accompanied by her Aunt Bessie, joined his party. Some of the holiday was spent on Lord Moyne's yacht *Rosaura* in the Mediterranean. Was someone missing? It was Ernest Simpson! He pleaded the need to attend to his business affairs. Poor Ernest. And Lady Furness was banished from any communication, her Prince refusing to receive her phone calls, letters, or intermediaries.

Wallis was triumphantly riding her crest of the wave, ignoring the danger signals, utterly consumed with her self-importance. Society and the power brokers were discovering that the only sure way of getting the ear of Prince Edward, Britain's future King, was through her. Her power was far more than Thelma Furness's had ever been, but Wallis was far cleverer and more ambitious than Lady Furness.

One late night in September of 1934, Wallis and her Aunt Bessie were dining together, the subject being her relationship with the Prince. "Isn't all this very dangerous for you?" asked Aunt Bessie.

"You don't know what you're talking about," retorted Wallis. "I'm having a marvelous time … I know what I'm doing."

Aunt Bessie, by now a good friend of Mother's, reported her conversation with Wallis and was obviously very upset over it. Mother, too, was disturbed, Johnny having brought back papers and magazines from the United States, with one magazine headline calling the Prince "the Prince of Love."

For the benefit of my younger readers, I must explain that, while all these royal activities were being closely watched and reported on by the world press, Britain was under a complete news blackout regarding any activities involving the Prince and Wallis, as the government under Mr. Baldwin feared that the public disclosure of the Prince's ardent relationship with a once-divorced and still-married American woman could dangerously divide the country, not to mention the church, and even possibly bring down the monarchy.

So in the meantime, England went about its business, enjoying a pleasant and sunny summer.

Mother, through all the years 1931, 1932, and 1933, had been delighted with her friend's social success. Wallis had been free with her, not only discussing her relationship with the Prince, but also reporting with considerable glee the more and more respectful attitude society and the power brokers were showing toward her, as they finally realized that, if they really wanted the ear of the Prince and future King, they would have to go through Wallis.

Wallis had had Mother and Johnny to dinner at Ernest's and her flat with the Prince and other friends four times in two years, and Mother and Johnny had had Ernest and Wallis and the Prince over three times, plus just Wallis and Edward once at the beginning of 1935. Indeed, it was not unusual for the Prince and Wallis to drop by for a drink around 6:30 if they knew that Johnny was in town, before going out to a restaurant afterward, Ernest being excused as usual for business reasons.

On a day that I came up from Eton to go to my dentist for a filling in 1935, I actually met the Prince, though I wasn't in my best form, with half of my face frozen and my body exhausted from the tension of sitting for an hour while the dentist drilled and drilled. Just for the record, I am a complete physical coward in the dentist's chair, having canceled at the last moment many dentist appointments all over the world on some transparent excuse or other, out of pure, unvarnished fear.

After the visit to the dentist it was still only six, and I had a little over one and a half hours before having to catch the train back to Slough, the nearest station to Eton, so I decided to see what was going on at home. My taxi deposited me not quite at the front door, since there was a rather splendid deep-maroon Rolls-Royce directly in front, the chauffeur appearing to be in conversation with our local bobby. As I stopped to greet the bobby, he saluted me, and I was about to comment on the elegant car when I saw the royal flag on the vehicle, fluttering in a light breeze. I was twelve years old, in first half at Eton, and rather shy, and the thought of meeting the Prince of Wales with one side of my face numbly expressionless scared me to death. If it hadn't been for the bobby, I would have kept going, but he knew me and my family: He was always invited, at Mother's instigation, to have Christmas dinner with our staff, at which time we would come downstairs to wish them and the bobby a merry Christmas and pass out the Christmas bonuses, plus one present for each staff member. The bobby also regularly received a monetary gift and present for guarding our street so well.

So I clenched my teeth – still no feeling – climbed the steps, and rang the bell. A liveried footman opened the door, for a moment seeming at a loss for words. Then he asked if I might be Master Peter. I replied that I was and asked him his name, which surprisingly turned out to be Edward, meaning we now had two Edwards in the house, one upstairs and one downstairs.

Edward escorted me up to the drawing room, where he announced me in a very sonorous voice, much to my chagrin. Everyone stopped talking, and Mother leaped out of her chair to greet me, followed by Johnny and then Wallis and the Prince. I rushed into Mother's outstretched arms, wishing desperately to die, right there on the spot.

But I was not to die yet. Next came Johnny with a bear hug, also to my surprise and gratification, and then Wallis with a kiss, and the Prince with a handshake and a warm smile. The Prince must have been told of my dentist's appointment, for the first thing he asked me was how my tooth felt now. I told him I couldn't feel anything yet, since I was still numb, but that I hated going to the dentist. He assured me that he did, too, and that dentists were much to be admired for taking care of our teeth while being avoided at all costs and certainly feared by the vast majority of their patients in those days. Today I have a splendid dentist, a lady who rarely hurts me, and if it hurts at all it's only very slightly. Dentistry has come a long way since 1934.

We all sat down, and I was given a glass of lemonade. The Prince moved from the chair next to Wallis to the chair next to mine, and started asking me about Eton and my activities and friends there. I winged it pretty well, telling him not only about Eton but also St. Peter's Court, where two of his younger brothers, the Dukes of Kent and Gloucester, had gone. The Prince sighed, saying that he wished he could have gone to St. Peter's Court and been treated just like his brothers. He had envied them so much, but he and his next brother in line, George, the Duke of York, had been educated by private tutors. York, being rather frail, had also not been rushed into any of the services.

After I had told him as much as I could think of at that time, he told me, and the others, that he had had a wretched childhood. Neither of his parents was demonstratively affectionate, but as a boy he was actually afraid of his father, the present King George V.

According to the Prince, his education – for what it was worth – was the responsibility of a tutor named Henry Hansel, who provided "a mild scholarship with a muscular Christianity." He had played football at Oxford, excelled in golf, and was a good shot, which was Edward's father's favorite recreational pursuit. In fact, the King was a crack shot himself, thereby ensuring Hansel's appointment as tutor.. After a reasonable time, the King had insisted that Edward follow his father's example and take his Navy exams, which Edward assured us was accomplished only because a Naval cadet of considerable scholarship was placed next to himself, the Prince copying just enough of the answers from the cadet's examination papers to pass, with no one close enough to supervise them. The Prince admitted that he was ashamed of this subterfuge, but he also said it was the only way he could have passed his exams. If he had failed his father's ambitions for him right at the very beginning of his adulthood, he added, any future regard from his father would have been destroyed.

Living in fear of his father was not a happy situation. His education was very limited, and except for his brothers and sisters and relatives, he rarely if ever had the joy of a normal friendship. Following in his father's footsteps, he was sent to the Royal Naval College at Osbourne, which he detested, and then to Dartmouth, which he liked a bit better, but he never felt that he was liked for himself. In sum, he was starved for companionship and felt very much alone.

The Prince sat in his chair next to mine, looking into space, the words flowing on and on, with sometimes a catch in his throat and sometimes a smile. We were all struck dumb, for he had inadvertently given us a powerful impression of an undereducated man, a pampered man, a self-centered man, a man who had little control over his many appetites, a man who felt everlastingly put upon, a nice-looking man who could charm a boy called Peter with his smile and the warmth of his presence; yet I felt also that he was more child than I was, a Peter Pan in a world of Captain Hooks, and with a compass that pointed nowhere. He was living a life of great wealth and power and prestige, with the love of his life, Wallis. But undermining his joy was the inevitable challenge: Could he, would he, be able to become King and keep Wallis by his side?

He stopped his soliloquy for a moment. Then, turning to me, he took my hand in his and said, "I envy you, Peter. You don't know how lucky you are. You can make your own decisions, act in your own natural way. I am the Prince of Wales and future King. I confess I enjoy the trappings of my rank, but not the constant demands of that rank. You, Peter, are a free soul, with good and loving parents, the opportunity of a good education, and the world is your oyster. I cannot do what you can do; I cannot be what you can be, and never could. Treasure your mother and Johnny Dodge, two wonderful people and good friends whom Wallis has enjoyed longer than I have. You are a nice boy, Peter. I like you. I would like to see you again."

With that, the Prince rose, as did Wallis, though looking uncomfortable, and so did Mother and Johnny. We all went down the stairs together and watched them being driven away in the Prince's car.

I hadn't thought to drink a drop of my lemonade. Nobody had touched their drinks during the Prince's unburdening of his demons. Now I realized that the Prince had spoken longer than it seemed, and I asked Edward, the footman, to get me a taxi pronto or I would miss my train. He had the taxi in just over four minutes; I bade my mother and Johnny goodbye, with hugs from both of them, and was driven to the station just in time.

What a day: first torture, and then a Prince! In spite of his failings – and who doesn't have failings? – I found him rather endearing, and I was very flattered by all the attention he had paid me during my visit. The more I thought of how he had described his life up to now, the more I realized the advantages of not being royalty.

At twelve years of age, I was a very happy boy, enjoying my life to the fullest, frustrated only by my cursed inability to do well in class, though I did love history, English, and writing, for all of which I did receive decent marks.

Everything was coming up roses for Wallis. She and Ernest spent a weekend in 1932 with the Prince at Fort Belvedere, after which the Prince went on a goodwill tour of Malta, Paris, Copenhagen, and Stockholm. It was in 1933 that Wallis joined her Prince and his guests for the very first time without Ernest, who was purported to be in New York to discuss business with his father. On his return, he and Wallis gave an Independence Day party, with the Prince as Guest of Honor and Mother and Johnny in attendance. The Simpsons by this time were widely acknowledged as being among Edward's most intimate friends.

Mother and Wallis remained good friends, though Mother was becoming wary of Wallis's constant affirmation of her relationship with the Prince, while asserting that her marriage to Ernest was in no way affected.

"I'm only going along for the ride," Wallis said. "Could you have imagined when we met in that storm in front of the Hungarian restaurant that one day this little old Baltimore girl would be the closest and dearest friend of the future king of England? He needs me, Minerva. He really and truly needs me. He lights up when he sees me. He confides everything to me, including things I'd prefer not to hear, but he trusts me, he really and truly needs me."

"But Wallis, dear, where do you think this will lead?"

"I don't care where it leads! I'm on the crest of a wave, and as long as I can be there for him to lean on, and confide in, what harm can it do? It's like having caviar and champagne every day, and I love every minute of it."

"But Wallis, he's smitten with you. You admit it. Suppose he proposes to you?"

"Oh, Minerva, don't be silly. He couldn't marry me, a divorced American woman, even if he wanted to. No, darling, this relationship will finally run its course, like all his other liaisons, and in the meantime I am his trusted mentor and friend."

"More than friend, perhaps?"

"All right, more than friend."

"Well, Wallis, you know I'm your friend, and I wish you everything good, as I do the Prince, but I also like and respect Ernest, and it seems to me that he is the odd man out in this situation, although certainly handling himself like the gentleman he is."

"Minerva, dear, you don't know Ernest like I do. He adores me, and wants nothing more than for me to be happy. This part of my life will end, maybe sooner than later; when Edward's father dies, our situation will almost certainly become untenable and I will still have Ernest. Let me have my fun while I can, Minerva, please."

Such was the nature of the relationship Mother and Wallis continued to have, though Wallis was becoming less approachable because of her increased absences from her Bryanston Square flat. For Wallis, 1935 had been a heady year. It had included two holidays with Edward and friends, one skiing in Kitzbühl, Austria, and the second in the south of France. If there was anything negative in Wallis's picture, it was her Prince's father's animosity toward her; he referred to her only as "that woman."

The King had also informed his son that that woman was not welcome at the Palace. The Prince, no doubt bolstered by Wallis's man or mouse encouragement, disregarded his father's ultimatum and brought her to the State Ball at Buckingham Palace celebrating his father's and mother's Silver Jubilee. He danced with Wallis, while the King looked on in dismay, angered by his son's disobedience.

Wallis really didn't care about the King. She cared only for her Prince, and thrived on the many rewards of that relationship, where anything and everything was possible, where all doors were open and welcoming, and where Edward's protection ensured her invincibility. She was having a ball.

The year 1935 ended as every year ended for Prince Edward: at Sandringham, where most of the royal family was obliged to celebrate Christmas with the King and Queen. Edward felt lonelier than ever, his parents and brothers barely speaking to him, with the exception of George, Duke of Kent, recently married to Marina, Princess of Greece and Denmark, his only real friend left of the royals. Edward wondered why he had been invited at all, when he could have been with his beloved Wallis beside him, sparkling for him, keeping his backbone straight, complimenting him, inspiring him, nursing his resolution when he had yet another public duty to perform.

The royal family had reason for worry, for this was no normal affair such as the one he had enjoyed with Lady Furness and, before her, Mrs. Freda Dudley-Ward. This was an out-and-out obsession; where it would lead, nobody knew. Nobody? Edward knew. He had already sounded out his brothers, and in particular the next in line, Albert George, Duke of York, a quiet family man with a loving and charming wife, and two young daughters.

The Duke of York was stunned by his brother's request that he become King, and his wife, Elizabeth, fairly bristled at the suggestion that her husband, being the next in line, should take over Edward's responsibilities, just for some divorced American tramp whom she wouldn't deign to receive in her home. Furthermore, her husband was handicapped by poor health and a stutter, as well as utterly untrained and unprepared for the role of King.

"How dare you even suggest such a thing?" she told him. "You have been groomed to be King. So be King!"

Edward, somewhat chastened, next went to his mother, Queen Mary, who gave him short shrift, refusing to believe he would even consider giving up the throne for yet another mistress, and this one a divorced American woman. As soon as he could, a deflated Edward departed Sandringham and headed for Bryanston Court and Wallis.

Wallis, in the meantime, had already visited Mother in a high state of anxiety, telling her that Edward was dead set on marrying her, hopefully as King, but if his Prime Minister Baldwin and the government did not accede to his demands, he would abdicate and leave the country. "What should I do, Minerva? What should I do?"

"Your Aunt Bessie and I both warned you not to get in over your head, darling, and now I think a one-way ticket to the good old USA would not be such a bad idea. It would seem that you have made yourself, in your prince's eyes, indispensable to him. In his eyes you can do no wrong, and the thought of not having you in his life is unbearable to him. He will not let you go, Wallis. But if you really want to try to break up the present arrangement, you are going to have to do it soon. I will help you in any way I can, though I fear it may be too late."

Wallis hugged Mother and told her what a good friend she had been to her from the very beginning of their relationship. She promised to think over her advice very seriously. After Wallis left our house, Mother called Molly, who had been within earshot in order to mentally record the conversation, into the drawing room, and gave her an inquiring look.

"I don't know, madam," said Molly, diplomatically.

"I do know," said Mother. "It's too late."

Sure enough, a few days later Mother got a call from Wallis, full of joie de vivre, informing her that she would be going with the King onboard the yacht *Nahlen* for a cruise during the months of August and September. Mother and Johnny were invited to go along as well but sent their regrets, having made arrangements to take me to Europe during my summer holidays. I was now fourteen years old.

The possibility of Edward's abdication had caused his brother George, Duke of York, to go into the depths of depression. He considered himself a family man, leading a quiet life, simply doing the things that dukes do, including a lot of ribbon cutting.

During the previous March of 1935, a meeting had been held between the King and Ernest Simpson, where Ernest, under enormous emotional distress, agreed to end his marriage, asking only that the King give his word that, in taking Wallis as his wife, he would love and cherish her. The King agreed. Ernest then retired to his private study, lay down on the sofa, and wept until there were no tears left. He was humiliated, and helpless to do anything about it.

Under the circumstances, the divorce had to be arranged quietly. Finally, in the ninth month of 1936, in the peaceful town of Ipswich, Wallis was granted her degree nisi. That very same day, Edward formally proposed marriage, sealing his promises with a nineteen-carat emerald engagement ring from Cartier, at which time he installed Wallis in a house of her own in Cumberland Terrace, Regent's Park.

I personally find it unfortunate that, if you are born into the British royal family, and you are male and destined to ascend the throne, you may take advantage of your position; thus, if coveting the wife of another man, generally a friend of yours, is on your mind, you may lose your friend's friendship, but he can lose his wife! The poor friend, if not a member of royalty, has no standing, his apparent duty being to hand over his wife to you for your social and sexual pleasure. I don't know what a wife would do if she did not want to share the royal personage's bed, but you can be sure that no one in her right mind would ever own up to such an ill-mannered response.

To some degree, I sympathize just a little bit with Queen Victoria's eldest son, the future King Edward VII, who spent years and years and years with practically nothing to do except eat enormous meals in England and the French Riviera and bed down with some of the greatest beauties of his era, some of them other men's wives.

One true story about the portly King Edward VII that tickled the Parisians' funny bone was of a visit he made to the Ritz Hotel, his regular address while in Paris. The King and César Ritz were good friends, the King having long been an admirer of the hotelier's business acumen. Apparently, His Majesty was in the bathtub enjoying the company of two nubile young ladies, when suddenly they found themselves locked together underwater such that none of them could extract themselves from the others. The King, in desperation, finally had to bellow for help. When Mr. Ritz heard of the King's predicament, he personally carried a pail of soft soapsuds into the bathroom and poured it into the tub, a procedure which, with the occupants' help, finally broke their tight squeeze.

Can you imagine the scene?

The King, remembering his manners, insisted that Mr. Ritz help the ladies out first, followed by himself, also with the help of Mr. Ritz, whereupon all three of them were duly wrapped in enormous Ritz towels. That very day, Mr. Ritz ordered all the bathtubs in the Ritz Hotel replaced with bigger and wider tubs, so that none of his guests could ever be embarrassed in such a fashion again. Whether the King ever took advantage of Mr. Ritz's efforts to please is not for me to say.

Interestingly enough, when his mother, Queen Victoria, died and he became King, his wife being the beautiful but unloved Queen Alexandra, he turned out to be a very good and diplomatic ruler, creating the entente cordiale with the French, who became crazy about him and his lovely wife. He went on to become enormously popular in his own country. Look at all those wasted years!

Prince Charles, England's current heir to the throne, has trod the same purposeless road and suffered the same consequences. Fortunately, he learned to create projects that he enjoyed and with which he achieved considerable success, and he is also helping to head up some important international causes.

No sooner did Wallis and the King return from their summer vacation than King Edward called upon his mother to tell her of his betrothal. Queen Mary promptly gave him a verbal thrashing, reminding him of his responsibilities to the Crown and his people, and the sacrifices that were expected of him.

"This woman is a seducer; she has already married and divorced two men in her life – do you want to be the third? Who is this woman? She was a nothing, contributing to nothing. She came out of nowhere; let her go back to nowhere. She has a black heart. You were destined to be King. Edward, follow your destiny: Give up this woman, my son. She is no good for you."

The King kissed his mother's hand and took his leave, close to tears, not having expected quite such a cold and scornful reception, but sure of one thing. He was not going to give Wallis up. Wallis, in the meantime, had once again sought Mother's advice, knowing by now that in not many more days the British press would break its self-imposed silence, putting her in fear for her very life if the public turned against her.

Mother told her that she should leave her home no later than early December, when the dreadful news would break upon a dumbfounded British and Dominion public, and move into our house while the King arranged for her safety. Already Wallis had had stones thrown at her house in Cumberland Terrace, and threats had been yelled at her in the street.

Wallis gratefully accepted, but Mother's invitation was undercut by the King's own concern for Wallis's safety; he arranged for her what turned out to be a miserable trip by road and sea to the south of France and the safety of her closest friends, Herman and Kitty Rogers, at their villa in Cannes.

In the meantime, his Prime Minister, Stanley Baldwin, and the Archbishop of Canterbury, and others had failed to prevail upon the obstinate King. Finally, on December 3, the British press made its presence known with headlines of almost copycat content: "Grave Constitutional Crisis," Grave Crisis," and "Constitutional Crisis." The country, shaken to its core, fell into a state of gloom, the majority feeling let down by the much loved Prince of Wales, who had chosen to give up being their King for the hand of a common American divorcée.

The following evening, Winston Churchill dined with the King at Fort Belvedere, "finding him down to the last extremity of endurance." Three days later, the King advised his government that his decision to abdicate was final. He signed the Instrument of Abdication in Fort Belvedere.

The next day, the Instrument having become law, ex-King Edward VIII, styled for the moment Prince Edward, was informed by his brother, now King George VI, formerly Prince Albert, Duke of York, that he intended to settle upon him the title of His Royal Highness, the Duke of Windsor. Wallis was not extended the same honor of "Royal Highness," much to the Duke of Windsor's consternation and bitterness, causing a rift between the brothers until the end of Windsor's days.

After dining with his family at Royal Lodge, Windsor Great Park, the Duke of Windsor proceeded to Windsor Castle to deliver his abdication broadcast for the BBC.

I was back at Eton, and Gavin and I and all the boys in our house gathered in our housemaster's study, in somewhat cramped quarters, to listen to the former King's farewell speech. It was sad, and I felt both sorry and glad for him: He was finally free of a monarch's responsibility to his people, and the royal harness was lifted from his shoulders, even though he was still anchored by his titles and expected conduct. But he had Wallis, and to him that was worth more than a crown and an empire. It was she who had given him the key to escape. In fact, she was herself the key.

It was actually good for England and the Empire, for England deserved better, and George VI, despite his health problems and his stutter, proved to be an earnest king, steadfast to his responsibilities and duties. With his charismatic wife, Queen Elizabeth, at his side, he proved to his people that he was worthy of their trust. The family, with their dogs in tow, became beloved and respected as the quintessential Royal Family.

Europe, Full of Surprises:
Paris, 1936

F isk, Uncle Lionel's chauffeur, had been loaned to Johnny to take our car by boat across the Channel to France, and then drive to Paris and leave it in the care of the Crillon Hotel to await our arrival by plane two days later. Fisk accomplished his task and returned by boat and train to Ferring.

I was, to say the least, an excited young man. One of the Crillon Hotel limousines met us at the airport, and we were soon driving along the wide boulevards and spacious intersections, past some of the most sublimely structured buildings on earth. No wonder Washington, D.C., is such a gloriously laid out city: it, too, was designed by a Frenchman!

In those days of the older and most cherished hotels, there were only two that stood out above the others, the Ritz and the Crillon, both providing fantastic service, sumptuous rooms, and great locations. Johnny, on one of his rare leaves from his regiment at the front during the First World War, had chosen Paris for a change. On the advice of a fellow officer, he had managed to check into the Crillon, where he had an hour-long bath, a change of fresh clothes, and a wonderful dinner; after taking a brisk walk, he had returned to his suite, undressed, and gotten into bed, where he slept the longest he had ever slept – twenty-five hours – which, given what he had been through day after day after day, was not that surprising. General Fryberg once observed Johnny at the head of his soldiers, marching down a shell-blistered road in France, so completely exhausted that he was actually walking in his sleep! His second-in-command kept him on course.

There's another interesting point about the Crillon. Eight years later, in

1944, when we had just liberated Paris, the United States Embassy reserved one whole floor at the Crillon for people on Embassy business and VIPs. The Embassy offered half the suites on that floor to the SHAEF (Supreme Headquarters, Allied Expeditionary Forces) Diplomatic Mission to the French Government, of which I was a member, while proper quarters were being arranged for the American, British, and French staff. We drew straws for the prized rooms, and I got a beautiful suite to share with a good friend who had also been lucky.

Our offices were in the Chase National Bank, which was a part of the Rockefeller Empire. David Rockefeller and his wife were good friends of Johnny and Mother. David had attended the London School of Economics while I was attending Eton. I had been included with my family on three occasions hosted by David and his wife. He was older than I by five or more years, but he was always very kind and gracious to me. In 1954 he helped me accomplish a "bringing together" with him of a client of mine, the former Governor of São Paulo, who was running for President of Brazil. I felt that my client could receive some good input from David, the Rockefeller family having considerable interests in Brazil, Winthrop Rockefeller in particular. David received us at the Knickerbocker Club in New York, where my client and David had an informative meeting, which I hoped benefited both of them. My client was very impressed and grateful.

Long after the Second World War, in 1979, President Carter's first choice for the chairmanship of the Federal Reserve Board was David Rockefeller, who turned him down twice, both times deferring to Paul Volker, who accepted.

There will be more about this part of my career later in these memoirs.

Our Paris visit was to last us three memorable days. We had barely arrived in our rooms when the phone rang, and the Viscount Evan Tredegar, honorary Colonel of the Welsh Guards and supreme host of the most wonderful long weekends at his magnificent estate in Wales, Tredegar Park, Newport, Monmouthshire, announced that he was also staying at the hotel and that he had just seen us getting into the elevator as he came in the front door. He was giving a dinner party at Maxim's this very night, and would we please come to his suite first for drinks around seven o'clock before going to the restaurant, and "Make sure to bring Peter."

Why me? Johnny and Mother and I had been to one of his weekend parties in the past year, which was perfect beyond imagination, but I wasn't aware that this super host had paid any more attention to me than any of the other younger members of the party who sat at "the nursery end" of the very long table, hosted by either Harry Ware, his estate manager, or "Mother S" (for Sutherland), as everybody called her, Evan's private secretary. They were both delightful people, who kept the nursery end in a jovial state of contentment.

There was always a special guest of world renown to anchor the occasion. At the weekend party we attended it was H.G. Wells, the internationally acclaimed writer, a small man with a rather high-pitched voice and a homely presence, but who was known for being surprisingly successful with the ladies, and who had brought his present mistress along with him. Much later, after the war, she became Sir Alexander Korda's "reader," while I was also working for Alex. She was a brilliant lady, and I enjoyed her company on the rare occasions that our paths crossed. She was responsible for bringing books and scripts that she considered filmworthy to Alex's attention, and he valued her opinions highly.

Every night of that weekend, at Tredegar Park, after the ladies had left the room as was the custom, the men and boys moved closer to the guest of honor and listened to him, with proddings from Evan, talk on many different subjects, all with great conviction and considerable intensity. Some of his opinions I did not agree with, but it was exciting beyond measure to listen to this genius expound on so many subjects, some incredibly complex, and all with total confidence. It was an experience I will never forget, and we had Mr. Wells's company for three whole nights.

But tonight I am in Paris, my first night, and already we have been invited to the most renowned and celebrated restaurant in the world, Maxim's. What a way to start our vacation!

After we had all rested awhile, and then bathed and dressed – black tie, of course – we reported to Evan's suite, which was more like an apartment, with a small entrance hall leading into a sizeable drawing room. It was decorated with mirrors, brilliant crystal chandeliers, rich fabric-covered walls, and furniture representing the Louis XIV period that I found to be quite comfortable. There was also a Steinway grand piano in the room, and, as if to complement it, there were Edith Piaf, the most famous singer of love songs in France – mostly sad love songs, but rendered exquisitely – and Maurice Chevalier, who needs no introduction. What a coup for Evan! And what an honor for us! What a way to begin an evening!

Most of Evan's sixteen guests were familiar to my mother and Johnny, and I knew six of them from one or another dinner party in our home, though I did feel a little like a fish out of water. But Piaf took me under her wing and, speaking very fast French to me, of which I couldn't understand a word, inveigled me over to the piano, where she sat down and, very softly, so as not to disturb the guests, played and sang love songs to me, her eyes as sad as her songs. I decided she felt her songs in her very being, every time she sang them, no matter how many times, and that was part of her genius. Even if I understood hardly a word, there was no question of her talent, or the mood she wanted to convey to her audience.

After about ten minutes, guests started gathering around the piano, and Piaf's voice grew louder and more dramatic; after another ten or fifteen minutes, she finished with a portion of the French national anthem, the most inspiring anthem in the world, bar none, leaving us all somewhat exalted.

Chevalier, who had remembered to bring his top hat and his piano accompanist, took over from Piaf, who joined me on a love seat after two members of the hotel staff had rearranged some of the furniture so that Chevalier would have some room in which to perform. And perform he did, mostly the songs that had helped to make him famous, including a couple from a movie that he had starred in the year before in Hollywood. He was wonderful, but both artists had to perform later that night in separate theaters, so Evan thanked them both, in French and then in English, and requested that they stay for just a few more minutes to honor someone in the room. Since there was a vacant chair on my side of the love seat that I was sharing with Piaf, who was holding my hand in hers, much to my surprise and delight, Chevalier took the chair, so that I had the two stars of the evening sitting on either side of me. Was I dreaming or what?

Evan shushed the room, and when silence reigned he started to speak, looking straight ahead. I can recall his words almost as well today as when I heard them. "A couple of months ago, on one of my weekend affairs, a deed was done that I was totally unaware of until sometime after the doer of the deed had departed. This is the deed he did, as revealed by one of my gardeners to Harry Ware, my estate manager, who finally told me about it ten days later. Apparently, the doer of the deed was in the boathouse preparing to take one of the rowboats out, when Romona, not one of our brightest dogs, and one who could not swim and was afraid of water anyway, was chasing a small but swift little mouse across the lawn. Being a very smart little mouse, he dashed toward the pond, at the very last minute applying his brakes and taking off in another direction. Romona's reflexes were not so quick, and the poor dog went charging over the grass and into the pond. Fortunately, the doer of the good deed heard the splash and noticed that, since Romona's velocity had carried her well out of her depth, she had panicked and started going under. Our good deed doer quickly got into the boat and rowed out to Romona, who had gone down once; leaping out of the boat, he swam to Romona as she was going under yet again and reversed course, swimming with one hand holding Romona as he used the other to maneuver. The swimmer, now sopping wet, placed Romona in the boat and then himself, and paddled back to the boathouse, by which time Romona had recovered enough to kiss her savior's face and wag her tail. The do-gooder, seeing that all was well again, took off, I hope, for a hot bath, a change of clothes, and a hot toddy."

I knew after a minute that he was talking about me, but I was very surprised, because I hadn't seen the gardener, and the only error in Evan's story was that I jumped into the water to rescue Romona. I did no such thing. While reaching for Romona, I lost my balance and fell into the water, and the reason I didn't tell anyone about it was because I didn't want to own up to having been the cause of my own presence in the pond. Somehow I managed to get to my room unseen, where I hung my wet clothes in my bathroom; it being summer, they were dry by morning and quickly placed away out of sight.

"And the doer of this wondrous rescue of Romona is none other than the son of Minerva and Johnny Dodge, my friend Peter. Come here, Peter." I got up and went to Evan, who was holding a small jewelry box in his hand; when I opened it, it displayed a beautiful porcelain medallion in a gold case, with a colored picture of Romona somehow reproduced on its face. On the back of the gold case was written in carved letters, "For Peter Sherman, who rescued Romona. From Evan Tredeger in gratitude."

I was thrilled. Everyone clapped. Mother hugged me, and Johnny shook my hand and patted me on the back. Piaf embraced me and showered me with kisses. Chevalier asked me what I would like him to sing for me, and I said, "Louise"; the pianist began playing and we all got up and started heading for the door, singing the song with considerable abandon, with Maurice Chevalier leading the way and Evan and Edith Piaf bringing up the rear, all the way to the elevators.

This was pretty heady stuff for a fourteen-year-old boy. I was in seventh heaven!

Maxim's was wonderful. Josephine Baker was wonderful, the Eiffel Tower was wonderful, the Louvre was wonderful, as were the boulevards, the houses, the shops. Eating and drinking at tables on the sidewalks, the tantalizing smells, the clothes, the girls – I really loved Paris. Only a few years later, as an adult in uniform speaking French, I would be able to enjoy its temptations and its beauty for one whole year, by which time the world was on the brink, but not yet changing.

Incidentally, I later learned that Evan Tredegar had paid what was, no doubt, a hefty fee for the services of Maurice Chevalier and Edith Piaf, for world stars don't come cheap. But it's all relative, and he certainly gave his guests an evening to remember.

Vienna

Vienna was beautiful, of course. The pastries were to die for. But there was an apathy about the Viennese people, a lack of expression in their faces, as if they had a palsy, which put something of a cloud over the visit.

The first night we dined at our hotel, because Johnny had been delayed by an appointment that he had arranged before leaving England. Even in Paris he had disappeared for a whole afternoon. Much later we learned that these visits were part of a program that Johnny had taken upon himself in cahoots with a wing of the British Government that had used his services in Russia sometime before. They had drawn up a list of certain VIPs in the top echelon of the governments and military of the countries we were visiting who were deemed favorable toward the British; Johnny was to sound out their preparedness for war, and what they would do in case of war. The protagonists were Hitler, of course, with Stalin next and Mussolini way in the distance. Naturally, Johnny's credentials were impeccable, and he continued to pursue his task in each country, even into Germany.

Johnny was sick at heart, and even sicker when his Viennese connections told him that morale was at the bottom there, too; while the head of state was a brave man, he appeared incapable of bringing Austria out of its misery, and a homegrown Nazi Party, instigated by Hitler, was adding to its numbers by leaps and bounds. If Hitler wanted to, they said, he could probably take over Austria without firing a shot.

This is exactly what happened two years later, in 1938. On March 15 of that year, Chancellor Hitler rode triumphantly through the streets of Vienna, the imperial city where he had lived as a penniless third-rate artist nearly thirty years before. It was the annexation of Austria – known as the *Anschluss* – carried out under threat of invasion by the German army.

Munich

Hitler had first joined and then taken over the Nazi Party in its infancy in the beer halls of my favorite German city, Munich, the capital of Bavaria. I found myself impressed with the people of the city, who were celebrating life with good food, good beer, and good humor. And yet they appeared to be hard workers, whether laborers or executives, and we saw both.

And the uniforms! You would have thought you were already in a war, as one in every five or ten people displayed a uniform from one or another of the military services, not to forget the policing services. And then there were the Nazi posters displayed in wearying profusion on almost every wall and building, exhorting the multitudes to ever higher goals for the Führer and the Fatherland.

The civilian populace looked content. No doubt they felt a great joy in being a part of Hitler's great plan for the German people. He gave them a socialistic form of government in theory, but a pure dictatorship in practice, glued together by the inhuman power of fear. This weapon of fear was not apparent at the time of our visit, for in 1936 Hitler was exploiting his economic and industrial triumphs by taking a leisurely grand tour of his country, enjoying the fevered acclamation of its citizens wherever he went, flying home to the Berghof above Berchtesgaden only on weekends.

Hitler was also looking forward to the 1936 Olympic Games in Berlin, which were being masterminded by Joseph Goebbels, his Propaganda Minister, to be the most triumphant spectacle of the glory of National Socialism ever presented to the world. The Games were to provide Hitler a dramatic presence on the international stage.

To Hitler's credit, though labor unions had been banned, almost all workers were receiving an adequate paycheck, plus free medical and hospital care, plus subsidized vacations at seaside resorts that they would never have dreamed of visiting before his rise to power. Furthermore, there was no unemployment.

Hitler was also the first world leader to take a position on pollution, demanding that factories reduce pollution to a feasible minimum, whether in the air or pumped into the rivers, lakes, and oceans. He made the penalties severe and he made them stick. He enacted many decrees benefiting the workers, as well as the industrial leaders who had helped put him in power. The latter also believed that they would be able to control him. Fat chance!

It wasn't until 1938 that Hitler's plans for world conquest went into high gear. At that time, his financial advisers warned him that the German financial structure supporting his regime and its industrial and military complex were showing the first signs of fatigue; he had less than two years, they advised, to go to war or suffer the consequences of a severe economic breakdown.

From that moment on, Hitler became both a "warlord" and an "appeaser," switching roles as it suited him, until that fated day in the most beautiful summer that Britain had enjoyed in many a year, September 1 of 1939, when his troops invaded Poland. England promptly declared war on Germany. The world would never be the same again.

Berchtesgaden

But this was 1936, and Mother and Johnny and I were traveling in our car through pretty Bavarian villages, some on lakes or rivers, many seeming almost theatrical, they were so true to the drawings in fairy-tale books with their colorful characters and houses with a gingerbread touch. The women were generally dressed in their native costumes, either being slim and pretty or plump and not so pretty, and the men were partial to leather shorts and a harness over their shirts. Nowhere were we treated with anything less than respect and curiosity; even our lack of facility with their language was usually resolved by one of them interpreting for us. We liked the Germans we met and they seemed to like us; any fears we may have had in hearing of the Nazi regime's Jew-baiting and political concentration camps were put on hold for the time being. Every aspect of life was clean and efficient, and the people with whom we came in contact were polite and helpful.

Our final German destination was to be Berchtesgaden, above which sat Hitler's Berghof, his favorite home, where he returned whenever possible, and where his girlfriend Eva Braun resided, her suite next to his. Mother did not like this idea of going to Berchtesgaden at all, and she and Johnny had had quite an argument before she acceded to his insistence, on the condition that the visit would be limited to one night and a day.

We arrived at the hotel around five in the evening. Since it had been a long day's drive, Mother and Johnny decided, upon checking in, to rest up for an hour or so before having dinner. I, on the other hand, having done nothing but watch the countryside flow by all day, decided to take an exploratory promenade outside the hotel and get some fresh air. There had been nobody except the desk clerk in the lobby when we arrived, and only later did we discover that he was also the manager.

When I stepped out of the elevator, I saw that he was having an animated conversation in German with a large man I had not previously seen. The conversation came to a halt when the manager saw me. I started to walk toward the door leading to the road, when the large man turned around and, in good English with only a slight German accent, asked me if my father was the Colonel J. B. Dodge who was such a hero of the First World War. With a real sense of pride, I acknowledged that he was, and the big man then asked me if it wasn't true that he was also a good friend of Mr. Winston Churchill. "Of course," said I. "Everyone knows that."

The big man came across the lobby to me, and I said that I was Colonel Dodge's stepson, not his son. "No matter," said the big man. He had a nice smile, and he asked me where I was going. I said I didn't know, and he offered to take me for a quick tour of Berchtesgaden, including a glimpse of Hitler's home on the side of the mountain. I was thrilled. He introduced himself as Dr. Schmidt. We got in his car, and he described all the points of interest, including a restaurant with a folk-dancing show that he thought we might enjoy.

"Your hotel manager will make the reservation for you if you decide to go," he said.

We proceeded to Berchtesgaden, which was quite small in those days. Dr. Schmidt then drove partway up to the Berghof but said he couldn't take me any farther because the Führer was in residence, this being the weekend. After he brought me back to the hotel, I thanked him for the guided tour, and he thanked me for the company and drove off into the dusk.

As soon as I came back into the lobby, I saw Johnny getting out of the elevator. He looked surprised to see me coming into the hotel, and asked me where I had been. Full of myself and my outing with Dr. Schmidt, I told him the whole story. Johnny didn't say a word until I finished, but his expression changed into a look of anticipation – of what I had no idea.

"Peter, on no account do I want you to say a word of this episode to your mother," he said. "She's already on edge enough as it is, and I don't want to add to her worries. Promise?" I promised, although I was disappointed that I could not regale Mother with my tale.

Johnny had the manager reserve a table at the restaurant recommended by Dr. Schmidt, and Mother finally came down to the lobby, having bathed and changed, looking great, if edgy. We drove up to the restaurant, where every table seemed to be occupied by German families in their native costumes guzzling what appeared to be gallon beer glasses of foaming German beer and eating enormous plates of sausages and other meats and fried potatoes and beets and sauerkraut and I don't remember what else. It was a regular orgy of food and drink, and the bellies of most middle-aged and older Germans at that time reflected their eating habits. But they were having fun.

After we were seated at our table, Johnny joined in singing along with the band and the crowd, even if he didn't know the words. Mother smiled theatrically for Johnny's benefit, although obviously wishing she were in a somewhat less noisy and coarse atmosphere. Making the best of it, she joined the crowd with that marvelous whistle of hers, which soon attracted some other whistlers from other tables to our table; when the band finally took a break, they turned in our table's direction and applauded Mother and her group of whistlers, as did the rest of the patrons, much to Johnny's delight. He immediately ordered all the whistlers another gallon of beer, and they finally returned to their tables, leaving Mother and me free to peruse the menu, while Johnny retired to the men's room, having drunk a whole glass of beer himself. One of the amazing things about Johnny was that he never got drunk, no matter how many drinks he had, though I must confess that three was generally his limit, and it was more likely to be one or two at the most.

Johnny returned with another man in tow, a nice-looking fellow about his own age, and it turned out that not only could he speak some English, but he and Johnny had faced each other in battle in France in 1917. According to them, each side would gain a few hundred yards of sodden earth and freezing trenches, then lose it back again to the enemy, while the best of their youths were being decimated, the dead bodies of both sides sometimes stacked in piles for days as the battle went back and forth for a few hundred yards of dirt.

Johnny introduced his friend to Mother and me, and they continued to talk while we tried to make out the menu, Johnny's friend finally suggesting his favorite plate, which we ordered for all three of us. With its arrival, Johnny's guest stood up to leave, first accepting one of Johnny's Romeo and Juliet Cuban cigars, which Johnny clipped for him with his personal cigar clipper, and then lit. Johnny had a silver cigar case for four cigars that my mother had given him on their fourth wedding anniversary, which he generally carried on him for just such an occasion.

His guest must have known a good cigar when he smoked it, because he walked back to his table with a swagger he had not shown when he and Johnny had returned from the men's room. It was a nice touch. We watched him sit down and say a few words to his wife, a rather grim-looking woman with big hips and breasts, barren of any appeal. Her husband drew appreciatively on his Cuban cigar, blowing the blue smoke slowly toward the ceiling, a happy man.

And then it happened. His wife, obviously a dyed-in-the-wool Nazi and resentful of his fraternizing, in her mind, with the enemy, lost her cool. She grabbed the beautiful cigar out of his mouth and snapped it in half, crushing the two parts into a large ashtray while suffocating the burning end.

We stared, shocked, and Mother said, "Oh, my God!" Johnny smiled his dry smile that he kept for emergencies, and we finished our dinners, fully aware that his friend and his wife had left the restaurant without having spoken another word to each other since the incident.

Johnny finally paid our bill, tipping the waiter and sending the band leader a generous tip as well. As we walked between the tables and across the floor toward the exit, the band leader abruptly stopped the music and said something in German to his patrons, who burst into tumultuous clapping and banging of beer glasses on the tables. Johnny reached up and shook the band leader's hand, and we all three waved happily to the room as we exited through a throng of well-wishers onto the street and into the sanctuary of our car.

"My, what an evening!" said Mother, as Johnny drove the car into the road and back down the hill toward our hotel.

"I didn't know whether we were going to be lynched or lionized," Johnny noted. "I'm glad it was the latter."

Just then our car's lights picked up a couple on the sidewalk about a hundred yards ahead of us, a man beating up his wife with considerable pleasure. Johnny, ever the gallant knight, immediately slowed the car and said he must stop this wife beating. Mother screamed at him that, if he dared to leave the car in the middle of Hitler's stronghold to do such a crazy thing she would take me on the first plane back to London – that is, if all three of us hadn't immediately been put in a concentration camp where no one would ever find us. Mother was so vehement that Johnny backed down; when we passed the couple and realized it was the same couple of the cigar incident, I think Johnny must have been glad that Mother had restrained him.

When we reached the hotel, the manager was still on duty at the desk, his night manager having been taken ill, he explained. It was now eleven, and Mother excused herself, saying she was worn out and was going to bed; she instructed us not to wake her up before eight in the morning, because she was going to take a sleeping pill, since she had not been sleeping well since we started on the trip. Johnny promised. Noting that he wasn't sleepy yet, he said he would take a seat in the lobby and smoke one of his Cuban cigars before coming up to bed.

I took Mother to their room, where I bade her goodnight and walked through the door connecting our suites. This was generally kept ajar in all the hotels on our European trip, so I knew when Mother finally got into bed and went to sleep. For me, the whole evening had been so out of the ordinary and so stimulating that I found it impossible to relax; finally, I looked at the clock and saw it was almost one a.m. and Johnny hadn't yet returned to his room. This I did not like, so I dressed again and went down to the lobby, which was empty, except for the manager, whom I found asleep on a cot behind his desk. I woke him and demanded to know what had happened to my stepfather. He said that Colonel Dodge had been picked up by Dr. Schmidt just twenty minutes before, and that they would be back before dawn. I wasn't to worry; Colonel Dodge had instructed him that, should I come looking for him, I was to be told not to wake Mother and to go back to bed myself. On no account was Mother to be made aware of his absence. I didn't understand any of it. I just hoped Mother's sleeping pill did its duty.

I sat down in a chair with a German picture magazine, most of its contents being dedicated to the upcoming Olympics, but I couldn't stop worrying about Johnny and wondering if he had fallen into some ghastly Nazi trap and we would never see him again. That nice Dr. Schmidt might not be so nice after all.

The more I pondered the situation, the more scared I became. What if …? What if …? Why had Johnny been so insistent on coming to Berchtesgaden, in spite of all my mother's anguished pleas? Why would he let a complete stranger, Dr. Schmidt, take him away in the middle of the night, and to where and to whom? Johnny could be so prudent in some scenarios, and so risk-taking in others. He had survived so many dangerous escapades successfully in his life: Was this to be the final, fatal one?

At four in the morning a lady arrived on a bicycle at the hotel's entrance. Leaving her bike propped up outside, she entered the lobby with a small case and woke up the manager. Though sleepy, he seemed to know the lady and quickly ushered her through the door into his office at the back of the desk.

After a few minutes, the manager came out of the office. I got out of my chair, where I had been napping off and on through the night, and asked him, "Who was that lady?"

"She's my secretary. She speaks English, types, and is a stenographer in both English and German. A very good lady."

"But why is she here at four in the morning? Isn't that an unusual time to come to work?"

"Perhaps," said the manager, looking a bit uncomfortable. "But she has an appointment with one of our guests."

"At four o'clock in the morning?"

"Well, not necessarily at four o'clock. But as soon as he gets here."

I wanted to ask the manager why he didn't call the guest and tell him the secretary was here, but thought better of it. After all, who was I to tell the manager how to run his hotel?

At ten minutes after five, I saw Dr. Schmidt's car pull up to the front door with Johnny sitting beside him. They stayed in the car, talking, for another ten minutes and then they both got out of the car and came into the lobby. When Johnny saw me, he looked stricken and asked me why I was there. I told him I was waiting up for him. He looked over at Dr. Schmidt, who was smiling, and suddenly he grabbed me in his arms in a bear hug, and said, "That's my boy!" – the first time he had ever said "my boy" to me. I was thrilled. Whether it was because we were both so tired or for some other reason, we both had a tear nestling in the corner of our eyes.

Dr. Schmidt shook my hand and said how much he had enjoyed our drive the evening before, and I thanked him again and told him what a good time we had had at the restaurant he recommended to me. Johnny asked him if he could finally get some sleep, and he replied that the Führer generally slept until noon, but since there were no English, French, or Italian dignitaries on the engagement book for this day beyond Johnny, he would have the day off.

The bade each other farewell and it was obvious that they had enjoyed each other's company. Also, it had become clear to me that Dr. Schmidt was Adolf Hitler's official interpreter, and that he had been interpreting for the Führer and Johnny for the last three hours.

But I was not to hear a word of what had gone on until Johnny got his digest down on paper while it was fresh in his mind, and that is what he did for the next one and a half hours with the help of the manager's secretary.

I had been instructed to return to my bed and go to sleep. I peeked into Mother's room, and she looked like she was having a beautiful dream, her face peaceful, a slight smile on her lips. Thank goodness for sleeping pills!

An Extraordinary Conversation

A DIGEST
Written by: J. B. Dodge
Participants: Adolf Hitler, John B. Dodge, Dr. Schmidt, interpreter
At the Berghof
Dr. Schmidt ushered me into an enormous room, at the other end of which was a wall of glass, opening onto a large terrace and a breathtaking view of the surrounding mountains, bathed in the light of a star-studded sky and a full moon. If Hitler had wanted to create a good first impression, he had to go no further than that view.

Hitler was sitting in a large armchair, official-looking papers on his lap, with more on the side table near where we entered. He immediately placed the papers he had been studying back on the table and walked energetically across the room toward me. He was dressed in civilian clothes – a dark green jacket, black pants, and a white shirt and black tie with a swastika tie pin on it, and another swastika on the lapel of his coat. There was no one else in the room besides our interpreter.

Dr. Schmidt made the introductions. Hitler shook my hand effusively, and led me to a low table near the scenic view, where three comfortable chairs had been set up, a large silver teapot on the table, a flame beneath it to keep it hot, and a set of German-made cups and saucers to drink it from. There were also English cucumber sandwiches, the cucumbers cut wafer thin just like we have at home, and rice biscuits. Dr. Schmidt did the honors, pouring the tea and passing the sandwiches; I thanked the Führer for remembering this English custom, and he smiled and said there was a lot he liked about the English and their customs Then he launched into endless stories about the 1914 – 1918 Great War, and I told him some from the British side. I was just beginning to fear that this extraordinary occasion was going to be a complete waste of time, when he said, "Winston Churchill was crazy to fight the Turks. The Gallipoli invasion was a complete fiasco, a bloodbath for the British, and yet he is still a voice to be reckoned with, and he seems to have plenty of followers, in spite of being out of office. You are one, are you not, Colonel Dodge?"

"He is my friend, yes," I said. "We have been friends since before the war."

"And you think alike?"

"We both love our country, and want to protect it."

"But you are an American by birth. Americans do not like to fight other people's wars."

"I was an American, sir, and proud of it, but when war began, I had already become a British subject and sworn allegiance to the King. I am a British citizen."

"You are related to Winston Churchill?"

"Not by blood, but by family connections, yes."

Hitler paused, and took a sip of tea. Dr. Schmidt passed the sandwiches. The Führer's voice rose a decibel and his expression became intense, his eyes hypnotic.

"Colonel Dodge, you and your friend Mr. Churchill have completely misinterpreted my intentions. You think because I am building up my military forces I am going to war? It is exactly the opposite! I am a man of peace, surrounded by warmongers. Look at France. They have more troops than I have. Look at Russia, the Red Menace; Stalin has more men, more guns, and far more tanks than we have now. True, he exterminated most of his officers, but in time he will have them replaced. Germany is surrounded by potential enemies, and you and Mr. Churchill are fanning the waves of hatred against us with your diatribes. And don't forget, Colonel Dodge, I have brought my country out of chaos into a standard of living that is the envy of the world.

"Look at America. Look at France. Look at England. You are all floundering with high unemployment, high taxes, still paying off debts from the last war. You have no captain at the wheel to control and run a country with a firm hand and a goal that is backed by all his people, as I have with Germany."

Dr. Schmidt was doing a brilliant job of translating.

Again Hitler paused, and took a sip of tea, the better to moisten his lips, and his eyes remained riveted on mine. He truly had a tremendous presence, charming one moment, impossible the next, but always fascinating. He was absolutely confident, accustomed to obedience, and perfectly happy to follow his own intuition against all odds and all logic. So far, he had been quite successful.

"Colonel Dodge, I would like you to take a message, a private message, to Mr. Churchill from me. I am a winner, and God looks favorably on winners. England still has its Empire, and so you will come through in spite of your present condition. The enemy is not Germany; it is Russia! If Great Britain and Germany could become allies, France would quickly see the necessity of entering the alliance in order not to be left alone without Great Britain as an ally in case Germany found the need to become belligerent. With us three allied, with such an advantage of men and weapons, the rest of Europe would have no other recourse but to join with us. With this formidable array marshaled against Stalin, I think we could make any terms we wanted without the loss of one soldier! And what a prize! We would have subservient to our authority a vast country with the richest mineral and oil and gas deposits, plus a wealth of other resources, and an enormous peasant labor force in place that under our joint direction could be trained to run the programs. I'm told that we would have vastly more diamond mines than South Africa, so we would be pleasing the ladies as well!"

Hitler smiled. It was nearly five o'clock in the morning.

"That, Colonel Dodge, is why I asked you here tonight."

He stood up, as did I and Dr. Schmidt. Coming around to my side of the table, he cupped his hand under my elbow, leading me toward and through a glass door built into the glass wall and out onto the terrace, Dr. Schmidt in tow. We stood there for a while in silence, the view so splendid and peaceful at this hour, and then Hitler turned to me and said, "Colonel Dodge, you were a brave man in the war. Dr. Schmidt told me of some of your exploits both then and afterward in Russia, and I admire your courage and your bravery. I am trying to stop another war. We men of destiny must more than ever bring the message of peace, as I have described it to you, to men of goodwill. Be brave, braver than you have ever been in your life; convince your friend, Mr. Churchill, of my message of peace and all of his and your admirers and followers. If you and Mr. Churchill can move a majority of your friends in Parliament to our way of thinking, you will have made history, not only for yourself and Great Britain, but for the world."

With that, he shook my hand, less effusively but more firmly than before, and bade me goodnight and good luck. He turned back into that vast room toward a nearby door, through which he disappeared. Dr. Schmidt walked me back to his car, neither of us saying a word, until we were locked inside and driving back to the hotel.

"We have an agreement with France that, if either country is attacked, the other one will go to war against its attacker," I said.

"That is the point of our Führer's plan," Dr. Schmidt replied. "No one will go against France. No one will go against anyone. Russia is the enemy. According to the Führer's plan, even that could be obtained without bloodshed."

On the way up to the Berghof, Dr. Schmidt had pressed upon me the importance of not getting into an argument with Herr Hitler and not touching on delicate subjects, and I understood what he meant by that. I had come to listen, and listen I did.

Dr. Schmidt told me that some years after the war he had obtained a copy of *Who's Who* in Great Britain. By chance he had come upon my biography, a mere eight inches in length, but he became so intrigued with my career up until the date of its publication that he had continued to follow my career through newspaper clipping services on both sides of the Atlantic, including my marriage to Minerva.

Dr. Schmidt had also made a habit of checking the hotel's guest list, it being the only hotel at the time, on the chance that someone of real interest to the Führer might have a reservation, but he had not had any luck until I came along. I was flattered, but I told him the truth, that I was a very small fish in a very big pond, and I advised him he would find many more worthwhile personages in his *Who's Who* than me.

Venice

I really liked Dr. Schmidt, though I didn't envy him his job, and I was sorry to have to say goodbye to him. But we were fated to meet again, under far stranger circumstances than my visit with Hitler, and with a far greater burden of responsibility than I will ever have again, thank God.

Budapest was a unique and fascinating city, and we spent two days and nights there before leaving that beautiful city for Italy.

Venice, like Paris, embraces you from the moment you arrive to the moment you, very regretfully, leave. It is magic. It is romantic. It has a certain feel and an incredible setting that set it apart from all other cities. I was utterly seduced by Venice, as I was by Paris. And what seducers!

We were ensconced in a beautiful suite overlooking the canal at the Royal Danielli Hotel, which along with the Gritti Palace was aged and very grand. There, to our utter amazement, we found Johnny's sister, Lucy, and her husband, Walter Rosen, along with their children Walter Jr. and Ann, staying in a suite even grander than ours. I had never met this family. Ann and Walter Jr. were both older than I by three or four years, but I was pleased to have people closer to my age to do things with.

Walter Sr. was a supreme example of a perfect, cultivated gentleman. His father a former Supreme Court Judge in New York, Walter Sr. had been educated at the best schools. He had entered Wall Street as a young man with a special talent for banking, investment banking in particular, and had been for some time afterward the President of Ladenburg Thalman, among the largest and most prestigious private banking houses in New York. He was already enormously wealthy. He and Aunt Lucy were both involved in the arts, music being Aunt Lucy's thing, the playing of the theremin in particular (about which more later), and architecture and antiques of all kinds were Walter's specialty.

Their main activity during their summer vacations was casing some of Europe's great castles, mansions, and chateaus that had fallen on bad times. They would purchase from the financially strapped owners, at a fair price, a room from a French chateau, and maybe an unusual floor from another, or a set of crystal chandeliers possibly from a grand home on the canal right here in Venice. These rooms and artifacts were carefully removed and the walls replaced at no cost to the sellers; once they had been professionally broken down and packaged, they were taken back to America, where they were unloaded and rebuilt into the architect's plans as dictated by Walter Sr. The whole operation took some years, ending as a fabulous mansion on a large estate in Katonah, north of New York City, its name being Caramoor (dear love).

The house itself was the frame, into which Walter inserted superlatively restored antique furniture, some of it acquired along with the rooms themselves, as well as paintings, rugs, tables, and special conversation pieces, one of which was an enormous Bible sitting on the stand in the corner of our bedroom, when, in 1959, my wife Clementine and I were spending a long weekend at Caramoor as part of our honeymoon. Turning the opening pages, I found an inscription in English (not German): "To my beloved Vicky, from your loving husband Albert." From Prince Albert to his wife, Queen Victoria! Another oddity was the bed that four Popes had slept in during the Middle Ages, now the Walter Rosens' bed. Clementine asked Lucy if she and Walter hadn't found the Popes' bed a little unnerving at first, and Lucy replied with a laugh that Walter had carefully investigated the history of this emperor-size bed at the Vatican before obtaining it. He had discovered that it was the favorite of four Popes who, ignoring their oath of celibacy, had taken wives and mistresses unto themselves, with the normal consequence of producing children, one of whom was made a Cardinal at the age of eight. There was no doubt why the Vatican wished to be rid of the bed. It certainly was the most splendid bed we had ever seen. If only it could talk!

Aunt Lucy founded the Caramoor Festival, to which New Yorkers in particular come in droves every summer for the concerts. André Previn was one among many distinguished directors and conductors over the years. Joan Sutherland, the greatest opera singer of her time, gave her first performance in the United States at the festival.

Aunt Lucy was a knockout of a lady, about five feet eight inches tall, with a pompadour hair style that increased her height by another foot or so, it seemed, and with a beautiful, elegant face on a long neck, plus a slim figure. Like her brother, Johnny, she had a presence that could get the attention of a room full of chattering people without her saying a word. She was graciousness personified, and yet, like her husband Walter, a down-to-earth person, generous with herself and her influence in the world of young, underfunded artists pursuing careers in voice or instrumental music, never denying a more than generous scholarship if the professors in their field verified that talent was indeed there.

Aunt Lucy found joy in almost everything she was interested in, and, like Mother, she loved to laugh. These two sisters-in-law got along wonderfully well, mainly, I think, because they were both very giving of themselves and poured their energy into any project, big or small, that they felt worthwhile and worth doing.

Walter Jr. and I got along swimmingly. Ann Rosen, his sister, a very nice young lady and a good tennis player, joined us part of the time, particularly when we took a gondola for an afternoon, lazing on the well-pillowed sofa-like seats through the many canals and bridges that we never would have discovered by ourselves. Other times she would be with the adults, as Walter Jr. and I would on occasion, and in the evening we would all gather together for dinner at some marvelous dining room or restaurant.

It was on the third day of our visit to Venice that Johnny got a phone call from Count Ciano himself, the son-in-law of Benito Mussolini, Italy's Fascist dictator. Count Ciano was, I believe, the Italian Secretary of State at that time, and he wanted Johnny to have lunch with him that very day. Johnny was flattered and curious, so he accepted, and Count Ciano, who spoke reasonable English, Johnny told us, said that he would send his own motor launch to pick him up at one that afternoon.

Walter Jr. and I had visited the Palace of the Doges, from which Venice ruled and enriched itself beyond measure for centuries, via the shipping commerce of that part of the world; we had also seen the Bell Tower, St. Mark's Square, the Bridge of Sighs, and so on. In Italy it isn't possible not to see beauty, whether in a city, a village, or the countryside, all different, all beautiful, the most magnificent of all being Rome, a city I had to pass up this time but would see many years later, still in all its glory. Actually, Florence became my favorite.

But today, the day that Count Ciano had invited Johnny for lunch, Walter Jr. and I had said we would take the motor launch out to the Lido, maybe a mile or so into the ocean, featuring a nice beach, tea dances from four to six in the Excelsior Hotel, and a great place, so Walter Jr. informed me, for picking up birds (girls!). Not being as adult as my family member and new friend, I wasn't so sure about this proposition, but he went off birdwatching, as he called it, while I sat on the sand, wishing that I had a few more years under my belt so that I could be as worldly as he.

As I gazed around the Lido Beach at the vast semi-naked humanity spread before me, much of it asleep, soothed by the soft sounds of the waves spewing onto the sand and then retreating slowly back into the sea, I was startled to see in the distance a veritable walking goddess in a white bathing suit with a very hairy male accompanying her up the beach toward me at a leisurely pace. Behind me I heard raised voices; turning, I spied a group of photographers talking excitedly among themselves and starting to aim their cameras in the lady's direction.

Who could this person be who was worth all of this admiring attention? Suddenly I knew. Marlene Dietrich! The Movie Queen! The word "glamor" must have originated with her: There she was, with her gorgeous figure, her long legs, and that commanding presence, coming straight at me. I sat there transfixed, incapable of movement, my mouth dry, and suddenly realized that she was talking, but not to me. In those days, the news media showed some respect for their subjects and were not nearly as aggressive as today, and I realized that what this glamorous movie star was doing was escaping the burden of yet another interview by telling the photographers and newsmen exactly what her itinerary was for the next few days. It apparently worked, for without appearing to slow down, but cramming a lot of information into a brief space of time, she assuaged the media's hunger for news of her; then she stepped into her motor launch, safely wrapped in a large beach towel, the hairy beast still at her side. Actually, he was probably a hard-working press agent.

Anyway, Walter Jr. finally returned with two young ladies in tow, not as young as I, American college girls, but they were nice, and we went for a swim and showered and changed back into our clothes in the Excelsior Hotel. We were escorted to a table in the Tea Room, where we spent the next couple of hours drinking tea and eating finger food with our new friends, ending with a yummy chocolate cake and some dancing. Dancing was one of the few things I was good at. Mother had taught me to dance, she being a great dancer herself, and I even won first prize in the dancing class at St. Peter's Court, though it wasn't much fun dancing with another boy in my arms.

To Walter Jr.'s disappointment, the two young ladies were returning to Connecticut the next day. We shared a boat and dropped them off at their hotel, and then returned to ours, each retiring to his own suite. I lay down and went straight to sleep: Sun and sand and a lot of foxtrots, not to mention the thrill of seeing Dietrich so close to me that I could have touched her, had worn me out.

When I told Walter Jr. about my near encounter with the great movie queen, he gave an anguished cry, "Oh, no!" and asked me why I hadn't come looking for him the moment I saw her in the distance. I told him that, with five thousand bodies or more reclining, kneeling, or standing on the beach, I wasn't about to go looking for him; anyway, he was looking for his "birds," so we ended up even. Grudgingly, with a twisted smile, he agreed.

Walter Jr. was brilliant, a genius scholar, at the top of every class he took. He was also very grounded and modest, not impressed with himself, just a well-bred, well-educated, and delightful friend, who treated me with great kindness, and who had almost certainly a great future ahead of him.

That evening at dinner Johnny told us that Count Ciano had emphasized the great regard that he and his father-in-law Benito Mussolini had for the British nation, and how much our good relations meant to the Italian people. Whatever Hitler might say or do, he had stressed, Mussolini was a man unto himself and would do the right thing for Italy as he, and not Hitler, saw fit. We were not to be afraid. Of course, it was easy for Count Ciano to speak thusly, for Hitler would not be ready for war until 1939 and could afford to give Mussolini a long rope, knowing he was there and in place. Mussolini knew it. Count Ciano knew it. Hitler knew it. All it would take would be one healthy tug.

At the end of lunch, Count Ciano had asked Johnny to give his best regards to Winston Churchill, and to tell him how proud Mussolini and the Italian people were to be friends with the British people.

"We must keep the peace," were Count Ciano's last words, spoken with an embrace and firm handshake.

Johnny liked the Count, but, as with Hitler, didn't trust him.

We left for Switzerland two days later, our final stop. I had had a perfectly marvelous time, particularly with Walter Jr., though I really had grown to love both Walter Sr. and Aunt Lucy very much. Both were outstanding characters and beloved people, and it had been a really superb week in a city unique in all the world.

I never saw Walter Jr. again. He died, like my good friend Richard Spencer, in an airplane accident while in flight school during the Second World War. What an unutterable waste.

Switzerland

Chateau d'Oex
Lausanne and Montreux, both beautiful cities nestled on the shores of a fabulous lake, seemed somewhat bland after our previous destinations. Even Gstaad, only a few miles from our final rendezvous, a city that was fast becoming a favorite haunt of the jetsetters of that period, failed to grab our attention more than any of the other Swiss places we had seen. It was only when we drove into Chateau d'Oex, a mere hamlet compared with the others, that we felt relaxed and exhilarated all at once.

Chateau d'Oex in those days was nothing more than a small village, set high among the surrounding mountains, with verdant slopes that supplied herds of bell-ringing cattle with fodder during the summer. It boasted one medium-sized hotel, run as smoothly as the works in a Swiss watch, and delicious pastry shops that we ravaged between long walks in the mountains. Our program for each day was mapped out for us by our concierge at the hotel, whose directions led us to magic waterfalls, secret caves behind the falls to be explored, bubbling brooks to be crossed, and wildflowers scenting the intoxicating air. We broke our walks only for a delicious picnic lunch prepared by the kitchen staff, the menu different every day.

It was a wonderful way to end our fabulous but demanding trip, and the utter peace of the mountains' countryside, marked only by the soft sound of water tripping down whatever mountain or valley we were exploring and the distant sound of the cattle bells way below, enfolded the three of us into a relaxed and loving unit, and finally pushed aside for all time the curtain that had existed between Johnny and me.

At breakfast, the day before we left Chateau d'Oex, Johnny asked me if I would consider living there for a year or so, except for vacations back home, in order to learn the French language fluently. I was stunned, but I answered, "If that's what you want me to do, of course I'll do it. But what about Eton?"

"You'll stay at Eton until 1938, Peter, when I would like to give you a year, at least, in a very well-established and successful private boys' school right here in Chateau d'Oex. It has been highly recommended to me by two friends, both of whose sons are being tutored here now. I have an appointment for you and me to meet with the headmaster at five o'clock this afternoon; that will give us a final day in the mountains before we go back to the hotel by four o'clock, so we can bathe and change in time for our date. Eton hasn't taught you much French, and neither your mother nor I have ever had the time to learn a new language, but you'll still be at a formative time of your life in 1938; it seems to me a big plus to add to your résumé when you finally are ready to go out into the world and make a living. But don't be swayed by anything I've said. It's your life. I will abide by your decision."

Johnny continued to amaze me. He was evidently not satisfied with sending me to the two most prestigious schools in England, St. Peter's Court and Eton, the latter a place where the parents of newborn baby boys put their sons' names down immediately after birth in order to get on the waiting list. Johnny Dodge, with a stepson about whom he knew very little beyond the fact that I was his wife's firstborn and the only child of my father, had enough influence and sense of responsibility that he had successfully entered me at Eton when I was six and a half, and into B. G. Whitfield's house at Eton for the year of 1934.

And now this. He had done so much for me, way beyond what he might reasonably have been expected to do. I was so grateful to him, and I prayed silently that the afternoon meeting with the headmaster would prove a success.

It did. The headmaster was pleasant, and the school, with twenty-four boys in all, was comfortably sized and intimate; in fact, every boy had his own private room, considerably larger than mine at Eton. According to two separate boys attending the school with whom I spoke, the food was good, the teachers were very good, and Chateau d'Oex was a wonderful place to live. It had tennis courts and a large swimming pool; bicycling, walking, and mountain climbing in the summer; and skiing, skating, and bobsledding, among other sports, in the winter.

The wonderful Swiss trains pulled into the Chateau d'Oex station on time almost every half hour during the day, going in whatever directions you wished to go, providing you were back in your room by ten at night on Saturday and Sunday. During the week, trains were forbidden to the students.

Joyfully and gratefully, I accepted Johnny's offer and was entered for the first term of 1938. I was thrilled by the whole idea and concept of learning French under such congenial circumstances, and of living in such wonderful surroundings.

I had recently seen the film, *Lost Horizon*, based on the book of that name written by James Hilton. It was set in an imaginary paradise high in the Himalayas called Shangri-La. The English actor, Ronald Coleman, had played the lead, and I had found everything about that movie uplifting and inspiring; naturally,I yearned to live out my days in such a paradise. It wasn't to be, not exactly, but when I returned in 1938 to Chateau d'Oex, it became my Shangri-La, if only for a little over a year.

Mother had remained at the hotel while we were at the school, and she and the maid had finished packing for our departure the next morning. She seemed as pleased at my decision as was Johnny, though privately she urged me that, after all Johnny had done and continued to do for me, the least I could do when 1938 rolled around would be to make darn sure that, when I finished my schooling at Chateau d'Oex, at the end of 1938, I knew enough French to speak, read, and write it, and be able to conduct myself confidently in a room full of nothing but French men and women.

Actually, I did one extra term, February, March, and April of 1939, "a final polishing," as the headmaster described it. By then, I was ready to meet my first Parisian lady!

Five months later, Hitler launched the Second World War.

The Musketeers

That great American, Theodore "Teddy" Roosevelt, 1858–1919, adventurer, politician, and gung-ho President of the United States of America from 1901 to 1909, had three sons whom he loved dearly. But only one of them was the apple of his eye, Kermit R. Roosevelt. Unbeknownst to each other, Johnny and Kermit had both received tickets to a much-in-demand football game in New York when they were in their late teens, their tickets placing them next each other; within two hours they were firm friends, having exchanged telephone numbers and addresses and seen little of the game. Their friendship grew over the telephone, and soon they were visiting each other's parents' homes, cementing their relationship even further.

Kermit finally went on to Harvard and Johnny to McGill, after which Johnny's mother, Flora Dodge, divorced his father, and sailed to England with Johnny and his sister Lucy. Flora Dodge, as we know, later married Lionel Guest, a fine man in many ways but bedeviled with poor health. He was a gentleman of very good stock and plenty of money but lacked the strength to stand up to Flora's overbearing personality.

With the outbreak of the First World War, Johnny, now a British subject and eager for action, volunteered for service in the British Army. In spite of being an American, Kermit managed to join the British Army, as well. He served as an officer with the British Expeditionary Force in Mesopotamia and was awarded the Military Cross, while Johnny won his DSO in the Gallipoli fracas and the DSC in the battle of the Somme, France.

Kermit and Johnny's strong friendship continued up to the early part of the Second World War, the period after Mother and Johnny and I returned from our European trip.

After that trip Johnny reported to Winston Churchill, who conceded that Hitler's proposal was an arresting and interesting idea, but completely ridiculous, for who would come out the winner if Hitler's plan was carried out? Hitler, of course! He would have a base of such enormous power that no one would dare say him nay.

"No, sir," said Winston. "But I think you ought to tell Franklin Roosevelt about your meeting with Hitler. America is in the grip of isolation; it might give Franklin a wake-up call. Of course, Johnny, it must be done in absolute secrecy, without any official authority or normal channels involved, and no slip of any kind where the news media are concerned. Leave me out of it. I know you'll work it out; you always do. But if any part of Hitler's plan leaks out, it would put Great Britain in a terrible diplomatic mess for even knowing of such a plan. Be very careful, Johnny, please. Good luck. Let me hear from you when you get back."

Johnny had accomplished his mission, though Hitler's idea had apparently been stillborn from the very beginning. Neither Churchill nor Johnny's connection with a certain arm of the British Government trusted Hitler or his grand visions for longer than a few well-reasoned minutes of their time. Besides, Hitler's plan was deceptive and amoral. Johnny had done his duty, and now he had been given another task: to report on his visit to Franklin D. Roosevelt, President of the United States of America. But how could he do this when all normal lines of communication were forbidden to him?

He pondered his dilemma for some time before a light went on in his head and a big grin appeared on his face. Kermit Roosevelt, his long-time buddy in many adventures between the end of the last war and Johnny's marriage to Mother, would be his bird dog and find a way into the White House – that is, if he wasn't on some safari in deepest Africa or scuba diving in the Bahamas.

Johnny checked his private telephone book, picked up the phone, and called the overseas operator.

Having received the go-ahead from a charged-up Kermit, he cleared matters at the office and pushed up his normal scheduled itinerary to the States by one month, advising his clients of his new schedule. He also let his Washington clients know of his imminent arrival just two days hence, because they provided him with the perfect cover.

Kermit Roosevelt, who had planned to leave the next day for Tibet, had promptly put his trip on hold; instead, he was out on the airfield in his car, parked within one hundred feet of where Johnny's plane would stop. He had already arranged for Johnny's baggage to be immediately cleared through Customs and transported in the hotel limousine, to await Johnny's arrival.

The plane, almost on time – a good omen – landed and eased over to its designated parking area. A silver ladder, with side rails to hold onto, was pushed to the exit door, which soon opened. Johnny Dodge was the first passenger off, descending the stairs into an enthusiastic bear hug from his old buddy, who obviously had some pull at this international airport.

Kermit was a portly gentleman, with a florid completion, but his appearance was deceptive, as it did not reflect his physical fitness, his incredible stamina, or his deadly fists. He, like Johnny, had slain many dragons in his life, with gusto. They were truly two peas in a pod.

On the way into town, Kermit explained that he had closed down his residence two days before. His furniture was draped in sheets, his home immaculate, and the servants already on their long paid vacations, during which he had intended to visit Tibet, study its religion, and climb a few mountains. As a result of Johnny's urgent summons, he had booked him into a suite at the Madison Hotel next to his own, from which Kermit had originally expected to depart that very day.

After Johnny's bags had been unpacked and put away, the two had a drink at the bar downstairs and then went into the restaurant for a lengthy lunch, catching up on each other's recent lives. They did not discuss the reason for their reunion until they were safely back in Johnny's suite. Here they settled into comfortable armchairs, both entrance doors being double-locked and the dividing door between their suites left open, so that any sound from the other room would be quickly detected.

Johnny marshaled his thoughts into a proper sequence. He began by describing the night he spent talking with Adolf Hitler. Kermit's eyes grew bigger and bigger as the story unfolded. At the end, he finally exploded.

"A raving lunatic!" he said.

"I wish he was."

"But how could he expect …?"

"You'd have to be there, Kermit, to feel his presence, to hear him, to have those eyes envelop you with that hypnotic stare of his, demanding attention, subservience, adoration. He spoke with great tenderness of his devotion to little children, so innocent and so vulnerable, and of his Alsatian dog Blondie, so loyal. No mention of his mistress, Eva Braun.

But he still harbors great resentment on account of the Versailles Treaty, over which he went into a screaming tirade. I actually sympathized with him; but he only wanted to hear his own voice criticizing all the true and untrue punishments that had been heaped upon Germany at the end of the war. He had so many challenges to overcome, and so little time, or so he said. I never did find out precisely what he meant by that.

"It was four thirty-five in the morning when I looked at my watch, at which Hitler stopped dead in the middle of a sentence, his mouth still open, and I had a prickly feeling run down my back. I wondered if I had overstayed my welcome. I wondered if I was a dead duck.

"But no, Hitler composed himself and returned once again to this desire for a grand alliance with England and France, and finally all of Europe, with Stalin a mere pawn in the grand plan to keep his countrymen employed in vast mines and industries, under the supreme direction of Hitler and his allies."

"But where is he going with this, Johnny?"

"To hell in a handbasket," I hope. But also to war, inevitably. In another two years he will be practically invincible, if he keeps his rearmament program going full steam ahead and we do nothing but wring our hands and envy his country's miraculous economic recovery. He has to go to war before his money defaults and his banks start printing one thousand or even one million marks for every single mark, as they had to do after the last war. He is committed to war, and the only hope I can offer is that he turn on Russia first and, while he is occupying the vast distances of that country, gives us the opportunity and time to bring our three services, plus the British Merchant Navy, up to snuff. But if he decides, once again, to first smash through Belgium and into France and we are not prepared, I do not wish to predict the end. I also fear for the United States."

"Good Lord, Johnny, why?"

"Our beloved USA, according to an internationally available report from the League of Nations, is in seventeenth place in Army numbers and equipment; eighteenth in Army Air Corps planes and pilots; and fifth in naval vessels and manpower. None of your services are recruiting, for lack of funds, and when one soldier or sailor retires, many times his place is not refilled. America is as unprepared as Great Britain and France. Your one big advantage is your distance from the European continent, though you, like us, could always be vulnerable to massive groups of U-boats such as those that the German Navy used to great advantage in the last world war. I am told that Hitler is spending unbelievable sums on devilish new submarines, which no doubt will be used to ever greater advantage in the next war, if we haven't found some better way to destroy them than we had the last time."

There was a long pause, and then Kermit grunted, "It's this damned Depression,

Johnny, a real malaise in all our countries. Perhaps the only way out would be another war."

"God forbid, my friend. But that's why I'm here, to report on my meeting with the Führer to your President, and lay out my personal, in-depth view of what may be ahead of us if you don't take steps pretty soon, along with Great Britain and France and

Belgium, to rearm and improve all your services. The idea would be that in another two years Hitler would not be so keen on taking on the West. I hope that he will then look to the East, where, like Napoleon, he and his army will be worn down and defeated by the devastating Russian winters, and the expendable millions of serfs that Stalin would happily sacrifice in order to break Hitler's back and hobble his army by extermination or retreat."

Johnny could see that he had made an impression on Kermit, who, realizing how secret this approach to the President had to be, took himself out of the picture, being too well known and too often photographed by the media to risk putting in an appearance in public. He therefore decided to use a distant cousin of his who worked in the White House in a very secret and highly classified office, his main function being liaison officer between his office and the President. This meant that he would sometimes see the President two or three times in a day, and over time he had become quite cozy with the President, because they shared the same surname, were Democrats, and had been born a few blocks from one another. Indeed, the President addressed his aide as cousin, knowing that his "cousin" was related to President Theodore Roosevelt. Kermit said that he would try to arrange a luncheon with this man the following day, after which he would report back to Johnny. In the meantime, Johnny would be setting up appointments with his Washington, D.C., clients for the next few days.

And so both gentlemen went about their business. Kermit's cousin readily agreed to broach the subject of John Bigelow Dodge's meeting with Adolf Hitler to the President; the subsequent meeting with the President, he was told, was to be held in absolute secrecy, with no media attention, and was not to be spoken of again. This might be quite a challenge for the President, but it was necessary, even if the meeting had to be turned down.

It wasn't.

Johnny was going about his business, counseling his exclusive list of clients. At the same time, he was being lavishly entertained by these selfsame clients, who were also proud to call Johnny their friend, a no-lose situation that his firm back in London later handsomely rewarded. In the meantime, Kermit and his cousin were feverishly concocting one scheme after another to set up an utterly safe and secret meeting between the President and Johnny Dodge. Each idea seemed brilliant in first light but was finally shot down for one reason or another, and it was back to the drawing board.

Finally, it was President Roosevelt himself who reminded Kermit's cousin that he would be leaving the White House in three days to inspect a major part of the home-based US Navy fleet. His visit with Colonel Dodge had to be now or never. In desperation, Kermit had to admit to Johnny that neither he nor his cousin had succeeded in coming up with a sure-fire way to smuggle Johnny into the White House and out again without his presence being noticed.

Johnny was silent for a long minute. Then he took a deep breath and had Kermit call his cousin to arrange a time and place that he and the President could meet. Within an hour the word came back: ten-thirty on the very next morning. FDR had been well briefed by Kermit's cousin about Johnny, his family background, and his achievements; upon discovering that Johnny's grandfather had been President Lincoln's ambassador to France, he had suggested it would be only fitting for Colonel Dodge to be received in the Lincoln bedroom.

At Johnny's request, Kermit obtained the plans of both the interior and exterior of the White House, with all rooms named or described. (I believe it was produced by the National Geographic Society.) With Kermit's assistance, Johnny spent the next three hours studying the plans and the possible routes to the floor where the Lincoln bedroom was located. In addition, he had Kermit drive him, slowly where possible, up and down and back and forth along all the streets and boulevards that led to entrances and exits at the White House. Finally, Johnny said that he knew what he was going to do. Kermit asked him what the plan was.

Johnny looked at his old friend wistfully, for they had been the perfect team in so many adventures together, both for their countries and for the pure joy of beating the odds.

"Kermit," said Johnny, "you and I have always respected each other's judgment. Please, respect my judgment this time, too. Only I will know how I pull this off. That way, no one will ever be able to replicate my plan. That's the way it has to be. Surely you can see that?"

Kermit huffed and puffed, but he had to admit that his friend's reasoning made sense.

Johnny looked at his watch; in one hour he had to be at a dinner party in his honor, given by a friend and client. He'd better get showered and into his black tie and dinner jacket. "I've got another engagement in an hour," he said. "I'll be lonesome without you, Kermit. In my book, you're the greatest. Pray for me, and take care of yourself. I'll see you sometime tomorrow."

"God bless you, Johnny. I'll be waiting for you here."

"So be it," said Johnny, and gently closed the door behind him.

At three in the morning, Kermit, who had heard Johnny come in around one, and who himself had slept listlessly from then on, decided to remain no longer in his bed without checking on Johnny. Taking his flashlight, he quietly opened the door between their rooms.

Johnny's room was tomb-like. Not even his breathing was audible. Kermit turned on his flashlight. The bed had not been slept in. Johnny's dinner jacket had been hung neatly back in the clothes closet.

Johnny himself was long gone.

His troops during the 1914–1918 war against Germany had called Johnny "the Dodger," mainly for his nightly excursions behind enemy lines, sometimes bringing back one or more German officers at gunpoint; at other times, with the help of his Sergeant Major, he might be shepherding a whole group of German soldiers, surprised out of their sleep, all sent back up the line to finally be interned in Great Britain or across the seas in Canada.

Johnny didn't believe in killing for the pure sake of killing, but these risky proddings into enemy territory were his way of achieving some balance between chivalry and death, the saddest part being the enormous casualties that trench warfare produced. Only at Christmastime did the killing stop, when the soldiers crossed into each other's lines, sharing Christmas food and drink and tobacco and songs, a camaraderie heightened by the urgency with which it came and went. Then it was back to "either thee or me."

Johnny had used his secret skills of concealment and speed, reaching the White House while the guards and internal duty staff were supposed to be changing shifts; in fact, they had all been attracted to attempts at putting out a fire that had suddenly erupted on the West Wing lawn, the flames blazing with great intensity but little height. The White House volunteers, though enjoying an unexpected escape from their regular duties, were losing the battle with the flames. Then out of the night came the sudden clanging of many fire engines cutting through the darkness and up the driveway; as unexpectedly as the fire had begun, it abruptly went out, leaving not even a red cinder. The firemen were stunned; after checking that the fire was definitely exhausted, they returned to their fire stations bewildered and perplexed. The cause of the fire was never discovered; presumably it must have burnt up in the flames.

In the meantime, Johnny had reached the Lincoln bedroom. Finding the electric
switch with his flashlight, he turned it on and was surprised to find that a table with two chairs, one across from the other, had been set up in the room, one chair a normal, comfortable chair with upholstery matching the colors of the room, and one bearing the seal of the President of the United States. It was of recent design, and definitely not an antique, as was the rest of the furniture. A good sign: At least Johnny knew he was expected.

Johnny had been determined to give the room the respect it deserved. As much as he yearned for a comfortable night's sleep on that prestigious bed, he considered himself unworthy of such an honor. He did not believe that he was a major player in this strange drama, but that he was simply the messenger and, like Dr. Schmidt, an interpreter of Hitler's proposal. So, instead of the bed, he slept in the guest chair.

At seven a.m., Johnny awoke, having slept for only two and a half hours, following a grueling afternoon, a dinner party, and a double change of clothes, the last one being into the uniform of one of the major plumbing companies in Washington, D.C. It had come from one of his clients, who was a good friend as well as president and owner of the company. The uniform was a great disguise, consisting of black trousers, black socks, black shoes, and a black jacket with a polo collar, with only the company's name in wine-red mounted on a small patch over his heart. His friend, the company president, knew better than to ask Johnny the what or where or why of his request. He could hope only that when the uniform was returned, it might give some clue as to its purpose or destination.

It never happened. Anything Johnny borrowed was always returned spotlessly cleaned; anything damaged was generally replaced.

On this occasion, Johnny was happy to find that the bathroom needed no plumber's attention. Having opened his plumber's bag and taken out his straight razor, , shaving soap and brush, and toothbrush and paste, and taken a French bath, he climbed back into his uniform. It was then seven thirty-five a.m.

No newspaper; no breakfast. Almost three hours to go, and nothing to do. He didn't dare show his face. He was nameless, faceless, invisible. Last night was fun, but not now. Until 10:30 he would be in purgatory. Better still: He went back to sleep.

At 10:25 Johnny awoke to the sound of voices outside the bedroom, followed by a rat-a-tat-tat on the door. Bouncing out of his chair, he stood at attention, as he answered, "Come in, Mr. President!" The door opened wide, and there stood the President of the United States, holding onto the arm of an aide … Could it be Kermit's distant cousin?

"By golly," said the President, grinning at his aide, but embracing Johnny in his gaze. "You were right all along, cousin."

He gave Johnny his left hand, since he was holding onto his aide with his right hand, which suited Johnny just fine, since he had forced him to shake hands with his left hand ever since his right hand was shot. Or had Kermit told the mutual "cousin" of Johnny's predicament, and had he then alerted the President to the situation? If so, and it did turn out to be so, it certainly was a wonderful gesture.

"Colonel Dodge, I don't know how you did it and I'm not going to ask you, but I have been briefed fully by my friend here, and I am in awe of you and your incredible career. You are an amazing man. I honor you sir, as I do the man whose room you have

occupied this night."

With that, the President was led by his aide to the other side of the table, where he sat down. Then the aide retired to stand outside the door, awaiting instructions.

Johnny thanked the President for receiving him under such secretive and unusual conditions. After inquiries from the President as to Kermit's health and present pursuits, Johnny brought up the subject of the meeting, giving him a full rundown of Hitler's proposal, as well as Winston Churchill's response. He emphasized the pathetic imbalance between the military power base being built up by Hitler and that of most of the rest of the world. The latter, he pointed out, appeared to be largely at Hitler's mercy, particularly if no real effort was made to make up the difference in military strength before Hitler was ready to go to war. For war it had to be or Hitler would have bankrupted his country without having anything to show for it.

The President sat in silence for a while, finally asking some questions, the majority of which Johnny was able to answer. He then turned to Johnny, full face, and said, "Colonel Dodge, I'm going to be absolutely honest with you, and you are not going to like much of what I have to say, but it's the truth, damn it, it's the truth. America, like Europe, is in a Depression. These are sorry times. We are a rich country, but to make money you must have money. I have put many measures into place that are providing employment to millions of my people, building dams and roads and subsidizing farmers and providing social services, all of which are a positive sign. But until we get a really strong, independent grassroots commercial and industrial initiative going in this country, we are not going to overcome our monetary dependence on the US Government and the US Mint, which is depleting itself at an uncomfortable rate. We have become strongly isolationist, partly because of the last war, and partly because Americans like being American and do not trust foreigners, even though all our families were originally from other countries.

"I know we have a small army, a small navy, and a small army air corps. There is no money to add to their budget. An army is a luxury until you go to war. I don't know whether Hitler will go to war. You tell me he will, and I am inclined to believe you, but with this country's overwhelming isolationism there is no way we would be able to enter a war. I would be hanged from the nearest tree for even suggesting such a thing. The only way we would come into a war would be if we were attacked, and at least for now, I don't think we have an enemy in the world!"

"I'm thinking in two years, sir," said Johnny.

"You've told me a lot of truths today, which I appreciate. Germany, Italy, Russia, all dictatorships, all militaristic. If I lived in your part of the world, I would probably be saying the same things you're saying. They make sense. But not for America. Not yet. Winston knows I'm an Anglophile. My heart would be with you if you became involved in another war. I would manipulate like crazy to find ways to help you, but I must say that, without an enemy attack on American soil, the American people would see no justification for going to war."

The President leaned across the table and grasped Johnny's left hand with his. He said, "You are a good man, sir. I appreciate men like you. There are far too few of you left these days. Keep up the good work, Colonel. God put us here for a reason, and you are certainly fulfilling yours."

"As are you, sir. I thank you most humbly. America is blessed to have you," said Johnny.

The President called to his aide to come in, who lifted him out of his chair. He turned and gave Johnny a final look, saying, "I'm glad your grandfather was Lincoln's ambassador to France. Otherwise, I never would have met you. My best to Winston and Kermit."

Johnny heard the President instruct his aide to come back for Colonel Dodge and accompany him safely out of the White House.

When he returned, however, the Lincoln bedroom was empty. Its overnight guest had departed.

After returning to his hotel, Johnny had gone to his suite to be welcomed by a very relieved Kermit Roosevelt. He removed his plumber's cotton uniform and sent it immediately to the hotel's laundry, to be returned to the president of the plumbing company by that afternoon, along with a note of thanks in Johnny's handwriting. He then showered and got back into a business suit.

Lunch was served in Johnny's suite, at which, under oath of silence, Kermit was told of FDR's good wishes to him personally and the ensuing report and conversation. Again, Johnny had done what was required of him, even though the outcome had not met his hoped-for expectations. Nonetheless, given his authority, which was minuscule under the terms of absolute secrecy that had been imposed upon him, he had achieved the purpose of his trip.

In the afternoon, Johnny visited his last two Washington clients, having already made a reservation for the next day's train from Washington to New York, where he would reside at the Plaza and continue to attend to his clients' requirements and counseling. He also invited Kermit to bring his cousin to dinner that evening, at one of Washington's gourmet-oriented restaurants, where Johnny would play host.

It was both a sad and a joyful evening. Kermit, who had rescheduled his trip to Tibet, was likewise departing their hotel the next day, and Kermit's cousin, the point man, who had played such a vital role in the operation, sat through dinner practically tongue-tied from being in the combined presence of two such extraordinary men. He did, however, comment on the fire that had burned a piece of grass on the lawn in front of the West Wing of the White House and had suddenly extinguished itself just as the fire trucks were arriving.

Kermit looked at Johnny in surprise. Johnny said nothing. Kermit looked hard and long at him, and Johnny still said nothing. Finally, they could hold their secret no

longer, and both broke into uncontrollable laughter. It was Kermit who had taught Johnny how to create last night's fire, though they had used the technique only once before, as both had been badly burned on their hands and lower arms, necessitating skin grafting, the new skin plucked surgically from their derrières. They had sworn that they would never use it again, though I think Johnny's fingers must have been crossed behind his back when he took that oath, for one of the cornerstones of his beliefs, often repeated to me, was, "Never say 'never.'"

Unbeknownst to Kermit, Johnny had experimented since that time with unusual fire-producing materials until he got it right, safely on this occasion, enabling him to proceed. Kermit forgave him for breaking his vow.

The two men toasted Kermit's cousin with fine wine and sublime cognac and dropped him back at his apartment, a somewhat bemused and happy fellow. He must have gone to bed feeling the effect of sitting for nearly three hours with two men of such enormous mental and physical energy, their relationship honed over the years to a smooth accommodation of each other's strength and quirks and to that warm and satisfying confidence that comes from sacrifice and success.

It had truly been a day to remember: a day that never happened.

Farewell to Eton

I floated through the last year and a half at Eton with my coterie of friends, some of us having shared our tenure together at both St. Peter's Court and Eton College, adding up to almost ten years. Life continued to be good. Not caring about mortality, we were free souls living up to the height of our expectations and opportunities. Only the threatening clouds of end-of-term exams marred my enjoyment of life and living.

The holidays, as always, continued to be spent at each other's homes every summer, swimming, sailing, walking, riding horses from our host's stables, and – a new fad – being flown in small open-cockpit biplanes for two (one wing being above the other) by one host or another.

It was a really marvelous experience, because you flew only at a comfortable height, the countryside maybe five hundred or a thousand feet below you, and, wearing your leather jacket and goggles, felt like a veritable superman. You could relate to all the beautiful and interesting territory passing below you, because you were going only at about sixty to ninety miles an hour. There is no joy, now, is there, in flying at six hundred miles an hour thirty-five thousand feet up!

When I was ten, Lady Dashwood landed at an airport near St. Peter's Court in her DeHaviland Moth and was driven over to take her son out for lunch. She remained dressed in her flying clothes – that is, trousers with a black leather jacket and headpiece, her goggles pushed up on her head. Talk about sophisticated glamor! She completely won my heart. She really was beautiful – except for Mother, the most beautiful creature I had ever seen. Lady Dashwood's image stayed in my heart for many months. I even made a friend of her son, just so there was an imagined contact there. I was ten years old.

I was also fortunate enough to be taken up in George Easton's airplane. He had

recently won the world land speed record, taking it away from Sir Malcolm Campbell. Odd how my first two personal plane flights had been with Ann Morrow, later Mrs. Charles Lindbergh, and George Easton, holder of the world speed record.

During the winter, those of us who had homes in London joined forces to attend concerts at the Royal Albert Hall, our favorite conductor being Sir Thomas Beecham, who had also conducted at Eton. Our favorite male singer was Paul Robeson, a black American who could defy gravity with his deep and honey-smooth voice. We loved going to musical comedies starring Leslie Henson, Bobby Howes, Florence Desmond, the Crazy Gang, and Flanagan and Allen, and seeing *Peter Pan*, which remains my all-time favorite, even though it wasn't a musical. I must have seen it half a dozen times, including, many years later, the Mary Martin version in New York.

And then there were the morning rides in Rotton Row. I had progressed to a smart-looking, dapple-gray horse named Fiddler, who managed to do everything right and utterly won me over. He was at my service, on loan from my old friend Mr. Bruce, the stablemaster whom Johnny had chosen for me when I was seven years old.

Of course there was also the rare weekend at Ferring, when Molly and I would return for one whole day of glorious fox hunting with the Crowley and Horsham Pack, sandwiched between the night of our arrival and the night before we returned to London.

Molly was enjoying a pleasant relationship with Harry, the groomsman to whom I had introduced her (as you may remember, in a very ill-mannered fashion, of which action I have only recently expiated myself). During the summer months, when our main residence became "Florida" Ferring, Harry would sometimes visit Molly on her day off and take her to tea at the Bluebird Café, followed by a bus ride to Worthing to see a movie. They were both crazy about Ginger Rogers and Fred Astaire films, and their favorite actor was Ronald Coleman. Mother, ever the guardian angel, realized that these outings with Molly must be straining Harry's purse, so she arranged a private account for Molly, to be used mainly for her to pay her own way while she was with Harry. He was at first indignant, but when he realized that they could have twice as many outings as before, he capitulated. They enjoyed each other for two years, but the spark just wasn't there, and during those long winter months Harry finally found the girl of his dreams; he married her, and as far as I know they lived happily ever after. Molly, whose life with mother was her real reason for living, continued in attendance for some years to come.

Finally, 1938 came around, and I did not return for the first-term half of that year. I had at last been freed from the structured environment of the finest British boarding school in the land, full of good memories and not a few tears, to study French at the private school in Switzerland. My wonderful housemaster, B. G. Whitfield, had, like the Reverend F. G. Ridgeway of St. Peter's Court, become my father and mentor, always encouraging me when I was feeling down. Until I learned to live with my learning disability, I had been down a lot, though I did not let my friends know. Mr. Whitfield was a dear man, a fine example of a very good housemaster whose boys meant everything to him.

Eton had been good to me in many ways. It had taught me much about living, especially about living up to certain standards in both behavior and trust, and that a man's integrity should be the cornerstone of his life. I had been a poor student, apparently not destined to ever attain scholastic heights of any kind, but I was blessed with a happy nature and a good attitude. These two attributes have been my sword and my shield and have opened my way both directly and indirectly into a world of fascinating characters and personalities from all strata of society. The foundation and connections were originally laid by Johnny and Mother, and my own innate talents have taken me from here to there and there and there!

Next stop: Chateau D'Oex, my Shangri La.

The train from Montreux ascended gradually into the mountains through valleys and tunnels and hairy twists and turns, the snow dense upon the passing terrain, the sun striking the earth's white mantle into fields of dazzling diamonds. This was not city snow, coarse and pigmented with city dust, but pure as the air one breathed. It was all so beautiful, it almost hurt.

Finally, the Chateau d'Oex train station came into sight, not big and imposing like European and American stations, but small and intimate and truly welcoming. A chauffeur from my new school, who was there to meet me with the car, took over the responsibility of my trunk, my personal bag, and me, and drove back to the school past the small stone Anglican Church that I would sometimes attend on Sundays.

This school, like Chateau d'Oex itself, being somewhat high up on the side of a mountain, was on occasion immersed by the very clouds themselves. Today, however the view from my new room swept across the valley below and up to the peaks of the snow-covered mountains beyond. A fantastic sight.

My teacher, Mr. Bender, intuitively detected my lack of concentration, thereafter exerting all his teacherly cunning to make the subject of learning the French language both entertaining and compelling.

It was a wonderful year, an incredible year for me, for I was now becoming in command of the French language, and I had finally overcome the lost faith in myself caused by failed exams and bleak report cards, saved by Mr. Bender, my confidence in myself finally restored.

My last term went quickly, and I passed the headmaster's final judgment with flying colors. It was May 1939.

Our country home at Ferring was full of guests from all parts of the world, enjoying packed tennis courts; on one exciting occasion, Jack Crawford and Fred Perry, the Australian champions of the world, gave a tennis exhibition for our privileged guests.

Johnny's yacht *Minerva*, temporarily berthed back at Worthing took his seagoing friends across the chanel to the French Riviera, while mother entertained the tennis players and the beach crowd. All went well in our piece of heaven. I was now seventeen years old and helping mother with her hosting duties, even sitting at the host's place at the other end of the dinner table. It was tremendous fun, and I took to this task like a fish to water. No one ever had better examples of perfect hosts than I had in my mother and Johnny.

Those of us living at that time would never forget it, the last weeks of a unique era that we who remain will remember until the day we die. It lasted only twenty-one years from the end of 1918 to September of 1939, a mere flick of an eyelid in time, but it was my time, when I was born and grew into early manhood.

Yet even as June and July moved on in sun-filled days, guests were beginning to shorten their visits, because some feared to be caught away from home or country should the worst happen. Grim expectancy was in the air, a foreboding that crept under one's skin, as Hitler zigged and zagged, promising peace and threatening war. People were now talking nervously about the prospect of war; recruitment stations were beginning to appear in cities around the country; and gas masks were being manufactured and stacked in warehouses. Conscription was suddenly for real.

Could it be that, very soon, the ground would move beneath our feet and the sounds of death would be heard in the fields of battle and the skies above?

We were, indeed, living the overture to the greatest and most devastating war in the history of humankind.

The Phony War,
1939 to 1940

T he whole British Empire listened on their radios to an elderly, exhausted, and mortified Prime Minister, Neville Chamberlain, declare that, with Germany's invasion of Poland, a country that Great Britain had given its word to protect in the event of an invasion by any nation – meaning Germany – Great Britain and its Dominions were now in a state of war with Germany. We had been holding our breath for so long, hoping against hope that Chamberlain and Hitler would be able to work out some peaceful accord that would be to their mutual advantage. But it was not to be.

Hitler had been waiting only for his secret adviser, a fortuneteller, to give him the good word. The bad word came from his financial advisers, who told him in great panic that, because Germany was teetering on the brink of financial disaster, he must declare war now or never. Hitler still hesitated; and then the words he was waiting for lifted his spirits beyond belief. His fortuneteller, a lady supposedly well versed in astrology, gave him the good news that his stars were now in ideal alignment, signifying overwhelming success in any venture or ventures that he decided to take.

Hitler, with fire in his eyes and supreme confidence in himself, gave the command: "March!"

Almost immediately, Johnny put in his request to be recommissioned into the Army. He was, however, put on the back burner for several months, because the recruiting officers were more interested in Britain's youth than in a middle-forties-something recruit, even though he was a hero of the First World War with a record of leadership and valor second to none. Finally, his good friend Winston Churchill became First Lord of the Admiralty, where he quietly arranged matters so that Johnny's request to serve his country was accepted and he was commissioned a Major in the Middlesex Regiment.

Johnny didn't really care that he had been demoted to Major because of his age, but he did remark to me that if he continued in this manner he would surely end up a Private in the next war. After a brief training stint, he and the rest of his regiment were transferred to France; part of them were stationed behind the Maginot Line, and part along the border with Belgium. Johnny was intensely frustrated to be put with the former group and went almost out of his skull doing nothing day after day but forced marches, military parades for visiting mucketymucks, and target practice.

General Gort was in charge of the British Army in France. He was a fine soldier and a gentleman, but not exactly imbued with strong leadership qualities or a commanding presence. Every morning he took his morning walk with his aides, greeting his troops with clipped salutes, meanwhile agonizing over when the enemy was going to strike and where, apparently under War Office orders that he was on no account to be the first to make the decision to attack.

Equally at sea were Mother and I, neither of us having found an opportunity where we might be useful. For me in particular, the problem was that, not only was I under age for any of the services, but on my soon-to-be eighteenth birthday I would still not be able to join any British Military force without swearing allegiance to the King, thereby losing my American nationality, which I was not about to do. At the same time, most of my school chums, the majority a year or so older than I, were volunteering for service, many of them in the Royal Air Force, including Gavin and Richard and Henry C. and Peter Steele, with Patrick Plunket and a couple of others joining their chosen Guards Regiment.

Back at Ferring by the Sea, our house was being systematically cleaned, mothballed, and put away for the winter. It was no longer the center of entertainment and laughter, with guests from all over the world coming and going, enjoying the company, the various activities available, and above all the presence of their hosts, Johnny and Minerva.

I sometimes look back on those golden days before the war. What heady and glorious times they were, our wondrous summer home under the direction of Mother and her majordomo Charles, both taking enormous pride and joy in their endeavors, along with Johnny. My life then was so full of exciting people, from Gandhi to George Bernard Shaw, from Winston Churchill to Pierre Laval – the latter a very influential cabinet member in the French Government, both before and during the War, when he threw in his lot with General Pétain, Hitler's puppet and President of the French Government operating from the city of Vichy. M. Laval ended up at the end of the war being judged a traitor, at which time he was put up against a wall and shot.

With Mother's Broadway connections, and her and Johnny's own celebrity, it was relatively easy for the two of them to attract stage and movie stars from both sides of the Atlantic to our weekend parties at Florida, adding a splash of glamor to the occasion. Among our many other guests were Laurence Olivier and Vivian Leigh, and Robert Donat, winner of the 1939 Hollywood Oscar for his brilliant performance as Mr. Chips in *Goodbye, Mr. Chips*. We became good friends after the war, when I was working for Sir Alex Korda's London Film Productions. Others were Ralph Richardson and even Ronald Coleman. Molly, mother's personal maid and good friend, went into paroxysms of nervous excitement while he was under our roof, Coleman being her favorite actor. Even our guests were somewhat starry-eyed in his presence, some becoming tongue-tied, including me. He was an elegant person; after I stopped treating him as if he was the Holy Grail, I found him very easy to get along with and great fun.

Other guests included Anthony Eden and his first wife; Lord Beaverbrook, the newspaper mogul and future member of Winston Churchill's war cabinet; Emil Pfizer, Mother's and my good friend; and Kermit Roosevelt, Johnny's best friend. Also Lord Evan Tredegar; Lady Emerald Cunard; and Charles and Ann Lindbergh, when they were living in England after the tragic kidnapping and death of their firstborn: They told Mother that their weekend with us had given them their first real desire to get on with their lives since the tragedy. Mother was pleased.

What bliss those years had been. What memories they still provide. The house was like "the temple of joy," as a guest had once written in our visitors' book. Florida would now remain closed for the duration; after the war, it was sold and reverted to its former raison d'être, becoming once again a hotel. I miss it still to this very day.

With Johnny away in France, the family was now back in London. Mother and Johnny's children, my half brothers, four-year-old David Dodge and two-year-old Tony Dodge, who resided in the nursery with Nanny, a sweet lady whom we all enjoyed. But my world was changing fast, for I was no longer the youngest member of the family. I was caught in a strange seesaw world between wondering when the bombs would descend on London and our beautiful home, and what had Bertha made for tea in the nursery.

The Real War, at Home and Abroad

Both Mother and I were up a creek for a while, and then, shortly before the war began in earnest, she found a cause, and soon after that I was offered a job! Mother's cause was created by her fury when the Russian Army suddenly attacked tiny Finland without provocation or a declaration of war. Mother thereupon founded and directed the Finland Fund, created to raise money and goods to prop up that country's war economy. The Finns, to everyone's complete amazement, then threw the Russians' gigantic army back across the border, hemming them in for many weeks, helped by the snow, sub-freezing weather, and their superior skiing skills.

Kermit Roosevelt must have had a very powerful civil service member at the Foreign Office to do his bidding, both in the First and Second World Wars, for he had rejoined the British Army (strictly forbidden to US citizens) about the same time that Johnny was received back in. On dining with Mother one night and hearing what she was up to, and under what growing success it was operating, he decommissioned himself back out of the British Army and, at Mother's invitation, set himself up at a desk in her office. There he used his name and connections to start an enlistment office for Finnish immigrants in England wishing to volunteer for service in the Finnish Army. With a target of five thousand fresh soldiers, he arranged for their travel to Finland at his own expense.

Mother's Finland Fund was incredibly successful, collecting money, food, winter clothing, pharmaceutical products, and on and on. The cause, and the tremendous goodwill toward that cause, induced banks and accounting firms to volunteer some of their paid staff to control the many gifts and money that were pouring in to support little Finland's defense and hold back the Russian ogre.

Mother proved once again her amazing organizing capabilities, finding many new and powerful connections. Although both the Finnish Fund and Kermit Roosevelt's enlistment office were finally disbanded after Russia's overwhelming numbers again broke through the Finnish front, the Finns had already proved to themselves and to the world what heroes they could be.

Mother's staff continued in place until all the money and goods that had been donated but not yet sent to Finland were returned to their original donors. Before his own return to Finland, the Finnish Ambassador presented Mother with his country's highest honor, before a crowded room at the Finnish Embassy. Present were all those fine people who had loaned out their staff, along with numerous friends of Mother's, the most treasured one being Clementine Churchill, standing in for her husband, Winston.

Kermit, who had succeeded in raising eight hundred and sixty-two volunteers, who had not yet been sent overseas, released them with bonuses, but was deeply saddened by the outcome. He quickly rejoined the British Army and was sent first to Norway and then to Cairo. After the United States declaration of war following the Japanese attack on Pearl Harbor, he again decommissioned himself and became an American army major. In that role he took part in the first action against the Japanese in the Aleutians. He died there in 1943. Like his father, the former President of the United States, he was one in a million, with an enormous zest for life.

When told of Kermit's death sometime later, Johnny could not hold back his tears. These two good friends and warriors had lived their lives to the fullest, and what exemplary lives they had been. God love them both, for we will not see their like again.

As for me, I was rescued from my frustrations by a former teacher at St. Peter's Court, John Green, who had tutored me one summer at Ferring and who was now the headmaster of Selwyn House. He had married Joan, the oldest daughter of the previous headmaster, and they had acquired twins and a dachshund. Selwyn House and St. Peter's Court were separated only by a large stone wall running between them. Now, under war conditions, both schools had been evacuated to new quarters in different parts of the country, hopefully away from danger.

I liked John Green quite a bit, and I liked him even more when he invited me to become a teacher of history and English for boys from seven to nine. It certainly wasn't a lucrative job, but then neither was I a very imposing candidate, considering that I had never even thought of teaching before.

But I was thrilled, as was Mother on my behalf. I accepted with alacrity, and two weeks later I was on the train for Selwyn House Private Preparatory School, now ensconced in a large Manor House near Oswestry, in Wales. I was saddened to leave Mother alone with just my young brothers and Nanny and a much-reduced staff of four. This had come about because Mother had encouraged over half of the staff to volunteer for factory work or farmwork, three of them taking up the former and two the latter. Left were Molly and her sister, Kitty, a new girl named Rose, and Bertha, thank God! Charles, our majordomo, had, with Mother's encouragement, already enlisted in the Navy. I was sure that it would not be long before Mother would find some situation that suited her talents, and that would help to fill up the empty times without her beloved Johnny.

Johnny, for his part, was in the middle of writing a letter to Mother when it happened. With a tremendous roar, the very earth moving beneath his feet, the guns exploded into life. For a brief moment hey shuddered in surprise. Then he realized that the war had finally begun.

Johnny fought as bravely as ever in the Second World War, winning the Military Cross, Kermit having won it in the First World War. It is second only to the Victoria Cross, the British equivalent of the American Congressional Medal of Honor.

Again France was the battlefield, the German tanks having once more smashed through Belgium into France at amazing speed. The French and British forces were pushed back across that country, until only a watery grave awaited the British Forces: the French with British assistance had established a holding pattern to enable the British soldiers to get through to Dunkirk, but then what?

The delaying action was bloody, but it held long enough for the troops to reach the shore, while an incredible fleet of boats of every size and shape was being organized, literally overnight, by the British Government under the direction of the new Prime Minister, Winston Churchill. Every port on the west coast of England and even further afield disgorged its volunteer boat owners with their boats; most of the crews, of course, would never have dared to risk such a voyage across the English Channel under normal circumstances. But these were not normal circumstances. The very heart of Britain's best was in the extremity of danger, dependent on rescue by a very large bunch of holiday skippers, amateur boatmen for the most part, but with a core of professional seamen.

It was an incredible achievement, with both the troops and their rescuers operating under murderous conditions, being constantly strafed and bombarded from the air. The giant land-mounted German guns finally got their range, turning many of the beaches into blood-soaked sandpits, with uncounted bodies blown to smithereens. It was a nightmare, as troops were placed aboard boats only to be strafed and sunk from the air, those left alive having to repeat the process, sometimes more than twice.

Johnny had spent all day and every day, once the boats were ready, leading large groups of men from his Middlesex Regiment into the water, swimming out to the nearest boats, returning again and again with weary, wounded, and shell-shocked, half-naked and tattered soldiers, many of them having their first swimming experience. When a few soldiers refused to go into the water at all, they were left to take care of themselves as best they could. Feeling sorry for them, Johnny ignored their behavior. He had led as many of his troops off the land and into the boats as there were boats to fill; with a few good swimmers from his regiment, he was spared to fight another day.

The number of troops that the Whitehall experts estimated would reach England's shores was thought to be approximately twenty-five thousand. The true figure came to over two hundred and fifty men! Winston Churchill had been Prime Minister for only two weeks when he heard the final numbers of those actually rescued. He took a deep breath and smiled, while facing the horrific fact that most of Britain's weapons of war had been left behind in France. Britain was practically defenseless, save for what had not been sent to France in the first place, and was an easy target should Hitler decide to finish it off before returning to other conquests.

Churchill, facing the abyss, raised his voice in a mighty roar. With inspired speeches, he laid out to his people his scenarios for victory, stirring their hearts and assuring the world that Great Britain would never give up the battle, come what may.

Captain Frank, skipper of Johnny Dodge's good ship the *Minerva*, got the call along with all the other motorboats in port, the authorities apparently unaware that the *Minerva* was a sailing ship. Perhaps they were misguided by the description of the vessel as having one diesel engine; at any rate, Captain Frank, with the help of his daughter Pam, weighed anchor, the sails billowing in a north-northwesterly breeze, and joined the fleet of motor boats, all of them unknowingly and uncaringly sailing into the mouth of hell, united by desperation and a magnificent esprit de corps.

The *Minerva*, because of her keel, had to be anchored farther out than the smaller boats, which brought to it load after load of rescued soldiers, until Captain Frank yelled "stop," fearing that the yacht, already dangerously low in the water, would sink. With the help of Pam and two soldiers who fortunately knew what they were doing, the boat turned back across the English Channel, its sails full, the diesel engine running at top speed, though with the weight of all those soldiers the voyage took six times what it had taken on the trip over.

According to Captain Frank, the discipline aboard the ship was excellent, in spite of there not being enough food or water to go around. The Lieutenant in charge of the troops had explained the situation: it was either all, or no one at all. The really amazing thing that day was the fact that the *Minerva* had not been bombed, nor had its decks been raked by machine-gun fire from the air, nor had it been fired upon from the land. It was as if the boat were made of cellophane. It was a miracle!

Captain Frank had a theory as to why the *Minerva* returned unscathed while so many other boats had gone to the bottom. It was the sails! Who in their right mind would want to destroy such an elegant white sailing vessel with its beautiful lines and breathtaking sails, its Royal Yacht Club burgee fluttering in the breeze? Apparently, no one.

Several Escapes, Including the Great One

Poor Johnny; he was so involved and focused on getting his surviving soldiers out to the boats at his particular section of the beach that he never knew about the amazing feat that Captain Frank and his daughter Pam had performed until he was a civilian again, after the war, when a friend in government told him. He was thrilled, and proud of the *Minerva*, but even more so of Captain Frank and his brave daughter; he let them know his pride in their service to their country, and happily rewarded them in substantial ways.

Johnny was not to be among those whom he had rescued. He led as many of his men off the beach and into the boats as there were boats to fill – a great many men over a lengthy period of time, a brave few having remained behind to delay the German advance. By now, on the beaches themselves, their ranks were whittled down and they had no glimmer of hope in their future.

The enemy was here, on the beach, in the darkness. The guns were silent, the only sounds heard being German voices rounding up the last remnants of the British Expeditionary Force. The Germans were loud, their prisoners' voices subdued.

Johnny had thought of going back into the water and swimming away from Dunkirk until he could reach a quiet part of the shoreline, maybe finding a sympathetic farmer who would give him food and somewhere to sleep for a night, after which he would try to escape. But it was hopeless. On this night, he was incapable of any more physical action. He was no longer a young man, and his strength had finally been drained to the last drop.

A small contingent of the Luftwaffe (German Air Force) loomed out of the darkness. With their torches aimed into his eyes and their guns at the ready, the contingent's Kommandant, a small wiry man, introduced himself with a strong Lancashire accent, telling Johnny that he was here to collect enemy flyers and take them back to his prisoner of war camp in Germany. Apparently, his mother was from Lancashire, hence the accent.

Something about this English Major intrigued the Kommandant. Realizing Johnny's weariness, he sat down beside him on the beach, much to Johnny's surprise, and interrogated him in a decent and respectful manner, which Johnny appreciated. Then the Kommandant finally stood up, walked some distance away, and told his communication officer to call Military Intelligence in Berlin, to find out if they had by any chance any information on a Major John Bigelow Dodge.

Half an hour later the Kommandant was reading a report that had been given to the Military Intelligence back in 1936 by a Dr. Schmidt, on the orders of Adolf Hitler himself. Stunned by the report, which included Johnny's connection with Winston Churchill, now Prime Minister of Great Britain, the Kommandant realized he had a very special prisoner of war on his hands. Despite his awareness that Major Dodge should be turned over to an army prisoner of war camp, the Kommandant decided to keep this prize in his own prisoner-of-war camp; that was how Johnny ended up as the only army man in a camp full of Royal Air Force officers.

Johnny had already escaped once from his Lancashire-accented, English-speaking jailer, by jumping off the train while on his way with the Kommandant and other British airmen to the prisoner-of-war camp. Eight hours later he was nabbed by an inquisitive policeman with a gun, demanding his identity papers. Naturally, Johnny didn't have any; after offering some futile explanations, he was escorted back to the train, where an exasperated, but still polite, Kommandant awaited, hoping to be able to reason with him. Instead, Johnny explained to the Kommandant that it was a British prisoner of war's duty to escape from a military prison belonging to the enemy. Indeed, according to Johnny, it was a natural act, like a baby bird taking its first flight.

At the Kommandant's camp in Germany, Johnny proceeded to escape two more times. The last time he was free for three days before being caught and brought back, but the Kommandant's patience had finally run out. As much as he liked and respected his VIP prisoner, he realized that Major Dodge's propensity for escaping was not doing his own record any good. Johnny ended up being transferred to a recently created prisoner of war camp for enemy airmen, Stalag Luft III, at Sagon in Silesia, located between Berlin and Breslau.

Paul Brickhill, one of his first friends at the new camp, described Johnny's adventures in his brilliant and classic book (and later enormously successful movie of the same name), *The Great Escape*, in these words:

"The artful Dodger, Major John Bigelow Dodge, had been born an American. His mother, Mrs. Charles Stuart Dodge, was a daughter of John Bigelow, US Minister to France under Abraham Lincoln.

"In the first week of the 1914 war, the Dodger, a smooth-cheeked youngster of twenty, took ship to England with his mother and sister Lucy, to get into the fight as soon as possible. Five years later he was a colonel with the D.S.O. and the D.S.C. When the lethal bickering started again in 1939, the Dodger's friend and family kinsman, Winston Churchill, soon had him back in the army and the Dodger was trapped some months later with the BEF [British Expeditionary Force] in France, down the coast from Dunkirk.

"Now in his forties, he swam miles out to intercept a ship, missed it, swam back, was caught, escaped again, then caught again, this time by the Luftwaffe, and always thereafter stayed in Air Force prison camps (when he wasn't escaping). A tall and courtly character, the Dodger had an incredibly charitable nature and a strange insulation from fear. I don't say that extravagantly. I think fear didn't bother him."

The Kommandant of Stalag Luft III was Oberst (colonel) von Lindeiner, a slim, handsome man in his sixties, with a Prussian background. Air Marshal Hermann Goering, the Supreme Commandeer of the German Air Force, was also in command of all enemy airman prisoner-of-war camps. He had appointed his assistant at that time, Colonel von Lindeiner, to command the newly built Stalag Luft III, because he knew him to be both firm and humane. Goering had followed Baron von Richthofen – the Red Baron – into the top spot when Richthofen was shot down in the First World War. He had proven himself a brilliant operational pilot and was thought to have a soft spot for Air Force prisoners.

The determination of the prisoners to escape, generally through incredible underground tunnels, and the challenge to the Kommandant and his guards to ensure they would not escape, was multiplied in all of the German prisoner-of-war camps for British and later American prisoners. The siutation once caused a heated meeting at Hitler's Berchtesgarten retreat, with Hitler in an absolute rage, because he had just been advised of the great escape from camp Stalag Luft III within the hour.

It just happened that Keitel, Goering, and Himmler were staying overnight, so Hitler called them into an immediate conference, giving orders that no minutes were to be taken of the meeting. Hitler stopped an argument among the three men as to who was to blame, saying, "They are all to be shot on recapture."

Goering protested. To shoot them all, he explained, would make it quite obvious that it was murder. Besides, there might be reprisals on German prisoners in Allied hands.

"In that case," Hitler said, "more than half of them are to be shot."

Those who escaped that day, only to be caught and returned to camp at Stalag Luft III early on, were the lucky ones, including Johnny Dodge. Their number was about twenty-three, of whom only three were able to make it back to England. It was the biggest and last major escape of the war, with some fifty flyers escaping out of seventy-six, all later captured on different escape routes. After they were assembled at a halfway prison, then loaded up in trucks, they were finally dispatched, supposedly back to Stalag Luft III. Instead, halfway to the camp, the trucks were stopped on the pretext of allowing the prisoners to urinate, whereupon they were commanded to stand to attention, facing away from the road. Out of a black van emerged a small detachment of Gestapo marksmen, who immediately opened fire into the backs of the fifty defenseless British RAF officers, killing them all.

To put this cold-blooded massacre into its evil context, Himmler, Chief of the Gestapo, on the early morning after the escape and on orders from Hitler, spoke to his second in command, Kaltenbrunner, in Berlin. Later that morning, Kaltenbrunner issued the text of what has since become known as the Sagan Order.

"The increase of escapes by officer prisoners of war is a menace to the internal security. As a deterrent, the Führer has ordered that more than half of the escaped officers are to be shot. Therefore, I order that Kriminalpolizei are to hand over for interrogating to the Gestapo more than half of the recaptured officers. After interrogation, the officers are to be taken in the direction of their original camp [Stalag Luft III] and shot en route. The shootings will be explained by the fact that the recaptured officers were shot while trying to escape, or because they offered resistance, so that nothing can be proved later."

It was a crime of such magnitude that, even before the end of the war, British Intelligence, along with auxiliary branches, went into full operational mode to track down and bring to justice every living perpetrator of this appalling deed. And track them down they did, one by one, slowly but steadily, until the last one had been brought to justice. It was a painstaking, time-consuming, often dead-ended operation, but in the end it proved successful, though that provided little comfort or justice for the brutal murder of fifty of England's finest.

Johnny, when he was told of the Gestapo's slaughter of his comrades, vowed he would avenge them. If you want to see his role in that scenario, rent or buy the movie *The Great Escape – The Untold Story*, starring Christopher Reeve as Major John Bigelow Dodge. It might surprise you.

Coming back to Paul Brickhill's book on the escape, we read the following: "Johnny the Dodger accompanied ten other escapees, going by train to Hirschberg and then down to Czechoslovakia, all wearing cloth caps and dirty clothes. They got out of the train at a little station just before Hirschberg and then they split up.

"The Dodger, with Werner and their escaping officer, set out to walk to Czechoslovakia, but it didn't take more than a couple of hours to see that the snow was going to beat them. They went back to the Hirschberg station that night, had a little trouble getting their tickets, but collected them eventually, and were sitting in the carriage, waiting for the train to start, when the police came through looking very closely at their passes and said, 'Komm mit.'

"Taken to Gestapo quarters, they found half a dozen old friends in the same situation. After interrogation they handcuffed the Dodger and pushed him into a cell by himself.

"One by one the Stalag Luft III escapees were rounded up, and a fortnight after the break, out of the seventy-six who got clear of the tunnel, only three were still free. The Germans never did find them. Two were already in England; the third was on his way.

"It is not easy to follow Johnny Dodge's sequence of escapes, but the final one ended with his imprisonment in the forbidding Sachsenhausen Concentration Camp north of Berlin. It was the adjutant of Sachsenhausen himself who arrived by car with guards and handcuffs to take him to the concentration camp, where he was put in a solitary cell, completely isolated from the rest of the prisoners. Here, except for an hour's walk in the yard in the middle of the day, alone, he was left incommunicado, without reading matter, conversation, rarely a change of clothes, malnourished and plain miserable for months on end."

Johnny had been in many desperate situations before, but by its very repetition this was the worst. He would beat it, if he lived that long, he told himself, over and over again. The things that kept his sanity in check were his memories, particularly of Mother and their life together. But that was about it. That, and hope.

The Conspiracy, 1944

It was in 1960, a year after I had married my beloved Clementine, a marriage that lasted forty-four wonderful years, when Johnny and Mother, while on one of his USA business trips, stopped off at our house in St. Petersburg, Florida, for the weekend. We were in the middle of a glorious spring, with temperatures during the day in the mid-seventies, at night in the fifties, and they both enjoyed themselves enormously, on land and on our boat, the *Clementine*, with which we happily voyaged on the waters of Tampa Bay and the Gulf of Mexico.

The third and final night when I took Johnny out on our boat for a ride on Tampa Bay, a full moon was shining on the water, our wake shimmering like ruffled snow spewing out behind us and a light breeze ruffling our hair. Our wives had had their fill of the boat and decided to sit out on our dock, and do what women do most naturally – that is, talk!

After we had been cruising for about twenty minutes, he suggested we cut the engine and drift for a while, and then he told me the incredible story that follows. He had first made me promise that, if ever I told anyone or wrote about it for public consumption, it would be long after his death. Forty-something years after should be enough.

I have kept my promise.

≈

Johnny Dodge was awakened as usual by the sound of the guard coming with his breakfast, a monotonously ersatz coffee, with half a piece of black bread or a biscuit so hard as to break a tooth if he didn't crush it underfoot until it was broken into small pieces and then softened in the coffee. Neither the bread nor the biscuit was really edible, but he ate one or the other, for he knew the alternative and would not consider it.

Johnny was holding out for the end of the war to come, for this concentration camp was escape-proof, of that he had no doubt. He had plotted and planned, in his head, all the possibilities for escape, each one turning into a dead end. Dispirited and hungry, always hungry, he had put his mind into keeping his sanity and exercising his legs and body in that one hour at noon allowed him by his jailors.

His guards remained cocky and confident, particularly after hearing one of the Propaganda Minister's belligerent tirades over the radio, assuring his people that victory would soon be theirs. He was a good speaker, Johnny conceded.

Hitler was silent, though he was telling his cronies of his secret weapons that would soon bring his enemies to their knees. I imagine he was speaking of the Buzz Bombs and the V2s, both weapons of destruction, the first the more intimidating by the fact that they were jet-propelled and pilotless, making unbelievably scary sounds until the jet's computer turned them off and they immediately fell silent until crashing into their targets with an enormous explosion. Immediately after would follow the sounds of sirens emanating from fire trucks and ambulances, signaling one more gift from the Führer that had found its mark.

The RAF was able to explode some of the Buzz Bombs in the air, though we lost pilots in the early stages when they flew too close to the bombs while blowing them up, with dire results. The Londoners' nerves were becoming very frayed over time by these bombs' intensive intrusiveness into their lives. Our invasion of Normandy on D-day brought a welcome relief to the city, as the aerial onslaught soon began to diminish.

The V2s were much more deadly. They could not be seen since they were flying at a speed beyond anything we had, at least at that time, so there was no defense against them. You would not know they were there until you were actually blown up, so what did it matter? As a result, there was very little fear of them.

And then there was Hitler's top card, the atomic bomb, which had been under development for over three years. Now his scientists were assuring him that, within a very few months, he would have his atomic bomb, and God help us all.

This particular morning Johnny was surprised to be taken to the showers, a rare event indeed. He was also supplied with fresh prison clothes and a barber to cut his hair and shave him, the barber being another prisoner. What omen did this portend, he wondered, both bemused and hopeful, for hope was really all he had left.

Midmorning, the same adjutant of the Sachsenhausen Concentration Camp who had personally put him in solitary with no regard for his rank or the Geneva Convention's rules of war, had the guard open the cell door. They walked in silence through the prison passageway to a car drawn up at the prison entrance. A young German officer was standing beside it, and the prison adjutant extended his hand to Johnny who gave him only a steely glare.

The German Air Force officer introduced himself, they shook hands, and Johnny was ushered into the front passenger seat. The car headed off the grounds of the concentration camp and onto the road to Berlin. Johnny naturally asked the young officer just what was going on. What was his situation? The officer smiled and put a hand to his mouth, meaning he could not tell him. After they finally reached Berlin and the lieutenant found himself in a tonier part of the city, he drove down one side of the street that had not yet been bombed and pulled up in front of a men's clothing store.

The officer beckoned Johnny to get out of the car, and they entered the store, where the officer instructed an elderly man immaculately dressed in a well-cut suit to take Johnny's measurements for shoes, socks, shirt, tie, underwear and a suit. The officer asked Johnny if he had a preference in suits, and Johnny said that he favored a single-breasted dark grey suit. And then he suddenly realized that he could be falling into a trap, for, if caught in civilian clothes with no credentials, he could be accused of being a spy and possibly shot on the spot. The officer gave his word to Johnny that he could wear his new clothes without compromising himself. Counting on the officer's honor, Johnny went into the changing room and came out a new man. The despised convict clothes and cardboard shoes had been placed in a bag for disposal in an incinerator; his appearance, though he was a shell of his former self, was lit up by a beautiful smile, his first relaxed and sincere smile in eons of blighted, formless days of purgatory.

"You look good," said the lieutenant. "Handsome indeed. What you need is some good food, and that is very scarce now. But at least it will be better than what you have been getting, I hope."

"So do I," said Johnny. "Where to next?"

It was after midday, and the lieutenant suggested going to his officers' club for lunch, which sounded good to Johnny. They were soon seated at a table for two in the club, an attractive oval room with tables set for two or four, and a long table down the middle with a variety of hot dishes arranged on top from which to help yourself. To Johnny it looked, smelled, and tasted like a royal banquet, though he took only a large tablespoon of each of four choices, for fear of suddenly overwhelming his stomach and losing his lunch before it could do him any good. The dessert was ersatz ice cream, which the lieutenant wouldn't touch, but which Johnny enjoyed enormously, much to the officer's amusement.

Now that they were back in the car, Johnny refrained from questioning his keeper anymore, for he had deduced that the lieutenant, though an honorable man, was on a delicate mission of which he had been told very little, except that his life depended on being both courteous and cautious that Major Dodge did not escape. If the latter should happen, he could expect to be returned to the ranks and dispatched to the front, a powerful threat to any soldier who misbehaved. So far, the lieutenant was happy that everything was going as planned. He prayed that it would remain that way.

Johnny, on the other hand, was not about to try an escape. He was much too curious to find out what all this was about. The only thing that he was quite sure of was that he must be very important to someone in an extremely high position in Germany – someone who was obviously playing a secretive hand with dangerously high stakes. It looked like Major John Bigelow Dodge was the only person capable of bringing this particular game plan to a successful conclusion.

They drove up in front of the Adlon Hotel, Berlin's finest, though Johnny could see that a part of the building had been badly damaged by Allied bombers. They got out of the car, entered the lobby, and crossed to the desk. The lieutenant picked up the in-house phone and was put through to someone with whom he spoke briefly in German; he then replaced the phone and led Johnny to the elevators. They got off on the fourth floor and walked to the end of the corridor to a door marked 403.

The lieutenant knocked, and the door was opened almost immediately. Framed in the doorway was the last man Johnny had ever expected to see again: Dr. Schmidt, interpreter to Johnny's nemesis, Adolf Hitler. For a long moment, he stood, unbelieving, yet knowing that his eyes were not deceiving him. Finally, Dr. Schmidt grasped Johnny's hand and ushered him into the suite. Johnny had already thanked the lieutenant for his services, and Dr. Schmidt then dismissed him.

Dr. Schmidt pointed to a chair angled toward another chair, which he had been occupying while awaiting his guest.

"Major Dodge, you have escaped from almost every prison in Germany," Dr. Schmidt said.

Johnny smiled, but said nothing. He could not comprehend his present situation, and the last thing in the world that he wanted to do now was to have another face-to-face meeting with Adolf Hitler. He finally asked Dr. Schmidt if Herr Hitler was here in Berlin now.

"No ... the Führer is at headquarters near the Russian front. I am no longer his interpreter, for he really does not need me anymore."

"Then what are you doing now?"

"I am working for Air Marshal Hermann Goering, and that is why you are here. Tonight you will be the guest of the Reich Marshal and you will understand why I have scoured the entire chain of prisoner-of-war camps and captives, only to find you at a camp not even approved for prisoners of war, especially one such as you. I am terribly sorry this happened. The adjutant was dismissed immediately after you left this morning and is now on his way to the Russian front."

Again Johnny was silent. The morning had happened too quickly. He had gone from numb desperation to suspicion to a tiny speck of hope, to a rush of freedom, to a good meal. And only then had he realized that there really was a reason for it all, which he would learn tonight. It was almost too much for Johnny, and Dr. Schmidt, a sensitive man, suggested to him that he get out of his clothes and into bed, adding that he would call him at seven that evening in plenty of time for him to bathe and change into his gray suit, or another complete wardrobe that included a good-looking blue business or evening suit with black shoes. The gray suit had come with smart brown shoes, obviously expensive. There was also a handsome new leather suitcase on the luggage stand and fresh flowers by the window, the lieutenant having arranged for the clothier to personally bring the suits and extras with him to the hotel, while Johnny and the lieutenant had lunch together. The flowers were courtesy of the hotel. A complete bathroom kit was in a leather case in his bathroom. Should he need anything else, all he had to do was to call the desk, where all the clerks spoke English and would be sure that his requests were answered immediately.

Johnny thanked Dr. Schmidt. He told him how glad he was to see him again, shook his hand, and let him out the door. After such an interminable period of repetitive nothingness for months and months and months, this incredible morning had overwhelmed him. It was like a beautiful dream; it was many wonderful, inexplicable things happening all at once, but all positive and civilized, so he undressed and got into bed, a real, comfortable bed. Before he could appreciate its newness and its actual luxury, his eyes closed and he was fast asleep.

Little could he imagine what lay ahead of him.

Johnny awoke from the first really good sleep he had had since he couldn't remember when. He felt relaxed and calm and more like himself. His first impression upon opening his eyes was that he must be dreaming. But the phone beside his comfortable bed had rung, and Dr. Schmidt's cheerful voice had greeted him, verifying that he was real and this beautiful room was real, and all he had to do now was to fill the enormous bathtub with warm water and soak for a while, and then soap himself all over, and finally turn on the cold shower, a constant practice with Johnny throughout his life.

Energized by his sleep, his bath, his cold shower, and his spiffy new blue suit, he was dressed and ready by ten minutes of eight that evening, pale and undernourished but relaxed and comfortable in his own skin for the first time in a very long time. Sure enough, at eight there was a knock on the door, and he let in a smiling Dr. Schmidt, who seated himself at Johnny's invitation and told him that the Air Marshal's plane had landed and he should be there in another twenty minutes or so, providing Allied bombers didn't arrive ahead of them.

They talked about the war, and gradually Johnny got the impression that Dr. Schmidt was already reconciled to the thought of defeat because of America's entrance into the war following the Japanese attack on Pearl Harbor. The US declaration of war had been directed not only at Japan, but at Japan's allies, Germany and Italy. Because America and Great Britain now dominated the skies over Europe, and had destroyed so many of Germany's petroleum sources, which were required to feed that country's weapons of war, particularly on the Eastern Front, the odds had become vastly more favorable to the Allies than to Germany.

The Eastern Front was now, just before April 1944, a quagmire, a constant heavy rain bringing practically all mechanical movement to a halt with the exception of the tanks, most of which were anxiously waiting for petroleum supplies. Only the frigid cold earth beneath the battlegrounds prevented the belligerents from sinking into the earth, while both sides threw spasmodic destruction at one another.

The Russian soldiers were much better clothed than the Germans, who were now worn out not only from the fighting, but also from the atrocious winter weather -- the temperature often registering ten to thirty degrees below freezing -- and the complete failure of the German Supply Corps to furnish them with weather-resistant apparel.. The morale among the troops and many of the officers was in the basement; some soldiers were actually deserting or simply giving in and letting the elements release them from their suffering.

The phone finally rang again, and Dr. Schmidt went to the side of Johnny's bed to answer it. He listened for a moment and then turned to Johnny. "The Air Marshal awaits you," he said. "I shall be the interpreter."

Johnny smiled to himself, took a deep breath, rose to his feet, and followed Dr. Schmidt down the corridor.

The Gambler had had a long string of successful gambles to his credit, from the First World War to the Second, having joined the National Socialist Party in the early years. With his heroic background from the First World War, bringing kudos to Hitler and his party, Hermann Goering attended to anything that Hitler needed doing, whether legal or not, with relish and a professional business attitude. Hitler was impressed, and Goering stepped up the ladder along with Hess, Goebbels, and Himmler, as Hitler's political career ascended, until finally these four men were Germany's most powerful, utterly beholden to their leader.

Until Hitler went to war, Hess had been considered the leading candidate for Hitler's position should he die in office, since Hess had been with him longer than any of the others. Of course, Hitler never let any of them feel absolutely certain that their position was rock solid. After the war began, there was really nothing much for Hess to do, and his expectation of being Hitler's heir withered away, driving him to make a desperate unauthorized flight to England to seek to unite England with Germany against Russia, exactly as Hitler had once tried with Johnny as his go-between. Both plans came to nothing. Hess languished in jail, first in England and then in Germany, during and after the Nürenberg trials, finally dying, still under the Allies' jurisdiction.

Now that Goering's Luftwaffe had been beaten in the Battle of Britain, Hitler's relationship with Goering had cooled. Although the Royal Air Force had been outnumbered twenty to one and had lost a plenitude of pilots, they had finally routed the Luftwaffe and, to a major degree, won back the skies over Great Britain, prompting Winston Churchill to pronounce his immortal words, "Never was so much owed by so many to so few."

Despite Goering's failure, Hitler knew he could not afford to cut him out of the inner circle. Even though Goering was living an autonomous life within his own fiefdom, Hitler still valued Goering, for he had been a loyal and successful Nazi bigwig and was, after Hitler himself, the most popular Nazi leader with his countrymen. Moreover, if there was ever a time when Hitler needed cohesion among his toadies, it was now. His Eastern Front project was cracking, and his cities were being pummeled by a much larger and more devastating dose of what he had inflicted upon his enemies in recent years. Now America was in the war. The odds had changed, and the stakes were no longer certain.

The large polished wooden doors to Air Marshal Herman Goering's suite were wide open. Two costumed footmen stood at attention just inside, wearing blue and gold knee-length breeches with white stockings and shiny black pumps on their feet, their jackets of the same material as their breeches; on their heads were white wigs such as certain British judges were accustomed to wear. The room, the hotel's most elegant, was furnished in faux Louis XIV furniture (reminiscent of Evan Tredegar's from the Crillon Hotel). An enormous and superlatively brilliant chandelier illuminated the room, with large candles in six-foot-tall holders lit and evenly spaced a foot away from the brocaded walls, while a gigantic Persian rug covered most of the marble floor. At the end of the room were an ebony dining table and chairs, the chair frames inlaid with patterns of ivory and precious stones; it was a table for twelve, tonight set for three. In the center of the room stood the host, a warm, welcoming smile on his face, his dinner outfit more becoming to a Straus operetta than a deadly serious effort to resolve an almost impossibly complicated dilemma.

Johnny could not help but smile. The Air Marshal's presence and charm were almost overwhelming, but his evening wear, on a body of Falstaffian girth, simply asked for ridicule. Only his extraordinary self-discipline saved him from exploding into uncontrollable laughter. The Air Marshal had chosen an all-white outfit, with voluminous riding breeches descending into white riding boots, with abbreviated spurs so that he would not be tripped up by them – what a delightful thought! – and a military jacket buttoned from top to bottom. On one side of his chest were his medals, some well earned from the First World War, others somewhat less impressive, but all correctly arranged on a dark red velvet backing on his tunic.

"My dear Major Dodge, this is a pleasure and an honor," said the Air Marshal, grasping Johnny's hand and leading him to the table at the end of the room. Johnny was seated by a footman at one end, and his host was seated by the other footman at the other end. Dr. Schmidt, the interpreter, sat between them.

To Johnny Dodge, this whole picture was beyond his comprehension. He had started the day with absolutely nothing but negative and mind-blowing monotony seemingly stretching forever into his future, a pathetic shadow of his former self; how could it be that now, within a matter of mere hours, he was sitting at a table with one of the four most powerful men in Germany, as his honored guest?

His host was jovial, affable, majestic even, and Johnny wondered if, with the faux furniture and trappings of the King Louis XIV period, Goering was not playing out a fantasy of his own, copying effete gestures that belonged in the French royal courts with grace and accomplishment, but utterly ludicrous in these circumstances. Even the venerable Dr. Schmidt permitted himself a pained expression from time to time.

Johnny was fascinated, and embarrassed. It was a side of his host that he had never in a million years expected to see. But the sirens had not yet sounded, the food was superlative, and Johnny had even taken a sip of the red wine that the bewigged servant had poured into his crystal glass. All this monarchist extravagance had rejuvenated him, and, as Goering ate his food with hilariously delicate motions, Johnny, careful to eat in moderation, found his voice. In the same warm mood that Goering had set, and with his brain finally beginning to feel the effects of sudden nourishment, he managed, with Dr. Schmidt's help, to blend some of his personal experiences into those of Goering, who proved to be a good and delighted listener. When they had finished their dinner, they adjourned to a smaller room with more modern furniture, featuring statues and paintings of nude boys and male-female couples in sensual liaisons. There was also a large round table, where you couldn't help but see that the tabletop was held up by six erect penises.

Johnny wondered why Goering had chosen this somewhat distracting room for their meeting, and also whether, as we Americans might say, he was AC or DC or both?

Johnny knew that he had a wife, a former German opera star, but it seemed that he swam in other pools as well. It was only after the three of them had sat down in the sexually oriented room did Johnny realize that the charming Goering playing out his lust for majesty as the foppish King Louis had suddenly changed to Air Marshal Goering, a stern-eyed, icy-brained Machiavellian tyrant.

"Major Dodge," said Goering, "Dr. Schmidt has told me a great deal about you, most of it good, though I understand your mission on behalf of our Führer failed miserably. I am going to give you a chance to make amends and save a half million to a million lives. How does that appeal to you?"

Johnny realized, only a few hours out of interminable months of hell and semi-starvation, that he was in no condition to negotiate with this man, but that at least he could listen to his proposition, whatever it might be.

"Depends," said Johnny. "Whose lives are we going to save?"

"All of ours: Germans, Russians, Americans, British, not to mention the civilian casualties, which in this war have become enormous."

Johnny almost said, "I wonder who started this war," but discretion overcome valor. Instead he asked, "And how does the Air Marshal propose to achieve this?"

"First, Major Dodge, you must swear an oath, as an officer and a gentleman, that you will never speak a word of what I am proposing until the deal has been effected. If we cannot make a deal, you will never tell a soul, while I am alive. Do I make myself clear?"

"Perfectly, but I shall not make that promise until you tell me the deal."

Goering flushed and yelled angrily at Dr.Schmidt, who waited until Goering had vented his wrath and then, in a soft and soothing voice, calmed the Air Marshal down. Goering settled back in his chair and pressed a bell by his side. Cognac glasses containing Courvoisier were brought in, but neither Dr. Schmidt nor Johnny accepted them, giving Goering an excuse to drink from his guests' glasses on top of his own. (I have heard that the fatter you are the longer it takes to get a buzz on.)

Dr. Schmidt did not interpret anything that had been said between them after Johnny had made his condition for his oath to Goering. It had obviously displeased the Air Marshal, for it had shown that Johnny, weak though he was, was not a pushover. Furthermore, Johnny's mind was becoming clearer by the minute, until he finally realized that, right now, he held the winning card, for only he was available to promote or not promote Goering's desperate need to reach a man whom he had hated above all others, but now needed above all others, a man who was no longer out of office but was now the Prime Minister of Great Britain, Winston S. Churchill.

"I am a realist," said Goering, taking a mouthful of cognac and rolling it slowly around in his mouth before swallowing it appreciatively. It was well after ten p.m., and he was about to explain his plan to Johnny. "I deal with facts as I see them," he continued, "and unless Hitler's eggheads can perfect an atomic bomb very, very soon, Germany will have lost this war, as it did the last, by fighting on two fronts – a mistake that even Hitler made in spite of writing in his own book, *Mein Kampf,* that Germany must never again fight on two fronts or it will once again lose the war. Even so, Russia would have proven a hard nut to crack: Although its front, taken by surprise, was brought to its knees, it survived to crush the German army with vast resources of soldiers who knew the terrain and accommodated the winter weather. The German troops, meanwhile, were dismally unprepared for such devastating cold; being accustomed to a richer culture and a more civilized way of living, they found acceptance of the barbaric conditions on the Eastern Front harder to bear.

"My air force, it turns out, was of little help, for the frigid conditions made flying very dangerous. We never had enough petrol, anyway, to do much damage to the enemy, or bring food and warmer clothing to our own troops. Hitler would rarely admit to any of this, living in his own little world with his yes men and his generals. None but Rommel stood up to him, plus maybe one or two of the rest who were forced to retire afterward. Rommel himself was made to take poison for disloyalty to the Führer, simply for daring to speak out on the true facts of the situation. And so it goes.

"If the war is allowed to continue much longer, all sides will become more desperate, with more killings than ever before. Hitler is, even as we speak, about to issue an order that, whenever the enemy approaches, everything – whether homes or factories or hospitals or schools – is to be flattened, burnt to the ground, destroyed, a policy of absolute scorched earth. Anyone failing to do his duty is to be shot as a traitor. It will destroy Germany beyond resurrection."

Goering paused, as if considering his words. Then he continued, "One of the scientists working on the atomic bomb has reported to me that they haven't yet collected enough 'heavy water.' If ever they do, it will still take some time to put it all together, not to mention testing it without blowing ourselves up, and finally placing it in the bomb bay in one of our heavy bombers. I do not believe that will happen, because the scientists are not fools, and they, too, can see the writing on the wall; the longer they manage to stretch out the time, the longer they will be able to live and hopefully survive the war.

"I am suggesting a much more peaceful solution to our quandary, one that demands much goodwill among all the participants, friend and foe alike, but it could bring an immediate conclusion to hostilities and save all those precious lives that would otherwise be lost. Think about it, Major Dodge. We Germans have the capability to continue this war for six months at least, maybe more. That's going to cost a great many lives of both military and civilians on either side, as the end is always fiercest, with even more slaughter and desperation than the beginning or the middle of a war."

Goering sighed, accepting another glass of water from Dr. Schmidt before he continued. "My plan is this. The wording of the peace terms of the present treaty will have to be changed from 'unconditional surrender' to 'conditional surrender,' the reason being that Mr. Churchill and his cabinet will be dealing with me, rather than Adolf Hitler, who will either have committed suicide or been assassinated, both of which I am capable of arranging at any time.

"Though I despise him, Himmler has given me his backing, after first testing the waters himself but receiving little response. Even though he approached Holland with a plan not too unlike my own, it was not acceptable to the Netherlands, or to me, and quickly died. Before the war is over, Himmler and his cronies will be out of the country or dead, and his agents will be judged by Allied courts.

"As for me, my countrymen like me. I am popular with all classes. I have not been tainted with Hitler's atrocious killings of his rivals and even his friends, and I am still well regarded on the basis of my reputation from the First World War. If the Allies give me a caretaker appointment, my first objective will be Germany's surrender to them. Then I'll need a year as Head of State to arrange for the restoration of political parties by the sixth month of my tenure, followed by elections set at a time chosen jointly by the Allies and me.

"During my time in office, I will restore order over the land, revive commercial and industrial activity, encourage the arts, clean up the rubble of war, and entice the middle class back to pursuing employment. This will go a long way toward ensuring the normal functions of a peaceful society. Even then there will be an enormous problem, with power stations destroyed, roads obliterated, factories gutted. But I am the man to lead this country, at least at the beginning, on the road back to normality. And when my one year's tenure is up and I am brought before an Allied court, I would have it that my service to the Allies and my own country will be recognized and considered in determining any punishment that might be brought against me."

Goering turned to Johnny and looked him straight in the eyes. "Well, Major Dodge, what do you think? Have we a chance?"

Johnny's eyes never wavered from Goering's. While he thought that the chances of Goering's plan being approved were about a thousand to one, he knew that sometimes that one won.

"Not great," said Johnny, "but there's always a chance. At least, I will give you my oath." They both smiled, and Goering gave his hand to Johnny, who took it and thanked the Air Marshal for his hospitality.

Goering had one last thing to say. "Major Dodge, this war cannot be allowed to go on. I have men of my own views who now, before it is too late, have decided to make a real effort to save Germany from Hitler's insane policies and edicts. I have people in every arm of government, on every army staff, and even on Hitler's daily agenda. If you, Major Dodge, can convince our friend Mr. Churchill of my plans – their practicality and their potential for salvation of so many soldiers and civilians of all our countries, friend and foe alike – then you will have rendered all of us a great service. I realize that you are only the messenger, but you know Mr. Churchill very well, and he knows and respects you. Since there is not a word written anywhere of my plan, only you, Dr. Schmidt, and I are the keepers of it. Until it is agreed upon, God speed you!"

Dr. Schmidt said he would take Johnny back to his room. While en route he congratulated Johnny on the way he had handled himself, particularly after such a hectic day. He also told him that he and another gentleman, a Dr. Thost, a high official in the German Foreign Office, would meet him at ten in the morning. Dr. Thost also spoke English. Dr. Schmidt would introduce them, and then he would be leaving with Air Marshal Herman Goering on his plane back to the Air Marshal's headquarters. Dr. Thost would personally explain his own responsibilities for Johnny's safety and lead him out of Germany.

In the meantime, if the sirens sounded during the night, he should immediately get in the elevator and descend to the basement, like all the other hotel guests. "The Air Marshal will always be among the first," said Dr. Schmidt with a twisted smile. There was great pain in the translator's eyes, and Johnny could not help but feel a touch of sadness for him, with his whole world falling apart around him, while Johnny was starting out with a new deck of cards and an enormous responsibility on his shoulders.

Pajamas were laid out on his bed, a dressing gown beside them, and slippers beside the bed. His chest of drawers was filled with four shirts, six pairs of underwear, four pairs of socks, and ten handkerchiefs; a wallet had been placed on the chest, with considerable German money in part of it and Swiss currency in the other, plus an identity card with his picture taken when he first arrived at his last concentration camp. Johnny looked at it and felt ill. Did he really look that bad? He undressed, went to the bathroom, and used the toothbrush and toothpaste he found there, a first for many months. Why his teeth hadn't fallen out, he didn't know. He came back and climbed into bed, a real bed, and sank into a deep sleep.

Even more fortunate for our exhausted Johnny, no sirens sounded that night.

By ten a.m. Johnny Dodge was back in his gray suit, bathed and breakfasted, and feeling a lot brighter than this time yesterday. He was still somewhat bemused, everything having happened so quickly, but at least his brain cells were operating at a considerably more energetic pace than before, and his buoyant attitude had returned.

Dr. Schmidt arrived at Johnny's suite shortly after ten, with Dr. Thost in tow. Dr. Thost was a robust-looking gentleman who had been a London correspondent for a German newspaper before the war. He was now a rising civil servant in the German Foreign Office and apparently in cahoots with Goering.

After being introduced by Dr. Schmidt, Dr. Thost took a seat, as did Johnny. Dr. Schmidt had commandeered a footstool. Dr. Thost spoke fluent if guttural English, and, though obviously not in on the reason for Johnny's trip out of Germany, he was impressed enough that he had been given the honor of being responsible for the VIP's journey by none other than Air Marshal Hermann Goering himself. He had met and spoken with Goering at a party given at the Foreign Office, and had flattered him so effusively for his achievements that the Air Marshal, being excessively vain and egotistical, had later made Dr. Thost his inside man at the Foreign Office. His record and value to the Air Marshal had proven incalculable. Thus had come about Dr. Thost's present mission, resisted by his superior -- lasting mere seconds, for who would long resist Hermann Goering? Only Hitler.

In response to Johnny's inquiring expression, Dr. Thost began. "Major Dodge, I am responsible for bringing you safely from here to Switzerland, from where you will be flown back to England. The Air Marshal has given me instructions through Dr. Schmidt that this is a matter of the greatest urgency, and that is why I will need your complete cooperation. The Air

Marshal had considered having you flown over in one of his own Air Force planes, but decided it might be too dangerous. So we have to take a circuitous route, for reasons I am not at liberty to say, but it will be for your protection and you will be given every consideration, I assure you, Major Dodge."

Johnny couldn't resist a happy smile: At the very thought of England, his sons, David and Tony, and Minerva, his chest swelled as if to burst and his eyes became entranced with the vision of his beloved wife, the one, the only, true love of his life.

Johnny suddenly came back to the moment, and apologized to his two protectors for his behavior. Dr. Schmidt, always sensitive to his guest, stood up and put his hands on his shoulders. "You don't have to apologize, Major Dodge," he said. "We are the ones to apologize for the terrible things that have happened to you these many months. It is a disgrace. I only wish I had found you sooner. The kind of incarceration that you, a British officer, have endured for so long is outrageous, and those responsible will be taken care of, that I promise you. As you know, one is already being punished, quite possibly with his life."

Dr. Thost asked if Johnny was packed. When he assented, Dr. Thost took his bag. Giving a last look back at the comfortable suite, Johnny left the room with his companions and took the elevator down to the ground floor. There he received a bear hug from Dr. Schmidt, who wished him good luck and Godspeed, and then turned and walked briskly away.

Dr. Thost placed Johnny's bag on top of his own in the trunk of his car and motioned to Johnny to get in. Little did Johnny realize, as the car pulled away from the curb, that he was about to be taken on the wildest journey of his life.

Dresden, among Germany's most beautiful cities, was the first stopping point on the route programmed by the Air Marshal himself for Johnny's edification. All his hosts had been instructed as to the subjects to be discussed and those to be avoided at all costs, as well as told to be on their best behavior.

Dr. Thost had made arrangements for two rooms with bathrooms on a lower floor of the hotel, in order to be close to the bomb shelter in the basement. They used the hotel as a base for the first two nights, but relinquished it on the third night, having been invited by the State Governor to attend a small reception and dinner at his home and spend the night. Dr. Thost considered this to be a great honor, and Johnny considered it just one more proof of Goering's creeping power play and the amazing speed at which the Nazi idealistic front was crumbling. Ordinarily, the State Governors were among the most vicious and fanatical members of the National Socialist Party.

What was more important to Johnny and Dr. Thost was that the Governor's invitation saved their lives, for that night Dresden was bombed and firebombed, their hotel pulverized to rubble, even the basement bomb shelter being smashed to pieces. There was a heavy death toll.

Johnny soon found himself being treated as an overnight celebrity. Dr. Thost drove him to the S.S. Administration headquarters outside Dresden, where he was greeted by an S.S. General who spoke warmly of the historical links existing between Germany and Great Britain. He explained that the British Royal family, up to and including George V and Queen Mary, were of pure German blood, and that, furthermore, the grand German Army had played a vital role in helping Wellington defeat Napoleon at Waterloo. These comments left an incredulous Johnny, who had fought for the British in two wars started by Germany, completely speechless.

The General then invited the two men to his home for dinner, where his wife, considerably younger than he, provided a delectable meal, and he filled the air with pleasant platitudes regarding the cozy relationship between their two countries. Johnny almost wondered if the General was hallucinating, or if he himself had somehow missed something while incarcerated.

Dr. Thost, now having taken Dr. Schmidt's place as interpreter, did a good job, but he was corrected on two occasions for not interpreting the General's remarks correctly, showing that the General knew more of the English language then he was letting on. Johnny also realized that his host's superior was none other than the dreaded Himmler, top man of both the Gestapo and the S.S. If so, the General must be reflecting his boss's political leanings at this time, which meant that Hitler's team leaders were quietly splitting away from their leader's aspirations, which by that time really came down to "do or die," or, perhaps more correctly, "do *and* die."

With Hess, Hitler's oldest comrade, having flown to England and now lodged in prison; Himmler weaving his own conspiracies; Goering in the wings ready to move against Hitler on a moment's notice if his plan was accepted – that left in place for Hitler only Goebbels, his fanatical loyalist and Propaganda Minister, whose power was limited to the media and film industry. He was, moreover, totally dependent on his Führer.

To Johnny, this analysis came as an amazing revelation, obviously one that could be of tremendous importance to Churchill and his cabinet. Hitler's Nazi machine was showing definite signs of splintering, and the mood among his leaders was no longer that of certain victory, but rather the opposite, one of desperately searching for ways to survive to the coming end.

Wherever Dr. Thost took Johnny, he was greeted with considerable warmth and constant references to the so-called brotherhood between the two countries. Apparently, this was all on Goering's agenda for Johnny, for they kept going for three days outside Dresden. Johnny was entertained by seemingly endless nice Germans, all profoundly attracted to the British people and desirous of bringing the war to an end. Johnny wondered what these nice Germans had been saying when Germany had conquered a large part of Europe, and Russia was still an ally.

Now they were going to leave Dr. Thost's car for a while and take the bus to Weimar, where once again they were heavily bombed. Nevertheless, they spent a couple of days being entertained by more nice German people.

Next, a chauffeur brought Dr. Thost's car back to him, and they then drove to Regensburg, where they stopped to eat in a café. Since no one was eating there at the time, it being around three-thirty in the afternoon, the proprietor, after serving them, had retreated into his office. Thus they spoke together in hushed tones, in English. Unbeknownst to them, however, someone overheard them talking in English, probably the owner of the café, curiosity getting the better of him. Suddenly the police arrived, handcuffed them, and marched them off as suspected spies.

Dr. Thost was crimson with rage, admonishing the police with his importance at the German Foreign Office in Berlin, and raining every possible kind of threat of punishment upon their heads if they weren't freed immediately. All of this the police ignored. Johnny, jailed once again, though with Dr. Thost sharing his cell, spent two days and nights awaiting execution. He felt utter bitterness: Having come so close to freedom, it seemed terribly unfair that death should come like this from petty local officials, when the very German Foreign Office itself was bowing to him in his prospective role as mediator.

Poor Dr. Thost was going out of his mind with frustration and fear. If he wasn't allowed to get through to Berlin by that very night – the orders already having been approved and read to them – they would both be shot at seven the following morning.

It was the local Gestapo that freed them, after a message had finally penetrated to Berlin and the answer came back clearing the two "spies."

Dr. Thost and Johnny then went on to Munich, and finally left for the Swiss border at Lake Constance. That night Johnny said his goodbyes to a jubilant Dr. Thost, who, in spite of every obstruction, from bombs to police – and faced with the immediate prospect of being shot – had accomplished his duties successfully. He could now report his triumph back to Dr. Schmidt and hopefully await another promotion in the German Foreign Office.

Johnny then introduced himself to the Swiss police at St. Marguerita. After arranging with British Army Intelligence in Bern to alert the Prime Minister to Major John B. Dodge's urgent need to meet with him on vitally important business, that very afternoon the RAF flew him back to England.

Dr. Thost's last gesture to Johnny had been to hand him an envelope, to be read only when he was back home. When Johnny opened it, he read a phone number and the words Green (for success) and Red (for failure). "Dear God," he thought, "what an impact one little word can make!"

When the RAF plane landed at the airport outside of London, Johnny was welcomed by the commanding officer, and a chauffeured limousine transported him and his suitcase to the district of Whitehall, where he was deposited in front of an imposing building of the same ilk as most of the other buildings in that section of London. Here he was greeted by a red-tabbed Brigadier Ponsonby, a friend from before the war, who greeted him with a smart salute and warm handshake. "I've heard that you've been through one hell of a lot," he exclaimed. "And you're too thin. We've got to put some meat on you, Johnny. The PM is excited about your coming. He has a very high regard for you – you know that, don't you?"

They had reached the reception room, where the Brigadier asked him if he had lunch. Johnny replied that he hadn't eaten since a continental breakfast hours before.

"Not to worry," said the Brigadier. "We have the best teas in town. I'll send one of the tea ladies with your tea right away, and if you want to wash up, the bathrooms are over there. And Johnny, don't ask any questions. Down here you are incommunicado until the PM arrives from the House [Parliament]. Understand?"

"You mean I can't even call Minerva?"

"I'm afraid not, old friend. It's the same for everybody. This is probably the most top secret building in the city, or the country for that matter. Only the business of war goes on here. Nothing personal. Of course the

PM lives by his own rules, and that's fine with me. I hope to see you around, Johnny. We must break bread at my club one of these days."

"I'd like that," said Johnny, fretting silently over his inability to make contact with his wife. The Brigadier shook Johnny's hand, saying that he was going off duty in twenty minutes, now that Johnny was secured in the reception room. Within another fifteen minutes, the tea lady arrived with her mobile tea cart, setting up a portable table in front of his chair, on which she placed a silver tea tray with a teapot, lemon, sugar, and milk, plus an appetizing array of finger sandwiches and an enormous piece of chocolate cake. Johnny managed to eat the lot.

An hour and a half later, the table and the tea tray having been removed along with crumbs from the floor, Johnny was about to doze off, when in charged Winston Churchill with Anthony Eden, back in the saddle at the Foreign Office, and the newspaper titan and now Cabinet Minister Max Beaverbrook. All three looked tired but triumphant, Churchill having blunted all the criticisms of his opposition with his facile tongue and appeasing good humor.

For a moment the three stopped dead in their tracks, staring at Johnny's sunken face and undernourished body. Then Winston grabbed him by the shoulder, looking deep into his eyes, and said, "Oh, Johnny, I am so sorry. I had no idea." He turned away in shock, while Tony Eden and Max Beaverbrook took their turns making Johnny welcome. They all went through the reception room and into Churchill's office, where sturdy tumblers were filled with Scotch. Johnny bowed out, fearful of muddling his mind. For the next twenty minutes, he recounted some of his experiences since they had last seen him, seemingly, to Johnny, many eons ago.

Finally, Winston called them to order, asking Johnny what the urgent business was that demanded his attention right away. Johnny began, and within five minutes all three men had put down their glasses. They remained glued to Johnny's account of his meeting with Hermann Goering, and his further observations regarding the obvious disaffection among Hitler's trusted deputies.

When Johnny finished, there was a long silence. Finally, Churchill said, "I've heard vague rumors, none verified, along the lines of which you speak, but nothing as solid as you have presented. This is incredible! My God, Johnny, you have done us an enormous favor. From your inside observations alone, we now know we are at the final stages of this dreadful war. As for Goering's plan, I will have to have you lay it out, along with your comments, to my Cabinet tonight. Is that all right?"

He had already pressed a bell at his side, and a uniformed Royal Navy secretary appeared, her expression calm and authoritative.

"Call my Cabinet members right now," Churchill said. "I want them here within the hour – top priority, understand? And move the meeting to the other building. We'll need more room. Add these people to the list." He had been scribbling while talking and tore the sheet with the extra names from the pad and gave it to the RN secretary.

"Top priority, you understand?"

"Yes, sir."

"And bring your notebook to the meeting."

"Yes, sir."

When the secretary left the room, Churchill ordered whatever was on the menu for dinner for three right away. Johnny turned to him and said, "I cannot report to your Cabinet on the Goering plan, Winston. At the Air Marshal's request, I gave him my oath that not a word was to be copied down about the plan. Even if we agree to it, we still would have to consult with the Allies; and if we don't agree to it, we certainly don't want a soul to know that we ever considered it, do we?"

"You shouldn't have given your word," Churchill said.

Johnny sighed. "If I hadn't been told about the Goering plan, I never would have imagined the deep defeatism that I saw spreading through the German populace, from top to bottom, giving me those firsthand impressions that you appear to value so much."

"He's got a point," said Tony Eden.

Churchill pulled out a cigar. After puffing on it for a minute or so, he finally said, "You're right. I was wrong. You have always honored your word. I was out of order, Johnny. I'm sorry."

Johnny accepted his friend's apology. The PM ordered Goering's plan off the table, meaning it could not be discussed until he put it back. They settled down to a simple repast that gave Johnny just enough energy to carry him through the remainder of the evening. In the meantime, while dining, they returned to the more intimate details of Johnny's journey from the concentration camp to the plane carrying him back to England, all being amazed that he had survived the experience.

I cannot report to you what went on in that Cabinet meeting, for Johnny refused to give me any of the important details, except that it lasted much longer than he expected. He added that he had never before seen so much passion expressed by so many brilliant and highly esteemed Englishmen on both sides of the issue. Winston had brought in a few additional colleagues whom he felt were needed to round out the occasion, including three eminent judges, and Clement Atlee, leader of the Labour Party. In spite of being on opposite ends of the political spectrum, they enjoyed each other's company when away from the House of Commons.

Of course, there had been no recording secretary in the room, and all attending participants had given their personal oath to Winston Churchill that they would never speak or write of the meeting again, if the vote on the issue was no. If the vote was yes, the same rule would apply until an agreement had been worked out between Churchill's group and Goering's appointees.

As we all know, the vote was no. Johnny was congratulated by one and all for his presentation. Winston thanked him with a little speech covering Johnny's career, referring to him as "my very dear and faithful friend from before the First World War to now, who has been my valiant right arm, without whom I do not know what I would have done, or even if I would be here in my present position right now."

Johnny quickly stood up on a chair, and in a clear voice, with a smile on his face, said, "I promise you, Winston, with or without me, you would be right where you are now standing! We need you, remember?" At that there was much laughter, and much clapping, for both of them.

Johnny then went to another room that had been reserved for him and put through his call to the telephone number that he had been given. A man's voice, sounding very much like Dr. Schmidt's, answered. Johnny spoke the word: "Red." There was a moment's silence, and then the phone went dead.

At Winston's request, Johnny remained overnight in a small bedroom, for the PM had arranged for Johnny to be debriefed the next morning, after which he was to have lunch at 10 Downing Street, the Prime Minister's official residence. Churchill had made sure that Johnny would be occupied in the underground office by the debriefing until well after midday.. Then Johnny was to be transported to 10 Downing Street in the PM's own official car. Johnny knew none of this at the time. It had been a long and eventful day, and Winston wished him a good night's sleep – a generous gesture by the PM, for the night hours were his favorite time for talking.

Johnny, though he was aching for his wife's presence, had no trouble falling asleep.

It was the beginning of October 1944, some seven months before the end of the European war. Mother was in her element, riding the crest of her own wave. In 1942 she had been appointed to the position of Director of the Information and Hospitality Centre for American and Dominion Forces and Visitors, housed in the English Speaking Union building on Charles Street. It was a non-paying position, but it was tailored for Mother's many talents. With a superb paid staff chosen by Mother, all working their hearts out under Mother's benign example, she was sitting pretty.

Mother had also created welcoming hospitality satellite offices in every major city in or around which US or Dominion troops were stationed. Their purpose was to introduce officers and men of the US and Dominions into compatible British family homes on their days off or on weekend passes. Mother started with a bang, renting the offices, staffing them, training and supervising the office staff, building an ever-growing roster of hosts, carefully cataloguing interests and backgrounds, and making herself available for any office in crisis. It never happened.

Mother's organizing skills had helped her over many obstacles in the early days. Given, in addition, her connections to the seats of power, she soon became besieged with invitations from the top brass, who appreciated what she and her staff were doing for their men. So she never lacked for social lunches and dinners with the many generals passing through town, not to forget the American ambassador, John Gilbert Winant, whom she admired greatly. They were good friends, he seeking her advice on many subjects pertinent to his duties. Mother refrained from inquiring about his social life, knowing of his ongoing love affair with an adorable English lady a few years his junior, whose pedigree was spotless and whose situation was "free." He was married, but had left his wife out of danger in the States.

It was a joy to see him and his lady friend together, and most of what remained of London society was betting on their getting married after the war was over and an amicable divorce could be arranged. At the war's end, Ambassador Winant did indeed return to his wife and asked her for a divorce. She refused, remaining adamant; finally, in desperation and brokenhearted, he committed suicide. A sad tale indeed.

Mother, who was just back from one of her once-a-month weeklong trips to visit the satellites most needing attention, was on the phone to the Mayor of High Wycombe, Eighth Bomber Command's Headquarters, when her personal secretary gave her a hand signal, in the shape of a V, meaning someone of real importance was on the other line. Mother excused herself to the Mayor, saying she would call him right back, and picked up the red phone on her desk.

It was Clementine Churchill on the phone, asking Mother's help in entertaining a VIP whom she felt sure Minerva would enjoy; she herself was not feeling up to snuff that day, and anyway Minerva was so much better at this kind of thing than she was.

Mother agreed to her request. She would be there at one o'clock. She then reconnected with the Mayor of High Wycombe. Finally, she also called the office of General Ed Betts, the commanding officer of the Judge Advocate's Office of the Eighth Bomber Command; with some embarrassment, since the general was out of the office at that time, she left word that her luncheon with him on that day had been checkmated by 10 Downing Street; it would have to be postponed until another time.

Mother arrived at the PM's residence almost on the dot and was ushered into a smaller room than she had expected, used as she was to the drawing room and the dining room. Taking a seat, she wondered why she hadn't asked for some background on this guest of honor, but this was her first day back from her trip to the satellites, so she already had more than she could cope with as it was.

There was a rustle behind her chair, as if a curtain was being opened. She rose, turned around, and screamed. Johnny came forward, and put his arms around her, neither saying a word, both holding each other tight, Mother finally bursting into tears. Johnny then caressed her, saying over and over again, "My darling, oh, my darling, oh, my darling."

Having waited a respectable time, Winston and Clementine then entered, their faces wreathed in smiles. Winston said to Mother, "Minerva dear, it's been a long time, hasn't it?"

"Too long, far too long," said Mother. "Can I keep him now?"

"For a while," Winston said. "I've got something I want him to do, and he wants to do it, but first he needs to have a complete checkup by his doctor, and you are going to feed him back to his prime again, aren't you, Minerva?"

"That I promise," said Mother, wondering what in the world had caused Johnny to come home in this condition. Not that it really mattered. Johnny was home again, and if Johnny was home, all was right with Mother's world.

They moved to the dining room. Over lunch, Winston told Mother about Johnny's new assignment, which was to take over the search for the remainder of the perpetrators of the cold-blooded massacre of fifty RAF airmen, many having been good friends of Johnny's. It would require some time away from Mother, but London would be his base of operations to which he would return after every field operation. Winston also told Johnny, in front of Mother, that he would have the assistance of an American officer from the OSS [the predecessor of the CIA], whom he would find very helpful, the officer having had similar experience against the Japanese, who had also committed atrocities against American forces.

Mother accepted Winston's and Johnny's agreement. What else could she do? But for now, she would have Johnny to herself, her desire and her duty being to bring this physical wreck of a man back to normal in mind, body, and soul. With bountiful loving and caring, she intended to effect a miracle for this man, her man. He was emaciated physically and mentally from months of abandonment and helplessness and semi-starvation, his spirit hanging between life and death, enduring an utter sense of aloneness, with only a faint glimmer of hope to sustain him. And here he was – alive.

Mother vowed to herself that she would somehow accomplish both her work for the troops and the rehabilitation of her beloved Johnny, whatever it took. She sat back and looked at Winston, sitting at the head of the table talking with Johnny, both in a relaxed, jocular mood, Johnny laughing appreciatively with his friend and longtime mentor.

Mother, who appreciated Winston's amazing energy in the face of the unbelievable burdens of the war and of his office, decided that her sacrifices were minute when compared with his. After they said their thank yous and goodbyes, Mother took Johnny for a leisurely stroll through Hyde Park, breaking up their walk on a bench by the Serpentine. There they sat, hand in hand, with the need to feel the certainly of each other's presence.

Together again at last, they watched the ducks and the swans swim slowly by, and, for the first time in a very long time, they felt a loving sense of peace. At least they were back together again. For now, that was everything.

On the School Front

As mentioned above, Selwyn House had been evacuated from Broadstairs, Kent, like most of the other private preparatory schools in the flight path of the enemy bombers. The Manor House, in a village not far from Oswestry, Wales, had now become a school that easily accommodated its seventy-two boys plus domestic staff. It had many rooms that were quite large enough for dormitories and classrooms, plus a large dining room, a recreation room, a private master's room, a big kitchen, and – for the moment, at least – a full staff.

John Green, the headmaster, had sent ahead the material that I was to teach the young students – seven to nine years old, in classes of eight – so by the time I arrived at the school I had prepared myself as well as I could. At the end of the mid-term examinations, Green, who had taken quite a risk in employing me, complimented me on my teaching, all my students but one having passed with good marks. The lone holdout was cursed, I believe, by the same handicap that I had. He was such a nice, well-behaved little fellow, and my heart went out to him.

Rationing was in full force, with one egg every six weeks, and limited amounts of butter, sugar, meat, candies, and so on: everything that had been a normal ingredient of our lives was being restricted or given up entirely for "the duration," however long that might be. Mother told me that Flora was having Fisk deliver a box to 10 Downing Street every week containing butter, eggs, milk, and cream, plus some of the vegetables she grew, including American corn on the cob. Palmer was still working the farm for her, his job being characterized by the government as necessary to the war effort, with the remainder of Flora's produce being dispensed by local authorities. Winston, being Winston, kept only the vegetables, but had the butter, cream, milk, and eggs sent to a Restorium for badly wounded soldiers. His private secretary sent a note of thanks to Flora at the end of every month.

The Squire, owner of the Manor House, had moved into a much smaller house on the grounds; soon thereafter he was called to duty by his regiment, the Welsh Guards. The Guards' Honorary Colonel, Viscount Evan Tredegar, our friend and super host, had recently been appointed Master of the Pigeons, or some such title; this gave him the responsibility of caring for and programming the carrier pigeons, who were capable of flying between England and camouflaged destinations in France, protected by members of the French Underground Resistance. After the pigeons made their landing, a tiny cylinder attached to the bird would be opened; after its message had been read, another message would be inserted into the cylinder in response. The bird would be fed and allowed to rest, following which it would return to its home base with its new message attached. These were very special pigeons, extremely well trained; they provided a conduit for the exchange of vital information and directives between the British Military Intelligence and the French Underground Resistance, all at little cost or danger in transit.

Only one schoolmaster at our school was called up, a very healthy and energetic gentleman. However, he failed his physical exam because of hemorrhoids. He seemed quite happy when he returned.

On arrival at the school, I discovered that the domestic staff was lodged in the school building or, if local, in their own homes. The teachers were placed in cottages already occupied by tenants on the estate, with only one bathroom per cottage to be shared by all its residents. Maybe John Green wanted to sugarcoat my remuneration, which was a pittance, but I was glad to have it, and even gladder to be given my own private bathroom, my cottage being the only one that actually had two bathrooms.

I was not the only new teacher. Along with me was a very attractive young teacher named Gabrial Palethorp, the daughter of the famous sausage (banger) maker. We clicked right away, and enjoyed long afternoons on our bikes and even longer horseback riding periods, thanks to the generosity of another squire living close by who had his own stables and let us use his horses whenever we wanted. That was usually once a week, weather permitting, on a Thursday, our chosen afternoon off.

Gabrial was a delight, warm and affectionate, but neither of us stepped outside the recommended bounds of propriety, keeping things going with hugs and kisses but no more. Fortunately for both of us, my hormones hadn't yet seen the light of day! I hope she had a happy, fulfilling life after our brief and chaste romance.

It was only after we had liberated Paris while I was with the SHAEF Diplomatic Mission to the French government in 1944, that a French gentleman and real friend gave me the key to enjoying and being enjoyed by the fairer sex. He introduced me to Jacqueline, whom I would surmise was in her mid-thirties to my age of twenty-two. The most gorgeous, sensual, intelligent, lovely lady I could ever have imagined, she took me under her wing and, with great tenderness and affection, taught me the joys of physical love, along with the art of fulfilling a woman's desires. The male's preoccupation with his jewel beneath his bellybutton should, I learned, be put on hold until he fulfilled his lady's wants, his hands, lips, and tongue far more exciting to her then his throbbing member. He was also always to go slowly, building the tension gradually. Only then might he enter the gates of paradise. Above all, he was not just to desire her, but to LOVE her. This advice, so freely given and with such passionate results, carried me through some wondrous affairs in different countries, of which you may hear later.

But for now, I am wet behind the ears, an impressionable young man in his eighteenth year, who enjoys his employment more than he ever thought, constrained only by a schoolmaster's pay from making it his life career. In short, I closed the door on that idea and turned my attention to a more immediate challenge. Great Britain was in dire peril, stripped of practically all weapons of war, with only the far outnumbered RAF fighting valiantly in the skies in what should have been a complete rout but was not yet. Our pilots were performing miracles in the air war, but with great loss of planes and lifes. The only bright spot in the picture was the fact that the German Luftwaffe was losing three of their planes to every one of the RAF's. It was a grim and scary time.

Hitler's enormous military might was drawn up close across the English Channel, where it waited for Goering's Air Force to destroy what little remained of our defenses. The Air Force was to bombard our cities into submission, leaving the projected invasion as a mere mopping-up affair. Clearly, it was time for me to join the Home Guard, a civilian volunteer force created to watch over the entire country, with orders to report any unusual activity to the nearest command center and to defend its area to the best of its ability, should Hitler's admirals and generals invade by air or by sea.

For me this would mean a six-hour service span, twice a week, day or night, in the hills around Selwyn House, my eyes trained on the skies, ever watchful for enemy forces parachuting into our peaceful, green, and pleasant land, with murder and mayhem on their mind. In the event, what were we to do? I soon found out.

As the new man on the Home Guard Security Detail, I started out being given the hours from midnight until six in the morning – the graveyard beat – every Monday and Friday night. For my first night my commander had done me the courtesy of coming to the school and leading me on our bikes to the rendezvous, where we were all expected to be in attendance at midnight on the dot, to be given our instructions, which were to keep awake and on no account to lose our weapons.

Our commander, Sergeant Archibald Smith, turned out to have been in the cavalry in the First World War. He was obviously shell-shocked then and certainly now, for he constantly contradicted his own orders mid-sentence, with devastating repercussions.

He was middling sized, with an enormous black moustache – far too large for his size, but his pride and joy, nevertheless – and with eyes either vacant or intense. He wore a kilt of no particular clan day in and day out, with nothing underneath.

We arrived at the headquarters on the top of a hill surrounded by other hills, where I was introduced to my fellow warriors as Corky, a name my commander had laid upon me halfway to our destination. I had no idea why he chose it, but I soon felt at home among the others, whose nicknames were all somewhat ribald but descriptive of some trait in their behavior. There was, for instance, Big Bertha, originally the name of an enormous gun the Germans had used in the First World War; that name, which soon evolved into Bertha, served to dignify a portly member of the Home Guard who suffered from extreme flatulence; he could actually play bizarre chords that reverberated off the hills in an elephantine concert when he was in the mood, a feat that always brought on amazement and reverence for the man's unique talent. And then there was Pee Wee, a little man with a weak bladder, who would stand for ages waiting for the last drop to drop, while his pals made bets on when it would end, the one nearest to the minute winning the pot.

It seemed to me that all these men – and the others were all way beyond recruitment age – had strong and very independent personalities, so that our commander had serious tantrums of exasperation on every occasion when he tried to turn us into soldiers. Of course, it didn't help that halfway through his command "Forward, march" he would contradict himself, and it would come out "Forward, reverse march," with half the contingent going one way and half the other. This meant that the entire formation would end up in a tangled mess of cursing guardsmen on the ground, their commander taking wild leaps into the air and shouting incoherently at the moon.

As to our weapons, they were an equal farce. I was given a three-pronged farmer's fork, used for digging or lifting things, with which I was supposed to wait until the German soldier dangling from the end of his parachute got close enough above me and then thrust it upward. Failing this, I was to leap upon him, my fork held at his throat, and hold him there until he was taken off to a prisoner-of-war camp. I had decided that the latter strategy would work better for me.

The only guns we had were for hunting birds and rabbits, and, for the majority who didn't have guns, there were some amazing groups with their own defense weapons. There was a bow and arrow group, half of whom were out of action because of misdirected arrows – they called it "friendly fire" – and a group that put together Molotov cocktails, small but easy to make explosives that could cripple a tank if placed between the caterpillar tracks and the tank itself. Happily, there was no need to use them.

We even had a so-called Military Band, consisting of one mouth organ, one drum, and one pair of castanets, an extraordinary mismatch that, although played with sublime enthusiasm by their obviously tone-deaf musicians, inevitably brought the entire Home Guard to out-of-mind hysterics. We had grown men actually rolling on the ground, completely out of control, laughing uproariously until their lungs were hurting, their rib cages aching, and their eyes flooding. And still they went on laughing!

I, too, was among that group of maniacs thrashing around on the ground. When I finally surfaced, becalmed, I began to wonder if this ridiculous three-piece band that had such an effect on grown British men and me wouldn't have the same effect on German men; if so, why not make a recording of its repertoire and let the BBC broadcast it continuously, day and night, on a separate channel, to both our friends and foes, wherever in Europe they might be. I am quite sure that you cannot laugh uncontrollably and shoot a gun at the same time.

Anyway, I still think it was a good idea.

My two-year involvement with the Home Guard was an exhilarating experience. The characters were so hilarious and endearing, and we all became such good buddies, that just thinking about them today gives me a giggle and a good feeling of those happy, crazy days with some of the most outlandish and wonderful friends I have ever known.

One of our masters on the staff, in his early thirties I would say, married, wrote a letter to some person of his political persuasion (Socialist) whom he obviously wanted to impress. In his letter he boasted that he was subversively injecting the ideas and purpose of Socialism into his authorized class agenda, since now was the time to sow the seeds before his students' minds could be challenged by the opposition, Liberals and Conservatives alike. The letter was returned for "no such address" and was put among John Green's letters, there being no name listed with the return address.

John, the headmaster, read it and, of course, was shocked. He called the letter writer on the mat. The master first excused it as nothing more than a bad joke, but finally admitted his guilt and was fired on the spot. I later ran across him after the war, when he was a salesman for a liquor company, and he told me that he was now a Stalinist communist.

Another teacher, who had been with the school for some years, never married, went to the headmaster and told him that he and his lady friend were soon going to be parents, and what did he think he should do? John, having had no clue that his master was even dallying with a lady, promptly called a friend and headmaster in another part of the country and asked him if he needed another schoolmaster. His friend said that one of his schoolmasters had been called up and was reporting to the army soon after; thus, provided that they arrived as man and wife, they could use a flat near the school and start fresh with the next term.

John and his wife, Joan, attended the simple wedding service of this couple in a church in Oswestry, with a small reception after, and saw the happy newlyweds off at the station with a generous bonus on top of the master's salary and best wishes for a new life at another school, many, many miles away. And so a scandal was avoided that in those days could have seriously affected the school's image.

As for me, I was becoming a very troubled young man. Every last one of my friends was either in one of the services or had been killed. I was nearing the end of my second year as a teacher – and a good teacher, John had told me – though my spelling left much to be desired. The Home Guard, so dear to my heart and an excuse for madcap lunacy twice a week, would have been wiped out in a few minutes by well-armed and trained German soldiers, however brave and resourceful we might be, with only our crazy military band offering a momentary diversion.

To Sea

I was feeling tremendously guilty at not being in uniform at my age. It was only when I saw a story in the American magazine *Time*, about the enormous loss of cargo ships and their crews, that I thought to question whether you really had to swear allegiance to the King in order to enter the British Merchant Navy. As usual, I called Mother, who called a Mr. Booth, an acquaintance of hers who owned the Booth Shipping Line operating out of Liverpool, who told her that no such allegiance was necessary; moreover, he said, the British Merchant Navy was desperate for seamen, the risk being so high now as to be giving former Merchant seamen second thoughts about re-enlisting in the Merchant Navy – a few trying to get into the Royal Navy instead.

Mr. Booth and Mother arranged for me to report to the ship two weeks after the end of my last term at Selwyn House, a matter of just over one month. My category as a seaman would be as deck boy, the very bottom of the bottom, with the entire crew practically empowered to give me orders. I began to have reservations, but knew that I could never look myself in the face again if I backed out now, so I decided to go for it, come what may. I quickly told the headmaster of my decision, and he took it very well, offering me a berth at the school if I ever wanted to come back.

In spite of the negatives, at least I would be able to hold my head up and know that I was on active service, on an equal footing with my friends, and possibly at considerably greater risk than they were. The German U-boat submarines were chewing up Britain's pipeline to our markets abroad with an insatiable appetite, Britain's very life depending on the goods brought back to England safely by the British Merchant Navy.

I packed up and said my goodbyes with some regret, for it had been a placid and easygoing two years, except for knowing that I could always expect the unexpected when among my buddies in the Home Guard. Soon it was time to go, first to London and Mother, then to the Adelphi Hotel in Liverpool, and finally aboard the ship that would be my home for many, many weeks, my world turned upside down.

But so what? I was finally in the war!

While I was back in London with Mother, we took to going to as many plays, particularly musicals and comedies, as we had time for. One play, a lush musical by Ivor Novello with Novello himself starring, gave us a very uncomfortable and suspenseful time. The scene on stage was of London being bombed – as I recall, with the hero and heroine seeking a safe shelter, faced with the blast of bombs bursting, the flash of flames, and the sound of antiaircraft guns going off while miniature searchlights pinpointed the stage's simulated night sky. It was impressive make believe, but what was even more impressive was the fact that a real bombing raid with real bombs was raining down on London just outside the theater building. Nobody spoke. Nobody moved. And when the real sirens' all clear rang out after the real raid had passed, we all clapped wildly, as did Ivor Novello and the entire cast on stage.

After the war I was told that that was the only night the two bombing raids, one theatrical and one for real, were synchronized. Just as well.

I also managed to get in half a dozen rides around Rotten Row in Hyde Park on my wonderful horse, Fidler, courtesy of Mr. Bruce, the ever-gracious stablemaster who had now known me for some fourteen years. I had also reconnected with Juliet McCloud, daughter of the McCloud of McClouds, whose heritage was woven into Dunvegan Castle on the Isle of Skye, where the family lived and entertained before the war, including Mother and Johnny and me for one long weekend. The experience was breathtaking, with bagpipes announcing dinnertime, seals lolling on the rocks below, and fairies sometimes seen in the gorse, a wild evergreen shrub with pretty yellow flowers and sharp thorns to protect them from intruders. The fairies also had their own flag flying at the top of a flagpole to confirm when they were in residence. When this flag was down during long, miserable winters, they were rumored to have been seen on the beaches of sunny Brighton, playing fairy net-ball with much enthusiasm.

Juliet was a delightful companion and a gifted portrait painter, not of people but of horses; after the war she made a very good living with a never-ending list of people wanting their favorite horse or pony painted by such a talented lady. During some of my time before leaving for Liverpool, we would spend afternoons together when she was not painting; we would go to the music room upstairs and put on records of romantic foxtrots to dance to, and for a brief hour or so life was awfully good.

During a couple of mornings, I was at the English Speaking Union, where Mother was the Queen Bee. She helped me to pick out the most suitably bedraggled-looking but serviceable clothes to wear on my trip, my tailor-made suits and blazers not being appropriate for my new and very subordinate station on the ship.

Finally, Benita, a particularly adorable girlfriend, and my beloved mother shared that last luncheon with me at the Causerie at Claridge's. Then it was off to the station for Liverpool, where with tears and hugs I left them to return to their homes, since the idea of their waiting on the station platform for the train to leave was too much for all of us to bear. Dealing with the staff at home had been bad enough, and the day before, at the English Speaking Union, it was as if they were sure I was never coming back again. Maybe I wasn't, but I didn't want to be told so right up front. Anyway, they all meant well, and I was very fond of our staff, not to mention my two half brothers, their dear nanny, and Mother's staff at the ESU. They were all good and hard-working people, whose memory I would cherish way into the future.

The Adelphi Hotel in Liverpool was quite luxurious, and I was pleased with my room and bath and the courteous staff. What was even better was that Fanny Ricketson-Hatt, who had divorced B. Ricketson-Hatt, the head of Reuters and our good friend, was staying overnight at this hotel with her new husband, who just happened to be the president of the company that owned a group of hotels including the Adelphi.

At dinner they had a hard time understanding why I had chosen the British Merchant Navy, in spite of my protestations that there was not another service open to me that I knew about if I wanted to stay an American. I reminded them that, without the British Merchant Navy, the entire population would be slowly but surely starved to death. The farmers would be incapable of growing enough food on their own to feed anywhere near what the population needed, since we depended on the safe importation of an enormous amount of food from overseas, plus all the other goods that held our lives together. Obviously, the German U-boats were not helping our situation one bit. We finally got on to less controversial subjects, and when we said goodnight and goodbye, I somewhat envied them, comparing my immediate future with theirs.

I had left a wake-up call at the desk, and sure enough the phone rang by my bed promptly at six a.m., giving me just enough time to shave, dress in my "go to work clothes," have breakfast, read the newspaper ("Coventry Badly Hit by German Bombers"), and order a taxi. The porter, who had been on duty when I had arrived the day before, was now giving me an almost critical look of disfavor.

I gave the taxi driver the address at which my ship was berthed and crawled back into my innermost sanctuary, where I gathered my strength together for whatever lay in store for me on this, my first day in the British Merchant Navy. I had the taxi driver drop me off a block from the Liverpool docks and walked the rest of the way. After all, I was only a deck boy now.

The S.S. Benedict

With my official documents and papers, plus passport and boarding pass in my care, I walked up the gangplank and was greeted by the ship's officer. After taking away all my documents and papers, leaving me with just my passport and boarding pass, he looked at me somewhat incredulously and told me to report to the bosun (boatswain) on the aft deck.

There were several seamen with mops and pails swabbing the decks, while others chipped away at the ship's rusted railings. Off to the side sat a wizened old man who could only be someone's great-grandfather returning to the old country to die. Since everyone else was working, I took a chance and asked him if he knew where the bosun might be found. For at least a minute he stared at me with considerable curiosity; then he said, "I'm the bosun; you're Sherman, aren't you?" I admitted that I was. He then told me to relieve one of the seamen whittling away on the ship's rails; I would have a ten- minute break at the end of every half hour, sounded by the bell on the bridge. At noon we would break for lunch and, this being my first day, I could have the afternoon off. After that, I was to be onboard promptly at eight a.m. every day to receive my assignment. By watching the other seamen, he indicated, I would soon learn how to be a good one myself.

The ship would be sailing very soon, but the crew would be given only three hours in which to hustle their bags aboard before we would stand by for departure. Only then would each seamen's watch be posted on the corkboard under cover midships. I prayed that I would have more bridge duty than working below deck in the cargo hold while in port, or stuck on deck with a pail and mop for mindless hours of boredom.

When the bell from the bridge rang at noon, I was plumb worn out, but rather than return to the hotel, I decided to see if someone other than the bosun would talk to me; until then, the other seamen had ignored me as if I were invisible. All but one of the seamen went below or exited the ship for a brief respite ashore; that one, after making sure that no one but I was left, crossed the deck toward me and introduced himself as Dunn, asking me where my lunch was.

I told him that I hadn't brought a lunch, whereupon he said he had a big sandwich that he would share with me. Since he had already found out that I and two others had been assigned to his cabin, why didn't I go below with him and choose my bunk before the other two showed – if they even showed, since some of them might be seeking other ways to serve their country.

Dunn was a rugged-looking man, two years my junior, about five foot nine, with a broken nose and brown eyes, his thick hair smothered with pomade, shiny like a veritable billiard ball, but nice. He seldom used the "F" word, unlike his companions, who seemed to have dispensed with all adjectives except that particular one. I suppose it makes the art of conversation easier.

Dunn took me into our cabin, a small space with a porthole and four bunks in twos, one up and one down. I took the up one over Dunn's bunk, having always enjoyed the upper berth from the time Mother had taken me with her to Reno, Nevada, where she had obtained her divorce. The train trip from New York was a three days and nights event, the clickety clack of the train's wheels transporting me to never-never land in no time at night, much to Mother's relief.. The views from the observation car during the daytime filled my memory with a multitude of impressions, many of which are still with me to this day. I wouldn't leave my viewing window until the uniformed attendant came through the train bringing us the good word that breakfast, lunch, or dinner was now being served in the dining car. At that age (four or five), I was always hungry.

On the good ship S.S. *Benedict*, things were somewhat different. The other two occupants of our cabin finally arrived within hours of our departure, both well groomed in the ways of merchant seamen, but completely at sea where I was concerned, neither one looking directly at me and both inclined to speak in whispers. After a couple of weeks, they stopped whispering and accepted my presence with some reservation.

As for Dunn, he was an enormous help, in spite of the fact that the first four days and nights of our journey at sea found me laid out on my bunk with *mal de mer*, not throwing up but feeling incredibly weak and helpless.

Truth to tell, I thought I had left my problems with seasickness behind when I was about fifteen and Johnny had begged me to go with him on the good ship *Florida* for an afternoon's sail in the English Channel. The sea was choppy, but I was so infatuated with Pam, the captain's daughter, that I completely forgot about my malady. In fact, I had thought that from then on I was cured. Apparently not; but Dunn, and even the bosun, who checked on me every day, had to admit that we were going through very heavy seas, and that most of the passengers were suffering as much as I was.

On the fourth day I began to get my sea legs, and on the fifth the bosun put me to work on the passenger's deck forward, scrubbing away while some of the passengers, particularly the females, insisted on engaging me in conversation. As soon as the bosun saw my brief social interlude, he sent another sailor to relieve me and put me to work on the poor old railings, followed by cleaning up my cabin. He finally relieved me to have my dinner (ghastly) and go to bed.

While I was feeling so ill, I missed the arrival of the British Navy's great ships forming in convoy to shepherd some forty to fifty cargo ships way out into the Atlantic – an enormous cargo fleet that would soon be released to go it alone to their own destinations through German submarine U-boat infested waters, many of them never to be seen again. We had one sailor onboard, the only survivor of his ship's sinking with all hands but him, much to our own sailor's chagrin, for the others took him to be a bad omen, sailors being somewhat more superstitious than others, maybe because they have more reason to be.

Wonder of wonders! I had been on the bridge in service on the graveyard watch for two nights in a row, an assignment that took me off deck-scrubbing, rust-destroying misery. If I could just keep my eyes open! Why did I always get the graveyard watch? I really wasn't complaining, for eventually I grew to love this watch, where, in addition to looking for signs of German U-boats, I could have a crystal clear view of those fabulous stars in the heavens, the atmosphere being utterly free of pollution, such that you wanted to reach out and pluck a star itself from that brilliant sky. Of course, there was always another side to things: A dark, cloudy night, particularly if the waves were steep, ensured a much safer passage than a brilliant, moonlit night with little waves and a churning wake.

The day after I returned to work, the Royal Navy exchanged flag signals with the beneficiaries of its protection and ever so slowly eased away from us. It then set course to shepherd another fleet returning from distant lands with a multitude of goods to support Great Britain's many needs.

We, it would turn out, were on our way to Brazil.

My duties on the graveyard watch were simple. First, I was to be constantly on the lookout for U-boat submarines, with binoculars if needed, roving in an entire circle of water every few minutes, always looking for that periscope, the one reflective object that could be the warning sign that your destruction was close at hand; indeed, the torpedo might already be on its way. We had a medium-sized gun, depth charges, and hope.

The officer on watch with me the first night, and every third night, was the senior officer, who was held in some contempt by the captain, I had been told. I stood on the bridge in the open, while the watch officer stood or sat on a stool by the helmsman. He rarely if ever said a word to the helmsman and rarely communicated with me, except to send me down to the kitchen for a mug of hot tea and a sweet roll, or sometimes a donut. Since the lookout sailor was not permitted to eat or drink while on the bridge, I had to go to the kitchen some distance away, drink thirty seconds worth of tea and eat thirty seconds worth of sweet roll, and then carry the watch officer's tea and bun back upstairs from the kitchen and then upstairs from the upper deck, which on rough nights was not an easy matter. This particularly strange officer timed me. Five minutes was the limit, there and back. I always made it, as did the others, so no one ever learned what the punishment for being late might be.

From the wheelhouse, the duty officer could see the bathroom door on the covered passageway of the top deck level, one stairway down from the wheelhouse. This senior officer, whom I will call Hector, rarely looked beyond the bathroom door while on his watch, even though he was supposed to cover the entire waterfront every five minutes with his binoculars; thus he left me with the responsibility of covering for him without being asked. His fetish, if word of it had reached the captain's ears, could no doubt have ended his career, although, since the Merchant Navy was in an emergency state with regard to more crew members, he might well have gotten off with a slap on the wrist. Anyway, I kept my mouth shut and glimpsed his shady performance briefly between the constant lookout duty which was imperative for me faced with this officer's gross negligence of duty.

What Hector desired was to see one of the young lady passengers come from her cabin in her dressing gown and bath towel and disappear behind the bathroom door. When that happened, he gave the helmsman a twenty-minute break, something he never gave me, since I think he felt I was there only to serve him mugs of tea, sweet buns, and, if he was lucky, a three a.m. sandwich. Now he stood at the wheel, no doubt feeling godlike, his mind flooding with desire; then, satisfied the ship was on course, he left the wheel and started tracing his imaginary conquest in the air, finally jerking himself in sexual thrusts. His body was apparently echoing what was going on in his inflamed mind, which was no doubt projected on the other side of the bathroom door, relieving the pretty young lady of her greatest asset, without her feeling a thing. He was transparent and disgusting. I doubt if he had ever actually enjoyed a woman. He was so obviously ill at ease and tongue-tied when in their company.

I was hearing much talk of women among the sailors, who by now had finally accepted me, not quite as one of them, but as an oddball who had suddenly appeared out of nowhere and needed guidance and protection, of which I am glad to say I received plenty. The bosun turned out to be self-educated, well read, biographies being his favorite, with Bulldog Drummond and Lord Peter Whimsey being his thrillers of choice, and finally Charles Dickens for historical fodder. He was eighty-two years old and had been a sailor since the age of fourteen. He was not quite comfortable with me, nor I with him, but we grew to enjoy each other, and I couldn't help but remember my first meeting with him. Sometimes appearances can be deceiving.

As for the two seamen sharing our cabin, they were reasonably normal. The smaller one, Bert, had a uniquely wavering snore that was actually soothing and did not disturb our sleep at all. His pal, Scotty, was a big, strapping man with a slow and steady approach to life. When we reached the waters of tropical Brazil, in the height of summer, we all slept naked, with no covers, and I, who was usually up before the others in order to get to shower and shave first, was always amazed to see that Scotty, although sound asleep, would be empowered with a full erection! I discussed this later with the ship's doctor, who told me that it was not at all unusual and did not depend on a sexual dream for its instigation.

In order to do something constructive for the seamen, I created an hourlong discussion group that met once a week in the evenings, on deck if the weather was okay and in the kitchen if it wasn't. I encouraged Dunn and Bert and Scotty to participate, and spread the word. The first week it consisted solely of my cabin's occupants, but slowly curiosity got the better of some of the others, and in three weeks the number was up to six, including one wireless operator. I had hoped that I could lead them into worldly subjects that might coach them away from their normal "F"-sprinkled repertoire. Not likely! The repertoire included soccer, of course; movies, of course; girls, of course – in fact, anything but talk about the ship or the war or world events.

Soon after I started the seamen discussion group, the engineering department asked me to start one for them, which I did. Usually four or five attended, talking about their faith more than anything, apparently most of them belonging to a strict Christian sect, originating, I think, in Scotland.

But for now, in this fetid war, as the days passed slowly and monotonously and, for many aboard, fearfully, we were practicing using our mounted gun and increasing the accuracy of our depth charges. Sometimes the sea was heaving with forty-foot waves, while at others, it was calm as a sleeping baby, the beautiful flying fish sometimes landing on the deck, quickly fried by its temperature of one hundred and ten degrees, or a graceful porpoise swimming ahead of us or playing off our stern in the foaming tendrils of the wash.

We were finally approaching our destination, though still a couple of days out. I had never especially liked bananas, but out of the blue I got a great hunger for a banana split. My plan was to order a banana split at the nearest milk bar as soon as we landed in Brazil. When I told the seamen of my need, they appeased me with cries of "of course," although not quite in those words!

And then the duty watch saw a periscope, the sun catching its reflection in the distance, and all hands ran to their appointed stations, mine being the rescue boats, while others rushed to the depth charge stations, and others manned the gun and ammunition. The ship's engines were cut back to idle, and an oppressive silence enfolded us, as we wondered whether the U-boat had actually seen us or not.

Fortunately, the waves were high that day, and we waited for over an hour. Our ship did not dare to drop anchor, and the wind broadsided it, causing not a few of us to be touched by a little *mal de mer*. Finally, the captain gave the all clear, the engines slowly built back up to speed, and a lot of fearful passengers and some sailors returned to whatever they had been doing. The SS *Benedict* strove mightily to make up time, zigzagging until nightfall, a rough and rainy night providing a safety blanket for the ship. My wonderful English Speaking Union had provided me with rainproof and windproof clothing, plus rubber boots that closed at the calf so no water could enter. I was impregnable!

I was quickly coming to the conclusion that, though all aboard this ship could be in dire peril, we were no more so than Mother and everyone else living in targeted cities all over the war zone. It was plain that Hitler's *Blitzkrieg* (lightning war) had cleared the way for open terror upon not only the military combatants, but also the entire civilian population, a new and deadly concept of warfare, only at the turn of the twenty-first century to be carried even further by the activities of terrorists.

I am a fatalist – always have been. If death had my name, there was nothing I could do about it. If it didn't, there was nothing I could do about that either.

In London, for instance, the quickest way to get around town was by the Underground train system. During this period the stations, however, became overnight bomb shelters for Londoners and their families, who brought blankets and pillows and stayed until morning, returning night after night until the German air raids finally came to an end.

I heard of only one Underground station disaster during the war, when a German night bomber dropped a bomb that fell through the Underground entrance and bounced into the bowels of the station, exploding with devastating force and causing many casualties. I believe the same thing happened to HMS *Hood*, among England's biggest warships, when a bomb was dropped from a German plane and fell right through a funnel into the ammunition room. It blew this favorite of the Royal Navy right out of the water, with considerably more than eight hundred sailors lost. Only two survived.

In contrast, Hitler had had Paris mined with explosives that were to be blown up, should Paris ever be about to be taken back by the Allies. When it was obvious, even to Hitler, that the Allies – including me and my SHAEF Diplomatic Mission to the French Government (about which, more later) – were about to enter Paris, Hitler gave the command to destroy Paris immediately. The general in charge of Paris refused, instead ordering that the bombs planted under Paris be defused. He must have known only too well that by this action he was cementing his own death. Thus was Paris saved by a German general with a conscience.

The last days before reaching port were exceedingly tense, for it was on the last leg of our journey to Brazil that disaster was most likely to strike. The U-boats often hunted in packs off the coast of whatever country they were covering. As a result, the cargo ships had to use every trick in their bag to sail around the enemy; in some rare cases, they might even run into or over a U-boat, putting it out of commission or sending it to the ocean's bottom. The SS *Benedict*, for its part, zigged and zagged its way through dangerous waters, all eyes onboard scanning the sea for the sign of a bubbling torpedo's wake reaching the surface; in that case, we would pinpoint its direction and hope that a sudden change of course would save us to live another day. On this journey, however, no such event occurred. The previous periscope incident had shaken up the passengers and a few overly superstitious sailors, the latter fully aware that the only survivor of a previous ship's destruction was onboard this very boat – a bad, bad omen. Fortunately, the Brazilian state of Pernambuco was the survivor's destination, and it was with an enormous sigh of relief that we entered the port docks at Recife and tied up.The passengers were jubilant, ordering champagne for themselves and beer for the crew. None but the passengers were allowed off the ship until the next morning, so after the usual hogwash of a so- called dinner, and the taste of good Dutch beer, I stripped and showered and fell asleep, ready for whatever the new day would bring.

Those in the engineering room were able to take advantage of our stay; leaving only a quartet on duty, they took off down the gangplank with broad grins on their faces, to the accompaniment of loud groans from the seamen. It so happened that the seamen and the engineer room staff rarely spoke to one another, a ridiculous tradition dating back to the birth of a ship's engines when they began to propel the boats, rather then the sails, a transition that also cut back on the number of sailors needed to run the ships. Since I considered myself a member of both groups, and neither side had ever said a word of criticism – at least not to me – I was astounded when my good friend Dunn told me of the tradition. He added that he had first been afraid of what might happen to me for so openly breaking with it, but for some reason no one seemed to mind. I was relieved to learn that, but then neither did anyone follow my example.

We were finally in port, safe for now. As planned, the rest of the seamen and I got off duty the following day, leaving just two seamen and a duty officer to keep watch. I wore a white shirt, open at the collar, with gray trousers, socks, and comfortable walking shoes, which Mother had insisted I pack. It was just as well, since most of the other sailors were attired in similar garb. In my smart civilian outfit I felt a glorious sense of liberation.

Now all ten of us, including the wireless officers, were headed for the milk bar, to finally gratify my longing for a banana split ice cream with banana, and so on. This was fun. Unbelievable fun! I felt like dancing in the street, yelling to the world, "I'm free, I'm free!," hugging a stranger, any stranger. So I did, a little old lady with gray hair in a black mourning dress whose face broke into a grateful smile such as would break your heart. That made me feel better still. At last we found the milk bar, and my seamen took over some of the tables; the manager and his daughter brought us our orders, the radio was turned up, blaring music of the day, and the milk bar suddenly became part dance hall. Some of the sailors were dancing with each other in utter abandon, particularly when the radio blared, "Happy Days Are Here Again." We also had, still ahead of us, the excitement of shops and movie theaters and all the commotion that makes a city a city.

Dear God, it was wonderful again to be alive.

Uptown Recife was like the commercial core of most seaside towns, but with the added flavor of the Portuguese language, spoken in Brazil since that country had been a royal domain of Portugal. Brazilian history is, to my mind, fascinating. The country continued to be favored by immigrants from far and wide, though industry and commerce, in partnership with local powers, were led mostly by the British, Germans, and Italians, at least through the thirties and forties and into the fifties. America's influence and imprint became apparent only toward the end of the forties and thereafter.

There is even a town in the interior of Brazil peopled by descendents of Americans whose loyalty to the British crown necessitated their escaping with their lives during the War of Independence. They ended up in Brazil, where they found rich farmland and nary an enemy in sight. There they thrived in harmony with other settlers. Their language now? Portuguese, of course.

On this, my first visit to Brazil, Getulio Vargas was the President. He was a benevolent dictator adored by most of his subjects, who had brought his nation finally into the twentieth century during a term in office lasting more than twenty years. It ended while I was working in São Paulo with the Royal Dutch Shell Oil Company in the early fifties, when Vargas committed suicide, in response to the country's currency having taken a dangerous fall in value, a problem to which the President had been unable to find a solution. I remember feeling bereaved, for he had done so much good for his country, for so long. I think he was just plain worn out.

At twenty years old, I was anything but! Our passengers had been offloaded to go to their chosen destinations in Brazil, and a new group of passengers were returning to England aboard the *Benedict*. At the moment

I was having enormous pleasure, simple pleasure – the best kind – with Dunn and the other seamen plus the two wireless operators who had become especially good friends of mine. In the hub of Recife, a fascinating and extremely friendly city, a crazy bedlam existed, but joyfully, with car horns blaring; well-attended coffee shops on almost every block; ladies dressed in dresses colorful enough to challenge a peacock; and shop windows bursting with everything that England's shop windows were bare of.

At one, we finally stopped for lunch. Since it was Friday, the main food for the day was *feshuada*, a Brazilian dish that turns a simple rice and beans affair into an extravaganza that is delicious beyond belief. It is a good idea to drink plenty of beer or water along with it, or you may go up in flames.

Before entering the café, I had observed about twenty deck chairs stretched languidly out on the sidewalk begging to be occupied, with an overhead canvas roof to keep the hot sun away and a powerful fan blowing air over a block of ice to ease one's siesta. As we neared the end of our meal, I suggested to my companions that, since they had had quite a bit of alcohol, both before and during lunch – mostly Pinga, a national drink derived from sugar cane, I believe, with a piece of lime; or very good beer from German beer companies – it might behoove us to take advantage of the lounge chairs for an hour or so after lunch.

This idea met with approval. We paid the manager for our lunch, took over ten of the chairs, and were soon fast asleep, only the grunts or snores of three of the men acknowledging what a fine meal they had enjoyed. Afterward, some of them would be embracing their ladies of the night, including very pretty ones, indeed. After the nervous strain of our suspenseful voyage, it didn't take too much to make us happy again. But for me and my two companions, Dunn and Donald, the wireless operator, adventure lay ahead.

When we had finally recovered from our siesta, and watched our sailors heading for their favorite bordello – with one of the two wireless operators trailing along behind them, whether to just look or participate I never found out – the other wireless operator and Dunn and I decided to explore more of the commercial hub of the city. Away we went, window-shopping mostly, but just wallowing in the bubbling scene around us, with the Portuguese language (which the wireless operator with us could speak quite well) sounding to Dunn and me sometimes like a machine gun, sometimes like a love song. Their music was a mix also, though mostly sung with an exuberant beat. Many Brazilian songs have crossed the water to great success in both England and the USA. (Who cannot remember Carmen Miranda, whose funeral I attended in Rio, while working with Royal Dutch Shell in the 1950s? She was stupendous. I had seen her perform at the Palladium in London and had been bowled over by her talent and her energy, as I had been by the silent member of the Marx Brothers. Can you imagine performing for an hour and a half without saying a word and having your audience in the palm of your hand? Absolutely incredible! Also Judy Garland, pure genius. All three performed at the London Palladium at different times.)

Dunn had a small leather bag that his girlfriend back in England had given him, in which he carried a Swiss knife, his passport, and some money. I kept my passport in a secret pocket that my tailor had put in the only pair of gray trousers that I had brought on the trip and was now wearing; my money was locked up in my money belt, designed especially for that purpose. We were shaken out of our complacency when Dunn, who was walking next to the curb, suddenly let out a yell; as we turned to see what the matter was, a man on a motorbike gunned his machine and took off into the heavy traffic with his bag.

Donald, our wireless operator, immediately flagged down a taxi. He gave the cab driver instructions to follow the motorcyclist disappearing into the thick of a very crowded street, a charge that in my personal opinion was bound to be a ridiculous waste of time and money, since it was obvious that a motorcyclist could slither and slide through openings that our taxi certainly could not.

But I didn't know our taxi driver. Of course he must have been demented, or bent on committing suicide and taking all three of us with him. As he rounded street corners at the speed of light, the screeching tires themselves begging for mercy, the complete loss of gravity appeared to make us airbound, as hardly anyone ever ended up on the same seat he had started with. It was pure pandemonium, a group of two brave seamen and one brave wireless operator brought low by one crazed taxi driver.

But, by golly, he finally cornered the perpetrator of the crime in a narrow dead-end street, blocking any egress with his taxi, as all three of us tumbled out onto a wild-eyed and obviously terrified motorcyclist. With the bag back in Dunn's hands, and everything in the bag safe and sound, we let the thief go, though only after Donald scolded him violently in Portuguese with considerable thrashing of arms and many scary threats, until he finally released him, very definitely deflated.

To the taxi driver he gave nothing but praise, forgetting the nightmare of being subject to almost constant flight and seat changing, with certain death being the only way out. But all had ended well, so we asked the driver to take us to a movie theater that was showing a Laurel and Hardy film, which he turned out to have seen with his wife the night before. Though he drove a bit less aggressively, he still kept us white-knuckled and squinty-eyed until we pulled up in front of the theater five minutes before the matinee began. I demanded the taxi driver's bill and gave him double his fare, for, in spite of our trepidation, he had proven to be a brilliant driver and had done just what we had asked him to do. We couldn't have asked for a better man. He gave me a big smile of thanks, and we stood on the pavement waving until he was gone from our sight.

The Laurel and Hardy movie was hilarious, and we laughed uproariously, for the film was in the original English but with subtitles in Portuguese. It didn't deter the Portuguese patrons, who seemed to enjoy it as much as we did, After the movie we adjourned to a ritzy-looking restaurant where I bought my group a delicious French dinner. It had been a really great day for us. Since Mother had generously stuffed a quantity of Brazilian cruzeiros in my belt, it behooved me to share my ill-gotten gains with my two friends, who didn't seem to mind a bit.

And so, back to the good ship and day duty on the bridge for the next day, and finally our voyage to Free Town, West Africa.

This was our last port of call before returning to Liverpool, we hoped, and it was a hellhole if ever there was one, blistering hot and without a breath of air. I don't remember anyone leaving our ship to sample the town's attractions, if indeed it had any. And to make matters worse, on the second day the native workers unloading and loading our cargo went on strike. For two more days we were stuck with nothing much to do but leave the Booth Line representative to bargain with their labor union, while we tried to stay out of the broiling sun. Even though all the ship's fans were running at full speed, the perspiration poured off us, turning our clothes quickly to a soggy mess. The few showers onboard were tied up the entire day.

Though normally not allowed on the ship, because of the strike a couple of boys from the local missionary school, one fourteen and one sixteen, came aboard to earn a little pocket money by diving from the railings of the ship's upper deck into the inky water below. These were scary, high and long dives, but well rewarded, when the crew and passengers threw their small change, piece by piece, over the railings and into the water. Only when the swimmers found that the weight of the bag that was strapped to their chests had become a burden did they climb back up the rope ladder that the seamen had placed there for them and empty their coins into a box that I had provided and over which I now stood guard.

Late in the afternoon, the passengers and crew were no longer able to stand the heat. Even with umbrellas spread out over the passengers' heads, and stewards passing out cold, wet towels, it was just too much. A general exodus now prevailed; with only three passengers and two seamen remaining, I told the two boys, who must have been pretty exhausted by then, to drink some water and call it a day. They drank the water which I provided, in paper cups, but as long as they had an audience they wanted one final jump. I argued with them that, since they had such a good day's diving, why endanger themselves now?

But they were anxious to go in once more, and I really had no authority over them anyway. The few observers still remaining demanded "one more time," so I threw the last few coins I had and watched them disappear into the silken smoothness of the black water. One of the two boys soon bubbled to the surface, holding his bag of coins tightly to his chest. They really had done well this day, and I was so glad for them. We both went to the side of the ship to welcome his tardy friend back, but he was nowhere to be seen; after checking both sides of the ship, my sixteen-year-old, beginning to look nervous, said, "I must find him!" With that, he leaped off the ship's railings and back into the water. I watched the boy coming to the surface to breathe again and again, his time underwater sometimes lasting for three and a half minutes by my watch, and I was praying for his friend to pop to the surface; but it was not to be. Somehow, whether he collided or became entangled with some underwater object, or drowned from staying down too long, perhaps to grasp a particularly enticing coin, we will never know, for he never showed up, dead or alive, while we remained in port. His friend, at the end of his tether, finally climbed back over the rail.

I sat him down to talk. After a long silence, he finally told me that, after the ship departed, he would tell the drowned boy's parents that their son had taken advantage of an offer to join the crew and sail back to England and a new life. Since no one on the ship was aware of the calamity except me, no one needed to know. He warned me to keep silent on the matter, for if it leaked out to the dockyard workers, it could erupt out of control, turning into any excuse for a fight, particularly with the British. It could even lead to mayhem and murder, as the Europeans' sometimes condescending and patronizing ways might drive the dockyard workers mad with rage. That was the first time I discovered that Great Britain was not always regarded with the highest esteem.

On the second day, the strike ended. Two days later, in total darkness, we pulled up anchor and very slowly and silently put Free Town behind us. I continued to feel desperately sad for the boy diver left behind. For such a day of triumph to be followed by such a sad ending somehow didn't seem fair.

On the fifth day at sea, just after lunch, a U-boat surfaced not far from us and fired a torpedo at our ship. We all knew we were done for. I rushed to my station by the lifeboats; the passengers came scrambling up the stairs or out of the passageways, either with their life preservers on or carrying them, and the Captain started yelling orders over the loudspeaker system. The ship suddenly shook, as the second officer in command in the wheelhouse had personally taken the helm and turned the wheel with brute force at full speed. While that could make only a few yards difference in the ship's direction, it was enough to change certain disaster into escape, after which we zigged and zagged, expecting a second torpedo to do what the first had failed to do. But, amazingly, there was none, and I think I know why.

Our ship was smaller than most of the other cargo ships, a mere ten thousand tons, and I can just imagine the U-boat commander thinking to himself, "Damn, I've already wasted one of my torpedoes, and the ship's so small, it's hardly worth another. I'll let this one go and keep what's left of my torpedoes for the big cargo ships." Whether my surmise was accurate or not, the return trip was accomplished through rough seas that made ships harder to see and more difficult to torpedo, and we were so small, it was fair to assume that the enemy had to consider if it was really worth it to attack us.

As for me personally, my failure to partake of the cook's dreadful food was beginning to affect my energy level – not much, but enough to make me aware that my weight loss could be seen on my face, which had developed a pinched look about it. This was not unreasonable when one considers that I had subsisted mainly on dry biscuits and some rare raisin bread, sometimes a sausage (but not a Palethorpe sausage), and once a week, perhaps, an egg. The only time I ate a proper meal was when we had shore leave, and I took considerable advantage of it, but over the long haul of about ten weeks, it added up to very little real sustenance.

Added to this situation was a recent slip on the stairs going down to the engine room, which opened a gash in my left leg just above the ankle in the fleshier part of my calf. The ship's doctor cleaned it, applied iodine (ouch), and changed the bandage every day. He ordered me to have it seen to immediately by my own doctor as soon as we reached port. In spite of the doctor's ministrations, the wound would not heal, and I could see that he was genuinely upset about the situation. It didn't exactly hurt, but I became very much aware of its existence.

Finally, we joined the fleet's convoy back to England's shores and docked safely at the same dock and moorings as before. I bade all my buddies au revoir – both seamen and engine room staff – for none of whom did I have more regard than Dunn, who had truly been a friend in need. I later had the pleasure of taking him to the *Crazy Gang* show in the West End of London, and on to a supper at the London Casino, with chorus girls and a band, which he enjoyed immensely, curious about everything that was new to him. We met one more time, after which I never heard from him again. I did know that he wanted to try another shipping line, though he didn't tell me which one. I hope he survived the war to lead a good life, maybe serving on the *Queen Mary*. He, along with all the British Merchant Navy, deserved only the best. They were a brave bunch of men, and I really don't think they were given the recognition and the gratitude that they deserved.

Because we had docked so early in the morning, I was able to get through to Mother before she left for the English Speaking Union. After tears of joy from both of us, I asked her to make an appointment with our doctor as soon as possible, which made her very uneasy, but I told her that I was just a little undernourished and I was sure everything would be all right. She said she would make the appointment immediately, and then she asked what I would like to do on my first night back home. I told her I'd like to take her and Benita to the Savoy to celebrate my return with my two favorite ladies: a bottle of dry champagne, a good dinner, and Carol Gibbon's great band to accompany our dancing – what a way to go!

Mother said she'd book the table. I was to come to the ESU to pick up a spare key to her, and now our, flat in Halkin Street. She told me that, during my absence, she had mothballed the London house and rented a charming two-room, two-bath flat in Halkin Street, reasonably close to the ESU, releasing the remainder of the staff to go into their chosen war-effort jobs. Bertha, our wonderful chef, was now working on a very large farm in Devon, with many employees, who, in spite of rationing, were, I was sure, enjoying the best cooked meals of their lives. Tony and Nanny had been placed by Mother out of danger's way on a farm in Wales owned by an aged couple, Mr. and Mrs. Moon, who did all the work on the farm themselves. They provided Nanny and her charges with fresh everything, and the chance to take walks on the farm and in the woods beyond, and even to ride a pony, very old and docile, because the Moons preferred ponies to dogs.

Mother's kept Molly, her beloved personal maid. Molly was residing in a small flat with her sister Kitty in Maida Vale, only fifteen minutes away by Underground. Kitty was an aide in a hospital just ten minutes away by Underground. Mother's managerial talents were still going at full steam. I hoped that I could be half as good; that would be a lot.

I was both excited and drained. The excitement was due to being back, safe and sound – though not that sound, nor safe for that matter, for the war was still on and the buzz bombs were still dropping – but at least the subtle strain of constant tension beneath a surface of repetitive monotony was suddenly no more.

London was pretty much the same as I had left it, though with more buildings turned to rubble and parts of London firebombed. The military balloons were still holding London up and at the same time frustrating the German bombers from coming any lower to get a clearer view of their objects of destruction.

That night was a joyful occasion, the Savoy dining room filled with uniforms of every service, as even I was wearing my British Merchant Navy pin on my lapel. Indeed, I was asked by both military and civilian patrons of the Savoy just what it stood for. Feeling slightly resentful, I told them, and it gave me an idea, of which more later in the next chapter.

It was on my third dance with Benita, a slow and very romantic foxtrot – "All the Things You Are" – that my wounded leg went out from under me. With the help of Benita and our waiters, I hobbled back to the table and sat down. Since Mother had booked Dr. McKean for nine the next morning, we cut the evening short; after dropping a very worried Benita off at her home, I returned to Mother's flat, where, with her assistance, I got undressed and into bed.

The leg was beginning to pain me a bit, and she gave me two aspirins, which helped me to go to sleep, during which I had a terrifying nightmare that my leg had just been cut off at the knee. It woke me up with a yell, causing Mother to rush in. She wiped my forehead and stayed with me until I fell asleep again. We didn't know it then, but I already had a temperature of one hundred and one, and it was going up.

On the Edge, 1942

The day that Dr. McKean and the surgeon declared the need for early amputation of my lower leg, which was the day after our night at the Savoy, Mother, with the doctors' prompting, put me into a private nursing home not far from Harley Street, where Dr. McKean both lived and had his practice, and so would be easily available to me in case of emergency. After getting me moved from West Halkin Street to the nursing home in the morning, Mother kissed me goodbye, saying she would be back in the evening and not to worry.

I knew that Mother was capable of overcoming almost any challenge that could be put in her way, but now she would need a miracle, my doctor and the surgeon having both agreed that the gangrene could not be stopped by any medical means available. Amputation was thus the only thing left if I was not to die. Mother left me with a bunch of magazines, which I looked through with blind eyes, registering nothing. The nursing staff came and went, trying to distract me from my morbid fears: the loss of a large part of my leg, or creeping malignancy and the end of my life. Neither prospect appealed to me.

Later that afternoon, I learned what Mother had been up to all day. Apparently, some five weeks before, she had attended a dinner party given by the American Ambassador, John G. Winant, at which she and the American Surgeon General had sat next to each other. At the time, the Surgeon General had confided to Mother that he and his staff were looking for and inspecting structures, away from London, such as large manor houses and other buildings that could be adapted into hospitals for American casualties of war. Mother, having established a good relationship him, asked if he would like her to send him a list of estates she considered appropriate, such as large mansions having a smaller house on the grounds, where the owners of these mansions could reside and still keep an eye on their property.

The Surgeon General was very grateful and equally impressed with his dinner companion and the position she held. He saw that more and more of the US Military would be taking advantage of what Mother's office might offer, now that the first contingent of American Forces, the Eighth Bomber Command, was arriving and setting up headquarters not far from London in High Wycombe, a city where Mother had a satellite office already set up and working.

Since the houses she had recommended were owned by friends of hers, she gave the General permission to use her name in setting up meetings with the owners. The appreciative General told her that, if there was ever anything he could do for her, she had only to ask. Mother then mailed letters to all of those on her list, explaining the need. Since everyone knew how much Mother was doing for the war effort, they unanimously complied with her request when the General came calling.

Mother never expected to see the General again, but here I was in a life or death situation, so naturally she called the London office telephone number which the General had given her when they parted after the dinner party. An aide de camp came on the line and told her that the General was out of town on business somewhere between London and Sussex; he added that he always called his office at five in the afternoon, and her request would be transmitted to him at that time.

Mother then explained the urgency of her request and the reason why she had to talk with the General at the earliest possible moment. After a few agonizing minutes of dithering on the aide de camp's part, he said that he would try to find him and ask him if he would consider calling her back.

My crusader had lunch at her desk, at the ESU, fearful to leave the phone for a moment. It took the aide an hour and three quarters before he connected with his General, who called her immediately. Mother once again explained my condition and the plans to relieve me of my leg from the knee down; she was eager to know if the United States had anything new that could possibly save my leg but was not yet available in Great Britain.

There was a long silence at the end of the phone, and Mother's heart fell. Finally, the Surgeon General came back on the line and said, "Yes, Mrs. Dodge, I have something. It's an antibiotic drug that is going through its final trials, but has proven itself to the Army. We will shortly be stocking it in England. Fortunately, I have some with me, not much, but certainly more than enough for your son. I think it might be just the thing to save his leg and prove its potency at the same time. I cannot give you its name, for I am really going outside my authority; it is restricted only to the US Military, but you, Mrs. Dodge, are so well spoken of for your growing activities on behalf of our soldiers, that I hope you will accept it as a token of my gratitude for all your endeavors and accommodations to both me and our servicemen. Now I shall send one of my doctors with what is presently referred to as the 'miracle drug.' I shall also invite your son's doctor to be at your son's nursing home by late afternoon, after I have appraised him of the situation immediately after you put down the phone. Give me the doctor's phone number and your son's nursing home phone number and address, and, God willing, your son will be out of danger by tomorrow morning."

Mother thanked the General with tears in her voice. Just before ringing off, he told her that so far he had visited five buildings on her list of possible structures to turn into hospitals, of which two mansions were unsuitable, one could be used in an extreme emergency, and the other two were definitely usable, with the owners of both houses happy to move into smaller homes on their estates if it would help the war effort. Their husbands were already in uniform and the wives would thereby be released from running "the big house" with a skeleton staff or none at all. How providential!

As for me, the miracle drug worked: My temperature went down, my leg began to heal almost immediately, and within ten days I was home again, feeling all the better for good nourishment. I owed my life to Mother, to the inventor and creator of this wonderful healing drug, and to the Surgeon General, to whom I wrote a letter of true gratitude for having saved me from being an amputee for the rest of my life. How blessed I was.

As soon as I was back to normal, Mother set up an appointment for me, of fifteen minutes' duration, with Alfred Duff Cooper, top man at the Ministry of Information. His Ministry was a twelve-ring circus, involving all kinds of projects under his supervision. His wife had been one of England's great beauties, who though now past her prime was still a handsome woman.

Duff Cooper had a nice round face and a pleasant, relaxed smile. He was impeccably dressed in a dark blue pinstriped suit, urbane to the nth degree, and he gave me the impression that I had known him all my life.

I told him about my night at the Savoy, when I realized that no one seemed to know or care about the British Merchant Navy or its importance to Great Britain. We were the silent service, it seemed, but it was time for it to be recognized and given credit for what was its due. I reminded him that the British Merchant Navy was operating under just as dangerous circumstances as all the other services, and possibly more. I added that it should be put in exactly the same category as the other services when praise and compliments were being given, whether in written stories of their accomplishments or on posters or on radio newscasts. And what about medals for the deserving seamen and wireless operators and officers under fire who went beyond the call of duty and even died under heroic circumstances? This was their war, too.

Duff Cooper nodded his head and wrote notes to himself, seeming amenable to my suggestions. He gave me an extra ten minutes in which he quizzed me on my experiences on the good ship SS *Benedict*. He then thanked me for my input and promised me he would bring up the subject of the British Merchant Navy at his next board meeting. Finally, he assured me that at least one of my suggestions would be implemented, though he didn't say which one. What more could I do?

I gave myself six weeks to exercise my leg back to its full strength, with long walks around Hyde Park, riding in Rotten Row, dancing and dining with Benita and Juliet, and celebrating the final days of my civilian life with Mother, who was all things to me: mother, best friend, promoter, adviser, sponsor, connector – all this and more.

Johnny, too, had had an enormous influence on my life – a man for all time. And what a man! If only I could live up to half his standards. At least I would try.

The US Military recruiting office had finally opened on the third floor of Selfridge's shopping center. I enlisted in the Eighth Bomber Command of the Army Air Corps, the first and only American outfit available to join at this time. A week later, I and a bunch of other inductees were seen off by their families, mine consisting of Mother, Benita, and Juliet; since I was not going so far away this time, there were no tears, though none of us were feeling exactly happy, either.

The conductor blew his whistle. After waving until my support group was out of sight, I sat down in my seat by the window and opened a magazine. Ahead were Lancashire and boot camp. A new chapter in my life was just beginning.

Changing Places

B oot Camp turned out to be a breeze, and in three months my new orders were suddenly cut in some mysterious military office. I was to be attached to the Judge Advocate's Office at the Headquarters of the Eighth Bomber Command located in High Wycombe, just outside of London, a mere fifty minutes by train from the city. But why the Judge Advocate's Office? The only thing I knew about the law was to keep on the right side of it.

Our headquarters at High Wycombe had formally been a private girls' school. They provided officers' quarters and offices for the different components making up the headquarters, while we enlisted men continued to be housed in quonset huts. Since the atmosphere was considerably more relaxed than at my previous camp, my boots and bed were rarely criticized, though I must admit that my talent in both bed-making and boot-shining never reached that perfect boot gloss or billiard tabletop smoothness that distinguished my fellow servicemen.

The Judge Advocate Unit consisted of five officers under the command of Lt. Colonel Campbell, a beloved character whom I looked up to with awe and reverence. He was judge, diplomat, and gentleman, never raising his voice, always conciliatory. Both his officers and staff hero-worshipped him, justifiably.

The officers' support staff consisted of three men: a master sergeant, a corporal, and me, still a private. There were also two ladies from the WACS, both of whom were very nice and competent, anxious to do their part in the war along with maybe finding a husband in the process.

Our working quarters consisted of an office within an office. At the far end of the room were two separate cubicles, half glass-enclosed, so that

231

one could see into them without any trouble, and likewise see out into the main room where the rest of us, both officers and staff, toiled. The larger cubicles was allotted to Colonel Campbell, and the other to the second in command. I was given a large desk and chair in the main office, pushed up against another large desk, so that the two faced each other. Claiming the desk opposite me was an officer, who became a very caring friend, in spite of his being an officer and me a private. Two months later I could at least add the appendage of Private First Class.

The officer was Captain Robert (Bob) Wagner. His father had been a famous legislator in national political affairs for many years before the war; the son, who sat six feet across from me for about six months, sometime after the war also ran for political office. He won the political plum of being elected for three consecutive terms to the grandiose office of Mayor of New York.

Seeing that no one was coaching me in the art of being a file clerk, Captain Wagner took to coming in early, before the office opened, to tutor me in organizing and classifying letters, memos and documents, including those stamped secret, top secret, etc., etc. He had great patience with me, and coached me well. Captain Bob was one hell of a good and generous gentleman and a kindly friend, and I shall forever be in his debt.

One incident in my time as a file clerk woke me up to the fact that all men are not created equal in their sexual orientations, some preferring to cohabit with their own kind in preference to the female sex. This was considered "an unnatural condition" according to the mores of that time, before the World War and even into the sixties; it was, therefore, mainly practiced as a subculture. However, as time went by and I grew more sophisticated, I became aware that some of my social associates were consorting together. Furthermore, these men usually came from the higher echelons of our society, and I realized that it was not as unusual a choice as I had thought.

Anyway, a young officer was brought into our office under guard and seated just outside of Colonel Campbell's office. Since the colonel was still out of the office having lunch, Bob Wagner took the file from the guard accompanying the lieutenant. He perused it, then handed one sheet over to me, giving me a frown that meant it was for our eyes only.

The young lieutenant, who had been discovered in a compromising situation with an enlisted man, was being dishonorably discharged from the United States Army and sent back to the States. I returned the report to Captain Wagner and turned to look at our prisoner. He was so young, little more than my age, a nice, decent-looking man with a poet's face, obviously at the end of his tether, discharged and disgraced and emotionally fraught with anguish and guilt. He was from Atlanta, well educated, and from a good family background; I hoped his family would find it in their hearts to be compassionate and welcome him home without criticism, at least not initially. Such a tragedy.

Today, of course, it's another story.

My off-duty time, when I did not have a pass to London, was spent with Rosemary Carvill, the lady I saw in the street on my first day in High Wycombe and soon afterward as a volunteer in our PX. Ro, as I called her, was living in the rented Manor House with her mother and father, her father's company having evacuated from London. He had brought a minimal staff with him to carry on the business during wartime.

Ro's father was a fine man, a gentleman-squire kind of person, nice-looking and easy to be with; her mother was pleasant, but shy. The staff worked in the Manor House, rarely seen until they returned to their lodgings somewhere in the town.

I had many meals with the family, and managed to supply them with luxuries that they would no longer find in public stores. But I could never possibly make up for their generous hospitality, her father's in particular. I came to admire him for his wisdom, much of it acquired from his life in the business world, and much from his personal philosophy.

Ro was a good friend. After the war, when I was working with Sir Alex and Sir David, through a connection I had the privilege of finding a part for Ro in the dancing ensemble of a musical play that was coming to the West End. It came, and it bombed! But it provided Ro with new connections in the theater, which is what a great deal of life is all about. If you don't have what it takes, of course, you still won't make it, contacts or no contacts.

Being close to London, I spent most of my weekend passes there, operating out of Mother's flat, visiting with my two flames Betina and Juliet. Betina was working as a volunteer aide in a London hospital, and Juliet, I think, had joined the British Red Cross, also as a volunteer. That allowed her, for one week a month, to be free to earn her livelihood by painting oils of horses and ponies for grateful landowners, her waiting list of customers stretching way into the future.

Mother and I would have breakfast together, unless something important had taken her out of town. If ever I could find a day when she was not engaged, we would have a stimulating dinner together as well. My beloved mother was so happy in her work and her life. The only cloud – a very big one – that hung over her was Johnny's absence from the scene. She really worried about him, knowing through Churchill's office of his constant escapes and fearing for his very life; even the mention of his name would bring tears to her eyes and a pathetic sadness to her face. She loved him so much, and I knew she would give whatever it took to have him restored to her.

But for now her life was filled with action, and people, and winning the war, and taking good care of American and Dominion troops and officers who needed and deserved the warm company and matched interests that Mother's Information and Hospitality Centre for American and Dominion Forces and Visitors provided. She had offices in the English Speaking Union, Charles Street, London, and in satellites all over England, Scotland, and Wales, wherever a reasonable number of troops were encamped.

My life was pleasant enough, with really wonderful people in my office, particularly Colonel Campbell and Captain Wagner, and even in my quonset hut, where the inhabitants were all clean and educated. Yet, while I knew I shouldn't have complained, I was not an entirely happy man.

I was at a dead end. I wasn't a lawyer, nor had I started any other career, as a couple of years of teaching and ten weeks on the high seas were not much of a recommendation. Moreover, filing, at least to my way of thinking, was not inspiring, nor particularly rewarding. For me, it had become monotonous drudgery; though I knew I was much better off than I might have been, I longed to be somewhere where my limited talents could be put to better use than as a file clerk.

And then it happened!

Sometime in the first third of 1943, Mother was having lunch with Ed Betts, Brigadier General and head man at the Judge Advocate's Office. Toward the end of the meal, the General happened to tell Mother of a new outfit that had recently arrived from the States, named the SHAEF (Supreme Headquarters, Allied Expeditionary Force) Diplomatic Mission to the French Government. The legitimate French Government was currently in exile in London, under the protection of the British Government, its sole representative and standard bearer being General Charles de Gaulle himself, plus a small army of volunteers who had found their way to England from France and its colonies., The group was growing in size as the war progressed. Meanwhile, occupied France was being governed illegitimately from the city of Vichy under Hitler's French puppet, Marshal Pétain.

The SHAEF Diplomatic Mission to the French Government was presently quartered in Cadogan Square. According to Ed Betts, the only major problem this new group was having was finding Americans now serving in the military who could speak French. They also needed to have enough of the social graces to get along with and understand their French counterparts, whose leadership by General de Gaulle was fast straining that gentleman's relations with his allies, and in particular Winston Churchill, who complained that the Cross of Lorraine was almost heavier than he could bear.

General de Gaulle and his army of expatriates carried little voice in the business of power politics, his countrymen across the Channel preferring a peaceful occupation and retention of the status quo. The few pockets of resistance were provided by brave citizens whose numbers were limited but whose courage resulted in much rail and bridge destruction and some vital observations that were passed via carrier pigeon to British Intelligence.

De Gaulle made his presence felt wherever he went, for he was a ramrod tall man who could never be overlooked in a room. He had a burning patriotism for his country and a grand image of its return to its place as a major nation. But he had a difficult road to navigate, with little money or influence, and only his enormous belief in the certainty of his own leadership and final victory kept him going, in spite of knowing that he was, at least for the present, a lame duck in a pond of swans.

Mother, who knew of my frustrations in the Judge Advocate's Office, even though I was intensely proud and grateful to be sharing an office with such a high-caliber group of officers and men, immediately said "Bingo!" to herself. She told Ed Betts, whom I had met on a couple of occasions, that I spoke reasonably fluent French and was well versed in the art of diplomacy, having been brought up with a background of diplomatic hospitality. Our houses, both in London and Ferring, were really a miniature embassy, with Johnny and Mother as dual ambassadors, and people of many nationalities passing through our doors. It had been a wonderful education and experience for me, with two real pros to lead me, as I grew up and finally was allowed to understudy Johnny when for whatever reason he was unable to attend.

"Peter would be perfect," said Mother, giving the General a quick digest of my background and education.

He seemed impressed and agreed to arrange an interview for me with an officer involved in procuring and vetting new recruits for this mission to the French Government, upon which it would be up to me to make a good impression. Little did Mother know the impression *she* was about to make. She and the General finally finished their lunch and walked out of the Ritz. Mother signaled the doorman for a taxi. Since the General had an appointment in the opposite direction from Mother's English Speaking Union, he waited for Mother's departure. The porter opened the taxi door, at which moment the elastic band holding up her pink silk underwear broke, with said underwear almost immediately dropping over her shoes.

The General was aware of the situation, as was the porter, and no doubt a few bystanders. The General seemed unsure as to whether he should pick them up and return them to Mother or pretend he hadn't seen Mother's predicament, in which case he ought to just turn on his heel and step into his own military car, which had pulled up behind the taxi. Mother saved the situation by stepping delicately out of her pink panties, picking them up with a flourish such as a bullfighter would be proud of, and jamming them into her bag. She managed to chortle all the way, causing smiles to appear on the faces of Ed Betts, the doorman and the enthralled passersby, and turning a somewhat embarrassing moment into a comic one.

I waited for two long weeks before being given a pass to return to London and Cadogan Square, now the home of what I hoped would be my new quarters, if I could just get past a Major Lawrence Daly, my inquisitor and the man who would seal my fate. I was to report to him the very next day, at ten a.m. sharp.

The next morning I woke up with a hole in my stomach, realizing that today was the day. I was suddenly excited and scared, for what if my French was not good enough? Or if the interviewer didn't like me? And what if I failed to pass the interview and ended up back where I started, a file clerk trapped with an ocean of files and no escape in sight?

Major Daly was about my height, five foot ten and a half. He was also slim like me, and had a finely chiseled face with expressive eyes the dominant feature. He was sympathetic and encouraging during the entire interview, only once being interrupted by one of General de Gaulle's aides who just happened to be at HQ at the same time as I; he was forthwith ordered by Major Daly to test my command of the French language. Major Daly himself had admitted at the beginning of our meeting that he was only just now taking classes in French with other officers and men in a school classroom nearby.

I passed! Afterward, I told this French officer about my mother's office and what it did, and he was there the very next day. Mother introduced him personally to a French-Canadian lady whose background and interests were comparable with his own, and in no time at all they became an intimate twosome, enjoying each other's company until we invaded France. I rarely saw him in Paris, and finally never saw him again. Only he knows what happened to the tryst that Mother started.

Major Daly, who had dragged out of me most of my history almost from birth, told me that he would make arrangements with the Judge Advocate's Office to relieve me of my duties there and to report to him personally as soon as my orders were cut. At that point I would no longer be a file clerk.

As soon as I left Major Daly's office, I took a taxi to Mother's office in the ESU, where I gave her the good news. She leaped up from her chair and came around from behind her desk. She took me in her arms, and we danced a musicless dance around the office, accompanied by much clapping and hurrahs from Mother's entire staff. A few bewildered military visitors politely joined in the clapping. I was intoxicated with Mother's enthusiasm and my own, carried away with a profound ecstasy that needed no alcohol. It was a moment that I will cherish forever.

When I returned to my headquarters in High Wycombe, I discovered that I had been recommended and approved for the rank of Corporal. Unfortunately, since I was leaving the Judge Advocate's Office, Colonel Campbell had to rescind my promotion, since it would be one rank lost out of the limited promotions available to his office, and these needed to be given to men who were staying there. So be it.

Once again it was departure time. I was thrilled with my new assignment to SHAEF and its Diplomatic Mission, and London, and Mother, and all that London represented to the world at this still beleaguered stage of the war. As for Ro and her family, I would miss them, but we would certainly be able to communicate by phone. Incidentally, Ro and I had discovered that we had birthdays on the same day, as do my nephew Julian Dodge, who is also my godson, and now Laura Robertson, a very nice and competent lady who works at the Northern Trust Bank and watches over my bank balance with an eagle eye.

But the Second World War in Europe, and my own particular theater of war, has three years to go yet. Though it was certainly a momentous and devastating war, I will write only of some incidences and experiences in which I was personally involved or that I witnessed during my assignments in France, Belgium, and Germany. These will include my tours of duty in

Paris and Brussels, with the SHAEF Diplomatic Mission, and my time with the Military Government in Germany. The latter quickly led to my posting to the Information Control Division of Military Government, where I remained both during and after the war. It was in this last post that I finally realized my own expectations for myself and fulfilled a challenge of which I could be proud. I realize now that, in retrospect, I really and truly had a wonderful war, in spite of the bombs, the buzz bombs, the incendiary bombs, the V2s, and finally a torpedo or two that missed. I was almost always involved with a talented and gallant group of men and women, many of them becoming good friends, who survived the major part of the war, only to become casualties as the first real fruits of victory were becoming apparent. I remember that I often wept in the privacy of a bathroom for the loss of yet another friend, dispatched by some form of enemy fire. Waste, waste, waste.

But for now, a new world is opening up for me. Come along for the ride. It may surprise you.

Major Lawrence Daly, like most of the brotherhood of the Diplomatic Mission to the French Government, was a specialist. He was a highly qualified and esteemed negotiator and arbitrator, with a long record of having brought about successful outcomes of projected strikes or strikes already in motion between the unionized employees of companies and their employers, generally resolved in Chicago, Larry Daly's hometown.

I became his interpreter, aide de camp, and friend, and studied under his tutelage the French Government's rules and the boundaries within which the unions and employers could negotiate. I can't say I enjoyed the subject particularly, but I did my best. From time to time I was given opportunities to handle a difficult situation such as when the French military officer would bring into our office a seething employer in a messy union squabble, with Major Daly gone for the afternoon and only yours truly to face this red-faced ogre regarding me with contempt. What would Johnny Dodge do? I quickly slipped into his image, becoming gracious, courteous, diplomatic, eager to resolve his problems, knowing pretty well how my boss would have responded, had he been there. And it worked! The ogre quieted down, surprised and pleased with my advice, and thanked me most profusely, as did my boss's contact in the Army of the Free French, Major Louis de Gard, who remained uneducated on the subject of company strikes and too proud to learn. After all, he was a military man, his whole life had been given to the Army, and he trusted that with victory he would soon be retired back to his cottage in Normandy whence he had come so many years before.

Major Daly, like most of the other officers, treated us lower echelons – all well educated but for a few – with the same regard that they treated one another, for we were all dependent on each other, and it didn't take long for a real esprit de corps to spring up and bind us together, officers and men, in a manner that was unprecedented but proved superlatively successful. The Major permitted me to visit and socialize at the French Headquarters, where General de Gaulle reigned, and I made friends among the younger staff, including encouraging them to visit Mother's office, which they did. Many new friendships and romances began in earnest, and ever after I could do no wrong, always being welcomed with an embrace or a kiss on each cheek.

Once my Major grew accustomed to the unpredictable assault from the skies, he asked me if I would introduce him to some of the night spots. Along with one other officer and two enlisted men, I introduced them all to the White Room, a club that I belonged to just off Piccadilly. It had a longish but intimate-sized bar and an excellent bartender who managed to remember almost every habitual member's favorite drink. The White Room also had a great piano player: Mark Anthony, I believe his name was, or was there a "Caesar" in there somewhere? I can't quite remember, but the important thing is that he knew our favorite tunes – "Star Dust," "All the Things You Are," and "Dinah," in Mother's honor – and he kept his music loud enough to hear and soft enough for conversation. Downstairs was a tiny restaurant with four tables, where fantastic Hungarian food was served. We had dinner there the very night the English actor, Michael Redgrave, was sitting at an adjoining table with friends; he later became the proud father of Lynn and Vanessa Redgrave, both of whom ended up becoming movie stars in their own right.

My two officers immediately requested membership in my club, and by bending a rule or two, I got them accepted that very night. The two enlisted men decided to think it over.

On another occasion, I introduced three of them to Mother, the two enlisted men and the officer all falling under her spell; soon all three of them were fixed up with ladies personally vetted by her. (My major had a lady friend back in Chicago, to whom he remained faithful.) Later, the White Room barman told me that they had become members and regulars, and that he had overheard them talking about the fabulous Mrs. Dodge, who had brought them all together.

On our next outing, I introduced them to the Nut House, a nightclub where stage and revue luminaries from the West End would congregate after their show was over, with many of those who had attended their performances following them there. Earlier, in my Merchant Navy phase, while waiting for my ship, the SS *Benedict*, to sail, I had come down from my room at the Adelphy Hotel in the lift (elevator) with Robert Helpman, a major ballet dancer of that time. He was apparently taking his company on the road. To my surprise, he was the first person I saw when I entered the Nut House. We both seemed to get around quite a bit, though I like to think my trip to Brazil and West Africa and back put me a little bit ahead of him.

My days were mostly taken up with helping my boss to enlarge his French vocabulary and improve his accent. He was a good student, spending hours every week with his head in one of the many French classics he had bought from some Charing Cross bookstore. He usually brought me into the picture only when he had to admit defeat over some paragraph that sometimes proved impenetrable to me, too. In addition, I took him to all the major museums and art galleries, and showed him the many parks and squares with their gated miniature enclosures accessible only with a key held by each householder surrounding that particular square.

Altogether, in spite of the destruction and mayhem going on day after day and night after night, my life was good. I introduced my boss and some of our officers and enlisted men not only to the cultural side of London, but also to the Windmill Theatre marked by the sign "We Never Close." There they could have their fill of naked ladies with gorgeous figures, standing and sitting in various poses on stage, not allowed to move an inch while the curtain was up, on pain of having the theater closed if the Lord Chamberlain discovered that such a "blip" had occurred. Strange rules, the British have.

And surprise -- to my immense delight and some bewilderment, my hormones suddenly revealed themselves with a wondrous shudder, and I finally became a complete man, after which my relationship with my beloved Betina became more intimate and my life even more worth living. Looking back, I'd say that your first real love, and the consummation of it, so new, so fresh and innocent, is a memory that stays in your heart forever, no matter how many joyful dalliances and alliances you may enjoy in the future. I know it has been so for me.

Suddenly it was D-day, and the world held its breath.

In the depth of the night preceding the invasion, a large force of the

101st Airborne Division had been dropped in terrible weather behind enemy lines, their absolutely vital role being to take out as many of the reinforced gun placements anchored on top of the cliffs above Omaha Beach as they could. This was to be a surprise attack; the weather was so vile that the Allies were counting on the German officers and gunnery soldiers on duty discarding any idea of an enemy offensive on a day like that.

General "Ike" Eisenhower had chosen Omaha Beach to be the major American route off the beaches to the liberation of France and finally the defeat of Germany. It was essential that the 101st Airborne succeed in eliminating those armed pill boxes with their powerful guns ready to blow away whatever trespassed upon the beaches below. If they could destroy most of the German firepower, the Allies would have a reasonably good chance of taking the beach with limited casualties, there being only land mines and the normal mishaps of war standing in the way.

But it was not to be. Unbelievably, though our troops were indeed dropped over enemy territory, they landed seven miles beyond where they should have, in an area with only unmarked fields and hedges, of which few soldiers had any experience, and no maps of the region to help them find their way. There was considerable chaos, and some deaths, and a few skirmishes with German soldiers leading to casualties. Though disoriented, by the light of day and a compass, most of the men returned to their units within days.

The truth of the matter is that this miscarriage of events almost cost us the war then and there, for although Utah Beach and others managed to survive the initial landings, nothing positive could be done without the assault and capture of Omaha Beach. All the paraphernalia of war was anchored offshore from this beach, in enormous cargo vessels of every description, just waiting for the command to discharge the goods in their holds to the smaller ships standing by to receive them. In the meantime, a large base and docking facility were to be quickly built way out into deep water to receive all these goods and transport them from the ships to the docks to whatever their destination called for. But not until we owned the beach.

It was at this terrible moment of imminent disaster that two events occurred. General Eisenhower, already knowing that his parachutists had failed to wipe out the clifftop arsenals aimed directly at his soldiers, albeit aware also that the weather bore some of the blame laid on the pilots for overflying their objective by seven deadly miles, had received not one strong positive from the front, turning his expected victory into a probable catastrophic defeat. Overwhelmed, he turned to his aide and asked him to bring him a letter he had written some days before, one taking full responsibility for the failure of our landings and declaring that he was now ordering our troops back to England immediately. He asked for a pen to sign it, and lit a cigarette while his aide went looking for the pen.

Some two and a half hours before this, an amazing spectacle had transpired. A detachment of some forty or more men from the Rangers, the most skilled, competent, elite group in all aspects of warfare, arrived out of nowhere, these men also embracing the art of climbing unclimbable mountains and cliffs and making the feat look easy. These cliffs, from where the German guns had taken a heavy toll of our initial troops, were considered by both the Germans and Americans as utterly and completely inaccessible. But the Rangers hit the beach running. They raced across the sand in a zigzag pattern, à la S.S. *Benedict*, throwing the Germans in their pill boxes into confusion, so that they only lightly wounded two out of the forty or so men. Arriving at the face of the cliff, out of sight and out of range of the German artillery, and with silent prayers from those watching on the beach, surely and steadily and silently these extraordinary men climbed the flat face of the cliff with the aid only of rocket launchers to anchor the rope ladders to the top. Everyone on the beach knew they were witnessing a miracle, for this incredible scene could have turned into a disaster, if the Germans had suspected anything.

On reaching the top, the commander and his detachment took a circuitous route around the back of the unprotected pill boxes, taking the German officers and soldiers by surprise, after which they would be sent back to England and a prisoner-of-war camp.

The automatic gun fire from the German positions in their pill boxes on top of the cliff had been a deadly blood bath throughout D-day, but the six much bigger and heavier mounted guns that those soldiers still left alive on the beach feared the most, but until now not fired, turned out to be telephone poles, cleverly erected to impersonate the really big weapons that had been removed before the invasion and were soon found by the Rangers and quickly destroyed.

This little band of cliff climbers, in a brief space of time, turned the war around. What had been abject defeat hours before became a glorious and world-shattering victory. I find myself frozen in fear when I think what the future could have brought if these men had not arrived at the right time, with the right weapons and the right climbing skills.

Now the picture had changed. The troops poured onto the beach, the docks were built, and ashore came all the necessary implements of war. Our beloved Ike, one day to become our American President, could put away his unsigned letter and instead send his congratulations to the commander and his incredible men, who unknowingly changed the course of history in one perfectly executed military operation. God bless them all!

≈

Our exit from London had been silent, swift, and airtight. Mother was away in Scotland, setting up yet another office satellite for the American and Dominion troops, but I had managed to get her phone number from her office. We had a brief but loving farewell, and then I called Betina, who was immediately overcome by tears and couldn't find her voice. I told her I loved her and not to worry.

Travel to France was by bus to the coast – a medium-sized ship across the Channel, amphibious boats taking us from the ship right up onto the sands of Omaha Beach, buses and lorries again for the long haul to Paris. And then we had seven months in the most beautiful city in all the world.

Paris Liberated

We were soon moved out of our temporary accommodations and into a less luxurious but efficiently run hotel, where I resided for the next few months. Our location was near our headquarters, the Chase Bank Building, and within easy reach of the headquarters of General Charles de Gaulle, who was now the nominal Head of State. Marshal Pétain, the former head of the illegitimate government of France, was no longer beholden to Adolf Hitler; he and his cronies were now in prison, awaiting their judgment as traitors. Included among them was our former weekend guest from the war, Pierre Laval, who ended up as the only one whom I knew personally who received the death sentence and was put up against a prison wall and shot.

The immediate subject on our minds at this time was the Liberation Day Parade, two days away, which was being organized mostly by some of de Gaulle's military officers under General Leclerc's authority. General Leclerc was a major hero in France, being one of the few generals who had brought great honor to France in this war. The Leclerc Division had, in fact, crossed the deserts of Libya, fighting its way to Tunisia. Our mission's officers and offices were made available as a backup, should they be needed. They weren't. It was strictly a French operation, which really worked out very well.

Much to everyone's consternation, de Gaulle insisted on walking alone at the very head of the parade, where he would be an easy target for an assassin. General Eisenhower himself, Supreme Commander of the ETO (European Theater of Operations), begged him to reconsider, but with no success. He was unable to use his authority, since de Gaulle was now Head of State and soon to be elected President of France. His journey would be

245

protected by armed police stationed on the roofs of many of the buildings facing onto the parade route. All of their owners had been thoroughly investigated and double-checked, with a small but questionable group being ordered out of their homes and kept out of Paris under guard for the entire day and night of the parade. Providing further protection among the Parisians would be armed police in civilian attire, ever watchful, as well as police and French soldiers armed and in uniform, observing the crowd face to face, their backs to the parade, their eyes watchful for the slightest sign of trouble.

The lineup for this great day was found acceptable. General de Gaulle was to walk alone at the head of his free French troops, a break in the middle of the ranks being allowed for General Leclerc. Next would be the SHAEF Diplomatic Mission to the French Government, with a scarcity of professional soldiers but abounding in high IQs, splendid credentials, and some of the most brilliant specialists in their own fields in the USA. But soldiers they were not, and I, at twenty-two years of age, was just about the youngest member of this blue ribbon group. My main contributions to our mission were, as already noted, that I spoke French and that I had a facility for getting along with just about any two-footed being, whether emperor or beggar, and the knack of enjoying their company equally well. I was fortunate in having the gift of making friends easily, and Johnny and Mother's influence on me by example had had a profound effect. I did not expect ever to attain their heights of glory, but by emulating them in my normal life, I certainly had an advantage that benefited me and my career both during and after the war.

Behind our representation would be the American contingent, made up of our Army, Navy, and Army Air Corps, the latter name being changed to Air Force and a separate identity only after the war was over. Next came the British, the Canadians, and the Australians and New Zealanders, all of whom were well deserving of their enthusiastic reception.

But that was for tomorrow; today our Mission's higher-ups had procured a Master Sergeant from another company to rehearse us in our march the following day starting at the Arc de Triomphe. The only problem was that he was tied down by other priorities until approximately eleven-thirty that night, and we were instructed, every last man of us, to be in place and ready for instruction promptly at that hour. Failure to do so would bring severe repercussions. Our top brass had also alerted the gendarmes to our plans, and they proved a great help in providing a space large enough to encompass our rehearsal.

The buses arrived on time to pick us up, and we were at our rendezvous and all in place, one line behind the other – irregular-looking lines, but lines nevertheless – so at least we were there and ready when the Master Sergeant drew up on a splendid-looking motorcycle, with a very pretty young lady sitting on the passenger seat behind him. He spoke a few words to her, and she got off the machine; then he picked her up and put her back on his seat, only sidesaddle, so that she could watch our pathetic efforts from the very beginning. It reminded me somewhat of my merry band of Home Guardsmen, only this Master Sergeant didn't contradict himself in the middle of a command, nor did he howl at the moon when his troops at first closed ranks too quickly, causing a domino effect. Instead, our instructor stood there, open-mouthed with disgust, his lady friend bursting into hysterical laughter. Even the gendarmes couldn't contain themselves. Realizing that we were making a spectacle of ourselves, we buckled down and started to take our Master Sergeant and ourselves more seriously.

Slowly but surely we began to get the highly disciplined rhythm of the march. By the end of the third hour, nobody was laughing and we were all reaching a point where both we and our instructor knew that we were over the top. During that last hour, when he threw the book at us, trying without success to catch us in a misstep or a wrong turn, he knew and we knew that he had performed a miracle, our posture above reproach and all of us in perfect step. Indeed, if one of Their Majesties' Guards Regiments had been in attendance at that moment, I think they would have been mortified by our supreme perfection and compelled to turn their busbies around, front to back, and slink away into the night.

Even the gendarmes clapped just before we were dismissed, as did our Master Sergeant's girlfriend, getting so worked up in the frenzy of the moment that she shared her hugs and kisses with all those within reach, saving her biggest hug for our mentor. The Master Sergeant was, indeed, sent on his way with three enormous cheers from all of us. One of our captains with some experience in the Reserves was detailed to take the Master Sergeant's place in the parade later that same day.

We went to bed exhausted. Came the dawn, even though we'd had only three hours sleep, buoyed by the excitement of a just liberated city and the disciplined confidence the Master Sergeant had instilled in us (he deserved a medal, for he was worth his weight in gold), we once again formed up in order, our uniforms pressed and our shoes polished. Mine, by the way, were shined by a little French boy who had set up a shoeshine business with a wooden chair and footstool on the sidewalk just outside our hotel from the very first day we arrived. He was the one breadwinner in a family of four; his father, a Resistance fighter, had been killed when his grenade detonated ahead of time, and his mother, only twenty-eight years old, was dying of cancer. Our company's doctor had taken her under his wing but could not save her, so we were all providing the family with the necessities of life. Little Jacques, our shoe black, and his sister, Jacqueline, were finally put in a nice school near where they lived. Before I left Paris we had set up a trust with an American bank that would safeguard their existence and education until the children turned eighteen, because the mother had only a few months left to live. It was very sad, but something good came of it also, for Jacques eventually became a pharmacist, and married and had two children. His sister, Jacqueline, married into money, and now lives in the South of France, her home open to any of us who should be passing through her part of the country. Her husband died some years ago, and at the rate that our Second World War Veterans are dying off, I doubt if there are many of us left to accept her invitation.

But enough. Today is "the day," a day that would go down in history books, and our Diplomatic Mission to the French Government was very much a part of it. As the parade moved off in perfect cadence, we could distinguish by his height, way off in front, the familiar figure of General de Gaulle towering over the Free French military ranks behind him. The General opened his arms wide, as if to embrace any and all of the joyfully acclaiming crowds lining his triumphant way. Behind him, in the middle of his Free French soldiers, rode General Leclerc on his noble steed, whose heroic military history brought sustained applause from a grateful public. Next, as planned, came the SHAEF Diplomatic Mission to the French Government. We marched resolutely in disciplined cadence, proud to have our American flag flying at the head and to be part of this memorable occasion.

Since this was such a unique and distinguished day in my life, I needed some way to commemorate it. Observing the wildly enthusiastic crowds out of the corner of my eye, I discerned that a preponderance of French males wore a moustache on their upper lip. This would be my way of commemorating this glorious event, a moustache such as worn by Ronald Coleman and Errol Flynn, movie stars of the time, whose upper lip sported a slim slash of hair beneath the nose, elegant beyond words, and just what I needed!

I had observed that, for some reason, as I had grown into maturity, I was generally taken to be younger than I actually was, which irritated the devil out of me. Now, at last, I had the answer: a slick moustache would make me look older and, I hoped, more sophisticated. I started to grow it that very day and have had it ever since, though now, in my old age, it is totally white. I should really shave it off, as maybe my naked face would look more youthful. Vanity, vanity!

Behind our group came the American, British, Canadian, Australian, and New Zealand military participants, filling out the liberators' ranks, all having participated in the liberation of this great country. We finally reached the end of our march. But before we were dismissed, the French Military Band ended this grand occasion by playing their national anthem. I was thrilled, and emotionally knocked off kilter. My tears were released, and I was amazed to see that my unmanly display was being shared by many of my friends, including Major Larry Daly. There is no anthem in the world that compares with the raw, patriotic passion of France's anthem.

I'm happy to say that General de Gaulle survived his first parade of adulation on French soil. Later in his presidency he managed to escape two attempts on his life, and was allowed to die peacefully at home in his own bed – a very long one.

The French population, by British standards, had enjoyed a pretty easy, if not normal, life, going about their usual business without fear of attack by land or air. Of course, they were occupied by a considerable group of authorities; while their own government operated out of Vichy under the direction of Marshal Pétain, an elderly military carryover from the First World War, the real power remained with the German occupational forces. Pétain was mostly a blind tool of Hitler's skullduggery, but he was a figurehead, nonetheless, to whom a large majority of the population was grateful for keeping life reasonably bearable and certainly war-free. It can even be said that a lot of them resented the Resistance fighters for upsetting the status quo.

As a general rule, albeit with some exceptions, the German occupying army had kept its authority within bounds. It appeared to have been largely respected among the Parisians and their fellow countrymen. At the same time, the Nazi autocracy had spawned a vague fear just below the surface, because the French could never be certain that they might not be arrested someday in their home or place of work based on some false accusation brought by someone with a grudge against them, or picked up for no given reason and taken away, never to be heard from again. If they were Jews, they could at any time be taken off a bus and put on a train that took them straight to an immense compound with the name Belsen, where their clothes would be removed and they would be sent stark naked to the baths. What they did not know in advance was that, instead of water, the shower rained down a mysterious gas that quickly, though cruelly, would extinguish their lives. After being fleeced of any possible valuables found in their discarded clothes or upon their mute bodies, including any gold fillings in their teeth, their corpses were quickly dispatched to the Belsen ovens and a fiery end.

But Liberation Day remains as fresh in my memory today as it did more than sixty years ago. Jubilation sums up the wildly ecstatic mood of the Parisians and their liberators, and a night of triumph and Bacchanalian festivity lasted through the early morning and beyond. The usual moral safeguards were happily dispensed with for this one night, when everything was wonderful and nothing was out of bounds.

Free! Free! Free! It was a fantastic day and an even more fantastic night, every soldier, sailor, or airman in uniform being treated as a hero, nothing being too good for him, deserving only the best that Paris could offer, whether food or drink or entertainment or an amorous entente cordiale. It was jubilation. It was triumph. It was *fraternité*, it was *egalité*, following rightfully after *liberté*. It was truly a day and a night to be remembered for the rest of our lives.

It was during the mid-thirties that my mother had the good fortune to cross paths with Lady Jan Malcolm, widow of Sir Ian Malcolm. Lady Malcolm, "Jan" to all her friends, became one of Mother's closest and dearest friends, and played a role in my life in Paris during the war.

Lady Malcolm's mother had been the world-renowned actress and society beauty Lillie Langtry, born Emilie Charlotte LeBreton, in 1853 on the island of Jersey. She was nicknamed "the Jersey Lillie" by her adoring public on both sides of the Atlantic. She was the daughter of the Dean of Jersey and his wife, the former serving the island as the Reverend William Corbet de Breton. Little Emilie, who had six brothers, was educated by her brothers' tutor.

Emilie grew up and became a striking beauty with a special charm that set men's heads in a whirl. She was married at twenty-one to the Irish landowner Edward Langtry. One of his attractions was that he owned a yacht. She insisted that they leave the Channel Islands, and they eventually bought a home in London. She did not begin her stage career until several years later, after her husband went bankrupt. In fact, it wasn't until 1881 that she made her first stage appearance, but her figure, her deportment, her classically beautiful face, and her acting talent and charm took the theater-going public by storm. In no time she was the toast of the London stage and the New York theater. Just incidentally, she also became the semiofficial mistress to the Prince of Wales, Queen Victoria's son Albert Edward, the future King Edward VII.

In addition to having lovers on both sides of the Atlantic, she had many friends including Oscar Wilde and the American artist James McNeill Whistler. She was also a businesswoman, who managed the Imperial Theatre for a time and also manufactured claret at her forty-two-hundred-acre winery in Lake County, northern California, which she purchased in 1888. In 1887 she became an American citizen, divorcing her husband the same year.

Now, dear reader, remember this was the mother of Jan Malcolm, Mother's very good friend, who was born in 1881, the child of Lillie Langtry's lover Prince Louis of Battenberg (later the first Marques of Milford Haven, 1854–1921). He married Princess Victoria of Hess and the Rhine in 1884 and became the father of Louis Mountbatten, first Earl Mountbatten of Burma, the last Viceroy of India, great uncle of Prince Charles, and grandfather of Prince Philip, Duke of Edinburgh, the husband of Queen Elizabeth II.

Despite having buckets of blue blood and royal heritage on one side, and middle-class genteelness on the other, this Lillie Langtry had broken all the rules. She stood out above all the classes with her formidable personality, enormous talent as both actress and singer, and a star quality against which none could compete.

In 1899, Lillie married the very rich and much younger Hugo Gerald de Bathe, who would inherit a baronetcy and become a leading owner in the horse-racing world, before he and his bride retired to Monte Carlo. Lilly died there in 1929 and was buried in the graveyard of St. Savior's Church in Jersey, the church in which her father had been rector.

Lillie's royal, illegitimate child was brought up and educated in the British Royal Household. She grew up to be a very beautiful and personable lady, with strong undertones of her mother but with a more dignified presence that acknowledged her royal blood. Jean Marie Langtry eventually married Sir Ian Malcolm of Poltalloch in 1902, becoming known by her many friends as Jan.

On some occasions during the thirties, while on holiday in London, I would join Mother and Jan for tea in our drawing room. Even in middle age, she remained a very beautiful woman, with an extraordinarily compelling presence accompanying a delightful personality, a good mind, and a wonderful sense of humor. She and Mother together reminded me of Mother's very easy and joyful relationship with Lucy Rosen, Johnny's sister.

Now I have a story illustrative of Jan's famous outbursts when crossed by someone's laggardness.

I was now living in Paris, as you know, with Larry Daly and others from our Diplomatic Mission. Lady Malcolm, whom I was now able to address as Jan, was also in Paris, the Director of the British Red Cross. She had reserved a box at the Paris Opera House for the season at her own expense, partly because she loved opera and ballet, but also as a way of entertaining people in the French Government and the business world who could help the British Red Cross.

After inviting me to dinner and the opera – what could be better? – she asked me if I would consider playing host for some of the dinner and opera occasions. After we tried it out a couple of times, she claimed me as her permanent host at these affairs, which I enjoyed enormously. It cost me nothing, because the Red Cross underwrote the affairs, which were designed to promote the British Red Cross and make friends in high places. This was done with considerable success. My contribution, besides playing host, was being able to connect with certain VIPs whom I had cultivated for some time and was on good terms with, and enlist them in this effort. Jan later told me that I had more than earned the magnificent dinners that had been provided me, not to mention the operas to which I had been treated. Incidentally, Jan spoke Parisian French with a perfect accent and a vocabulary that put mine to shame.

On one particular night we had dined well at her hotel, after which her car and chauffeur drove us to the Opera House shortly before the overture. The chauffeur was instructed to be back in front of the Opera House at exactly eleven p.m. Jan, like her mother, was always a very punctual person and expected everyone else to be.

The opera *Tosca*, one of my favorites, was sad but glorious, and we both clapped heartily as the curtain came down. We then descended the stairs into the lobby, Jan's hand resting on my arm. To our chagrin, the weather had turned stormy and the rain was pelting down, literally bouncing off the boulevard. It soon began to overtake the drainage runoff, which meant that the boulevard began to flood. It was now eight minutes after eleven; Jan, looking at her watch, said nothing. Two minutes later the chauffeur pulled up in front and came rushing into the foyer, which had emptied itself of all but a few late stragglers, no doubt waiting for the rain to let up.

Making the weather the excuse for his tardy arrival, he held an enormous umbrella in his hand.

Jan still said nothing. We were in the car, our feet, shoes and socks, and my trouser bottoms a soggy mess from the street flooding. As we pulled away, other cars, vans and trucks passed us, pushing great waves of water against our car's windows. I was about to make some remark about the opera we had just seen when Jan leaned forward in her seat. With a steely machine-gun delivery, her head just behind the chauffeur's ear, she chewed him out profoundly for not having allowed extra time in order to be at the Opera House by the agreed time. Jan's every sentence was laced with the most descriptive swear words, most of them unknown to me, but not to the man receiving them, whose whole demeanor had collapsed into jelly. In fact, he appeared to be drowning in his own guilt.

For me, it was a fascinating glimpse of a facet of Jan's personality that I had never seen before. Obviously, it was rarely seen by anyone, but was clearly a hand-me-down from her glamorous mother, whose temper could be equally provoked by tardiness or stupidity.

Some weeks later, when the chauffeur had dropped Jan off at her hotel and I had moved to the seat up front with him while he took me back to my hotel, he, with considerable emotion, told me that he adored her ladyship, that he had deserved his chastisement, that she was a great lady and had a right to say what she said to him. She had been correct, he insisted; he hadn't allowed enough time, considering the weather, to pick us up before or on the dot of eleven p.m., a mistake that he would never make again.

And now, another tale, revealing another side of the Parisians.

I had a French officer friend at de Gaulle's headquarters who knew the second in command to the lady director of the French Red Cross. I asked him if he would suggest to his friend that it would be a nice gesture if the director of the French Red Cross invited the director of the British Red Cross – that is, Lady Jan Malcolm – to a ceremonial entente cordiale at her office's headquarters, which was within a few blocks of Jan's headquarters. The madam director thought it was a splendid idea, and wondered why she hadn't thought of it herself. Soon an elegant invitation arrived by courier at Jan's headquarters; though I never told her of my part in the invitation, she asked me to come along and witness the occasion. With Major Daly's permission and the good wishes of Jan's staff, Jan's chauffeur Ben (short for Benoit) drove us to the French Red Cross offices, where we arrived by elevator on the correct floor at exactly the time Jan had been given.

An elegant door taken from some French chateau greeted us first. We admired it before I opened it inward and let the guest of honor through. She was, incidentally, dressed and groomed to perfection, accented by her great beauty and powerful presence.

We entered a room of enormous size, with at least thirty young female secretaries sitting at separate desks with typewriters, suddenly hushed at our appearance. Then they all stepped aside from their desks and turned toward Jan, making deep curtsies; they stayed down for at least ten seconds before arising, after which they stood at attention while a small brass band from the gendarmerie played the British Royal Anthem, followed by the French anthem. Then the second in command greeted us, also with a deep curtsy, and led us through a path between the secretaries' desks leading to the director's office at the far end of the room.

I excused myself after Jan and I had been received by the director and left them to themselves, instead involving the young ladies in conversation. I also helped to bring one lady back to life with the aid of someone's smelling salts, as she had fainted from the excitement of the occasion. She was a sweet young lady, overwrought with the majesty of Jan and the impact of the brass band.

Jan came out of the office after about forty-five minutes with the madam director, all smiles. As they walked back to the exit door at the other end of the office, the same deep curtsies were repeated, one line after the other curtsying just before Jan and her hostess reached that particular line. It was great timing, and obviously well rehearsed. Even the Rockettes from Radio City Music Hall in New York couldn't have done better.

It has always fascinated me how the French, who guillotined their monarch and many of their nobility, and the Americans, who fought desperately and successfully to oust Great Britain's George III and his royal dominion over their country, nevertheless are in awe of people with titles. When kings and queens and nobility are received in France or the US, every French or American family with the means compete to play host or to be invited to meet people who, without their titles, would not be given a second glance.

The Parisians, as are most of us, are ever eager for scandal. Most of them had long known of Jan's ancestry, the very fact of its imperfection making them all the more eager to pay homage to this particular member of royalty. It seemed that Lady Jan Malcolm had the combined, irresistible attraction of being born out of wedlock, a true love child, and yet of royal blood. She was, moreover, a real beauty, with a personality and presence that demanded respect and admiration; in other words, she personified "majesty" at its best.

Paris, of course, is for lovers, and Paris is where I learned the art of making love. But I was so constantly busy that there was rarely time for an affair, and, being still anchored to Benita, I was that much less interested in starting something. I do confess that the Parisian ladies could be so wonderfully feminine and enticing that I was severely tempted sometimes.

Of the many things I admired about Parisian women, one was the fact that, though the clothing industry was practically devoid of things to sell, their customers made do with canvas sacks, garbage bags – you name it, they grabbed it. Before you knew it, they had created a unique little number that was adorable on them, their cute coquettish way of wearing their creation undermining your bravely made promises and inducing you to succumb on the spot. Or, of course, you could run for your life and jump into a freezing tub of water.

Don't ask! Actually, I usually took a cold shower, hating every minute of it.

Everything was running very smoothly between General de Gaulle's headquarters and our own. The early tensions and misconceptions had all been overcome, and the roiling river that had originally been characterized by intense interchanges and constant new surprises now resembled a placid pond, rarely disturbed. Our working speed even became somewhat sluggish, for we had undercut ourselves by attaining an almost perfect operation; we were all so experienced and attuned to our particular purpose on the team that there were rarely any challenges to tackle. The pizzazz had finally gone out of our jobs and our lives. This left time for more fraternization between our HQ and the French HQ, and that was a good thing, for we could integrate our social lives, of which we had had very little, with our French companions, and spark some competition between us at the Tennis Club, the Golf Club, and even the Jockey Club.

One morning, Major Daly had asked me to help him with a group of union employees and their employers, both sides being brought to him by his opposite number, Major Louis de Gard. The latter was still refusing to embroil himself in union matters, insisting that he was a military man and unions were a civilian issue in which a Major should not be involved.

The meeting lasted a protracted length of time in our borrowed boardroom. There was much emotion and Gallic temperament on both sides, but with Larry Daly's vast experience and a little assistance from me, everything came up roses. The enemy camps that had just been at each other's throats were now embracing one another with fervent kisses on both cheeks, both sides happy with the contract that Larry had worked out for them and each believing they had gotten the better of the other.

Since our office could only advise, Major de Gard would be the sole official name confirming the contract signed between the union representatives and their employers. It would be typed on French stationery with the address at the top of the page being that of General de Gaulle's headquarters.

After we had seen them out, the Major invited me to lunch, taking me to his favorite café within ten minutes walking distance of our office. After we had finished our main course, he patted his stomach – it had inflated quite a bit since he had arrived in Paris – and ordered a cigar. He lit it and took a slow and appreciative pull on it; then he pushed back his chair and turned his attention from the cigar to me. For the next few minutes, I was totally embarrassed and very grateful.

"Peter," he said, "you have been an excellent and responsible aide to me since we first met, and I have nothing but positive things to say about you, as have those of my fellow officers and men who have benefited from your help and connections. You have obviously been very blessed in your life, and you seem to be comfortable with just about anybody. All of this has been observed by me and my fellow officers. Now that our mission here in Paris is working so smoothly, we think it is time for you to take on yet more responsibility, in an organization that should be right up your alley. It's called Military Government. Like our own mission in the beginning, it's in desperate need of recruits. Its purpose is to take over running the German territory captured by the Allies, in order to ensure a peaceful transition of power from the former Nazi-empowered administrators to our own military administrators, in collaboration with German administrators untainted by membership in the Nazi Party.

"I think you would be perfect for this kind of work, Peter. You are diplomatic, you are sensitive to people, you are respectful to both the high end and the low, and you make a very good impression wherever you go.

"The military government operation will be just about the same as our mission. Officers and men will take care of one another. Although the opportunity for acquiring rank, particularly at your age, will be on a par with our regime here, you will be given considerably more responsibility. Here, as you know, I am a one-man show, as you will become when you have completed your limited training and receive your assignment, which I believe will be the making of you.

"General Clay, who has a formidable brain, will be in charge of the American Occupation. When I first got inquiries regarding personnel for this Military Government, your name came instantly to mind. You do not have to do this, but I think you will be missing a great opportunity if you don't. I have written a glowing recommendation for you, and two other officers have done the same, so if you accept it you will be on your way to a new and exciting challenge worthy of you. I have been told by the Military Government that, though you are an enlisted man, if you do right by your commitment to your assignment, you will be offered an opportunity to become a civilian War Department employee, equivalent to a First Lieutenant and earning a considerably higher paycheck than you do now."

"But I don't speak German," I said.

"You don't need to speak German. We are the conquerors, not the conquered. Once you have been given your assignment, you will be able to employ a secretary and two interpreters, who will also be your assistants. I've really looked into this matter for you, and I think it is practically tailored for you. Think about it, and give me your answer in a day or two."

I didn't have to think about it. I knew intuitively that this was for me, and that my guardian angels had come through for me yet again.

"Yes! Yes! Yes!" I said, and my wonderfully good friend and I shook hands on it. I thanked him with all my heart for being the conduit of a chance to enter yet another chapter in my life, one that would prove be the most challenging and rewarding chapter of my military career.

Incidentally, I hadn't heard from Betina in quite a long while. I finally found out why when I received a Dear John letter from her with the news that she had married a naval officer and was pregnant, and she hoped I would forgive her. Of course I forgave her, a lovely memory in my life, but she had been the only restraint on my desire to sample at least one lady while I was in Paris, and now at last I was free to sow a few wild oats. Only I really wasn't, for her news came just ten days before I was to leave for Brussels. My mood at the time varied from sadness at departing the secure world I had enjoyed at our Diplomatic Mission to the French Government to enthusiastic anticipation of whatever unknown challenges awaited me in my immediate future. My mood swings undermined my sex drive and kept me on the straight and narrow.

Major Daly told me that he was giving me a small dinner party the night before I was to leave for Brussels, Belgium, and he invited me to pick four guests. I chose two enlisted men whose friendship I had enjoyed, and the two officers who had tagged along with my boss and me when we were in London and who had always been helpful when I needed them, both in London and Paris. They were also the two who had written recommendations for me along with the Major.

First, we would go to the Ritz Bar, which had been off-limits to enlisted men unless accompanied by an officer. I had been dying to visit it ever since I had returned to Paris, but was too proud to ask my boss to take me. He learned of my desire only when one of my enlisted friends tipped him off about my urge to see the inside of one of the world's most famous bars – no women allowed –where you could count on being dazzled by at least one or two celebrities for sure, if not more. Larry acceded to my wish and, knowing my attachment to Maxim's, where I had taken him as my guest one evening soon after we arrived in Paris, booked a table for six at nine for the night before my departure.

One of my other favorite attractions was the Folies Bergères, a very elegant and
semi-naked musical show with a "colored" American singer of good voice and enormous vitality, surrounded by a medium-sized chorus line of considerable beauty and talent. The theater was intimate, and I always tried to get a seat in the sixth row center, which suited me just fine.

I never told anyone my birthday, but Mother had sent me a generous check with a birthday card, for my twenty-third, and the Folies Bergères seemed to be just the right place to enjoy it. By a small miracle, I succeeded in being placed in the sixth row from the front, almost in my accustomed seat. During the show, one lady in the chorus line attracted my attention, and I thought she was looking right at me, with a lovely smile on her face. Right on the spot I decided I would invade the stage door and take this pretty lady off to a birthday dinner that very night.

After a short break, with the music playing romantically in the orchestra pit, the curtain opened up on a bare stage, where stood a beautiful and gorgeously dressed lady wearing an empress gown in black, wide and flowing outward and downward almost to the ground. It was bejeweled and sparkling, low on her breast to the V between, with her soft white skin magnified by the blackness of her apparel. She was holding up a sign that introduced the next act. Slowly, facing the audience, she carried the sign from one end of the stage to the other and back to the center, pausing and then very slowly turning around to face the back of the stage, causing a four-star alarm sigh of desire from just about every red-blooded male in the theater, as they beheld the most glorious back and rounded buttocks that God and nature could create. Very slowly and majestically, she walked away into the wings, leaving us like gasping fish washed upon the shore, our source of procreation standing at attention in her honor.

After the curtain came down at the end of the show, I beat a path to the stage door and greeted my hoped-for partner for the night, the lady who had been smiling right at me from the stage. Or so I thought, as I introduced myself as she came down the steps. She stopped, looking bewildered, and I told her that she had looked at me quite steadily, smiling all the way, and she told me it was almost impossible to see that far back, with the strong stage lights directed straight at her, blinding the chorus girls but not spoiling their performance. She said her name was Julie, and she was curious to hear my English accent coming from an American-uniformed soldier. So she fell into step with me and, finally becoming more relaxed and comfortable, she allowed me to take her to Maxim's, where we naturally had a wonderful dinner. She turned out to be a student at Oxford, her hobby being dancing; she had come to Paris to improve her French, ending up earning her living in an all-English chorus line, a tradition going many generations back. It turns out that the French dancers, adorable though they were, were rarely long-legged, and it had been for many years the custom that English dancers were in command of the chorus numbers performed so elegantly and semi-naked on the Folies' stage.

Julie gave me a great deal of history of the Folies Bergères. After dinner I took her home in a taxi to her the boarding house where she shared a room with another member of the chorus line. This put finis to any amorous inclinations I might have had, my last impression before falling asleep in my own bed being those fabulous orbs of the lady's derrière, so perfectly rounded, so kissable and caressable, so utterly desirable.

I had a last dinner with Jan, a lady I would miss very much but would be able to see many times after I returned from Germany at the end of 1946. At that time she appeared not to have changed a bit. Moreover, she and Mother had returned to their custom of having tea together in one of their residences. By that time, Mother and Johnny had sold our big London house for a large three-bedroom, three-bath apartment in Kinston House, Princes Gate, that was separated by only five houses from the residential Embassy of the American Ambassador to the Court of St. James, Lewis W. Douglas. His daughter, Sharman Douglas, was making a smashing impression on British society, somewhat reminiscent of Mother's conquest of the Mayfair Set. She was also being courted by the kind of titled gentlemen that poor Aunt Flora could only dream about.

Sharman Douglas mesmerized the British aristocracy and even charmed the debutantes and their mothers, not an easy thing to do. In the end, she never married. She was so lovely, and I was so proud of her, and so sad when I read in the newspaper of her passing. I wonder what she did with her life. I'm sure it was something constructive, whatever it was.

Lionel Guest had died, and Flora finally showed her nasty side again. She begged Johnny, her only son, of whom she was deprived for practically the whole war (what about Mother -- wasn't she deprived, too?), to visit her on weekends. After all, Minerva had him all week. Flora was an old, sick woman, she said. Actually, she was as healthy as a horse and would outlive her son by quite a few years. With her London house sold, she was now living in Wookitipi with a maid/cook and a gentleman who lived in her guest cottage for free, earning his way by handling her financial affairs and paying her bills and taxes. Mother didn't like it, but she wondered how she would have felt in the same situation and let it go. After all, Mother could be gracious, too. Fortunately, Johnny had inserted one line into the weekend agreement with Flora: When Mother and Johnny received a weekend invitation from friends, they would be excused to go if they so wanted.

But for now I am being royally entertained by Larry Daly. Our Mission's commanding officer loaned his military car and chauffeur to us for the evening, a very gracious gesture; though packed in like sardines, we reached the Ritz Hotel and finally the Ritz Bar in good humor, and sat down at the empty end of the bar. Larry and I observed with delighted astonishment that none other than Ernest Hemingway, the most successful American author of his time, was sitting alone at the other end of the bar, a bunch of civilian males being all that separated us.

We ordered drinks. As we were telling the others in our group who was at the other end of the bar, Hemingway appeared behind us, a big smile on his face. Naturally, we invited him to join us, which he did, sitting between Major Daly and me. In no time at all, he integrated himself into our little group, the only uniformed men in the bar, which I think was why he picked us to drink with.

He told us of some recent experiences at the American front, and then of Spain during its civil war and his peacetime admiration for the bullfights and the brave matadors. After some forty-five enthralling minutes, he paid our bill and got up from his stool, saying that he had a date with Marlene Dietrich, at which point Larry told him what a great admirer I was of her and made me tell my story of my close encounter with her on the Lido Beach in Venice.

Hemingway then asked where we were dining. When we told him, he said that was where his reservation was, too, promising that, after he and his guest had had their dinner, he would bring her over to our table for a nightcap. I should save the chair next to mine so that I could enjoy her firsthand, he added; she had just returned from the front with her group of USO entertainers, taking a couple of days' breather before heading to yet another part of the front lines. She always made a point of sharing the same dangers and risks as those of the uniformed men and women, including the Red Cross ladies, who became more numerous the closer you got to the front. According to Hemingway, they were always ready with hot coffee and donuts and a cheery word or two.

We dallied over the remainder of our drinks, waiting to see if any more celebrities would appear, but none did. So we exited to our kindly commander's car and chauffeur, and off we went to Maxim's, where we told the chauffeur we would return to our quarters by taxi and he could take the rest of the evening off. By the time we got there, it was after nine and the restaurant was really buzzing. Our table still awaited us; with an extra leaf added to it, we could now seat eight people instead of six. Larry, as host, sat at one end, leaving the chair on his right empty for Hemingway, and I sat at the other end, the chair on my right remaining empty until Marlene Dietrich was to arrive. We had seen them at the opposite corner at the end of the room when we came in, their heads together in conversation.

It was after eleven when we finally finished our meal – manna from heaven – and, like everything else that had gone so perfectly, whom should we see but our celebrity guests walking across the large dining room in our direction? I beckoned to Marlene Dietrich to sit by me, and pulled out her chair. She came right up to me with a mischievous smile on her face. Stopping in front of me, she said, "So this is Peter," only she said it with an emphasis on the "er" making it sound like an "A" as in "Peta," after which she grasped me in her arms and covered my face with kisses. My table companions, with Hemingway leading and feigning jealousy, began sobbing loudly, bringing the tables around us to join in this crazy behavior. Meanwhile, Dietrich held me tight against her breasts and continued with considerable gusto to cover my face with her kisses. The other tables and my friends continued to make horrible sounds of frustration and rage, and the restaurant's photographer took a picture that I didn't dare show to anyone until many years later. The flash from the camera calmed us down, and I was able to seat Dietrich next to me. She brought out from her bag a large but dainty handkerchief with which she proceeded to remove all the lipstick from my face where she had planted her kisses, leaving just one beside my nose as a souvenir.

When we had all been served our after-dinner liqueurs, Hemingway begged Dietrich to tell us the story she had told him about her most recent tour of the front. After a sip of something green in her glass, she proceeded to narrate an experience that, though sidesplittingly funny now, I wouldn't wish on my worst enemy.

It appeared that she and her troupe of USO entertainers, with a band of four musicians, were performing for the troops well within hearing range of intermittent gunfire. They had already given two other performances that day at two other locations near the front, and had eaten once in an officers' dining room and once in a barn provided by local farmers, who were also providing staples for the military. No one knows whether it was one of the meals, or some contagious bug in the water they drank, but just before performing the last show of the day, they all became sick, dysentery-sick. Being real troupers, they decided the show must go on. Dietrich quickly worked out a plan to station one and preferably two performers in the wings, in case the one performing had to leave the stage in a hurry; in that way, there would at least be some continuity. It was a simple plan, but not perfect, so that sometimes almost everybody was on stage doing a big number, and sometimes nobody. The four-man band was cut down to one, three of them too exhausted to play. The one who appeared to be untouched by this plague was struck down only when they were making an eighteen-hour drive back to Paris from the front; this became a thirty-six-hour trip, allowing for plenty of stops for the beleaguered trumpet player and a couple of other musicians not yet quite over the sickness.

But the show did go on. It was a real hellzapoppin' situation, completely uncontrollable, but a crazy and hilarious sight for the soldiers in the audience, who thought it had all been rehearsed. They laughed themselves silly until they were falling off their chairs, telling the rest of their unit later that they must see the show if it came back, for it was even funnier than Bob Hope.

The retracing of Dietrich's experiences had us all in fits, particularly as narrated in that deep-cellar voice of hers. We were especially enthusiastic when she got up and gave a rendition of "The Boys in the Back Room," feigning alarm midway through her song, as she dashed madly across the dining room as if to claim an unoccupied toilet. She was brilliant. Her fans, mostly French that night, even if not understanding her words (though quite a few did), were able to connect with her theme and were laughing almost as much as we were. Soon we were all up on our feet and going through the same pantomime that Dietrich had provided, our group aping her voice and her grimacing expressions as we circled the table, leaving her and Hemingway gasping for breath, their eyes wet with tears of laughter. It was such enormous fun, and so great to be in the company of two such rare and honored icons. The perfect way to end my stay in the most beautiful city in the entire world.

Next stops: Brussels then Dinard, in Belgium, and finally Germany itself, though the war was still going on. That is where I would at last achieve my dream of creating something really good of which I could truly be proud.

Brussels was a delight. It was a smaller version of Paris, with beautiful downtown buildings and a large square in the middle. On Saturdays a variety of events took place, including the running of a complete pack of foxhounds with grooms. The master, in particular, was garbed in red, as was a six- or seven-year-old boy, perhaps the master's son, clothed in exactly the same splendid outfit, the only missing creatures being the horses and the fox, as a stuffed fox stood in for the real thing.

I don't know if this happened every week, but I do know that wedding bliss was procurable in the civic center on the edge of the square, the building being considerably higher than the square itself. I was privileged to see a wedding party descending an outdoor stone stairway, where a photographer was shooting wedding pictures while commanding his subjects to go here, there, and everywhere, which they did with docility. It was truly a great day in all their lives; the groom and his lady, though obviously filled with joy, were embarrassed by all the attention they were getting, not only from their family and guests but also from most of the onlookers out for the day's entertainment.

My job was a piece of cake. Nobody in Belgium appeared to need my specialty, leaving me without a reason to exist, until a week after my arrival, when I received in the mail a rough first edition of a Military Government Guidebook explaining what to expect and how to deal with many of the situations that would be coming my way as soon as I was activated. The guidebook was fascinating, and I ate it up, particularly when I heard that General Clay, the commanding officer of the American Zone in Germany, had himself provided much of the information, suggestions, and alternate suggestions for us to put to the best use.

When I was finally ordered to report to the Military Government in Dinard, a middling-sized town on a body of water nearer the enemy, I felt that my indoctrination from this guidebook would be worth its weight in gold. So I took it to a bookbinder, who weatherproofed it and bound it in such a manner as to make it practically invulnerable to attack from any quarter, human or inhuman.

And so to Dinard.

A Matter of Life and Death

After my few weeks in Brussels, I reported to the US Headquarters in Dinard, which would give me my assignment to Military Government, Germany. Unfortunately, for me, soon after I arrived at Dinard, several soldiers, two officers, and I were stricken with the Belgium pneumonia, a particularly acute form of the disease that left you feeling like a blob of jelly utterly uncaring as to whether you lived or died.

I was taken by jeep, along with an officer and another soldier, all looking and feeling more dead than alive, to the Belgian Hospital, where I was put in a very large room in which both American military and Belgian civilians were being treated for this miserable disease, as well as other maladies. I remained there in bed for ten horrible days, the only bright spot being a very caring Belgian nurse whose patient I was on alternate days with an American nurse, who was efficient but had no heart. Marie, on the other hand, was so encouraging and endearing, that she overcame my listless state and gave me back a desire to survive.

Because of the intense need for the beds, I was released early. But I was admonished by both words and a letter from the doctor to my commanding officer, whom I had not yet had time to meet, that I was not to return to the workforce until I was fit and ready. This included receiving official permission to return to duty from one of the American doctors at the hospital.

Little did I know at the time when I was bedridden that the Battle of the Bulge had just exploded from the almost impenetrable bowels of the Ardennes Forest, taking the American Army completely by surprise. The Germans' momentum overwhelmed all resistance, with the balance of power suddenly being in doubt. This turn of events shocked General Eisenhower into an immediate three-way phone conference with his main advisers, Generals Walter Bedell Smith and Omar N. Bradley, part of which entailed commandeering a great many enlisted men and their junior officers away from their office jobs.

What I'm reporting now is the story told me by the three officers who were there at the same time. They were sent for a brief training period at hurriedly created training camps, after which they were dispatched to the front to help stem our retreat and stop the bleeding. It was a pathetic bandage where real surgery was needed, so it slowed the enemy only temporarily. The death toll was dreadful, mostly affecting the fresh soldiers detached from office-related jobs. They were suddenly confronted with the strength of the mighty Panzer divisions and Hitler's prime military divisions, well schooled and well experienced, dedicated to winning this battle for their Führer. They knew, as did Hitler himself, that this was his last real chance of plucking victory from the ashes of defeat.

Two incidents that were part of this incredible battle show the desperation of both sides to win. According to those officers involved in the fighting, even though being beaten back, they had come upon more than one group of bodies of American soldiers lying in the fields beside the shattered roads, all having fallen in line, the back of their heads blown off. It was cold-blooded murder. There was no possible excuse for such diabolical behavior. Only when we began interviewing American soldiers behind our lines, who seemed a bit out of place, did we realize that they were actually German soldiers dressed in US fighting uniforms, with pretty good documentation to confirm their identities. These were discovered from one German soldier, who claimed he was not involved when the assassins had blown off the backs of the heads of our office boys. At that point, our patience ran out. Since they were caught behind our lines and in fake uniforms, they were fairly and justifiably guilty and condemned as spies; all but one were put up against a wooden fence beside an empty field and shot. Only the one who reported on his comrades was freed, though we doubted that he would be alive for long, for he would have a lot of explaining to do to his superiors.

The weather really helped to turn our situation around, according to the three officers. The Panzer Divisions leading the thrust into our territory had to slow down in order to conserve their tanks' energy, because the supply trucks had not yet caught up with them. There was a good reason. The trucks were stationed in an area where they were, along with every kind of mechanical machine, bogged down in a quagmire of slimy mud, caused by flood water from the long deluge of rain that had gone on for hours. It had completely inhibited the trucks, incapacitated by eight inches of water beneath them, from any form of activity. The ground provided no resistance for the tires, only sending up mud baths to cover drivers trying to dig out the trucks, with wooden boards and other implements placed beneath the wheels. The water was high; the ground, too soft. The Panzer Divisions and the transportation vehicles would just have to wait for the rain to stop and the ground to harden enough for the tires to grip. It proved our winning card, because it gave the opportunity for our tanks, though not half as good as those of Germany and Russia, to do some damage to the enemy, once the skies cleared.

And indeed, when the weather cooperated and American reinforcements came in, the Germans were forced to leave their tanks and mobile equipment behind. Practically all of them were either out of gas or very nearly, while the Army Air Corps and the RAF had a field day blowing them up. By that time, Hitler's forces were under orders to withdraw and regroup to fight another day. So what started with the sound of thunder ended with a hiccup, and thank God for it.

But I was aware of none of this at the time. My doctor told me at one point that he thought he was losing me, but, because of Marie's ministrations, I rallied. We did, however, lose one lieutenant who had been in the jeep that brought us to the hospital. As for me, my respite in the hospital possibly saved me from being sent to the front, where my life might well have been extinguished along with those of so many of my compatriots.

When I was finally healed, orders were cut for me to be sent to Stuttgart, in the State of Württemberg, Germany, where I was to meet my new commanding officer, Colonel J. H. Hills, Director, Information Control Division, Headquarters, Office of Military Government, Baden-Württemberg. I was finally going to meet my new leader and boss, and I was excited and scared all at once. I finally calmed down, becoming even serene, when I reminded myself that I was a fatalist and what would be would be. Two nights before I was to leave, a part of Dinard was bombed, including the section next to the hospital, where the nursing staff from outside of the town had their living quarters. It was almost midnight when we heard the German planes' engines. Then the bombs started to fall, and the nurses living in their quarters raced for the adjoining bomb shelter. One bomb hit the dormitory behind them before seven of the nurses could get out, and all seven died. They included my beloved nurse Marie. She was a real angel, I am sure. I still have her in my prayers to this day.

Before leaving for Stuttgart, I was given an exam based on the Military Handbook that I treasured and could now read with my eyes closed. I passed the exam with flying colors, and the next day I left Dinard by train. With a couple of changes, I finally arrived at my destination in the early morning, stretched mentally and physically from lack of sleep, my uniform rumpled, but anxious to meet my commanding officer, Colonel Hills, and be given my assignment. My very future depended on how I handled myself and my assignment. I hoped it would turn out to be a reasonable goal within the scope of my limited talents.

Little did I know!

My interview took place in Colonel Hills's office at the top of the Tagblatum, the only skyscraper then in place in Stuttgart, a towering office building where the Military Government occupied space for its headquarters. He greeted me warmly, introducing me to his aide and his secretary, after which he came from behind his desk and had me sit down with him at a coffee table with two comfortable chairs. After his secretary brought in two mugs of coffee and cookies – my breakfast – he turned his full attention to me. He addressed me as Mr. Sherman, informing me that that was how I would be addressed from now on in my office by both my staff and all with whom I dealt or who would come under my authority.

He then explained my purpose, and why I was needed.

"Today the German civilians as well as the defeated military are severely demoralized and quite moribund," he said. "They can see no future for themselves – indeed, they are in a state of shock, finally realizing they had put their trust in false gods. Their whole Nazi-injected social structure is in collapse and confusion, leaving them with neither direction nor purpose. That is why Military Government is here, and in particular why the Information Division of Military Government is here, and why you and I are here.

"General Clay, commander of the American Zone believes that the best medicine now for the German psyche is to restore the main staple of their cultural lives, the State Theater. I agree with him most heartily. In addition, we must stop this cancer right now, before it gets completely beyond our control. We have to separate the gung-ho Nazis from those who were forced to join the National Socialist Party in order to take up a specific position for which only Nazi Party members were eligible.

This responsibility is being carried out by an Intelligence Unit under the umbrella of our Military Government. That is one side of the coin.

"We, and in particular you, are on the other side of the constructive side of the coin."

Colonel Hills paused. He rang for his secretary and told her that he didn't want to be disturbed. She closed the door behind her as she left.

My new boss glanced at some papers on his desk as if he had already read them. Then, with a smile, he said, "You know something? I wish I had been the recipient of these recommendations of yours. You must be quite a man to engender such enthusiasm. Anyway, that's why you're here, so I might as well tell you that your office will be in Karlsruhe, the State capital, where the State Theater is naturally located. Unfortunately, since the theater became a victim of the war, we have transferred what we could still use from the theater to another building of similar size, a movie theater, but with a number of alterations now in place, reflecting the image of the original. Though from the outside it looks like just another movie theater, I have already had dressing rooms and bathrooms for performers put in, along with a rehearsal room for when the stage is occupied, private quarters with a bathroom for the Intendant (manager), and a better and bigger and more usable stage, all of which can be set up in the old theater when it is finally rebuilt. So you will have a usable theater, if you can find a good Intendant.

"The State Theater, when it's in operation, is a heady mix of all the theatrical arts under one roof. It is the mainstay of the cultural life of the Germans, partially subsidized by the State Government, and brings a fine quality and quantity of choices for the public's entertainment at a reasonable cost. There are stage actors, who perform mainly in plays, though they can be used with other groups if needed. There are also a corps de ballet, a grand opera ensemble, and an operetta ensemble, and of course a fine orchestra that can be used for any stage event that needs music.

"That's a lot of people, my friend, and they are going to depend on you to recreate their world of theater and music. It's your responsibility to find an Intendant and place the very best denazified artists and behind-the-scenes workmen in their proper slots as soon as humanly possible. You can work with the Intelligence Denazifying Office in Karlsruhe – the Mayor there is an honest and good man and can help you a lot – and with anyone else you want to use.

"Remember, everything you do is brand new, with no real pointers showing the way. I would suggest you move slowly at first, sizing up each challenge separately, and then move on rapidly to the next. If you take it piece by piece, and you select the right men or women to place in leadership roles, you will have already saved yourself a busload of trouble and time.

"I have made no effort myself to find an Intendant. Once he's in place, he will free you from the actual responsibility of creating and running the show. All the Intendants during the war had to be Nazis or they would not have been permitted to assume that position, so you are just going to do your best for now.

"I think you can do it, Mr. Sherman, and my phone is always open to you. The State Theater is the biggest and most important nut you have to crack, though there is one other theater, privately owned, whose owner and performers have already been cleared of any Nazi affiliation. You also have the Cabaret House under your jurisdiction, and for the most part they can take care of themselves once they have been cleared of any Nazi members.

"As soon as you have our State Theater up and running, I want you to do the same thing in Heilbronn and Pforzheim, two other German cities in our domain and under your authority. Each has a theater that is out of order because of our bombers, though both can be restored a lot quicker than our old State Theater. What do you say?"

I sat there stunned, wondering just what in the world I had gotten myself into. I was twenty-three, going on twenty-four, with very little knowledge of what happens behind the stage curtains, let alone any experience or ideas on how to put together and recreate a cultural icon for the German public that would be able to live up to its previous high standards. It was plain ridiculous.

For a long moment, I felt completely out of my depth. I even considered feigning a faint! And then, thank God, I reconsidered. It was the biggest challenge that I could remember in my life, and I had so many men whose good graces and influence had furthered my career to this point. Could I really admit defeat before I even began? After all, I did love the theater, and the ballet, and the opera, and the symphony, so why not give it a go? Other people seemed to think I could do it, and Colonel Hills seemed to think I could do it, so what the hell.

The Colonel was speaking again. "I am losing a very fine German assistant from Karlsruhe; he is retiring there, where his family lives, as he has finished an assignment which had to do with our main theater here in Stuttgart. He has offered to be your lead assistant and interpreter, though most of the people you will be dealing with already speak English, having learned it properly at school before Hitler came to power. I would encourage you to take him on, for he never was a Nazi and is well educated, though he doesn't know any more about setting up and running a theater than you do. When you choose and delegate your leaders, choose with great care, for a good leader will be an enormous asset for you, while a poor one could sink your ship.

"Think of this whole challenge as an adventure in re-creating a vibrant cultural atmosphere for which you and you alone are the instigator and director. A good general, and that's what you will be, makes sure that he places every appointment where he belongs and will serve you well. Be in command, but gently."

Whereupon he gave me an inquiring look. I told him how much I appreciated the trust he had put in me. I assured him that I would do my damnedest to prove my worth to him and the men who had signed those recommendations, and that I would be very grateful to have the services of the German assistant returning to his family in Karlsruhe.

The Colonel then pressed his bell, and his secretary returned. At his request she went back and brought in a blond-haired, blue-eyed man in his late thirties, who was introduced to me as Carl Reeser. He became my rarely used interpreter but constant assistant, friend, and adviser, who would work as hard and as long as I, which quite often meant eighteen-hour days, sometimes with little sustenance. But we were wildly enthusiastic, and hell-bent on returning to the people their cultural home. Even though it would have to be in a temporary theater, it would be a place where they could once again be transported into other worlds, be it through a play, a ballet, an opera, or an operetta, leaving their Spartan and colorless lives behind them.

Karlsruhe

I operated out of a three-room furnished office, in a building only a couple of blocks from where the Mayor and governmental offices were located. I now drove a jeep of my own, on loan from the motor pool. The office itself consisted of a waiting room, where one secretary was stationed; in addition to her normal work, she acted as receptionist and kept appointment lists and dates and times for me to remember. Her name was Rita, a sweet lady, homely, efficient, and incredibly sexy. I think that homely ladies are far more giving of themselves than the goddesses whose ego quota is naturally self-obsessive, though I have known one exception who combined beauty and talent and generosity that raised the stakes to pure nirvana.

The main office contained another secretary, Una, very intense and very efficient, and my two assistants, Carl as my right arm, and Herman, a miniature version of the Air Marshal himself, who spoke English like an Englishman. Herman had been a journalist before the war for an American motor magazine syndicate, covering the European motor and racing world. He was better educated, more cultured, and more diplomatic than Carl; he was also older, in his fifties at least, and suffered from some disease that kept him short of breath, so he ran out of steam by three in the afternoon. He was still worth keeping; though Carl worked for as long as it took, never complaining, and I depended upon him much more than I did on Herman, I enjoyed Herman's company more. But all three of us were compatible, and we all became good friends and tremendously enthusiastic about what we were doing.

What *were* we doing?

I had a forty-five minute talk with the Mayor, a very smart and pleasant gentleman, with Carl in attendance; after I explained my raison d'être, the Mayor offered his influence and aid in any area that I needed. I suddenly decided to ask him if he had any idea where I could find a really good Intendant for the State Theater, which was at the moment rudderless, because most Intendants had apparently not yet been denazified.

"Yes, I do," said the Mayor, much to my surprise. "He was an Intendant in three cities before the war. We were at school together and are still good friends. When war came, Hitler insisted that all German Intendants must be members of the Nazi Party or forfeit their positions. He resigned, and retired to his Bavarian home. He's almost seventy, as am I, but in good health, as is Elga, his wife. I think he would consider an interview if you would care to talk to him."

I cared. Ten days later we had an Intendant, an absolutely delightful gentleman, tall, slim, brimming with energy, speaking good English, very cosmopolitan and cultivated, with a quirky sense of humor. He had an eagle's kind of head, with a high forehead and a long nose, his eyes darting everywhere with curiosity, and a strong jaw. He laughed a lot, particularly when he was up against an apparent stone wall. How he did it, I do not know. But he almost always managed to melt that stone wall, and when he couldn't, he turned to me for help. Fortunately for this State Theater, one way or another I would come through for him.

The position of Intendant of a State Theater is considered a very high and exalted one by Germans, so the holder of that position is generally revered by those working for him, as well as by his public. I never called him by his name, and he always called me Mr. Sherman. I addressed him, in fact, as Herr Intendant, and all the State Theater employees and artists were very respectful of him. They could see that he was a man of action and would brook no interference in his quest to bring the theater back to its former glory, hopefully stretching that glory to even greater heights.

His wife, Frau Elga, was a perfect foil; where her husband was full of energy and wanted everything just so, she was a very gracious and indeed patrician lady. She taught me a lot about the German people and their contradictions, as well as about her husband's difficulties in organizing such an enormous conglomeration as a State Theater when he had to start again from the very bottom.

Helping my Intendant necessitated my going under and over many of the city's rules and regulations. Fortunately, with Carl to interpret for me when needed, I had early on managed to entertain at lunch every top section manager in the cumbersome government apparatus. Moreover, I had continued to visit each one at least once a week, and sometimes more often, with the result that they had generally acceded to my demands. It seemed to help to provide them with plenty of good things from the Army PX before I started asking for specific assistance. I never once had to use my authority to get my way. But they were really good people, living in desperate times, and over time we all became good friends. I gave a Christmas party for them and their wives during the holiday season on the two Christmases when I was responsible for the cultural life of the inhabitants of Karlsruhe.

By the third month the theater had been thoroughly cleaned to a pristine sheen, including the seats and the carpeting. The lighting came from Stuttgart with the help of my Colonel, the orchestra pit was rearranged, the costume workers were reinstalled at their sewing machines, and a thousand other demands were nailed down. The cabaret clubs were being denazified and would soon be up and ready to entertain their patrons.

Our Intendant had now gotten his stagehands, lighting men, actors, musicians, dancers, and singers back on the theater payroll of all the companies, each with its own half day for rehearsals. A whole new program was being prepared.

With my help and the Intendant's direction, a glorious bedlam had been created. A marvelous sense of exhilaration and esprit de corps had triumphed over any and all mistakes or missteps, and the whole theater was imbued with an energy and grace that had long been absent.

In the meantime, programs of the coming repertoire were almost ready for printing. Invitations had been prepared to be sent out to the local VIPs, including the mayor and his wife, and Colonel Hills, who accepted with alacrity, telephoning me to ask me how I did it in such a short period. He had been counting on six months minimum. Instead, it would turn out to be four and a half months. I told him about my wonderful Intendant and his wife, and he told me that he thought I must have something magical about me. I told him that my magic came from my beloved guardian angels, but that I wouldn't be completely satisfied until the curtain came down on the first night's production. He laughed and said he was looking forward to seeing me on that night.

I then made a reservation for him at the best and nearest hotel for the opening night, and reserved a table for twelve in the restaurant for afterward, waiting until closer to the time to fill in the names of our guests. In the end, I had two tables of eighteen each.

Herman was the liaison between the Mayor's office and the top section of government managers, who needed to be constantly brought up to date on the progress of the old and battered victim of the war, the original State Theater. Its location was now being rebuilt. Herman's constant exhortations to the workmen to speed up their work went unheeded. I finally went to the Intendant, and then the Mayor, suggesting that they offer the workmen a bonus of two free passes each to the first four productions on the site of the newly refinished old theater; these would be given to them when the last brick had been laid, only if they put more effort into each day's labor than they had been providing. Somewhat to my surprise, the workmen liked the idea, and the building's rate of progress improved by fifteen percent, definitely a step in the right direction.

There would still be over a year's work to go, mainly for lack of materials and skilled workmen. As the year passed, however, German soldiers whose profession had been in the building industry returned from the war and joined or replaced some of the less competent workers. Also, the distribution of needed supplies became more normal, at which point the whole building operation became more skilled and was implemented considerably faster.

One of my other responsibilities was to ensure that all those working under the State Theater's roof were denazified before being allowed to work. This was ridiculous, since anyone working for the State Theater under the Nazis had to join the Nazi Party to hold down their jobs. I insisted that all our employees, whether working at the State Theater, a private theater, or cabarets, fill out their Fragebogen (questionnaires), including their political identity. Those working on the building site returned their questionnaires to Herman, who then gave them to me, and I dropped them off at the Intelligence Office for Colonel Hills to decide how the workers could be reclassified.

My private life I at first kept private, now that I had an apartment of my own in a building a few blocks from the State Theater. The lead female singer of the operetta ensemble and I had been irresistibly attracted to one another from the moment we were introduced. She was gorgeous, five years older than I, a natural blonde, with a face and figure to die for, and a soft, gentle, very feminine personality, including a fresh and delightful sense of humor. She spoke both English and French fluently, learned before the war on a farm in England during a summer holiday and a boarding school in France. She was really beautiful, both outwardly and inwardly, with a strong spiritual side balanced by a sensual side that lit up my life with every kind of fulfillment.

At my invitation, she moved in with me. We became a twosome, and as such were invited to a number of parties and dinner parties. Most of our hosts and guests spoke English, and we found them interesting and appreciative of what I was in the process of doing for them.

But the best part of the evening was when we returned to our flat and participated joyfully together in the most natural and spellbinding occupation in the entire world.

Some three weeks before the curtain finally went up on *The Student Prince*, with my precious companion Kitty in the leading role opposite the Prince himself, a large envelope arrived for me from Colonel Hills. The contents asked me to answer some questions in order for me to go from being a Private First Class to a War Department civilian, with a rank equivalent to First Lieutenant and a vastly larger personal remuneration than I had been receiving. (Of course, everything I paid for in order to do my job on behalf of the Information Control Division of the Military Government was reimbursed from the MG's Finance Department.)

Needless to say, I filled out the questionnaire and sent it back post haste. For the next couple of weeks, I waited for the confirmation in a high state of anxiety.

And then the morning of the first night finally came, and a weird calmness – or was it terror? – settled over all who had been irresistibly drawn to work at the State Theater, which carried so much of our hopes and expectations. Suddenly, everyone seemed to be speaking in hushed tones, with nary a laugh being heard. Whether it was the bone-numbing fatigue resulting from our working way beyond our limits for weeks, I don't know, but it was a day that we had all lived for, and now that it had arrived we felt too drained to appreciate it fully.

When I returned to our apartment from the achingly quiet theater, I found Kitty at the piano crooning love songs, including "Peterlein," a German love song that she swore was written about me. She loved the sophistication of Cole Porter and Noel Coward, and the romantic joie de vivre of George Gershwin and Ivor Novello. In addition, she sang songs from the cotton fields of the Deep South that could bring tears to your eyes. She also did a great rendition of Mother's "Dinah Lee."

After lunch she took a nap in our bedroom, to rest up for the big night, while I tried to read a book in the drawing room (which we called the music room), for about fifteen minutes. Then I, too, fell sound asleep, not waking up until nearly five, when we made tea and biscuits to hold us over. We knew we would not be going to supper until after the curtain came down on the performance, which, with a twenty-minute intermission, would be around eleven o'clock, three hours after the curtain first went up.

Both of us were feeling much better after our sleep. I brought Kitty back to the theater about six-thirty, an hour and a half before curtain time, and gave her a big hug and kiss. In time-honored theatrical tradition, I told her to break a leg and hurried away, as she sat down at her makeup table. Backstage was already beginning to hum. It was time for me to take command of the foyer.

The first thing I discovered was that the programs were all set up in the foyer by the main entrance, when they should have been broken up into four portions, one each beside the four doors providing the entrances and exits for the four sections of the house. The elegant and unique programs were too large and cumbersome for the ticket collectors to hold in their arms. The collectors, meanwhile, were supposed to be in costume, so I sent them off to the sewing room to collect four costumes to tie in with the period of the operetta. I had a table installed at each door next to where the programs would be provided, making them easily accessible for the four ticket collectors to dispense.

By now I had been seen around town quite a bit, to the point where the Mayor, with a laugh, had asked me if I was running for his office in the next election. I knew that many of the attendees would recognize me, so I was glad I had set up a reception line made up of the Mayor and his wife, followed by the head of the City Council and his wife, then by our Intendant and his wife, and finally by me. Colonel Hills had vehemently refused to be part of the reception line, insisting that tonight was my night, the Intendant's night, and the Mayor's night – "three good men who had wrought a miracle."

The Colonel had told me that he liked being near the stage, so I put him front and center, which pleased him no end. He arrived from the hotel at ten to eight, with most of the audience already seated, having bathed and changed and eaten some nuts and had a glass of Scotch, or so he told me.

The reception line was a great success, many of our patrons never having met the Mayor and his wife, and certainly never having met our wonderful Intendant and his attractive wife. I was amazed at how many attendees called me by name and told me that they had heard good things about me, and to please keep up the good work.

The Student Prince, of course, has a lovely score. Kitty's voice brought tremendous applause at the end of every solo; moreover, her duets with the

Prince, expressing their rapturous and loving romance, touched the heart of everyone there. The audience's ovations lasted for minutes on end, so that at the intermission I phoned the hotel dining room to delay our dinner for a good forty-five minutes beyond the time I had reserved.

At the finale, the stage was filled with bouquets of flowers amid thunderous applause. The Prince and his lady appeared after the cast had been roundly applauded, until the Prince bowed out behind the curtain, leaving my beloved Kitty alone on stage, her arms full of flowers and her eyes sparkling in response to the constant waves of applause rising to a crescendo that went on and on and on. Heady stuff for even a star, I thought, and at that moment I knew that our relationship would finally end. But to have had, and continue to have, if only for a while longer, the opportunity of sharing this goddess's love and great company, was worth more than I could ever have imagined.

On our way out to the two buses I had ordered to take us all to the hotel, my Colonel came up to me and put his arm on my shoulder, saying, "You did well, Peter! This is a night we will all remember, and you can be proud of your efforts. The Mayor has told me how highly regarded you are in this city, and the Intendant told me that without you we wouldn't have been able to open the doors of this theater for many more months. Incidentally, your lady friend is a perfect dream. Lovely, lovely, what a talent! She's going to rise to the top, that I promise you. Enjoy her while you can."

My own sentiments, exactly.

The dinner, when it finally arrived, was a great success – the food good, the toasts happy. The Colonel's table, at his request, included the Mayor and his lieutenants, along with their wives. All my work, for so many months, had finally proven to be worthwhile. As for my table, I put Kitty to co-host at the other end, and settled in to enjoy the company of the major artists who had performed on stage that night, along with the chief of lighting and the conductor of our orchestra, which I had found surprisingly good.

At the end of dinner, after we had bade our guests good night, with only Kitty staying behind, Colonel Hills took us to his suite and presented me with my official papers and card verifying that I was now a legitimate War Department civilian, with the equivalent rank of First Lieutenant. The Colonel and I saluted each other for the last time. From now on, I was to be a civilian for the rest of my life, God willing, though I really had been treated basically as a civilian from the time I joined the SHAEF Diplomatic Mission.

It had been extremely helpful that my patient and daring commander, Colonel Hills, whose confidence in me gave me confidence in myself, had not interfered in my work. He had taken an enormous gamble on me when he threw me into the deep end to sink or swim, and his gamble had paid off. As we said our goodbyes, he gave me half a hug and a warm handshake, and my Kitty a kiss on each cheek.

Then we returned home to our flat, full of the success of the evening and Kitty's extraordinary triumph. Since neither of us could possibly go to sleep in this state, we did what could only bring this perfect night to a perfect ending.

Paradise!

Pforzheim and Heilbronn proved to be duck soup compared with my State Theater, because both of them had been only mildly damaged by our bombers. The main problem for the theater owners was persuading their municipal governments of the need for their help in getting the theaters open and running. It seemed that the Mayors of both cities believed adamantly that there were a lot more important priorities than uplifting entertainment.

Naturally I set out to change that attitude, having by now become well acquainted with all the obstructive arguments. I finally succeeded in convincing the Mayors of both towns of the importance of counteracting the deeply demoralized state of so many of their citizens by bringing joy and beauty, romance, and entertainment into their lives, thereby giving them a more positive and normal view of life as it could be. This should, I argued, encourage them to feel that, despite all their present privations, their lives would soon be improved by the revitalization of their town, and their present unhappy circumstances would soon pass. And so it did.

There's one thing you can always say about the Germans: that they are good workers, as are the Japanese. With the inauguration of the incredible Marshall Plan, instituted by the US Congress, benefiting both friend and foe alike, our two former enemies were soon restored to their prewar working efficiency. Their skills, initiative and man-hours led to improved techniques that lowered the costs of their exports and gave the winners of the Second World War a definite jolt of reality during the late fifties and, in many cases, almost up to today.

It was during the time that I was bringing the two satellite theaters back to life that I began to think about my future, specifically about my home and career prospects. The war in Europe had been over for some months, as we were into October of 1945. It seemed to me that, now that I was a civilian and a free agent, I had better set a definite time to return home and begin a career outside the War Department, even though I doubted if anyone could have had a better military life than I. I had to admit that, along with all other British citizens, London's devastation of bricks and blood had been my testing ground, too, but I had survived it with nary a scratch, never even using a bomb shelter, and, except for taking Underground trains from one station to another, always living above ground – a charmed life indeed.

After a lot of heavy thinking, and conscious of my gratitude to my boss, Colonel Hills, for his faith in me these many months, I wrote him a letter terminating my employment on October 16, 1946, exactly one year away. He replied, regretting my letter but fully understanding my reasons, and expressed his own gratitude that I would be staying for another year to manage the cultural life of my domain.

Though busy, life had become so much easier. The State Theater, under our superlatively fine Intendant, was already drawing attention from some of the national newspapers and magazines. Not only were our theaters beginning to prosper, but a dynamic and very definite return to a more normal commercial life was evident. Even the banks were getting over their jitters and releasing funds to daring entrepreneurs with solid backgrounds to forge new businesses or reignite old ones.

The year 1946 was a wonderful one for me. As my time in Europe drew to an end, many occasions were being hosted for me and Kitty by the major players of the three cities. The most rewarding, of course, was that of my headquarters, Karlsruhe, where a twenty- three-, going on twenty-four-year-old Peter Sherman had dared to take on a challenge about which he knew practically nothing; with his two assistants, both as ignorant as he, he had managed, over months of learning, improvising, planning, and going where even angels might fear to tread, to find enormous satisfaction while gradually gaining ground. At the end, he knew that the team had slain or subdued all the resident dragons, and everything was finally coming up roses. And they had made it happen!

We were, in fact, intoxicated with our success. We went about our work with the State Theater, the politicians, and the men running the government, with tremendous enthusiasm and zest, however many hours it took, though we always let Herman, our man with the breathing problem, go home at three.

When the two satellite theaters were up and running, and the State Theater was performing as smoothly as any State Theater can, with full houses for almost every presentation, I began to feel that I had achieved all I had set out to do, unschooled or not. I wanted to leave at the top, with no final dinner events in my honor, for there was nothing I disliked more than being the center of attention; rather, I always enjoyed being behind the scenes, working my magic out of sight.

So I told no one of the day I would be departing, having already thanked Colonel Hills for his belief in me and his support throughout my tenure. I knew that my life experience as Film, Theater and Music Control Officer of the Information Control Division of the Military Government headquarters in Stuttgart for three cities had matured me beyond measure and broadened my whole outlook of the world. Though I will always have a bit of Peter Pan in my make up, I knew that my personality, my ME, was finally anchored and ready for come-what-may, after these experiences.

The last year was filled with the most sublime honeymoon that a couple could ever have, married or unmarried. On the weekends when Kitty wasn't onstage, we would take a picnic lunch and explore the countryside, cherishing each moment of our wonderfully intimate friendship. We both knew that our blissful time together was running out, and that we soon would be parting, perhaps forever. This awareness made our love affair more intense and precious than ever, burning memories into my subconscious that I treasure to this very day.

I stayed with my beloved for the final week, and then stopped at the Colonel's headquarters to say a final goodbye. I received a wonderful letter of commendation in return, and left for London on October 16, 1946, as I had intended. It had all been the greatest challenge and most wonderful experience of all my life so far, and I felt that those last two years had not only tested me to the limit but would remain as a cornerstone from which I could gather strength and wisdom for whatever opportunity lay ahead.

Home Again, at Last

The drive from the railway station to our apartment at Kingston House, Princes Gate, might have taken no more than twenty minutes, had I not instructed my taxi driver to take me the long way around. The trip thus included the Mall, Trafalgar Square with its salute to Admiral Lord Nelson on top of his column, and Piccadilly, where I indulged in a quick walk through the Burlington Arcade, to which I have always been attracted, and Fortnum and Mason, where I once later saw the actor Rex Harrison checking out the jam section. And then on to Green Park and Albert Hall and finally Hyde Park, with its memories of Mr. Bruce and my splendid horse Fiddler.

As we were driving into the enormous section of Hyde Park where cars seem to crisscross in all directions and I was nervously sitting on the edge of my seat, I saw the royal automobile, flag flying, driving toward us parallel to the left side of my taxi. As it approached closer, I could see the Queen on my side facing toward me, with her husband King George VI on the right far side next to her. For a moment I was stunned, my mouth hanging open, and then, completely out of control and full of patriotism for this adored couple, I rolled down my window and thrust my arm and head out, waving with great fervor to their majesties. The Queen turned to her husband briefly to say something, at which he, too, turned in my direction, and then she, with that wonderful smile of hers, gave me the royal wave, while I, without realizing what I was doing, continued to wave madly back at them.

The whole experience could only have taken ten to fifteen seconds, if that, but to me at that moment it was breathtaking, and I couldn't help but think to myself, "My God, what a way to begin my new life!" Even my taxi driver was awed. "Cor blimy," he said, over and over again, "Cor bloody blimy!"

Mother herself opened the front door of her flat, welcoming me with a long and very endearing hug, after which I embraced Molly, still in attendance on Mother, though her sister Kitty (no connection with my more recent Kitty!) came in one day a week to clean the apartment and help with the laundry. Molly had turned out to be a natural-born cook, so that when Mother and Johnny were home they never needed for a delicious meal. For a while, that included me.

My half brother David was enrolled at Stow, thanks to his grandmother Flora's interference. She had managed to get him under her supervision on the ground that he would be safer at Wookitipi then anywhere else, and Mother, being so busy herself and not wishing to get into a war with Flora, let her have him. Tony, the younger of my half brothers, was now attending John Green's private school, where I had spent two years of my life as a teacher, after which he would be following in my footsteps to Eton.

Johnny was away, Mother didn't know where, but it had something to do with the criminals responsible for the assassination of fifty of our brave airmen prisoners. It was Johnny's last month of service, after which he would return to his prewar position with the stockbrokerage company Nathan and Roselli and become a bona fide civilian again, at long last.

Mother reported that Johnny was almost back to his prewar weight, and that he now looked as handsome as ever, his hair just beginning to gray. With his old friend Kermit Roosevelt no longer there to tempt him with some new adventure, and Winston Churchill out of office temporarily, Johnny now seemed more serene and comfortable in his life.

Mother also told me that Johnny was looking forward to restarting the Ends of the Earth Club dinners that had originated in the United States. They had been brought to London by Johnny Dodge himself and almost immediately became a great success, their purpose being to bring together Americans and Englishmen of the highest stature and prestige, whatever their occupation, in order for them to meet and exchange views and confidences. Above all, the dinners were to feature speakers of rare intellect and prominent positions. Then Hitler went on his rampage and Johnny had to close down the dinner club for the duration. Incidentally, the club was out of bounds to the press, giving the guest speakers, whoever they were, a freedom of speech that was available to them without any limitations, and of which they generally took advantage.

Although I had never been to one of these dinner, being too young at the time, I would now be able to attend, if Johnny invited me. He would be home for Christmas, and I would wait to see what happened. For now, I could stay in the guest room, Tony having the other room while on holiday, although he was spending the week of Christmas in the country with a school chum and family. At least until I found a flat of my own, I was all right.

As it turned out, I had saved practically all my vastly improved remuneration for the last year from the US War Department Civilian Section, and I had promised myself that part of it would go toward a one-month vacation before I started looking for a position. I needed to find out which of my friends were left, and where and what they were up to, and when I could get together with them. I wanted to walk the parks; ride in Rotten Row; eat some really good food without having to wolf it down on account of lack of time; see some of the new shows; see what was going on at the Albert Hall; check into the Windmill Theater for another opportunity to feast my eyes on pulchritudinous female flesh; and see if the Mills Brothers Circus was coming to town for Christmas.

I felt a little dizzy thinking of all that I wanted to accomplish in one month. To start with, I asked Mother if I could take her to lunch. She said, "Of course, I've already reserved a table at the Causerie, where Benita and Juliet and I had a miserably sad luncheon with you when you were leaving to go to sea, before we took you to the station, dropped you off, and left you all alone standing there waving as our taxi drove away. We were all wondering if we would ever see you again, or would you be at the bottom of the ocean? And now you're back for good. We'll celebrate, right?" Right! And celebrate we did.

The maitre d' at Claridge's Causerie welcomed us to our favorite table. After we shared a bottle of champagne to accompany our delicious luncheon, and I spent two and a half hours satisfying Mother's inquiries into just about everything I had done while away, we returned to Kingston House. Molly had left for the day, so we each went to our rooms and collapsed. My, oh, my, was it ever good to be home again!

It was important that I look to the future with clear eyes and a competent stand, for I knew what I wanted more than diamonds and gold, and that was a part of the action where I could justify my employment with my talents in diplomacy and public relations and my successful career in Military Government. Surely this all added up to something good for me. Or was I just chasing the wind?

There were really only two desirable film companies at the time, the first and foremost being London Film Productions, Sir Alexander Korda's company. The J. Arthur Rank Company, a much larger operation, was not nearly so prestigious, because Rank was mainly a businessman. It was true, however, that with his large bankroll he was capable of hiring talented professionals to run the company's filmmaking side for him.

I still preferred Sir Alex's company, though I was beginning to have doubts about myself, for Sir Alex was a film-producing genius and I did not know much more about filmmaking than I had known about re-creating a state theater in Germany. Obviously, I would not be the most desirable applicant to hire.

Nevertheless, I decided to write to both companies and see if either had the least interest in interviewing me. My letter included my family, education, and military background, along with copies of my recommendations and the history of my achievements as Film Theater and Music Control Officer with the Information Control Division of the Military Government Headquarters in Stuttgart. I emphasized my experience and authority in implementing cultural activities covering the State of Württemberg and Baden in Germany. I think it was a good letter. At any rate, it was intended to show my enterprising spirit and responsible attitude. Who knew? It might be thrown in the wastepaper basket, or it might not.

A week before Christmas, I mailed my two letters. I remained calm by reminding myself that what will be, will be. Since there was nothing further that I could do about it, I entered into the spirit of Christmas by offering myself for volunteer duty serving the poorer citizens in the East End of London – Johnny's former political territory – by helping distribute Christmas dinners donated for more than five hundred less fortunate individuals, all to be handed out on Christmas Day.

When Mother and Johnny discovered what I was planning for December 25, they decided to join me. The location for the distribution turned out to be the Club that Johnny and his friends had underwritten some years before and later presented to the British Legion. Johnny's picture was hanging in the entrance hall to commemorate his having been the instigator and accomplisher of the building itself.

We had a wonderful Christmas Day.

Into the Movie World

J ohnny Dodge had definitely mellowed. Our relationship soon became affectionate and buddy-buddy, particularly after he learned more about my wartime experiences and the extraordinary transformation of my identity from Private First Class to a civilian-equated First Lieutenant.

Of course, none of this was in the same class as Johnny's amazing bravery under the most demonic torture, both mental and physical. We knew that his mind and body had been starved of all communication and received barely a thimbleful of nourishment, the months of captivity running on into oblivion, his body more that of a scarecrow than of a human being. But he had survived, and now he was my walking companion during Christmas week, often with Mother accompanying us. She would be wrapped against the cold in the mink coat that she had been using for more than ten years, while Johnny wore his cashmere overcoat and I my camelhair coat, all of us walking with energetic strides against the cold. Hyde Park on a sunny day was Mecca for those hearty souls who shared in the joy and exhilaration of a simple walk in the park. Even the ducks on the Serpentine appeared to be more active than normal, while the frisky dogs, their owners, and everyone else seemed to be blowing smoke from their nostrils in the chill air of the wintry day.

The three of us soon became attuned once again to one another, our relationship falling into place as easily as our hands into warm-fitting gloves. Johnny was soon to return to Nathan and Roselli, while Mother was at long last relieved of her wartime duties: running the English Speaking Union's American and Dominion Division. She had done this with enormous success for more than three years, receiving many commendations and awards from both the American and Dominion forces, the biggest surprise of all being a handwritten letter from General Charles de Gaulle, thanking her for her services to his troops while they were stationed in London. Ditto from Winston Churchill, who included Johnny Dodge in his letter to Mother, calling them "the most remarkable couple I have ever had the honour to know, and whose friendship to me and Clementine I will treasure always."

For my part, I was waiting, somewhat nervously, for a letter to come from at least one, and maybe both, with luck, of the film studio headquarters. But it was two weeks after the New Year before I received an answer from J. Arthur Rank's central office, telling me that there was no opening at the moment, but that they would file my résumé in case an opening should appear that would fit in with my capabilities. Something told me that that was a polite turndown, so I put it out of my mind. One to go. Help!

The next few days dragged by, while I became more and more disheartened, wondering what would be my next step if I didn't receive a reply at all. A letter finally came from London Film Productions, though I was so sick to my stomach with dread that I couldn't even open it at first. Knowing that the odds were standing at 50/50, I finally picked up the letter cutter and slit the envelope open.

It was not from Sir Alexander Korda, but from Sir David Cunningham, who turned out to be in charge of practically everything except the filmmaking part of the studios, located in Denham, just outside of London. Sir David was second in command, next to only Sir Alex. His letter started with an apology for his late response to mine, noting that he had been on a skiing holiday in St. Moritz and had only now returned. I thought it was exceedingly nice of him to have even bothered to give an excuse. He asked me to call his secretary and make an appointment. That was duly arranged for four days hence, in the middle of January, on a Friday at two-thirty in the afternoon.

During those madly slow days before the interview, Mother and Johnny both did everything they could to keep me occupied and upbeat, though it was unnecessary, for my confidence in myself had returned and I was calm and determined that I would be at my best in my meeting with Sir David. I did, however, pray a little more than usual!

The offices on Piccadilly of Sir Alexander Korda's London Film Productions, in years gone by, had been the elegant London residence of the Duke and Duchess of York, along with their daughters, Elizabeth and Margaret. Their stepping stone to the monarchy had been the consequence of King Edward VIII's abdication from the throne in order to marry Wallis Simpson, because the Duke of York was next in line to the throne. The entire hall was marble, as were the stairs leading up to the second floor where Sir David Cunningham's offices were situated. I could not help but feel that I was in a palace rather than a working office building, where a considerable degree of brainpower was dedicated to the creation of high-quality, crowd-pleasing films and to the opening of new markets for distribution of these films all over the world.

It had all started with Alexander Korda, who began in the film industry in about 1916 as a very young and ingenious producer in Budapest, Hungary. He had gone on over the years to be associated as producer and sometimes director of some sixty films, among them *An Ideal Husband*; *That Hamilton Woman* – also titled *Lady Hamilton*; *The Private Life of Henry VIII*, for which Sir Alex earned a knighthood from his sovereign King George V; *Rembrandt*; *Things to Come*, an adaptation of the book by world-famous author H. G. Welles, who had been the star of the weekend party at Lord Evan Tredegar's home in Wales that, you may remember, I attended with Mother and Johnny; *The Four Feathers*; *To Be or Not to Be*; *The Jungle Book*; *The Thief of Baghdad*; *Knight Without Armor*; *Elephant Boy*; *I, Claudius*; *The Ghost Goes West*; *Sanders of the River*; *The Scarlet Pimpernel*; and *The Third Man*, acclaimed as the best film ever to come out of a British studio, to this day still holding that honor.

Even Sir Alex's own roster of actors under contract to him listed among the very best, including Leslie Howard; Merle Oberon, whom Sir Alex chose as his second wife in 1939; Wendy Barrie; Robert Donat, who won the Oscar for best actor in the original *Goodbye Mr. Chips*; Maurice Evans; and Vivian Leigh, star of both *The Hamilton Woman* and, though not one of Korda's films, that superb production, *Gone with the Wind*, also starring Clark Gable.

A lady came out of a door on one side of the second floor. She was crossing to the other side when I asked her where I could find Sir David Cunningham's secretary. She smiled at me, saying that she was Sir David's secretary, and I must be Mr. Sherman. Her name was Florence, and she had a phenomenal memory, as I discovered in no time. She took me to her office and called Sir David on the intercom; I could hear him reply, "Show him in," so she led me out of her office, back into the hall, and up to a large two-door entry. Opening the right-side door for me, she wished me luck and closed it quietly behind me.

I had, before the Second World War, seen a photograph of the Italian dictator Mussolini's private office, an immense room with an enormous desk at the far end some inches above floor level. Mussolini reportedly derived great pleasure in chastising his underlings with cries of "Hurry up, you idiots, I haven't got all day," at which the underlings or even petitioners would have to break into a run, arriving at his desk huffing and puffing and definitely cowed, their lofty hero gazing down at them with obvious disdain.

This was not the case in Sir David's office, though it seemed to take me quite a while to cross that endless floor. His desk was flush with the floor, mercifully coming into sight finally, whereupon its occupant rose from his seat and shook my hand. Pointing to one of the two seats on my side of his desk, he motioned me to sit down, as did he, while he perused what I recognized as my letter requesting an interview.

Sir David was mostly bald except around the edges, with a cherubic face and a very pleasant smile, of medium height, stocky, and was dressed, as was I, in a pinstriped dark blue suit with a white shirt. He was wearing a military tie, while I wore my old Etonian tie, for luck.

"You've certainly had a very unusual military career, if ever I saw one," said Sir David, giving me a curious look. I was about to respond, when he went on to say, "If variety is the spice of life, you seem to have had your fair share of it. How old are you now?"

"Twenty-five, going on twenty-six in April."

"Well, you seem to be very adaptable, which I need; you also seem to have an ingrained feel for diplomacy, which means you can get along with people in all walks of life, which I also need; you are dependable, or the military wouldn't have given you so many responsibilities; and you certainly wouldn't have received such recommendations without deserving them, on top of which you are not bad looking! I'm in need of someone with all these virtues, someone who can adapt to many different situations and occupations without becoming disoriented, and your record suggests that you have those strengths, indeed already well-tested."

He stopped and called for two cups of tea over the intercom. His secretary, Florence, brought them in on a silver tray, and over tea he talked about this multifaceted job. I was to become his assistant and liaison officer, and I would, if nothing else, find my working life full of variety and no doubt odd situations; furthermore, I must always be ready to travel on a moment's notice.

All of these as yet unknown and unspecified tasks that I was expected to perform were to be compensated with a very healthy monthly paycheck and an outstanding entertainment allowance. I would be on a three-month trial. If it worked out, I would be given a raise at the end of the year. If not, I would be let go.

What did I think? I thought it was the most exciting thing that had ever happened to me. I was so glad that I had already been through numerous unbelievable challenges without even a compass to guide me and my two assistants, as once again it seemed that I would be in such a situation, but this time without the assistants. I must give Sir David his due, however; he always let me know that I was to negotiate frankly and clearly, and when he was not sure of his facts, he admitted as much to me.

I accepted, of course, thrilled out of my skull, delighted with the opportunity to work for such an illustrious company as London Film Productions, and also to be a part of an organization that, though small in size, was regarded as among the very top film companies in all the world. Sir David then told me that he had to be in Hollywood next week, and I would be put on salary plus entertainment allowance a week from that coming Monday, by which time he would have returned.

We shook hands, and I felt good not only about my new job, but also about my relationship with Sir David. Although it had been brief, it was already warm, each of us having sized the other up and neither finding the other wanting. I thanked Sir David for giving me the opportunity to prove myself, and wished him well for his trip to Hollywood.

I stopped off at his secretary Florence's office to say goodbye, just as she was about to open her door to Sir David's office, and thanked her for her courtesy. She seemed pleased. I left it for Sir David to tell her of my employment.

I walked the whole way home, my head in the clouds, my feet barely touching the ground. I was transported with a joy of such fulfillment that I literally felt godlike, the whole world my oyster. When I finally reached Kingston House and our apartment, I found Mother and Johnny pretending to be reading, Mother's book upside down, their faces obviously hoping for the best and fearing the worst. It took only one look at me, of course, to know that I had prevailed, at which point they leaped out of their chairs and into my arms, a three-person embrace that went on and on as we rocked together in a supreme hug that I hoped would never end.

Such ecstatic moments, so very rare in our lives, must be a tiny flake dropped from heaven, to remind us of another world more beautiful than ever we can conceive, but ever there for us to come home to when the time is right. So be it.

My first assignment after Sir David's return from Hollywood was the easiest and one of the nicest I could imagine: that of being chauffeur-driven in a Daimler limousine from London Film Productions headquarters on Piccadilly to Heathrow Airport, to welcome an old and trusted friend of Sir Alex and Sir David. In the thirties, up to the beginning of the war in 1939, this man had been Sir Alex's main agent for marketing and distributing Alex Korda films; actually, these included some films that were not Korda's, their producers being willing to pay for the privilege of being distributed on Korda's pipeline throughout Europe. Of course, Korda picked only the best, so his agent had generally carried out most of his requests, including placing the non-Korda-produced films at the best movie theaters available, along with the Korda films themselves. Only the advent of war had curtailed and finally stopped all importations of films into German-occupied countries, until Germany was defeated.

I learned later that Hitler had actually ordered a copy of *The Great Dictator*, Charlie Chaplin's masterpiece trivializing the two dictators, Hitler and Mussolini, and that Hitler had seen it alone, with only the projection operator as witness. Right after the film ended, the projection operator was dispatched to the Russian front, and Hitler had the film burned, while never offering a word of public criticism or comment.

Sir David had given me a passport photo of the gentleman I was to meet. I am sorry to say I have forgotten his name, though I knew that he had been with Sir Alex from the latter's film producer beginnings in Budapest. I also knew that he was considerably older than Sir Alex, who was barely in his fifties, while his friend was then in his seventies.

Sir David had urged me to learn anything and everything I could from this gentleman, whom I shall call Little Giant, for he turned out to be a small man, possibly five feet four, with a roundish figure and face, his eyes his best feature, piercing and calculating and somewhat intimidating at first. But by the time we had returned to the head office, we had become friends, he being flattered that I had grilled him for information on his career and his day-to-day activities, I being thrilled with all the information and explanations with which he had rewarded me.

At the end, Little Giant urged me, if I really wanted to learn his craft, to suggest to Sir David that I be given a month's leave to spend with him and learn firsthand what his raison d'être was all about. "Hands on" was the best way to learn, he said, though he didn't tell me how incredibly dangerous and life threatening it could be, particularly behind the Eastern border into Berlin's Russian Zone, and with Czechoslovakia also under Russian occupation.

I delivered my newfound friend to Sir David, who wanted to debrief him before sending him on to Sir Alex. I later learned from Sir David that he agreed with Little Giant that on-the-ground training was the best way to learn, but that he couldn't spare me for more than two weeks at the most; so two weeks it was to be, and only when Little Giant had finished his business at headquarters would we leave London for foreign shores. Little Giant also had a wife and was given extra time to spend with her.

In the meantime, Sir David gave me a list of things that needed attending to, everything from introducing myself to the movie theater managers – which usually meant taking them to lunch – where I learned a lot about another fascinating side of the film business. They, in turn, learned of my position as Sir David's liaison between them and our headquarters.

I also introduced myself to my counterpart at J. Arthur Rank Films, an empty hole that needed filling. This brought about a much more cooperative and useful relationship between our two firms. With Sir David's permission, I introduced myself by mail to a blue ribbon group of insiders in the film industry as Sir David's liaison officer, adding that I would be happy to attend to any requests they might have, thereby, hopefully, relieving Sir David as much as possible of that particular responsibility. Of course, I was inviting trouble for myself, since I was such a newcomer to the film industry, but I was slowly but surely ingratiating myself into the coteries on Sir Alex's side of the building, as well as Sir David's helpers. With the advantage of being able to draw upon the knowledge of all their brilliant minds, and in particular that of Florence, Sir David's secretary, I was pretty sure that the blue ribbon group would be satisfied with whatever answer I gave to their requests, though I must say that I was relieved to find that my bank of geniuses never once let me down.

One time I was invited to speak about my company and the movie world to a rowdy but enthusiastic group of teenagers from a local public school in the East End of London, sponsored by a Catholic Church – not a "Roman" Catholic Church, though, but one led by priests who were not much different from their Roman Catholic brothers, except that they were allowed to marry and, I suppose, father children, if they wanted.

After a very wild welcome, my teenage audience simmered down, and I was allowed to talk about our two latest film productions and tell them about the stars and the scriptwriter and the director. But I talked mostly about the stars, for those demigods, American royalty and Great Britain's phantom royalty, next in line to the real thing, remain an obsession with the young and impressionable, as they have since the dawn of silent movies and the subsequent discovery of sound.

One of Mother's connections at the BBC, Sheila Wasey, on hearing of my appointment to Sir David's staff, and knowing about some of my war experiences as recounted to her by Mother, asked if she might interview me on air, comparing my previous war experiences with my new life at London Film Productions. Since both Sir Alex and Sir David had to be consulted as to whether this would be a positive thing for the company, that was how I finally met my ultimate boss, Sir Alexander Korda.

The meeting was duly arranged. Tall and angular, his face peering owlishly over spectacles halfway down his nose, there stood Sir Alexander Korda, my movie idol and top dog, seemingly about to depart the room if I would just get out of his way, which I did immediately. In a loud whisper, he said, "Sit down. I'll be back," and off he went out the same door through which I had just entered.

I didn't sit; I was too uptight. So I inspected photos and civic and film industry awards that were placed discreetly and unpretentiously on the walls and columns of his office, which seemed more like a library, with books and manuscripts bedecking the main wall at the back of the room. Imagine! I was in the lion's den, without the lion, though in the first few seconds given to me to access him, it was clear to me that he had a strong presence and an equally strong personality – a man who was very comfortable in his own skin.

Upon his return, he went around his desk and told me again to sit down. Then he asked me what I wanted. I was caught off guard, believing that he had already been advised of the purpose for our meeting; indeed, I later found out that he knew exactly what the meeting was about, but was testing me to see how I would handle it.

So I told him what the meeting was about, explaining why I thought the BBC interview would be an original way of presenting London Film Productions through one newly engaged employee with an unusual military background and an equally unusual position with Sir David Cunningham – more like that of a man Friday than anything. At the same time, it was a position that offered a varied mix of challenges, just as I had experienced in my previous job with the Film, Theater and Music Control Branch of the Military Government in Germany.

When I finished my presentation, Sir Alex stared at me for what felt like a full minute. Then he said, "All right, do a good job," and dismissed me with a wave of his hand toward the door. I exited, relieved that it was over, though not quite sure whether he had liked me or not. At least he had approved the project. Later he heard it on a tape provided by the BBC at his request, following which he sent Sir David a congratulatory note on my performance. I knew that Sir David had heard the interview on his office radio, but he did not comment on it to me until he had received Sir Alex's complimentary note. There was no question as to who was top dog in this company, though Sir David always stated his honest opinion, whether it agreed with Sir Alex's or not, and I learned that they had considerable regard for each other. Although each was responsible for his own province, they meshed well, whether a facet of their company was under duress or they were opening new and untried fields of promise that needed a daring and calculatingly cool hand at the wheel. The two men were very different, and yet so complementary to each other that their employees didn't care; London Film Productions was a runaway success, and the fact that I was now becoming a part in that success made each day exciting and rewarding for me, with no two days being the same. I was rarely without a smile on my face.

Only one thing threw a small shadow over my joy. If I wanted to go with Little Giant on his next trip behind the Iron Curtain, Sir David said, I should do it now, for he needed me for himself and wanted me back in two weeks from the time I left. Unfortunately, this was impossible, for Little Giant had returned to his home to find his wife in bed with the flu, too weak to do almost anything for herself. She was older than her husband by five years, and he would not be leaving until he was assured that she was well enough to take care of herself.

I was spending considerable time entertaining people from other companies who were a well-established part of the British Film Industry. I found them curious and eager to be entertained by me, clearly influenced by my connection with Sir David and their supposition that I was also in a minor but influential position under the patronage of Sir Alex. Fortunately for me, nobody actually questioned my standing.

In my position as host, I was able both to learn a great deal about what was going on in the film world and, more importantly, to give my guests some surprise tidbits about my own company and its present and future activities. The information shared had first been cleared by Sir David and Sir Alex, with the latter providing most of the material that I used. It was a form of gossip that would do my company no harm, while enthralling my guests and raising my status among them by quite a few degrees.

I also enjoyed the company of a friend of Sir Alex, another Hungarian, whose main duty seemed to be to keep Sir Alex's first wife as far away from Sir Alex as possible. This friend, though considerably younger than his boss, spent most of his time acting as a buffer between them, complaining to me that his life was in great disarray. He was a successful film scriptwriter, he said, but was never able to find the time to actually write a script. For confidential reasons, I will call him Justin.

Sir Alex's first wife was Maria Corda, who had been a movie star in the silent movie era. She had changed her name to begin with a "C" in order to show her independence from him, although she did appear in some of his early movies.

Justin and I both had lady friends at this time, so one Friday, after a heavy week of engagements and inner office routine, we decided to invite our present conquests to make a night of it, starting with the Grosvenor House dining room, where Sidney Lipton's band was playing and his daughter singing. There we enjoyed a fine dinner and some exuberant dancing. I loved foxtrots, slow or fast, and we all got along well and felt comfortable together. Since the band ended up playing its last number, "Goodnight, Sweetheart, See You in the Morning" – how many times have you heard that in your life? – I suggested, all four of us being still pumped up and ready for fun, romance, or whatever came down the pike, that we go on to the Churchill Club, a nightclub where I had been a member from almost its beginning, and where you could usually see one or more celebrities for sure. Furthermore, the service and band combined to give you a very pleasant experience. I kept my Scotch there under lock and key, though we had all been drinking champagne on this particular night, and the maitre d' sent me over an iced bottle on the house, which elevated our spirits even more.

Time passed. I had just looked at my watch, noticing that it was now a little after one-thirty, and began to consider leaving the dance floor – my lady friend was a good dancer, and cuddled nicely in my arms, but my throat was parched, and I felt the need for a tall glass of water. At that very moment I noticed none other than Ingrid Bergman dancing with a vapid-looking male, she as elegant and enchanting as I had imagined her to be. I propelled my partner closer and closer to my target, who suddenly looked my way and immediately guessed what I was up to, which was simply to get close enough to her to touch her, smile, and dance away. I was certainly not going to be boorish enough to accost her on the dance floor. Finally, I, with my unaware partner, since she had her back to my idol, reached Bergman, and I brushed my hand across her arm resting on her partner's shoulder; since he could not see any of this, my heart throb blew me a kiss and I blew her one back, both of us giggling as I steered my partner away from the dance floor, my heart pounding and my feet tripping over themselves as I returned to my table. Whew!

Bergman, so incredibly real and human, deliciously desirable and hauntingly personable, became a memory hidden away in the top drawer of my subconscious, to be brought out only on very special occasions. A passing incident for her, surely – but a treasured one for me.

I paid the bill, and we decided to take a walk in the park. However, before we had barely started, I had an inspiration: Though the weather was cold outside, the Lansdowne Club would be warm, and there was a beautiful swimming pool just begging for company at this time of the night, when no one else would be about. We were just the ones to fill that pool! We stopped a taxi and piled in. Unquestionably, I had had a sufficiency of the bubbly, my favorite drink, but I was still at the top of my form.

When we arrived there, at two, a splendidly dressed doorman standing guard opened the taxi door for us. After I had paid the driver, we walked confidently into the Club's entrance hall, the doorman wishing us goodnight, as he no doubt presumed we were out-of-town club members returning from a night of partying.

Peter Henriques had shown me the separate changing rooms and bathrooms for those desiring to take a swim, so I showed our ladies where to go and took Justin to the men's changing room. After undressing, we all four came together by the pool, naked as jaybirds. We were each familiar with our own partner, our lady's nipples slightly extended and our sexual appendages feeling a certain intensity, until we foolishly decided to jump into the pool. It was freezing!

We all swam furiously to the other end, popping out of the pool as if by projection. And talk about flaccid! We men cringed helplessly, our mighty weapons shrunk to a pitiful shadow of their normal size, our two female companions bent over in out-of-control laughter. In order to avoid any more embarrassment, we took off for the men's dressing room, leaving our partners to fend for themselves.

At least there were showers to warm us and towels to dry us. Once we were all finally dressed again, we let ourselves back out of the building, the doorman somewhat surprised at our reappearance but apparently lost for words. We moved on at a swift walk, finally locating a taxi to take us to our homes. (By this time I was now the proud renter of a flat in Maida Vale.)

During the ride, our partners, like embers that you think are out but suddenly come back to life, started up with their hysterical laughter again, and soon we, too, realizing how ridiculous we must have looked to them in our frozen state of shrinkage, became similarly convulsed, prompting our taxi driver to caution us that our exuberant laughter might hurt us if we were not careful. This only had the effect of causing more hysteria until we reached the first drop-off, at my flat, where we all embraced through scattered laughter and Justin and his lady proceeded on with the cabbie to his flat.

Being young and lusty, and adoring the ladies, I could afford to be choosy. There would be no one-night stands for me. It had to be a relationship, with love and affection and friendship, and would usually last many months; the end would always be mutually agreed upon, both parties being the better for the experience and remaining good friends until the end of time.

The greatest war in history was finally behind us. It was time to enjoy the banquet.

My beloved is gone down into his garden,
to the beds of spices,
to feed in the garden,
and to gather lilies.
I am my beloved's,
and my beloved is mine:
He feedeth among the lilies.
– The Song of Solomon 6:2-3

The Russian Berlin

F inally, after some ten more days, Mrs. Little Giant was over the flu and capable of caring for herself. I was packed and ready for takeoff. Sir David wished me good luck, instructing me to do exactly whatever Little Giant told me to do and to come back safe and sound within the allotted time.

Johnny's goodbye handshake was tinged with some envy, I thought, for he smelled the challenge of danger, irresistible to a man with his background, though he and Mother were presently deep into organizing the first Ends of the Earth Club dinner since the war, already set for twenty-one days hence, in a private room at Claridge's. As I had hoped, he had invited me to be his guest. And not only that, he had also invited the only man who had had authority over General Douglas MacArthur in the Pacific War with Japan and General Dwight D. Eisenhower in the European Theater of Operations, namely, the United States Armed Forces Supreme Commander, General George C. Marshall. As President Franklin Roosevelt's chosen Commander in Chief, he had steadfastly and brilliantly maneuvered vast armies of men under the command of his best officers to find victory in both theaters of war.

Not only was General Marshall a giant among men already, but he would soon be given the honor of having his name attached to his country's incredibly generous recovery plan for Europe, to be known to history as the Marshall Plan. It would bring both victors and losers out of their postwar apathy and bankruptcy by oiling the wheels of international commerce with American loans, grants, and investments, all packaged to provide a means to bring prosperity and goodwill back to the barren cities left after the greatest war in the history of mankind, the Second World War.

How Johnny had brought about the miracle of having Marshall accept his invitation I can only surmise, but it certainly showed Johnny's stature among the great ones who outlasted the Second World War. In fact, it would continue to the end of his life and beyond.

But for now, I am in the limousine with Little Giant, being driven to Heathrow Airport on the first leg of our trip to Berlin. My mentor was not being very sociable, no doubt worn out by playing nurse to his wife. He had a rather beaten-up black leather bag on his lap, attached by a steel chain to his wrist. He only commented, in passing, on some edifice or other that caught his attention, or grumbled about the English weather, it being a typically windy and wet morning, the rain heavy and the streets soggy. Those unfortunate enough to be out in it were well drenched despite their umbrella or raincoat.

Since Alex Korda valued his old friend highly, we both had first-class tickets. The brief delay we endured after arriving at the London airport was spent in a spiffy-looking clubroom; we enjoyed leather chairs and courteous service and, since it was after twelve noon, Scotch for my mentor and a gin and tonic for me.

Soon after taking off, our plane broke through into glorious blue skies, and our spirits lifted with the weather and a reasonably good luncheon. After that, Little Giant went to sleep and I perused *Punch* magazine, always good for a few laughs, whether inspired by a cartoon or an article. I particularly enjoyed H. P. Herbert's writing.

Berlin's weather appeared to be competing with that of London, for that city, too, was engulfed in heavy, slanting rain. The great umbrellas that were to protect us from the plane to the bus a few yards away did nothing but whip around in the attendants' hands; with just a bit more wind I think they and their umbrellas could have been airborne!

The hotel in the British Zone that Little Giant had chosen was small and intimate. It was his favorite choice from long before the war, partly because the owner had never been a Nazi, and partly because it was centrally located but on a side street. It boasted a smallish dining room serving delicious food, provided by a retired chef whose lifelong occupation had been as a gourmet chef for some of Germany's major restaurants. Although retired now, he kept his cooking skills up to snuff by feeding those lucky enough to enjoy his small restaurant. Without that outlet, he said, he would die of boredom.

The first three days we canvassed the major downtown movie theaters in the British and American Zones. Sometimes Little Giant would leave me in the waiting room for up to forty-five minutes or so, when he came out to collect me and take me back inside. There he would finally introduce me to the managers, most of whom spoke some English, one or two speaking it fluently.

It bothered me somewhat that about once in every three visits I would be left to twiddle my thumbs while he and the manager would discuss some subject that apparently was none of my business. I was not so much offended as curious. I finally took the plunge and asked him point blank what went on in the managers' offices that I was not permitted to attend. Little Giant laughed it off by saying that he first softened up the manager by reminding him of the old days and the old stars and the old ways, including making a bit of cash on the side without the bookkeeper ever knowing. I was not to give it another thought. Was I learning anything?

I told him that I certainly was, though to myself I wondered how and if this competition with other companies vying for equal space in the same movie theaters could be used to Sir David's advantage in any way. And yet, though forty-five minutes of reminiscence and brotherly love was one thing, our time was limited, and I could only surmise that this particular pattern of leaving me out of the action, though used in only about a third of our visits, could be justified by something other than an entente cordiale, something that neither protagonist wanted me to hear. It was weird, to say the least, and I was beginning to have serious doubts about whether Little Giant was as loyal to Sir Alex as he professed. Or was he involved in something more than the selling of Sir Alex's movies?

Over dinner that night he told me that we would be leaving by rented car the following morning. He suggested that I get a good night's sleep, for we were going deep into enemy territory, surrounded by Russian and East German patrols, with sentinels and checkpoints that moved from street to street, so that one was never sure just where they were. The East Germans were under Communist rule, with a police force guilty of terror, torture, and murder; moreover, the German police chief was the most feared, cold-blooded and brilliant one to come along in many a year, according to my mentor. I wondered how he knew so much about the police chief. Could he, in some way, be in cahoots with this devil? No! Ridiculous! He was Alex's old and trusted friend, for goodness' sake! I gave up and went to bed, but I didn't sleep well. Not at all.

The next morning after breakfast, we got into a Russian car that Little Giant had procured, taking with us only a change of underclothes and our toiletries. With my mentor at the wheel, we took off down the road, passing quickly through the British crossing and then the dreaded Russian–East German crossing, where we found the guards in a jovial mood. Little Giant had told me that four of the guards had been bribed, so that one of them would always attend to whatever vehicle he was in and let us pass after a few minutes of lighthearted banter. The bribes were better than, say, being caught handing out a basket of food, which would call for a search and would then be quickly distributed among the guards, followed by the certainty of a term in a jail cell.

Once we had passed the crossing, my mentor took off down the road at an enormous speed, scaring me half to death. Little Giant, seeing my apprehension – white knuckles, gritted teeth, pale complexion – pointed to a small red flag on the right mudguard, explaining that it was a gift from the Zone's Police Chief and I had nothing to worry about. I decided then and there that I was being driven by a crazy man, for not only was he breaking the speed limit, but he had as much as told me that he was, in fact, involved with the enemy.

Finally, he slowed the car and drove down a quiet street, the buildings on both sides of which had been demolished. The courtyard and one wing of a house at the end of the street were in ruins, while the other wing was untouched.

We were welcomed at the door of that wing, and it was in this residence that I would learn the secret of Little Giant's second life, and be pulled into one of the strangest and most traumatic episodes of my entire life.

A nice-looking German couple, undernourished, as were most German citizens, and in their fifties, I would say, greeted Little Giant with considerable respect. The wife actually made a brief curtsy, her husband standing at attention beside her, his eyes gazing upon my mentor as if he were some god come down to earth. I was impressed with their reverence, especially compared with the polite but disinterested attention they gave me.

Never mind; after introducing me, Little Giant asked me to go back to the car and bring out a large wicker basket that unbeknownst to me had been placed on the floor of the car's back seat, covered with a blanket upon which sat a funeral wreath of some size. It seemed very odd, but I rescued the basket, and we all entered the house and were led to the kitchen, where our hosts opened it. They behaved as if they had received a gift of a million dollars. To tell the truth, I could not believe that a million dollars would have aroused as much excitement as the contents of that basket, among its delicacies being a large cooked ham, two cooked chickens, potato salad and green bean salad, and a sizeable chocolate cake, enough for at least eight hungry people.

Not having looked in the back of the car at the start of our journey, I had failed to see the cemetery arrangement, thinking that the scent that I was smelling was cologne that Little Giant sprayed on himself before we departed. (The only cologne that I had ever used was given to me by Mother during my first trip through Europe with her and Johnny, a small bottle of the eponymous product from the German city of Cologne, a pleasant masculine scent that I probably used once or twice a year. I still have the original bottle.)

After being engulfed with gratitude by our hosts, we moved to the dining room, where we partook of small portions of the chicken and the potato salad and a sliver of the delicious chocolate cake. All had evidently been prepared and presented to us by our gourmet chef back at the hotel, God bless him.

At the end of our dinner, spoken entirely in German, which left me totally out of the conversation, we adjourned to the living room, from whence our host made a telephone call. It was now well after eight p.m., but a trickle of middle-aged and older German men, eight in all, and four ladies plus four more who arrived while I was out of the house – making sixteen in all – occupied Little Giant for almost three hours. They appeared to be members of some kind of secret organization.

After listening to the first couple of interviews that Little Giant had with each one separately, I had intuitively grasped his method of dealing with them. He started with questions, then followed up with a discussion, sometimes quite emotional, and finally gave each man or woman his instructions, repeated again if he suspected that his colleague had not properly understood them.

I had no clue what they were talking about, though the intensity of their respect and admiration for their leader was beyond question. I found myself once again left out of his confidence, until, in the middle of the meeting with one member, he stopped in mid-sentence, turned to me, and asked me in English if I knew how to drive a motorbike. I told him that I had driven a friend's motorbike a couple of times before the war, a BSA, but that was a long time ago. Why?

"A motorbike, Peter -- it is like a horse; once ridden, never forgotten. I've just had one delivered. It's sitting on the driveway. It's a BMW and old, and because of the lack of petroleum, little used, but I have made a deal that ensures we will have enough petroleum for our wants for the next few weeks, if not longer. So take this key and give yourself a driving lesson. An hour should be long enough, for there is little traffic at this time of night and most of the police are home in bed. The reason for this aged bike is that all the newer and more modern motorbikes were apprehended and sent to the Russian front some time ago. When you return, I'll tell you all about what's going on and the reason for my presence here today and your assignment for tomorrow. Whatever you do, Peter, don't get lost."

I couldn't even get the two-wheeled Satan started! This crude excuse for a motorbike almost broke my spirit then and there. Initially, the engine refused to turn over at all; then, if a cylinder did spark and turn over once, it died immediately afterward, completely exhausted from its effort. The gasoline apparently was not the problem, but the battery was. After seven minutes of utter frustration and exhaustion, I realized that the battery was finally complaining with a pathetic whimper, at which terrifying moment the engine suddenly burst into a full-throated roar and I didn't know whether to thank it or shoot it. If I had had a gun, I think I would have shot it.

The brakes seemed to have been put on backwards, and probably upside down, for I couldn't be sure when applying them whether they would stop this monster from hell in a distance of one foot and throw me over the handlebars with a happy little laugh, or contrarily refuse to brake at all, leaving me to run off the road into an innocent little tree. The alternative was to run into a local horse-drawn milk cart that had surprised me by trotting out of the gloom, unheard because of the roar of the bike's engine, all much to the milkman's chagrin. His horse first neighed hysterically, and then, deciding that there must be better and safer places ahead, took off at a madcap pace, the driver yelling what could only be damnation on both me and the traumatized horse, who was having his first real gallop in many a year and wasn't about to be censured with the whip, especially since the driver was barely hanging on to his carriage seat. No seatbelts in those days!

I had sprained my finger but the motorbike escaped unscathed, cursed thing.

I returned to the house within the hour, convinced that the motorbike was bewitched and praying to my guardian angels to protect me from whatever fiendish enchantments the devil and his disciples were planning for me the next morning. Little Giant was sitting in a chair in the living room, all the visitors having gone home and our hosts in bed, if not asleep. He was nursing a half-filled tankard of German ale, a part of its froth temporarily attached to his chin. Telling me to sit down, he asked me how everything had gone. After I shared my opinion of the motorbike and its disgraceful behavior, my leader sympathized with a chuckle, noting that, since this was the only motorbike available just now, it would have to do. I can't say that that lifted my spirits one iota.

"Make the best of it, Peter," he continued. "It's only one trip you will ever have to make on it. And remember that the contents of the box that will be strapped to the luggage rack on the back of your bike are unique and precious and vital to our side, so don't think your tour of duty is over until you have delivered the box to the recipients themselves, who will accept it after identifying its contents."

"How will I know the recipients are genuine?" I asked.

"Because I will be with them. Don't worry, Peter, that's my part of the bargain. Everything has been taken care of."

Everything but my motorbike, I thought, but not wishing to be judged a negative influence when my leader and his followers were all so positive, I then asked him what exactly was going on.

"It seems to me that you are somehow the leader of a transparently very dangerous operation of some kind," I said. "All this secrecy with some of the German cinema managers in both the American and British Zones, and even more so in this Communist Zone, plus tonight's visit from at least twelve people that I saw – what's it all about?"

"Four more came while you were practicing with your motorbike, Peter. All of these men and women are leaders of the liberation movement, with their own volunteers, as they are my volunteers. The leaders and their colleagues risk their own lives day and night. All are dedicated to liberating as many as they can of those desiring to go across to freedom and generally to their families, who had already found freedom before that cursed wall was put up. The German police, under Russian orders, have made a devil's bargain with thousands of German families: If the men of the family are indentured for a specific time, usually until they are no longer of use to their country or their family, their family is allowed to leave for the Free Zone, thus putting a considerable onus on the Western governments to provide the money and the services necessary to support those families, most of whom are trained for very little. Schools have now been created to teach these displaced citizens, in the hope of ensuring that they will, in time, be able to provide themselves and their children with a reasonable income."

Little Giant took a long pull from his beer glass, then asked if I would like one. I refrained, it being too late in the evening for me to enjoy a beer. My leader continued his explanation. "Also, we have scientists and educators who are forbidden to leave Communist Germany. Those who have not been already murdered and want to escape across the border with their families are part of our liberation efforts. Not all of these are successful, but those who try it on their own almost inevitably fail, brought down by a hail of bullets in the back. Our methods for escape are more original and more readily successful."

I was stunned by these revelations. "Is Alex Korda aware of what you're doing?" I asked.

"Of course," said Little Giant. "He was the originator of the idea. He wanted a cameraman who was refused an exit permit from the Communist Zone. Alex didn't get his cameraman, but it set him to thinking. After creating a broad plan of liberation for those waiting to escape from their Communist fatherland to freedom in the West, where Alex envisioned a new start in a new world, he handed his plan to me to fill in the details and set the liberation movement in motion. A percentage of the money garnered from our European films is drawn off and deposited in secret deposit boxes from which we take what is needed to pay bribes and smooth our way across the borders. We're always finding or creating new ways to bring our human cargo through safely. We also smuggle goods of considerable value, both in and out of the zones, a side operation that helps to serve and bring to freedom even more Germans, whether they be Gentiles or Jews. The box that will be strapped on the back of your motorbike is in a unique category, so take good care of it, for it is a very valuable cargo indeed."

Lordy, Lordy, I thought. How ever did I get myself into this pickle? This is Johnny Dodge's kind of game, I mused, not mine. And then I pondered a bit and decided that, if I pulled it off, I would at last have a tiny adventure of my own that I could share with Johnny, though in my present frame of mind, the odds for me and that crazy motorbike were one hundred to one against me. Despite my uneasiness, I decided on the spot to drop the first half of my friend's title from Little Giant to just plain Giant. Except by comparison with Johnny Dodge and maybe Kermit Roosevelt, my mentor was an absolute giant in my opinion, worthy to stand shoulder to shoulder with the likes of both Johnny and Kermit. Whereas Kermit had died and Johnny had returned finally to civilian life, a little man in his late seventies was still fighting a war of liberation as well as representing London Film Productions on both sides of the Iron Curtain. He was physically a small man, but a born leader of men and women, whose courage and perseverance left him endangered every minute of every day that he remained in East Germany, depending, as he was, on his loyal band of warriors to keep faith with him. Clearly, it would take only a brief remark, uttered in all innocence but overheard by one of the secret police, and Giant's brilliant reign would be over, his wonderful human liberation apparatus quickly destroyed along with its operators. "Good God," I thought. "He's been into this liberation business for months upon months upon months."

Giant turned to me and said, "I want you to follow me and my car tomorrow morning until we come to the East German crossing point, where you will wait out of sight, off the compound, while I drive to the guardhouse and get out of my car. At that moment I hope my car will self-destruct in a furious blaze of fire, which is your signal to drive your motorbike at full speed past the guardhouse and back onto the road leading to the British crossing point, where you will quickly be passed through. You are to return to our hotel, where you will wait for me in your suite with the box, which I suggest you open immediately when you reach your room, for the recipients of that box are going to inspect its contents closely before taking possession of it. Hopefully, I will not be too long after you. Now take that sofa or the chair and go to sleep. I've grown accustomed to this chair, so this is where I will stay. It's almost midnight, and we will have about three and a half hours' rest, so get comfortable."

I bade him goodnight and curled up on the sofa, a blanket pulled up over me by this extraordinary man. Somewhat to my surprise, I was out like a light.

My mentor woke me up at three-thirty. The night's darkness was exacerbated by an all-enveloping early morning mist that blocked out the landscape and put a slick and dangerous cover upon the road itself. Giant informed me that there would be no breakfast for either of us, in order to leave the stomach empty and not to disturb it, for once fed, the natural progression would be elimination or the runs, either of which could bring our mission to a deadly end.

Because of the damp weather, Giant handed me a voluminous windbreaker, a couple of sizes too large, but welcome protection from the mist that would soon envelop me and my motorbike in a cloying wetness. It actually delayed our takeoff because of my machine's failure to start, although I went through three towels in drying off every part of the engine.

Our hosts came outside to see us off. With warm embraces we thanked them for their hospitality, and Giant started his car, while I was becoming more and more demented. I jollied the starter and the accelerator and even the brakes, in the hope of waking the rotten machine out of its sleep before the battery gave up the ghost.

As for the box on the back of the motorbike, it was two feet long and three feet high and a good two feet wide. It had been well strapped onto the luggage receptacle, its shape giving me no clue as to its contents.

Finally, the magic sound we all had been waiting for broke into the darkness. With a screeching shifting of gears, I followed Giant in his car out onto the road and set my course one hundred feet behind the fast-disappearing taillights of my leader.

It was too early for the German police to be setting up their temporary, constantly changing, stopping points. After the first twenty minutes of our forty-minute trip I was just settling down for a reasonably relaxed drive before we reached the German checkpoint, when a loud bang erupted between my legs. My engine slowly chugged to a pathetic whimper, with certainly not enough energy to continue on. In the still heavy dampness and semi-fog, Giant was soon swallowed up and gone, confident, no doubt, that I was still on his tail. I put the transmission in park, and, fearful of not being able to start up again, left the engine running, barely. I balanced the motorbike, still putt-putting as if exhausted beyond reason, on its steel foothold, and took three long and heavy breaths to calm me down. What now?

If you searched the whole wide world over, you would never find a more mechanically undereducated, utterly helpless being than me, with no knowledge whatsoever of what makes a motor run. In the civilized world, if you get into trouble on the road there is always the AAA man ready and willing to come to your rescue and get you taken care of in no time at all. Unfortunately, there was no AAA man on this road or even in this country, which meant that I was now at my wits' end, concluding that the only sensible thing was to take the box and the motorbike and bury them deep in the woods running beside the road.

I looked in the gas tank to see if I was out of gas, but no, it had more than enough to get me back to our hotel. I was actually close to tears at my atrociously bad luck, when, in the silence of the forest, the most amazing sound emanated from somewhere not too far away, muffled, but clearly that of a baby not at all happy with its present condition. If there was a baby out at this hour, there surely must be someone in charge of it!

I called out a low "Hey," for I did not want to attract the countryside to my plight. I walked a few yards off the road into the woods beside it, but the deeper I went the farther away were the baby's cries, and the more perplexed and disconcerted I became, beginning to feel that I must be losing my mind. After all, a baby is a baby, and babies cry. This one seemed to be howling, as if it was mad at the world for not paying it the attention that it had the right to demand.

Suddenly I froze, my blood seeming to ooze out of every vein in my body, my pores closing tight, my heart castaneting furiously. Could these howling cries be coming from the box?

I walked unsteadily back onto the road, to the motorbike, still hiccupping demurely, as if deserving a pat. No pats for you, you diabolical spoilsport!

I approached the box, from where I now realized the baby's cries were coming, no doubt awakened out of a deep sleep by that loud explosion from something that had slowed the engine down. Clearly, I must now open the box and release the baby from its hiding place. What kind of an escape was this?

The box had been beautifully put together, with breathing holes out of sight at the back, and in no time I lifted off the top, to be met by the voice that roared, a sweet little head appearing with golden curls and bright blue eyes, at the moment squinting at the sudden light, over bright to her after coming out of an enclosed and blacked out space, a baby chair supporting her and soft pillows protecting her from any undue motion. She was adorable. I later learned that she was three years old and had been given half of a very mild sleeping pill, which was expected to keep her in dreamland for the entire trip to our hotel; indeed, it probably would have, if it hadn't been for the loud bang that had brought our escapade to a sudden end.

Thank God that children will be children. I had propped her up on the motorcycle saddle, my windbreaker protecting her from the elements, and let her play with the handlebar, trace her finger on the speedometer, and blow one honk of the horn. She now grasped the handlebars, her right hand suddenly twisting the accelerator forward, and the motorcycle's engine jumped from putt-putting to a loud roar. Crazed with relief, I hugged my little charge with enormous gratitude – out of the mouths of babes – and then pushed the machine off its stand and back onto the road. With a whoop from me and a joyful cry from the princess, we were off again, me praying that Giant had waited somewhere up ahead for me and not gone on on his own or canceled the whole operation in disgust.

Naturally, he had done no such thing, but waited for us, his car pulled over to the side of the road, though he did say that, with the sun soon coming up, he would probably have had to change the operation to another day if I had been a few minutes later.

"Continue with our plan, Peter," he said. "Go like hell, and God be with you."

Neither of us said a word about the little girl, and time was of the essence. We had lost forty minutes, all told, and the changing of the guard was well past. Giant's situation was now much more fraught with danger than before, but we simply could not turn back. Whatever happened would not surprise me any more than my being responsible for this little princess, who was turning our risk-strewn road into a land of new sights and sounds and fairy-tale adventures.

I had placed my princess again on the front of the saddle between my legs, hidden underneath the folds of my oversized windbreaker, with a peek-a-boo space for her to see through until all danger was behind us. As soon as we neared the checkpoint, I slowed the motorbike down, though still following, for the soggy mist continued with us, barging in and out of our view and making driving dangerous.

Suddenly what sounded like a sonic boom bombarded our ears. The princess screamed and looked anxiously up at me, and I soothed her and hugged her, just then seeing a flame leap from the Giant's car. A siren blasted the air, and soldiers were running from all directions toward the burning car. I wondered if a chauffeur-driven car that had been drawn up on the side of the road about fifty feet back of us was a part of Giant's plan.

I moved the accelerator on the handlebar forward, gathering greater and greater speed. I raced onto the compound past the burning car, Giant standing aside from it while fire hoses were beginning to pump water into it. A German guard tried to cut us off by throwing a ladder he had been carrying at us, but it happily landed behind us. Within minutes we were at the British checkpoint and given the goahead. Though I got lost twice on the way back to our hotel, we finally arrived. I put the motorcycle at the back of the hotel down some steps into the cellar, and walked my princess to the elevator and up to my floor and into my suite.

Not having eaten all day, I ordered a heavy tea, with sandwiches filled with ham and smoked salmon and raisin toast and jams and three kinds of cake. Princess had a tall glass of lemonade and I drank four cups of Grays

Tea, with a twist of lemon. It was a delightful time, and she was a perfect guest, insofar as a three-year-old can be.

Sometimes I think back on that time so long ago when gallant men and women were performing daring achievements rarely ever spoken about again.

An hour and a half later, Giant returned, his car apparently burned beyond recognition, but he had had a backup waiting on the road with the car that would bring him and his escapees to our hotel. The latter had been guests of the chauffeur, who was one of Giant's agents, parked in the very same car that I had seen when waiting for Giant's personal car's explosive and fire-gutted end. I had not noticed the two escapees in the back of the car, nor had I glimpsed the chauffeur himself. Giant's agent told me he kept them well out of sight until they got through the German checkpoint, the guards having been hoaxed out of suspicion by their feelings of sympathy for Giant losing his car. They were only too glad for him to have the other car to travel in, never dreaming that two escapees within it would soon be on the other side of the British checkpoint, their lives saved at the cost of an old motorcar.

Giant brought the child's parents to my suite, where they were reunited with great joy with my princess, their adorable daughter. They overwhelmed us with their gratitude, and my princess hugged and hugged me. When her mother gently took her from me, she burst into tears, and my own eyes filled up as soon as she was gone. I never saw them again. Giant would not tell me who or what they were. "The less you know, the safer they are, Peter." That was the motto by which these amazing heroes, who helped so many desperate refugees flee across the borders from Communism to democracy, lived, and it certainly made sense.

I left by plane the next day. Giant would be remaining for six more weeks, visiting Czechoslovakia, Poland, Hungary, and Austria. Upon his return, he would have a two-week vacation, part of it spent in long, private sessions with Alex Korda.

Two good friends. Two amazing men.

There were two wonderful people whom I had the good fortune to meet soon after I returned from my brief trip to Berlin. One was the Guest of Honor at the Ends of the Earth Club dinner, General George C. Marshall, Supreme Commander during the entire Second World War of all United States military personnel wherever in the world they might be. When Johnny presented me to him at the reception as "son, Peter," General

311

Marshall answered, "I'm glad to meet you, sir," looking straight into my eyes, with a very pleasant smile, his handshake firm.

I was dazzled. He had addressed me as "sir," even though I was the least important person in that entire room of great achievers, while he was among the very rare exalted ones.

Johnny and Mother had put me at a table of eight in the middle of the room, my chair facing the elevated platform upon which Johnny would sit in the center, with General Marshall on his right. The other places at the head table were taken up by the present Prime Minister, Clement Atlee, leader of the Socialist Government; the American Ambassador, Lewis W. Douglas; the British Foreign Secretary, Ernest Bevin; and others of comparable importance. Winston Churchill had sent Johnny his regrets; he was in bed with a bad cold, which turned into the flu and kept him at home for quite a long time.

Johnny and Mother had deftly arranged the table seating and place cards so that Beverly Baxter, MP, former editor of Lord Beaverbrook's newspapers the *Daily Express* and the *Evening Standard*, was sitting on one side of me, and B. Richetson-Hatt, former manager of Reuters News Agency and present Public Relations Director of the Bank of England, was on the other side. Both were longtime friends of the family, and both had watched me grow into manhood ever since I arrived on England's shores. Both gentlemen, along with their wives, had frequently been entertained at our homes in London and Ferring, and Mother and Johnny had been guests at their homes. So I felt comfortable with them, though definitely on my best behavior.

Incidentally, my youngest brother, Tony Dodge, later married Lord Beaverbrook's brother's daughter; they had two daughters of their own.

There was a sparse sprinkling of only the very top-ranking military officers of the British Army, Navy, and Air Force. The major proportion of the eighty assembled VIPs were leaders of business, banking, and industry from both sides of the Atlantic; indeed, from the sounds emanating from the tables during dinner, including mine, there was plenty of business being discussed, but also much merriment. Only when the dinner was at an end, and the silver and china removed from the tables, was Johnny finally able to introduce his VIP of VIPs.

The General was an extraordinarily decent-looking man, more fatherly than military, but with a commanding presence, for he had a strong jaw and piercing eyes. I would not wish to be the one who might anger him. He was at least six feet tall, his uniform immaculate, his presence on the podium confident, his accent more southern than northern. He knew his subject well and spoke about it clearly, without cue cards.

In fifteen minutes he covered the late war in Europe, a string of incidents that explained the failures and successes of the allies, and then, to everyone's surprise and delight, he unveiled for the very first time what the Marshall Plan was all about. At the end of his analysis, he received thunderous standup applause, everyone pumped up and excited beyond measure about this magnificent gift. The Marshall Plan was designed to provide succor on a huge monetary scale, to restore fiscal stability by many financial routes, with the money coming from the US Federal Reserves, American banks, businesses, industry, etc. This disastrous war had not been kind to any country involved, and only the USA's singular physical insularity had saved it from the demolition and devastation of its friends and foes across the Atlantic Ocean.

With Marshall Plan money in hand, Prime Minister Atlee later created the socialized medicine plan in the UK, along with nationalizing Great Britain's major industries – rail, electricity, and so on. But that was for later. This night was the opening night of the Plan, and all in the room were in awe of its purpose and potential, gratified that there was at last a real chance of continued recovery. For once in their lives, everyone in that room loved America.

Johnny Dodge's first postwar Ends of the Earth Club dinner had been a fantastic success. His many friends and acquaintances came up to congratulate him on the extraordinary spectacle they had witnessed. When General Marshall left the dinner table for a few minutes, the entire roomful of guests broke into clapping, shouting "thank you" from the floor. A line of guests formed in front of the VIPs' table in order to congratulate Johnny in person on organizing such a unique evening for every single person in that room. Mother, bless her heart, deserved much of the kudos, too.

When the General returned, and Johnny and he were again the center of attention, I moved to the end of the table. There Great Britain's Prime Minister sat alone, a half smile on his face, no doubt sharing in the excitement. I took my courage in my hands and greeted Mr. Atlee from the floor. He invited me to come up, which I did. After I introduced myself and explained my relationship to John Bigelow Dodge, he asked me to sit down. For twenty minutes we talked about Johnny, fly-fishing, the Second World War, and the Marshall Plan. Atlee was a small man with an insignificant appearance, but in person he was an absolute delight, with a quick wit and a definite charm. I fell under his spell, and will always be grateful for his generosity in giving me twenty minutes of his time, and treating me as an equal.

It wasn't long after I returned to London that Sir Alex called me to his office. I presumed that he wanted to quiz me on my recent trip to Berlin, but no, not a word on that subject. Instead, he informed me that the King and Queen would once again – as was their wont three or four times a year, the Palace not having the capabilities – be his guests in our projection theater, at around two-thirty this very Saturday afternoon, it now being Wednesday.

The film had been chosen by their majesties. "Unfortunately, both Sir David and I will be in Hollywood negotiating some delicate business matter," said Sir Alex.

I had heard on the grapevine that the trip had something to do with distribution rights in the United States, a project that Sir Alex wanted to have cemented at the earliest possible moment. The Hollywood moguls involved had signaled that they were now ready to talk.

I wondered whom he had honored to be in attendance with the royals, and my heart almost stopped when he looked over his glasses straight into my face and said, "I'm appointing you, Peter" – the first time he had ever called me by my first name – "to represent me, and to give my sincere apologies to their majesties, assuring them that only a matter of overwhelming importance to my company would keep me away."

Before I could say anything, he continued, "I'm told you have ambassadorial experience, so this should be right up your alley. Put it to good work this Saturday. I'm depending on you."

He smiled and waved me out of his office. I returned to my own office, in a total state of shock, and sat down heavily. I would be with the King and Queen for at least two hours, with the doors locked but no guards in sight. Only the projectionist and I would be there to protect their majesties should some madman or anti-monarchist try to take advantage of the situation.

But first of all I had to learn the drill, and the only person besides Sir Alex who could teach me would be the projectionist. I fervently hoped he could give me some pointers on what my duties involved.

I found the projectionist rewinding films and returning them to their containers. He said he could spare me a few minutes. It turned out that he had watched Sir Alex receive the King and Queen from his second floor window, which had given him an angled but clear view of their arrival and welcome. From behind a pillar at the top of the stairs, he had also

314

seen and heard the jocular voice of Queen Elizabeth exchanging polite nothings with her host, the King apparently happy to be relieved of that responsibility.

The projectionist was good enough to give me two quick rehearsals there and then, and I was very grateful to him for the run-through. At the end of the day, I stopped off at Mother and Johnny's Kingston House flat and told them my news, at which they both seemed very pleased. I wasn't, for it had just occurred to me that the King and Queen had both seen me behaving like a patriotic madman, leaning halfway out of my taxi window waving wildly in their faces. My driver had been so embarrassed and mortified by the spectacle that, when we reached Kingston House, he had thrown my bags onto the curb and taken off with a final "cor blimy," without even remembering to pick up the fare that was waiting for him to come back. Obviously, I had stretched the poor man beyond his limits. For me it had been a wonderful experience at the time, but what about Saturday? Would the Queen recognize me? And if she did, would she point me out to her husband as that crazy man whose manners needed much attention? Alas, I couldn't do anything about it now; I just had to wait until Saturday and take my chances. Lordy, Lordy: Why me?

The time till Saturday dragged monotonously on, each minute seeming like an hour. When I awoke on Saturday and realized that it was the day, I wanted to turn back the clock, or better still, turn it a day forward, when all would be over. Either I would have been held up to royal ridicule or, God willing, nothing would have happened at all.

At two twenty, I was dressed in my blue suit, white shirt, and red and blue striped tie, standing on the bottom step at our building's entrance. At twenty-seven minutes after, the royal car drove onto the driveway and up to the entrance. Since there was only the chauffeur up front, I opened the rear car door, from which the King got out, followed by the Queen. I assisted the Queen by holding her hand and arm for balance, and she thanked me, whereupon I introduced myself and offered a brief but sincere apology from Sir Alex. When I explained the reason for his absence, the Queen who seemed to be the King's mouthpiece, commiserated with Sir Alex for having to be on business so far away, and on a weekend as well.

Queen Elizabeth took my arm as we started up the marble steps, with the King close behind. This worried me, as I believed that the King was always supposed to be in front, but since they were not in public view now, I supposed they could do what they liked.

The Queen started to ramble something about the weather, when she suddenly focused fully on my face, her hand going to her mouth; looking at me intently, she said, "Your face is familiar to me, but I cannot remember where I might have met you. Can you help me, Mr. Sherman?"

I swallowed two or three times and broke into a cold sweat. "No, Ma'am," I replied, putting my foot upon the next stair, hoping to urge her majesty on up the stairs as quickly as I could. But she stayed put right where she was, a charming, beloved lady who had me at her mercy, while she pressed me to place myself in her memory. I couldn't tell her the truth, and I was trapped in my own deceit, so I stood stricken in silence until the King urged us on upward. The Queen again took my arm, and I ushered them up the last few steps, across the hall and into the projection theater to their seats, at which point the Queen turned to her husband and said, "Of course, Bertie; it could have been a dream. I have such strange dreams sometimes. Maybe that's where I saw him."

I couldn't quite see the logic of that statement, but I hoped to distract her from the subject by presenting them with a box of chocolates that I had bought for the occasion from the "in" chocolate shop of the period. I lifted the top off, placing it under the bottom, and offered them each a napkin from Mother's collection, which they accepted, the Queen insisting that I should have the first chocolate. Fortunately, it tasted superlatively good.

I sat down two rows behind them and pressed the button to start the movie, pleased to see the first titles successfully projected onto the screen and delighted to hear the happy sound of chocolates being separated from their crinkly paper wraps. As the film finally came to an end, I decided that the King had enjoyed the film and the chocolates, and the Queen had enjoyed the chocolates even better than the film. More than half of the top layer had disappeared, and I hoped the chocolates and the movie had dispersed all prior images of me in the Queen's mind.

We returned down the stairs, the King and Queen together, I bringing up the rear, as the King commented favorably on one of the actresses in the movie. The Queen, with a wicked smile, said, "Now, Bertie, watch your blood pressure. You know what your doctor said!"

At that the King actually grinned. She put her hand in his, and you could feel the real affection that they had for one another.

The royal car was waiting. I gave the chauffeur the box of chocolates to guard. Her majesty thanked me again, telling me what a lovely afternoon they had had, particularly with the added extra of the chocolates. The King assented, "Yes ... Yey ... ey ... yes," through his voice impediment, a burden since birth.

As the limousine pulled slowly away, the Queen leaned across her husband and gave me that wonderful smile and an abbreviated wave to accompany it. My cup runneth over! (P. S. In a memo to Sir Alex, I suggested that he continue providing a box of the best chocolates for the royal couple, that having proved such a success on this occasion. Indeed, it evolved into a tradition, which made me feel good, too.)

By 1951 I had met and become enchanted with Clarissa Churchill, Winston Churchill's brother's daughter, who had once worked for Sir Alex Korda. She was a very gracious, charming and down-to-earth lady, and we had a brief friendship shortly before I left for Brazil (about which, more later), she not knowing about her future suitor, who would soon make her his betrothed: Anthony Eden, our friend and neighbor.

I was now well favored by those I needed to know me in the film industry. Outside the film world, I still managed to keep my friends in other careers, including a gentleman considerably older than I whom I had met through Johnny and Mother. His name was Olaf Hambro. He was the President of Hambro's Bank, over which he lived in an elegant flat with a "daily lady" to run it and work for him. He also had a perfectly beautiful home in the country, where he weekended with me on several occasions, and where he would follow a Squire's routine of helping to judge horse shows, dog shows, beauty pageants, and flower shows. His favorite activity, however, was helping the Boy Scouts do whatever Boy Scouts are supposed to do. On Sundays he attended the local church in his own family pew and sometimes read the lesson.

Olaf had a butler and housekeeper/cook to run the mansion, both having to work harder and longer on weekends but able to lighten their load during the week. A gardener attended to the lawns and plants. His wife had tragically drowned in the family pool some years before. He also had a son, Charles, who would one day take over his position.

I tailed along with Olaf to all the functions on his calendar each weekend I visited him, and enjoyed all of it very much. Even more did I enjoy the many stories of his life that he shared with me at the dinner table or in his library. His comment on Alex Korda was that he was something of an artistic genius in his chosen profession, but that he was glad that he had a good CPA and Sir David to watch the business end of things.

Back in London we would often go to Prunier's, a favorite restaurant of ours, where he particularly loved the oysters, while I enjoyed the Dover sole bonne femme. I can remember one evening when he experimented with some wine that had been recommended by a friend. When it was delivered to our table and uncorked, the waiter handed the cork to him on a small silver tray. After sniffing it, he hurriedly returned it to the tray, protesting that the bottle was corked, meaning that the wine was no longer fit to drink. Another bottle was brought to the table, with the same result. Olaf then dismissed the embarrassed server with a sympathetic smile, along with a request for a certain other wine that proved to be just fine.

On another occasion, at a movie theater, when the Royal Anthem was played at the end of the picture and we all stood to attention, a young man tried to get out of the long row before the anthem was finished. Only Olaf's large stomach stood in his way. Olaf stubbornly refused to let him pass until the anthem was finished, out of respect for the Royal Family.

Speaking of which, Queen Mary, the Queen Mother and the widow of the late King George V, lived not far from Olaf. On occasion she would invite herself to tea, with a lady-in-waiting in attendance. She obviously liked Olaf, but even more, she liked antiques and knew that Olaf did likewise. So when she thought he had had time enough to acquire some new specimen or two for his collection, she would invite herself over. If she saw something that struck her fancy and for which she obviously hungered, he would grind his teeth in frustration, while putting on a great show of "what an honor it was to present to her majesty this *objet d'art* from my meager collection to join her majesty's grand and glorious collection of antiques."

Her majesty – and she really looked a Queen personified – would then put up a pretense of protestation at his largesse, after which she would accept his gift. Olaf would see her out the front door downstairs, because she refused to take the elevator. She and the lady-in-waiting, who never said a word during the entire visit, got in the car; as the royal limousine drew away from the curb, Olaf would bite his lip and acknowledge to himself that the Queen Mother really knew her stuff when it came to antiques.

Olaf was a wonderful friend. When I one day broached the subject of money and taxes – in particular, my money and my taxes – he immediately offered me a good position in New York with his bank's office on Wall Street. My problem was that, though I was living high on the hog on my very generous entertainment allowance, and my remuneration was nothing to sniff at, taxes during the years after the war were horrible. My bank account, like those of many other executives with good paychecks, was decimated by the dreaded taxman into a pathetic shadow of its former grandeur.

The war had put a great burden on Great Britain, coming a mere twenty-one years after the end of the First World War. The country had not even had time to pay off all of its debts before the new war was upon it. Truth to tell, I don't know or want to know what would have happened without the Marshall Plan.

Anyway, though I was exceedingly grateful to Olaf for his offer, banking was just not for me. For that matter, Johnny had offered me the opportunity to follow in his footsteps, into his firm on the Stock Exchange, and I had turned that down, too. I liked to make money but did not want to make a living with money as my all-embracing pursuit. Both banking and the stock exchange are extremely important and worthwhile careers. I am not criticizing them. They are just not my cup of tea.

I was beginning to think more and more of Brazil as a way of being released from the heavy hand of British tax collectors. I had even talked on the matter to Johnny and Mother, who to my relief told me they would both stand behind me in any decision I decided to take.

I knew that I would be giving up a wonderful life with friendly acquaintances everywhere, and even a few real friends, whom I counted on one hand. I would be stepping out of an exacting, varied, and incredibly challenging and rewarding career in my beloved London, where I had tried to make a small if subtle imprint. I knew that whatever would come would never be as thrilling to me as it was to wake up each morning with joy in my heart and a great willingness to take on whatever was thrown at me on that particular day.

New York, my birthplace, I would love, but first I wanted to return to Brazil. After explaining my decision to Sir Alex and Sir David – both of whom were upset, though Sir David the more so – I gave them notice that I would be resigning from London Film Productions in three months. During that time I was prepared to break in whoever was chosen to take my place. I went through two applicants whom Sir David did not approve, ultimately leaving the company without having hired anyone who met his standards.

Johnny asked me if I had really made up my mind, and I said yes. He noted that he was prepared to set up an appoint for me with a friend of his who was on the Board of The Royal Dutch Shell Company, which had offices in Rio de Janeiro, São Paulo and other cities in Brazil. The appointment was made for one week hence.

I was interviewed by a very nice elderly gentleman who ended the session by informing me that Johnny Dodge was the finest gentleman he had ever met. He also told me that, after a three-month indoctrination at various offices and cities in the United Kingdom, I would be put aboard a ship to Brazil, where I would be given a hands-on training course until I was finally approved for a position somewhere in that country. At my urging, he agreed that I should ask for a career as a public relations counselor, based on recommendations from Colonel Hills, Sir David, and Sir Alex.

So began my travels around England, moving under the auspices of Shell from office to service station to office. It was fascinating in some ways, and incredibly boring in others, for everybody had a set duty to perform, day in and day out. Until that time, my life had been exactly the opposite, as I never quite knew what would be coming down the pike for me to unwind on any particular day. However, being an eternal optimist, I learned what I needed to learn and hoped for the best.

Though I did not find this out until some months after I had joined Shell in Brazil, either Johnny's friend forgot to put my public-relations experience in the record that was mailed to Rio ahead of me, or it may have been regarded as a useless pursuit by someone in power in the company and quickly destroyed – who can say?

For now, I am paying my respects and farewells to all of Sir Alex's and Sir David's connections with whom I was acquainted. I was regaled with quite a few dinners in my honor, which I detested but learned to accept gracefully. I must admit that it gave me a bit of a charge when I looked around a dining room full of acquaintances who were there just because I was there.

The really elegant dinner parties were given by Sir Alex and Sir David, both having been honored by Johnny Dodge as his guests at one or another Ends of the Earth Club dinners. Both my mother and Johnny had been invited to their separate dinner parties, Sir Alex even including Clarissa, an appreciated touch.

And so I bowed out of my life at London Film Productions. I took my three-month training, after which I bade a tearful farewell to my beloved mother and now equally beloved Johnny. I shared a final subdued dinner with Clarissa, who, as mentioned, for now knew nothing about her future suitor and husband, Great Britain's Prime Minister, Anthony Eden.

When I returned from my three months of training, prior to embarking for Brazil, I found an envelope bearing Sir Alex's crest. I opened it to find a very cordial letter from Sir Alex and a very welcome check; it was large enough to permit me to pay off all my taxes in one glorious moment, leaving me free to take with me all of the salary I had deposited over many months and even years. For the most part I had been able to get by on my entertainment allowance, which had automatically grown each year, thus making me quite a moneyed man, enough to make me comfortably independent for at least a year and maybe more. But I had given my word to serve a year and serve I would. I was planning to live off my salary from my new employer, after depositing my financial substance in a well-regarded American bank in São Paulo or Rio, wherever I was to be situated. I would start with a financially clean sheet with my new employer.

I wrote a very sincere and grateful letter to Sir Alex, telling him how proud I had been to work with him and his wonderful company; and another to Sir David for being more of a partner than a boss. I could not have hoped for a better friend. Often, after a particularly heavy day, he would call my office and, if I was not already engaged for the evening, we would go to his favorite SoHo restaurant, where his wife would be waiting, a charming and very talented actress, well known in the West End theater world. We all three would soon unwind with a drink or two and a scrumptious dinner, after which we would pay our respects to the chef in the kitchen, who would wrap each of us in a great gorilla hug. At that point Sir David would always blush crimson, to his wife's hilarious laughter; the chef, a portly gentleman, clearly considered all this odd behavior to be part of the English people's way of saying thank you!

I had been living a life that few mortals could even imagine, an extraordinary kind of dream world, and yet enthrallingly real. Up next was Brazil, a beautiful country, where I would first face a great dilemma, and finally find a great opportunity.

Brazil

I enjoyed a fascinating voyage to Brazil with a delicious romantic lady who acted as if she thought I was God's gift to women. We had a delightful dalliance the whole way over, meaning at least twelve days, while the other single men aboard eyed us with envy, and a few husbands appeared to be groaning under their breath.

Kia – that was her name – reminded me quite a bit of my Parisian tutor, who had ensnared me most lovingly into the subtle arts of making love. By the time we reached Rio de Janeiro, I had lost two pounds and Kia three, despite the elegant meals we had consumed both for our pleasure and to keep our strength up. An Argentinean now returning to her homeland, she was a friend of Evita Peron, the wife of the President of Argentina. Her flat was located near the Presidential Palace.

We slowly entered the port of Rio de Janeiro, the sunset just an ember glow in the velvet sky. The stars, brightly mirrored by their reflection in the bay, surrounded us. Only something way off to the left provided competition to this view – the pearl necklace illuminating the promenade of Copacabana for miles along the beach. It was a lovely sight to behold, but still not as lovely to me as that magnificent sky.

The passport inspectors came aboard that evening. After having my passport checked and stamped, I asked if I could go back with them, for I was anxious to get to my hotel, the Copacabana. My reservation there was for the next night, but I was confident they would take me anyway, because my reservation had been booked through the American Embassy. The passport inspectors were agreeable to my returning to terra firma with them on their boat.

Kia was surprised and saddened by my decision, but I think we were both wearied by then. She did not insist on my remaining; we both knew that we had experienced a unique relationship that few could even imagine, let alone maintain. And so we parted, never to see each other again. Because neither of us was attached to anyone else at this time, our consciences were clear.

With a further assist from one of the passport inspectors, who kindly drove me in his car to the Copacabana, I brought him into the foyer of the hotel. After checking in without any problem, I gave him dinner in the dining room for his trouble, which we both enjoyed very much. Then I bade him goodnight.

That night I slept the sleep of the dead. I awoke at eight the next morning, with the sun streaming in through lacy curtains. My first steps were a slow walk across my suite to the large window facing onto the Copacabana Beach, where already the sand was filling up with pulchritudinous sirens in their skimpy bathing suits – no bikinis in 1952 – running, stretching, dancing, flirting, or flat on their backs after a rough night out on the town.

It was a glamorous sight, but it did not get a rise out of me, for my delightful Kia had drained me to the core. All I wanted to do that morning after breakfast was to put on my bathing suit, take a beach towel, and rest my weary bones upon the warm sand, with maybe a swim in the ocean to cool off.

I had arrived a day ahead of my official date. Since no one knew I was there, I had the day to myself. I had decided to rest up so I could be in better form on the morrow, when I presumed I would be officially received by Royal Dutch Shell and learn where my future residence was to be. I hoped it would be Rio, for this was the hub of Brazilian power; given my relationship with Hershel Johnson, America's Ambassador to Brazil – he was my godfather -- and my expertise in both diplomacy and public relations, it seemed to me that I could be of considerable advantage to this highly regarded company. I did call Hershel Johnson and was booked for a seven-thirty dinner that evening.

I had a very rudimentary grasp of the Portuguese language, but I still spoke reasonable French. At that time, from the early fifties to the early sixties, French remained the second language in Brazil; since I anticipated dealing with the more educated Brazilians, I expected to find a linguistic bond with them.

Following a delicious breakfast, with the sun, sand, and water beckoning, I got into my bathing suit – which came up over my shoulders!

Today I am told that a pouch covering the male's sexual apparatus is all that is needed. Since it is clear what it is, why not just go naked and have done with it?

I staked out a nice little patch on the beach, with an English lady and her nine-year-old daughter. The child intrigued me by moving from English to Portuguese and back again with her mother, already showing signs of near fluency in both languages. Little did I know at the time that this same lady was married to a Brazilian diplomat, who had had a lengthy career in London. There he had not only gone considerably up his State Department's ladder, but had also married this selfsame lady. Not only that, but in a zippered up pocket in my smaller bag was a letter from Mother to this very lady, introducing me to her and her husband. Mother had befriended her early in her marriage to her diplomatic husband, and indeed they had been at our house for dinner on more than one occasion.

For now, however, I knew none of this. After the light breeze and warm sun had coaxed me into a brief nap, I decided that I had had enough sun. Putting some sand on my beach towel so that it would not be blown away in my absence, I approached the water. Feeling the warm sand underfoot and then the cooler ocean, I experienced a serene feeling of appreciation for this moment, brief though it might be.

I swam languidly out to sea, surprised at the distance I had covered in such a short time, not to mention the fact that those in the water were now some distance away from me. I felt proud of myself and, for a brief, deluded moment, wondered if I was a better swimmer than I had thought. Then I decided to return to shore before I wore myself out completely. Suddenly I woke up to reality and I realized what I had done.

I was in an unforgiving undertow, just as Mother had faced so many years before, only I had no Johnny Dodge to come to my rescue. My British grooming had taught me that British gentlemen do not cry for help, but it did allow me to wave my arms somewhat frantically in the hope that some male would stop feasting his eyes upon the ravishing "bods" decorating the shoreline and come save me, please – pronto!

I don't know about the pronto, but I did hear a male Portuguese-speaking voice bellow at some point when my strength was down to its last brief moments. Shortly afterward I felt the arms of my rescuer turn me onto my back and guide me, with vigorous strokes and hefty pushes, parallel to the beach. When the undertow was weakened, he brought me up onto the beach; with a friendly look to see that I would live, he took off back to his post, for indeed he was a lifeguard, who had been summoned by the English lady who told him a damned fool Englishman was drowning right under his very eyes. Maybe he was asleep, but he had saved my life, and I later came back and thanked him with a good reward. How much is one's life worth? He was very grateful; according to a bilingual stranger standing nearby, my rescuer said he would rescue me any time I got into trouble in the water. I thanked him again, promising myself that I would never again go into the water, at least not the water under his supervision, or I would bankrupt myself in no time.

Later, when I presented Mother's letter of introduction to the lady at her husband's flat, and discovered that she was the one who had sent the lifeguard to my rescue, I embraced her warmly. Ever after I kept in touch with the family, all three of whom became my good friends.

I waited until the next morning to make myself known at Royal Dutch Shell's headquarters, where I was given an appointment for four that afternoon. The Englishman in charge of transporting Shell personnel from one place to another was my sole contact at Shell headquarters, except for one charming executive lady in her mid-fifties who received me in her office before I saw the Shell's travel agent. She was very gracious and gave me some valuable tips about the company, such as who was who and what to expect; then she took me to the office of the travel agent, a very nice and easygoing man to deal with. There I learned, much to my annoyance, that I was to be assigned to the São Paulo office. But I kept myself in balance, hoping that all the bad stuff would be thrown at me first, and then the sky would clear and the sun would come out and all would be well. Ha!

The dinner with Hershel the night before had been great. I filled him in on news of Mother, Johnny, and my life in recent years. He, who had never married, told me that, on becoming the American Ambassador to Brazil, he had appointed his mother to be his official hostess. She was a real character and a very distinguished and elegant lady, but at this time she had returned to Charlotte, North Carolina, for a brief vacation with her many friends at home.

Hershel offered me a suite, bedroom, and bathroom that I could use whenever I came to Rio, providing there was not an overflow of VIPs at the time. I can remember having to move to a hotel when President Harry Truman's daughter came to town, a perfectly delightful lady, and another time when a very wealthy lady with a pincushion of a husband – who else would marry her? – swept into the Embassy like she owned America. She was a veritable tyrant with her scared and insignificant other half and everyone else whom she thought beneath her, which included most of the land mass in the world. Lordy, lordy, how the staff and servants despised her, and despaired for her husband! Fortunately, they stayed for only three days, during which she trashed everything Brazilian and epitomized a thoroughly overbearing and obnoxious caricature of the ugly American.

But that was then, and now is now. After finishing my dinner, I viewed the sun go down and the stars come out in all their magnificence. (The air was almost free of pollution at that time, I surmised, for the stars looked much clearer in the Rio night than when I was in São Paulo the following night.) Following a leisurely walk on the Copacabana promenade under the illumination of the pearl necklace, I toddled off to bed, where I slept heavily, once again waking up the next morning in anticipation of whatever was in store for me.

That was to be quite a lot, I discovered.

The friendly travel agent at Shell headquarters had told me that, after my plane landed at São Paulo Airport, I should look out for a man holding a Shell Company magazine prominently displayed. He could not describe the man or give him a name, because he didn't know who would be sent from the São Paulo office.

My plane landed on time. With the help of a porter and his four-wheeled baggage mover, I came out to the reception area, where I waited for twenty minutes. Then a large young man with an intelligent face came walking briskly into the reception room, desperately trying to hold the Shell magazine up where it could be seen, but failing miserably. Obviously this was something new to him. I waved, and we shook hands and introduced ourselves. His name was Bart, short for Bartholomew. With my patient porter in tow, we reached Bart's car, stowed my luggage away in the trunk, and I tipped the porter somewhat more generously than usual for his having stayed with me for such a long time.

Bart's car was not a company car, but his very own. It was a shiny new Hudson, a large and comfortable American-made car of which he was obviously proud. He seemed to be enjoying his new toy immensely. I was impressed, since any new car coming into Brazil for sale would have cost many times its original price in America, with Brazilian federal and state taxes added on and, of course, the necessary connections to be suitably rewarded. I could only put Bart down as having a financially very well endowed and influential family, which later proved to be the case.

Bart asked me if I would like to share quarters with four other apprentices, or if I would prefer my own quarters. He added that his own apartment building had one furnished apartment available, and I said I would like to see it. Since the cruzeiro was so much devalued against the dollar, I found that I could more than afford it, for it would have cost me three or four times more if I were renting in any capital city in the world. São Paulo, however, was deservedly the industrial capital of Latin America, and my neighborhood was among the better neighborhoods of the city. The apartment's furnishings were new, though based on an image of the twenties; loving that period anyhow, I was more than pleased to sign a contract for one year and a day, with first option on renewal. After I had put away all of my luggage and other belongings in the drawers and cupboards, with Bart's help, he suggested that we go to his club for lunch. After lunch he would take me to the São Paulo headquarters of Royal Dutch Shell and introduce me to my new bosses and colleagues.

His club was definitely upper crust, with both Portuguese and English being spoken as well as French. He was greeted by both younger and older friends and two members of his own family, so that my head was swimming with Brazilian names that passed in and out of my skull as fast as I was introduced. Nonetheless, it was good to see how well he was regarded.

Bart was twenty-five years old to my going on thirty-one. Compared with all the experience that I had gained in my short lifetime, he was an innocent, having been saved from wars, semi-starvation, loss of friends, poverty, or disease. I had been pampered in much the same way, but I had been through the war, and what a difference a war makes.

I felt paternalistic toward him, and a little envious, for he was in his own territory with all the support of the good life I had enjoyed in England. When I told him that the American Ambassador to Brazil was my godfather, he was delighted, and when I further told him that I had the use of a suite at the embassy in Rio with two beds and a bathroom in it, he positively beamed.

I was more concerned with what the Shell Company had in store for me. Bart told me that he had been instructed to be my escort and show me the ropes, so that I might thoroughly immerse myself into the Shell way of doing things and the Brazilian lifestyle. I felt much as if I was going back to school. Very soon afterward, I knew I was.

I remained under the impression that the information about my public-relations background, along with my sterling references, was in someone's office at Central Headquarters in Rio. Thus I continued to hope that one day soon I would be reassigned to training that would be much more interesting than the dry and infinitely boring education I was currently undergoing. While anticipating a new assignment, I kept my eyes on the prize awaiting me if I just held out long enough and was given enough points to pass approval. Then I could get on with the real business at hand, namely, polishing Royal Dutch Shell's image and increasing the company's business – plans that I had shared only with my good friend Bart, whose shocked comment on hearing each new version was inevitably, "Why didn't I think of that?"

I was being trained to be a well-rounded Shell technician who would, if luck and ability triumphed, become a true blue Shell Company employee capable of climbing up the ladder of opportunity. I was none of that, nor did I want any part of it, for I knew that such a life would crush my spirit and my innate talent, and would certainly send me to purgatory.

Believe you me: This is no criticism of Royal Dutch Shell. Rather, it is a criticism of myself, who from the very first was convinced that, once my aptitudes were put to work on behalf of Royal Dutch Shell Brazil, it would be easy to move up both professionally and financially. I planned to secure my position and at the same time bask in the sunshine of Brazil's social life, with time out to indulge my idealistic side in support of some cause. Already, doing something to alleviate the ghastly poverty in one hellish outreach of Rio was my first choice, providing I could find a group already engaged in such work, hopefully with government and private support.

The real truth of the matter is that I should never have used Shell Oil as my means of coming to Brazil. I had plenty of money, and could have come and made myself known on my own. With Hershel Johnson as my conduit, and with my career papers and references in hand, who knows what could have happened? Fortunately for me, something great did happen, which wiped my slate clean. Indeed, I suspect that one of the best things that ever happened to Royal Dutch Shell was my eventual departure by mutual consent.

The drudgery in the daytime at Shell Oil headquarters and out in the field was balanced at night by dinner parties, restaurant and club parties, sporting occasions, and on weekends much sailing and yachting.

But daytime was repetitious, clerical, and to me, stagnant. The monotony of it made me all the more disenchanted with myself. Why had I ever talked my way into Shell on the false premise that I would be a good member of the team if Shell let me do what I could do best for them, namely public relations? Shell's point of view made perfect sense, whether they had my PR papers on file or not. They had hired me to learn the oil business, and to hell with anything else. From their point of view, they were absolutely right.

Besides Bart, my other good and influential friend was the former Governor of São Paulo, Dr. Ademar de Barros, a medical doctor before he put his feet into politics. After I left Shell, he became my very well-paying employer, whom I had been coaching ever since I had first met him at the French Embassy when it was celebrating Bastille Day. For a brief moment, we were standing near each other, but alone, so we introduced ourselves, in French, of course. While we were talking, the British Ambassador wended his way toward us and started a conversation in English. The recent Governor of São Paulo introduced me to the British Ambassador, who, on hearing my name, said, "Well, you must be Minerva Dodge's son." When I assented, he said that he had known Johnny Dodge since the First World War, and that he and his wife and Johnny and Minerva dined together whenever he was back in London from his postings abroad. Hershel Johnson had told him of my arrival some time before.

The British Ambassador, it turned out, had a daughter living in the embassy whom he would dearly have liked to be joined with some appropriate male. I did take the lady out a couple of times, and I liked her very much, but I knew she wasn't for me. Anyway, when Neusa came along, all bets were off.

Dr. Ademar was at least six feet tall and maybe more, big without being fat, but definitely big, a big head on a big body, standing out in a crowd. Like Johnny, he had a presence, was married to a fine lady, and had offspring. He had a keen mind; besides Portuguese, he spoke English, French, and German, the three dominant languages at that time. He had considerable charm and a good sense of humor. For some unknown reason, he took a liking to me that opened up a relationship that gave me back my confidence in my profession, along with opportunities galore for polishing his image and that of his political party.

A few months later, I met Neusa at a dinner party in São Paulo given by the owner of the city's newspaper, who went on to become the Brazilian Ambassador to the Court of St. James. Neusa and I were seated next to one another at the dinner table; somehow we became friends and lovers almost before the dessert, but certainly from that night on. She was a small but dynamic lady, beautiful to behold, with ebony hair, tanned skin, and green eyes. She was exceedingly smart, a great hostess, and a great lover, and if she was your friend, she was your friend for life. Incidentally, she was also an accomplished actress, having recently starred in the movie *O*

Cangaceiro, the first Brazilian movie to be honored by Hollywood with an Oscar for being the best foreign film of that year, 1953 or 1954.

Despite my eroding work performance, it took me almost two years to untangle myself from Shell and move on to greener pastures. I give Royal Dutch Shell much praise for putting up with me for so long, though I would have happily gone over to Ademar's camp earlier, had it not been that Shell had treated me better than I deserved. Except for the disappearance of my PR records, which may well have been misdirected or lost in the overseas mail traffic, I really could not fault them. I was well aware that this period in my life, though not my own cup of tea, would have been a great opportunity for a young man just starting out in the world, who could commit himself wholeheartedly to a future with this fine and growing company.

As for me, I had other kinds of challenges to confront: the kinds I knew I could beat!

At long last I was harnessed to my rightful profession. I had an employer who gave me my freedom to burnish both his own and his political party's image, not forgetting his radio station and airline, rewarding me with an exorbitant entertainment allowance and a more than lavish paycheck deposited into my bank account every month.

Ademar was a PR counselor's dream. Having seen the fruits of my work for both him and his Party over many months, he was now gung ho and pulling at the leash to announce his candidacy for the Presidency of Brazil.

Janio Quadros and Juscelino Kubitschek had already announced their candidacies, both being about as popular as Ademar de Barros. This meant that we were in for a very close race, which also implied a very dangerous and unpredictable race, for when it is that close all bets are off, and all manner of double crossing and outright lying enter into the process. Politics is a mean business, and always has been, the cream and the scum rising to the top of the bottle, a never-ending division of good and evil.

It was to be a deadly and complex time, with nothing certain except that we had nine months leading up to the finish line. Enormous amounts of money were brought into each Party's headquarters from self-interested organizations, including banks, companies, factories, labor, and the media, each leaning toward one or another of the candidates. Meanwhile, the junior candidates running for state and national offices were gnashing their teeth and wringing their hands in dismay, for this presidential race was too unpredictable to call, and what if you backed the wrong man?

Despite all the tension building in the coming months, the good life went on, and my life became once again almost as joyful as during my time with Sir David and Sir Alex at London Film Productions. Of course, my taxes were no longer so overpowering as to drive me out of the country – indeed, they were now only a small part of my obligations. I was managing to spend my entertainment allowance as abundantly and all-embracingly as I did at Korda's, most of it now going into my pursuit and persuasion of British and American business owners to Ademar's cause. I also arranged numerous dinner parties hosted by Ademar, either in his home or at his favorite hotel. He was very well read in both British and American history, probably better than most of his guests; the latter usually related well enough to him to forge a commitment of some kind to his cause by the end of the evening. Ademar truly had the stature and the attitude of a winner. When my English acquaintances asked me what I thought of his chances, I told them again and again that I believed he was the best of the three candidates, and that he would make a splendid President of Brazil.

I also had a reasonably private life with Neusa, but when a star is a star, and her film earns the glory of Best Foreign Film at the Oscars, she also has to be in Hollywood and attend first nights for the film in selected cities in both the US and Great Britain. Often there would be more than a week or even two when I would be without her. But when she was in residence, and Bart and his beloved lady friend, later to become his wife, were available, we four together did just about every sort of entertainment and party that I can think of.

One party I can never forget was located on a fazenda (plantation), a mere fifty minutes away in Bart's car from our apartment building. Our hosts had invited about sixteen of us; as the weather was perfect, the party was held outdoors. It featured a churrasco dinner, the meat having come from the host's own herd, with many fixtures and a sublime dessert. Our host steadfastly refused to share the recipe for the dessert, insisting that it was unique to his family, going way back to when his first relatives arrived in Brazil from Tanzania, many generations ago. I couldn't blame him. His dessert was close to a British delicacy that I was crazy about, but with a Tanzanian interpretation.

Everybody was in a happy mood after the two-hour dinner, though some seemed almost incapable of getting back on their feet. Nonetheless, we had a good fifteen-minute walk ahead of us to the Pavilion, of which our host was very proud; it was a large and graceful structure with many chairs and tables on the concrete floor, where a large table would be laid with hot coffee, liqueurs, cigars, and cigarettes. But first there was the plumbing to be examined, and a line quickly formed at the doors of the one toilet for the ladies and another for the gentlemen.

Neusa had been worried by the early departure of a young couple who were due to be married within the month, both coming from fine families without a shred of scandal in their backgrounds. The engaged couple had taken off for the Pavilion even before the delicious dessert was served, at which point Neusa became really anxious. She knew both of them, and their families, and was aware that they were young and in love, and desperate for each other. Both were presently living an introverted and chaperoned existence, at a time and in a place when sex before marriage was considered taboo; if they were discovered together before the wedding, they would face mind-boggling punishments from both their church and their parents. The daughter, if fortunate, would be incarcerated in a nunnery, while her swain would be sent abroad to cool his ardor until returning a year or so hence and being forced to move to some smaller town many leagues away from São Paulo.

Neusa was already three-quarters of the way to the Pavilion, with me a few yards behind her, when we arrived at last to the sound of two bodies in joyous participation of the world's favorite occupation.

"I knew it!" Neusa said. "We should have followed them when they left. It's too late now. Why didn't she have a chaperone?"

The couple was at the end of the room, with candlelight behind them, showing every amorous thrust and gesture in shadows on the wall. The man was sitting in a cushioned wicker chair, his lower body naked, while his loved one sat astride him, her lingerie on top of his clothes on the floor. Her cocktail dress was still on her, his presence already within her, as they rose and fell with one another in pure ecstasy, utterly oblivious to all about them.

The delirious sounds emanating from these young people's throats were anything but soft, and I could not imagine what Neusa would do now. The deed was being done in front of our very eyes, and suddenly we could hear the sounds of the other guests stumbling around in besotted merriment. Neusa quickly blew out the candles beside the couple, at which point they "came" together, he with a mighty groan, and she with a drawn-out shriek of complete fulfillment.

Neusa allowed them to remain there, still connected, for she well knew that the immediate after effect is as much a part of the experience as the consummation itself. Then, fearing the arrival of the other guests, she urged the man to withdraw from his beloved. She handed a large handkerchief to the young woman, as I handed mine to the young man. Neusa pressed them to get back into their clothes, as being caught in this compromising situation could brook severe complications. The lady's dress had been pulled down off her breasts, which were full and shapely, the nipples still puffed up; Neusa reminded her to cover herself up, and within a few short minutes all was back in order. The lovers looked pale but blissful, and so under the spell of their intimate encounter with one another that they remained in a daze, apparently feeling no embarrassment. They thanked us for our support and secrecy, and with warm *abraços*, they left us to return to his car. He took her home to the safety of her parents and the chaperones, to endure the last weeks of their engagement.

Bart and his lady, who arrived ahead of the rest, asked if we wanted to stay some more. We demurred; we had had quite enough of everything for one day. Bart gave a sigh of relief, so, after thanking our hosts for their hospitality, we returned to Bart's car and drove in supreme comfort back to our apartments.

Neusa and I, and Bart and his fiancée and his family, were all invited to the wedding, held in a splendid church in a very solemn and beautiful ceremony. It was followed by an enormous reception, with all the high society in their Parisian salon dresses, the men bedecked in formal suits reminding me of Ascot. Neusa and I were dressed accordingly, Neusa in a brilliant red dress especially designed for her by the House of Dior, I in a rented formal suit in step with all the other gentlemen.

Neusa's looks, dress, and film star appeal made her a particular attraction, especially with the men, but everyone there was thrilled at the award given to *O Cangaceiro*. When the men thinned out, the women moved in to share the glory with the star for the film that had brought such pride to Brazil, its first Oscar ever. Even Getulio Vargas, the President of Brazil, who would be retiring at the next election and was attending the wedding reception with his family, wanted to meet her. When she was told of this, she insisted on putting her arm in mine and walking over to the President. He was sitting with some of his family in a corner of the room, but rose to his feet when we arrived in front of him; after he had complimented her on her movie performance, Neusa introduced me and he shook my hand warmly, observing that all of Brazil was celebrating the Oscar and that I must be very proud of her. I said I was, in French, and he seemed rattled, so Neusa translated for me. He beamed and introduced me to his family, pronouncing my name "Pita Serman," losing the "h," but I was flattered that he could even do that. He asked Neusa more about the film and her promotional efforts abroad, and he thanked us for coming to his table. Neusa told him what an honor it had been for both of us to meet him, whereupon he kissed her on both cheeks, shook my hand again, and let us go. I was thrilled and pleased for the newlyweds that he had honored their family and their marriage.

A son was born to the now married couple eight months and four days after their wedding, a month short of the expected time. This was because the baby had been conceived a month earlier than anyone knew except for us and the attending doctors. It was seven and a half pounds, healthy as can be, with everyone happy to call it a "miracle baby." The doctors who delivered the child knew when to keep silent.

We two, Neusa and I, had been there at the very conception, and now we had attended their wedding. That's pretty unique, don't you think?

Politics

At my instigation, Ademar and I had discussed a trip to New York a couple of times while we were canvassing the major states to test his political and emotional reception in the field. He had been received well by many state VIPs, usually politely if not always enthusiastically. In the two states with their contending Presidential aspirants, he had naturally found most doors closed.

Interestingly enough, the *canaceiros* – meaning the cowboys and those at the bottom of society, a vast preponderance of what the Argentineans call "the shirtless ones" – greeted Ademar with much acclaim. We took special note of that, but they were chaff in the wind, glad for a meal and a place to sleep, untutored, unskilled, and illiterate, and available to do anyone's bidding when there was a possible reward.

Politically, they could be bribed with a pittance by those running for office. If only we could set them afire with some unique and simple goal that no one had thought of, a goal that could be uncovered only by a sensitive census in two or three parts of Brazil! If there were a common accord on some really worthwhile and previously undiscovered objective that would fire them up and could actually be brought to realization, then, by golly, we could swamp our competitors and claim the presidency based on the millions of votes from the very bottom of the pile, God bless them all. I began to give some serious attention to this idea, but then had to put it out of my mind for the moment.

Now we're heading for New York, where Ademar will be staying at the Waldorf Astoria Hotel, and I will be staying with Aunt Lucy Rosen. Aunt Lucy's husband and son were both deceased, but Aunt Lucy's grand home on West 54th Street continued to be run like clockwork with a full staff of butler, chauffeur, and maids (from Ireland), with half of the staff on duty at the Caramoor estate in Katonah on weekends.

I had called Aunt Lucy immediately after the date of arrival in New York had been set and told her the purpose of the visit. She immediately declared she would host an elegant dinner in her home in honor of Ademar. She also insisted that I use her lovely home as my residence while in New York, an invitation that I accepted with great pleasure.

I had advised the *New York Times* of our arrival time at the airport, for my job was to solidify the image of Ademar as a person of considerable stature in the world, and acceptance by the USA's most prestigious and influential newspaper wouldn't hurt.

The fact that my client had been the former Governor of São Paulo, the most powerful city in South America, and was possibly the next President of Brazil, made Ademar a genuine superstar VIP. Even before leaving Brazil I had made most of my arrangements directly with all the media news syndicates, as well as certain newspapers, magazines, radio stations, and the top three TV companies headquartered in New York.

I had had the good fortune to meet and play tennis with Jinx Falkenberg, a champion tennis player of that time, and a beautiful and most charming lady. She ate me up on the tennis court and spat me out without moving a hair on her pretty head, much to my chagrin. In spite of that, she was a very nice lady, and we became friendly, though not on the tennis court.

One day she told me that she had recently signed a contract to host a new morning TV show in New York. She would be leaving Rio in a week, and if I knew of any special people going to that city I should let her know, in case they would be amenable to being guests on her TV show. I was now very glad that I had been able to send her quite a few fascinating people. Jinx was grateful, and when it was my turn to need her, she came through splendidly. Not only did she have Ademar on her TV show, but she also arranged for him to be on her husband Tex's very popular radio show in the evening, airing from the Peacock Alley in Ademar's hotel. Tex's other guest was to be President Franklin Roosevelt's Postmaster General, Jim Farley, now a VIP with Coca-Cola. I was curious to see how these two giants would get along together.

Johnny Dodge had also been of enormous help to me. Though I had arranged our visit with David Rockefeller, of whom I have written in a previous chapter, Johnny had been calling his own top-level clients in banking and stockbrokering, including Mr. Morgan of the J. P. Morgan Bank, a wonderful gentleman and great friend of Johnny's. In fact, Johnny went one incredible step beyond and actually arranged the appointments, after discussing the arrangements with the principals, with their secretaries, so that there would be no confusion or mistakes. In return, he expected Ademar to adhere to his timetable.

Ademar adhered, for I went along with him. Although he knew he was meeting the cream of the crop, he was constantly amazed at the public fame and caliber of those VIPs to whom he was introduced. Johnny also called Lucy, his sister, and suggested certain special guests who he thought would be appropriate for the occasion of her dinner party. Lucy was grateful, as was I.

From our arrival on time at the airport until our sendoff, a week later, our path seemed to be strewn with roses. The *New York Times* had sent a young and earnest reporter to the airport on our arrival for Ademar's first interview; the reporter gave him a fine write-up with a photo in the next morning's edition. Representatives of the major TV stations were there also, and were given brief but pithy interviews for their evening newscasts.

Knowing what a triumph it would be if Ademar were to be invited to the office of the Mayor of New York City for a visit, I asked Jinx if she had any inside connections; she said she vaguely knew of one PR person on the Mayor's staff and would try to feel him out on the subject of a meeting between these two VIPs. As it turned out, the PR person thought it was a great idea, thinking that it would help solidify the Mayor's relationship with the Latinos now immigrating to and living in New York. So the day and time were set, and the meeting went very well.

Ademar's adversaries in Brazil naturally cried foul. The US State Department winged an incendiary missive into the Mayor's office ordering him "to run New York and keep out of foreign affairs, or else!" The deed, however, had been done, and no one could stop its effect on Brazilian politics.

A week later, polls were taken across Brazil to see if there was any change in the previous order of the candidates, which had been blurred head-to-head since the beginning. And indeed there was. Ademar was now running eight percent ahead of the others. I had achieved what I had set out to achieve ... but with what help, known and unknown, seen and unseen! I was so blessed with wonderful friends, and above all my wonderful Johnny and Mother, always there when needed, not to mention Aunt Lucy.

Vignettes from New York

The TV studio was intimate, and the show was live – meaning it was spontaneous, with no cue cards except for the hostess, though I noticed from where I stood behind the TV cameras that Jinx was oblivious of everything except her guest. Ademar was in his element, having a pretty and professional interviewer, and I was proud of both of them.

There was only one gaffe, and it was a doozy. During the interview, with everything going along bright and breezy, another pretty lady, dressed in a minuscule skirt and skimpy top, came onto the set holding a tray with two cups and saucers, which she placed on the table beside them. Ademar, being a healthy male, had eyes only for the skimpily dressed lady, who made a Marilyn Monroe exit, her walk and her derrière obviously entrancing him, leaving Jinx Falkenberg grinning.

As soon as the lady disappeared back into her dressing room, Ademar reached for his cup on the table and took a good mouthful of its contents. Unbeknownst to Ademar and me, Jinx's TV Show was the property of Lipton Tea, which is no doubt a splendid tea, but not at all what Ademar had expected. As quickly as he had filled his mouth with this strange taste, he blew it right back out, at which moment there was utter stillness in the studio. Then everyone on the set, including those behind the cameras, and even a shocked Jinx herself, broke into hysterical laughter.

Ademar, bewildered, though with a surprised grin on his face, demanded to know "Where is the coffee? Brazilians drink coffee, not this kind of stuff!"

It took a while, with the TV cameras now on hold, for the studio to regain its composure and settle down, and for Jinx to explain the situation to Ademar. At that point, being a good sport, he had the beginning of the scene re-rehearsed. This time, when the cameras started up again, he drank his coffee from the tea cup, beaming into the camera and swallowing the coffee briskly. Then he wiped his mouth and commented, "Very good tea!" That allowed Jinx to move into her prepared Lipton presentation, while Ademar enjoyed his second cup of coffee, served the same way.

Jinx kept the original filmed incident in her private collection, claiming that, even though it would have been embarrassing if it had been shown to the public, the original was still a priceless glitch that she would treasure always.

Except for the fact that one looked American and one looked Brazilian, former Postmaster General of the USA Farley and former Governor of São Paulo Ademar were both big men. Both had that serene composure of successful men who are at home in conversation whether with a shoeshiner or a reigning queen.

I had dinner with Tex before his show was to air that evening, to give him some background and suggested questions that Tex could put to Ademar that would enhance his interview. After our dinner, about half an hour before the show went on, Ademar and Farley were introduced to each other by Tex and me. After a few minutes, we realized that Tex's guests had instantly taken the measure of each other and liked what they saw; in fact, they had excused themselves and adjourned to the sofa outside the roped-off enclave, where they could have some peace and quiet and get to know each other better.

Tex and I were delighted with this turn of events. I walked around the hotel's ground floor, noting that everything was sparkling clean, which made a splendid impression except for the few memorial plaques honoring those Americans killed in action during the Second World War. The intention was good, but obviously it was sparsely funded or carelessly attended to: The lettering on the plaques was disintegrating, a pathetic tribute to those being commemorated.

Of course, the interviews with Tex were a great success. Ademar was his first guest, followed by Jim Farley, after which the all three discussed some additional subjects. When Tex closed the broadcast, we all adjourned to comfortable chairs in the bar, where we talked for another two hours, one of the most enjoyable events that I can remember.

With one exception, I had nothing to do with Lucy and Johnny's guest list, though Lucy gave me a copy of it three days before the dinner party. The list was impressive, including an Undersecretary of State and his wife;

two of the leading bank presidents in America, whom Ademar had already met, with their wives; presidents of the two largest stockbroker companies, whom he had also already met, again with their wives, because Johnny had wanted Ademar to feel comfortable with the guests rather than having to start all over again from scratch. The Brazilian Ambassador and his wife rounded out the table, except for one other person.

Sometime before I came to Brazil, I became a regular attender at the Palladium Theatre in London, which was presenting a series of tiptop stars on stage every few weeks. I had seen Maurice Chevalier there again, and had gone backstage afterward to remind him of our last meeting at the Crillon Hotel in Paris.

He was very kind, and much to my surprise insisted on taking me to my favorite London hotel, the Savoy, where he was staying. We had dinner there and watched the late cabaret, with the guests dancing to the great band of Carol Gibbons. Carol and my mother had become good friends some years before, when he discovered that she was the actual "Dinah"; by that time, the song that had been written about her had become something of a classic.

Judy Garland was fabulous. The silent Marx brother, who never spoke a word for the entire one-and-a-half-hour show, with no intermission, held every single person in that theater utterly fascinated and entertained by his genius, giving us the most unique, satisfying and hilarious presentation that I have ever witnessed.

Among those incredible stars shining at the Palladium Theatre was a more recent but no less talented star from Brazil, who had been making waves in Hollywood musicals and could now be seen on the Palladium stage. I had been attracted to her in the movies by her extraordinary way of singing and dancing and her incredible vivacity.

One evening I had managed to obtain a seat in the front row, which was amazing, considering that the house was filled. Then the music began, and the curtain went up, and there appeared on stage this tiny bombshell with built-up shoes, a jungle green costume and a towering pyramid of a hat decorated with Brazilian fruit and flowers. All of this effect made her appear considerably taller than she really was. But who cared?

She was Carmen Miranda, Brazil's powerhouse gift to the world, and she could energize that stage as few others could. She was dynamite, a fabulous entertainer with a really wonderful personality that crossed the footlights and affected just about every single person in that theater. The ovations at the end of every number were very loud and endearing, as if a tryst had been accomplished between the star and her audience. I knew I had to meet her.

After the curtain finally came down following a fifteen-minute ovation and yet another number, stretching the show an additional half hour, I was among the first out the door. I went backstage, where the doorkeeper remembered me from my previous visit to Maurice Chevalier's dressing room, which still had its star on the door. As for my interest in Carmen Miranda, he seemed to think I was an impresario, as he just pointed me to the door with the star on it and said, "You know everybody, don't you?" Lordy, Lordy, what stories that room could tell, if only ...

I knocked, and a voice called, "Come!" I opened the door and saw Carmen Miranda on a sofa, still in her costume from the final scene. Her hat was on a hat stand with many other glamorous pyramid hats propped up on other hat stands. Her shoes were off and a masseuse was massaging her feet, while her dresser waited patiently to undress her, shower her, and who knows what else. It was almost eleven o'clock, because the performances had gone into overtime. That probably would come out of her salary for the labor union's staff.

She looked at me with a surprised expression and said, "Yes?" I wondered if she spoke in one-syllable words for lack of an English vocabulary, but then she smiled. The room lit up, and she said, "What can I do for you?"

"Just let me look at you," said I, and her smile grew bigger. Deciding that this was my opportunity, and returning her smile, I added, "I think you are the most entertaining lady I have ever seen in my life, and you are so damned cute that you won your audience over in the first five minutes."

She looked at me, perplexed, and asked her dresser what the word "cute" meant. The dresser translated it into a compatible Portuguese word, and she brightened up again.

"I think you are cute, too," she said.

From there on we became instant friends, and it wasn't long before I invited her to dinner at the Churchill Club. When she accepted, I realized she must have been hungry after all the physical effort she had put into her dancing and singing that night. I took a lazy walk for forty-five minutes before returning to pick her up. Fifteen minutes after I arrived, we were in our taxi and on our way to the club.

She was wearing a very modest black dress, with black stockings and black pumps, and a gorgeous diamond cluster pendant above her heart. I think she wanted to be incognita that night, and I understood, but in spite of her appearance, she remained a petite version of her stage persona. We chatted away in the taxi as if we had known each other all our lives, which is saying a lot for an Anglo American and a Brazilian movie and stage star who had only just met.

But she was so easy and confiding! With our dinner, which she relished, followed by a few foxtrots and a Brazilian number that had just become popular, and which we requested again just before the band went home, we at last concluded the evening in extra good spirits, having no doubt that we had a good rapport.

I took her out three more times during the run of her show at the Palladium, and when she left to return to Hollywood, she gave me her home phone number, along with her agent's number. She insisted that if I ever returned to the States I was to call her, so that we could meet again and catch up with one another.

Our relationship was not a love affair, but rather a good and affectionate friendship. I later learned that she had just married an employee of her studio, an American, and I sent her a cablegram of congratulations and good wishes. She wrote me a lovely letter back, inviting me to their home if ever I should be in Los Angeles.

All of those memories came back with a rush when I put two and two together on the occasion of our trip to New York. As with Neusa, Ademar was very proud of the wonderful impression Carmen Miranda was making in the USA and Great Britain, not only as a star, but as a goodwill ambassador for all things Brazilian. At that moment of recall, I found her number stuffed in the back of the inside pocket of my wallet, and – to cut this story to size – let me just say that my enchanting friend dazzled all the magnates and their wives at this extraordinary dinner party. Ademar, with Carmen Miranda on his right, was puffed up with the joy of being able to share this extraordinary Brazilian lady, who had captured the hearts of her public wherever she went, with the others at this dinner party.

Aunt Lucy, uncertain in the beginning whether this was a good idea, finally gave a reserved yes. After it was all over, she remarked that she had never hosted a dinner that was more fun, and that she had never seen grown men of such esteemed position let their hair down and act like happy kids. That was Carmen's magic. She made you feel like a child again.

God bless Carmen Miranda, whose life was soon to be cut off so pathetically short. All of Brazil went into mourning, and large parts of the world as well. I went to her funeral in Rio, where I met her bereaved husband. I felt for him. I have never seen such enormous crowds of mourners; practically all the main streets of Rio overflowed with sobbing admirers of this tiny lady with the biggest, kindest, most giving heart in all the world. We will not see her like again.

Just about every Brazilian living in or around New York was at the airport to see Ademar off. The vast reception room was filled with excited Portuguese voices all speaking at once, indeed yelling above the din at one another, all pumped up with the knowledge of being in the same building as Ademar de Barros, the next President of Brazil. The same reception awaited us both at the Rio and São Paulo airports. Ademar must have felt enormously grateful for the extraordinary welcoming receptions, by now confident that the supreme prize – the Brazilian White House – was well within his grasp.

He gave me and our New York contingent a three-day break, and then he took off on a goodwill tour of every state in Brazil. For this purpose he had ordered one of his own airline's smaller passenger planes – jet planes not yet having been put into service at that time – to transport him on his journey, designed to build on his American triumph and keep up the momentum wherever he went. At this stage of the game he appeared to be unassailable and could only increase his majority.

In the meantime, I was to visit a friend of his, some thirty-five miles outside São Paulo. My assignment was to arrange with him to lease Ademar an enormous piece of his land to accommodate sixty to seventy thousand people, plus an area for at least one hundred buses and maybe more, plus trailers, cars, motorbikes in another adjourning area, and vehicles from out of state. It was a mind-boggling picture, and I felt somewhat embarrassed to be putting his friend in such a position as to having to deny Ademar his request, though I wouldn't have blamed him at all if he did.

I had met his friend before and liked him. He spoke English fluently, and was both well traveled and enormously rich. His father had left him this hefty piece of the State of São Paulo on his death some five years previous.

After our greeting, we sat down in the living room and I went right to the point of my visit. At first he was almost tonguetied, but I suspect that he finally convinced himself that having a friend in the President's Palace was worth leasing him some of his land for a few days. His price for the lease was really very reasonable for having a hefty chunk of his land taken over by transportation machines making inroads into his defenseless earth, not to mention regiments of possibly rambunctious civilians coming to knock at the door of their chosen president to be.

Happily, at the time of the Event, the drivers arranged their buses in a very orderly fashion, and the crowd, for such a big and enthusiastic mass of people, behaved admirably.

Since I was now, with a very smart sidekick from Ademar's radio station, contributing to the newspaper and radio ads, we set the date, with Ademar's approval, for three weeks ahead, to clear the vast public space needed – starting the next day! – and to get a boxing ring set up above the multitude in the center of this immense field. We also had to arrange for all the electrical lines for lights, generators, sound equipment, loudspeakers, food and drink concession stands, and a sufficiency of portable toilets. It was a monstrous job, and the details alone were almost overwhelming, though I did find pleasure when things began to fall into place. I knew that I was way out of my depth, and only my good luck was keeping me going. I desperately needed a professional ringmaster in this business to release me from my unwanted bondage. But where to find him?

The only unexpected thing that happened at this time was that none other than the wife of Argentina's President Juan Perón, Senora. Evita Perón, had just accepted an invitation from President Getulio Vargas of Brazil to come on a three-day goodwill visit. She was to return to Argentina three days before Ademar's great event. It didn't bother us at all. It wasn't even a bump in the road. In fact, I paid hardly any attention to this event, until the American Ambassador to Brazil, my godfather Hershel Johnson, called me up when I was visiting Rio to tell me that he had received a letter, care of the US Embassy, for me, and he thought I should see it right away. I told him I would pick it up at lunchtime, and he said, "If that's the case, have lunch with me." I accepted, and at one o'clock I entered the Embassy's front door and was ushered into Hershel's office, where a table was set up with two chairs and a light luncheon displayed on his mother's beautiful china.

Hershel came right to the point. "Peter, did you know Evita Perón is coming in a few days on a goodwill tour?"

"Of course."

"Well, then, the President is giving a banquet at the Palace in her honor, and naturally all the Ambassadors and their wives have been invited, as well as Brazil's most important and influential leaders. Here is my invitation."

He showed it to me. It was very handsome, in raised gold lettering, and with the President's crest boldly displayed.

"It's magnificent," I said. "I congratulate you."

"Have you ever met President Perón's wife?"

"Of course not. I've never been to Argentina. Why would you ask such a question?"

Hershel looked at me with a slightly surprised expression and said, "Because you, too, have been invited to attend the banquet at the request of President Getulio Vargas."

He handed me, unopened, my invitation, its envelope exactly like his, my name written in a beautiful handwriting as Charles Austin Sherman III. The Argentine Embassy had apparently checked with the US Embassy as to the correct manner in which to address me. I opened it and saw exactly the same invitation as Hershel's.

"A mistake, it has to be a mistake, a mix-up of some kind," I said, feeling partly elated and party disappointed, for I knew without any doubt that there was no way I would be possibly invited to an occasion in such august company as this.

"It's got to be some kind of mistake," I repeated. "Someone, somewhere, just messed up."

"I thought that, too, at first, Peter, and I called the President's secretary to see if I could find an answer. She remembered that the invitation for your presence at the banquet had come from the Argentine Ambassador as requested by none other than Evita Perón herself. She called you Peter Sherman, so she must know you."

My head was reeling. "I swear to you, Hershel, as God is my keeper, I have never set eyes on her, and she has never set eyes on me. I have seen pictures of her. She is attractive, and I believe she's more popular with the 'shirtless ones' than her husband is, but the idea of me having met Evita Perón is ridiculous."

Hershel looked at me long and thoughtfully. Finally, he said, "I give up. I believe you, Peter. I just can't make heads or tails of it. I will, nonetheless, add you to the Embassy table. Report here that night in your tux – that's what my two other staff will be wearing. We ambassadors have to wear white tie and tails, damn it!"

Then he said, almost as a postscript, "Incidentally, you certainly did your boss proud in New York, according to my sources. I congratulate you. But don't let up. You have still some time to go."

"I know, but in New York I received an abundance of help and influential goodwill from friends and acquaintances and even the media, including my stepfather Johnny Dodge and his gracious sister, Lucy Rosen.

I was a part instigator of the main event, after which I was mainly a liaison man to some very helpful friends."

I told him about the next venture at the fazenda, and he said, "It sounds like a good idea. But don't quote me, Peter. Ambassadors have to keep out of politics."

"Of course."

We finished lunch, hardly saying another word, both befuddled by this extraordinary, inexplicable conundrum. Since I was under heavy pressure as it was, trying to put together all of the many parts that were to make up the event at the fazenda of such colossal proportions, I decided "to heck with it!" Maybe I would never know how I got on Evita Perón's list, but Ademar was my bread and butter, and I knew I was going to put all my energy into my work for him, my friend and provider.

Neusa was still out of Brazil, though now on the South American continent, and I really had no one with whom to discuss my weird entanglement even if I could. Bart's love affair with his future bride was taking up most of his attention when he was not at work for Royal Dutch Shell, where two promotions over the last year had pushed him gently up the ladder.

But this was the night of the banquet, so I was dressed in my finery, a taxi in the street below waiting to take me to the American Embassy. From there I would ride in the Embassy's chauffeur-driven limousine, with Hershel and his two aides.

For a fleeting moment, I wondered if I should have the driver take me to the Rio Airport, where I could buy a ticket on the ten p.m. flight to Miami, thereby leaving my Evita Perón problem behind me. That would free Hershel from blame for anything connected with the issue, and it would also free me from my responsibilities at the site of the fazenda, which were quickly overwhelming me and destroying my sleep.

And then I reminded myself of what a wonderful life I was having with my delicious and adorable Neusa, and my wonderful friend and boss Ademar, not to forget Bart and his kind and helpful family, and of course Hershel, who – in spite of his present uneasiness with the Evita Perón situation – I knew would always be my friend and supporter.

So I took the elevator down to the street and got in the taxi and directed the driver to take me to the US Embassy, wondering what could possibly happen to me next.

What indeed!

Evita Perón

The reception line at the entrance to the ballroom seemed interminable, though it actually took our little group a mere twenty-five minutes to reach the announcer proclaiming the name of each guest, with or without a title, after it was whispered into his ear by the guest himself. I had decided that, since she had used the name of Peter Sherman, Evita Perón would hear that same name again, rather than the legal name on my passport, Charles Austin Sherman III.

The very experienced announcer had a fine voice. He was tall and beautifully outfitted in a deep green and yellow velvet tail coat, white ruffled shirt and black pants descending only to his knees, from which white stockings reached down to shiny black pumps.

From a distance of thirty feet, I could see Evita Perón standing alone, with a military guard in full dress uniform about four feet back of her on either side. The President was already at the dinner table. He was now aging and could spend only a short while standing. Walking he did just fine.

The President's guest of honor was about five feet three or four inches tall in her heels. She was dressed in a golden gown that had to be from a Paris couturier, her slim figure smoothly outlined, her jewelry limited to a diamond necklace and wristwatch, plus a fantastic emerald on her finger. Her hair was golden, tightly brushed to her head, and her face was animated. She had a look of curiosity in her eyes, as if she wished she could spend time with each guest, but that just wasn't possible.

While Hershel greeted her, I gave my name to the announcer, whereupon Evita Perón turned quickly away from Hershel and looked at me with the biggest smile I think I have ever seen. It literally radiated; as I kissed her hand, the custom on such occasions, she said softly, "Peter, oh,

Peter!" in the most endearing manner, and we held our gaze until I let go her hand and moved on.

Jim, one of Hershel's aides, who was next in line, said that Evita Perón had kept her eyes on me before turning her attention to him. I was flattered, but I could not think what more could ever come of this occasion, for I was in a room full of Brazil's greatest and most powerful leaders, including Ademar and his contenders.

Because our table was that of the United States, it was arranged with a central view straight up to the extraordinary VIPs' long table on an open balcony, at least fifteen feet up and goodness knows how long. President Vargas was sitting straight and center, awaiting Evita Perón, who by now must have been almost two hours on her feet. Yet when the drums rolled, and the trumpets blew, and the doors at the end of the balcony were thrown open, with the searchlight turned on her, in came this golden goddess with a light step and that glorious smile, bringing everyone in that enormous room to their feet with tumultuous applause. She walked with a springing step until she reached the now standing president, her chair on his right proffered by a footman in livery, similar to that of the announcer.

Even after she sat down, the applause roared in great waves up to her still smiling presence. It calmed down only when everyone stood, first for the Argentine anthem and then for the Brazilian.

Our table was just off the dance floor, but arranged so that its guests were facing up toward the host and honored guest, and away from the dance area itself. I surmised that, after all the speeches, poor Evita would have to dance with many of Vargas's major players in the government. I later learned that Evita had cut the list to four, claiming that standing for more than an hour greeting the reception line was too fatiguing for her then to be expected to dance with all the members of his cabinet. Indeed, poor Getulio Vargas had had a bitter squabble with his cronies as to who would make up the chosen four.

Hershel was not at his best, drumming his fingers on our dinner table as if playing a complicated piece of Mozart. He had apparently not heard Evita's endearing "Peter, oh, Peter," because he asked me if she had said anything to me, and I said no. There was no point in raising his blood pressure any higher than it was already.

"I think we should be safe now," he said, patting my shoulder. "I still cannot fathom the situation, but there is no way she can do anything to you now, not in front of all these people." He smiled, and I smiled, and I wondered.

As the evening wore on, Hershel became more comfortable and amiable. He started recounting to me and his aides the story of growing up with my mother in Charlotte, North Carolina, and of their friendship that had held together ever since. Some of his stories of their relationship were really quite funny, though the two aides were laughing together a bit more loudly than the stories deserved. It was part of their job, no doubt.

The dinner itself was better than I had expected. Afterward, the President of Brazil gave a splendid speech, according to its reception. Then the star of the evening, Evita Perón, showed why she was well known far and wide for her oratory. In Argentina, she was the most adored of women, only the resentful blue bloods resisting her advances. Her popularity surpassed even that of the President, her husband.

Her speech must have been impressive, for she was interrupted many times by cries from her audience and tumultuous applause at almost every point, each of which was indented with a brisk chop of her hand, indicating that her next point was now coming up. It was, indeed, a glorious speech. Though I understood only parts of it, there was no doubt that she had her audience of brilliant and successful men and women in the palm of her hand. She was magic!

Now the final four of the President's cabinet each had his ten-minute dance with her, after which poor Evita rested her feet under the dinner table and entered into a conversation with her host. The floor now became full of couples dancing to a very good band, mixing American and English romantic music along with thrilling music from Brazil and the Argentine. It was irresistible.

I had seen the British Ambassador and his wife and daughter at their table, along with one uncomfortable-looking young man, obviously the daughter's date. I asked Hershel if I could be excused to give the British Ambassador's daughter a whirl, and he was delighted. The British Ambassador was also delighted, and off we danced together, for I had taken her out to dinner a couple of times at Hershel's suggestion. She was a nice companion, but soon afterward I had met Neusa, and that was another story. Anyway, away we danced, albeit a little unsteadily, for the lady in my arms had her head on my shoulder and was a bit tipsy. On the whole, though, she was handling it reasonably well, with my firm grip around her back. She told me that her date had never learned to dance, and with this great band's music she was dying to get out on the floor, so we danced three dances quite well. I returned her to her date, now glowering at me with an expression that suggested I had better not meet him in a back alley.

I returned to my table. Its occupants appeared somewhat subdued, and also somewhat in their drinks, but not enough to have them dancing with each other.

Hershel of course, was sober, refined, and bored out of his skull. While he intermittently talked embassy business, I kept my eyes on Evita, who was still talking animatedly with Vargas. Every now and again she had her host present friends of his to her. I knew that she knew where I was, because she had given me a brief wave and a great smile right after she sat down. Fortunately, Hershel did not see it.

I resigned myself to an evening of embassy gossip, along with some great music in the background.

And then the gods smiled.

I watched Evita whispering intensely and secretively in her host's ear. He smiled at her, nodding his head approvingly, and turned to the footman in attendance behind their chairs. After the President gave him his instructions and pointed to our table, the footman went out the side door and came down the stairs and back into the banquet hall, where the dance floor was now being enjoyed by many of the guests. He walked with considerable dignity over to our table and asked, "Señor Peter Sherman?"

I stood up. As Hershel's face tuned crimson, I moved away from the table to go with the footman. Hershel put out a restraining hand, but I was already out of reach and following the footman around the dance floor and up the stairs and along behind the dinner tables to where Vargas and his guest were once again whispering together.

I waited behind their chairs, until Vargas turned his head up and saw me. He actually got out of his chair and shook my hand; then he snapped his fingers at another footman, who was also his English interpreter, who asked me if the President hadn't met me before. Flattered beyond measure that, with all the people he had to meet, he had remembered me, I told him through the interpreter that I had been at a certain wedding reception in São Paulo. The President's eyes lit up, and he said, "You were with Neusa Vargas, weren't you?" I said yes and he then explained to Evita, who had also stood up, who Neusa was. She obviously recognized the name, being a great admirer of Neusa's films; she had already seen the film that had won the best foreign film award.

This seemed to be our cue to go to the dance floor. I bowed to the President; through the interpreter, he said, "Have a good time!" The interpreting footman led the way around the dance floor to my table, as I had asked Evita if I could present my godfather, the American Ambassador to Brazil, to her. As we walked over, Evita's arm through mine, Hershel and his aides came to attention in a state of shock. I introduced Hershel to her Excellency with a flourish. Evita started right in with a string of positive comments about America and all things American, and how she would like to see New York one day, and she had been told how beautiful the city of Washington was, and so on. Through this very good interpreter, Hershel and Evita ended up in a congenial and happy conversation. Though asked to sit down, she realized that we were wasting good dancing time, so she shook hands with the two dumbfounded aides and with Hershel, who, with a slightly dazed expression on his face, told her how honored he was to have met her.

And so we twirled onto the dance floor. A rapturous half-hour ensued midway in our dream world, with the other dancers observing our smooth synchronization and obvious fascination with one another. I stopped at the end of one musical number and asked the conductor, who spoke good English, if he would have his band play "All the Things You Are." I wanted to offer a heartfelt salute to this fabulous lady who was giving me a high in my life. He translated the title for Evita, who knew the words in her own language, and she became very emotional, holding me close and kissing my ear and blowing on it. We both knew that this had been a night to remember, and also that we would probably never see each other again.

At this moment she whispered in a mixture of Spanish and French that her friend Kia had told her of her relationship with me on the boat to Brazil. Evita had been so fascinated that she wanted to meet me: what better opportunity than during her official invitation to Brazil? Hence her request that I be invited to the banquet. I asked Evita to give Kia my affectionate good wishes and an *abraço*, and Evita said that Kia had asked her to give me the same, which she then acted upon.

I brought her back upstairs. The footman pulled her chair back, but she wasn't quite finished with me, so the President remained standing, as she motioned me forward to the front of the dinner table facing the ballroom. All the eyes that had been focused on us when we were dancing were now looking up at our return to the Presidential table; with a flourish, she kissed me, first on one cheek, then on the other. I kissed both her hands, the second palms up, and we tightened our grip. Then she sat down, and I bowed to the President, who had a big smile on his face. He shook my hand quite energetically, and jovially waved me goodbye. By the time I had returned to my table, the President and Evita were once again in animated conversation. I was so glad and so relieved that it had all ended so well.

The press were dismissed after the reception and the speeches had been recorded, so I didn't get any photos of us together, but what a memory!

Hershel's greeting was, "Her Excellency just saved your life! Did you know that?"

"No, I didn't know that."

"Someone here, maybe more than one, as my name is Hershel Johnson, would have put a bullet in you by tomorrow morning, for you are an American, or an Anglo as we are sometimes called, and you dared to allow yourself to be taken over by the honored guest for more than the limited ten-minute span. Indeed, I timed you two on the dance floor for thirty-two minutes, three times as long as was allowed, though I must confess, Peter, that I really don't know that I would have done differently if I had had the pleasure of being in your shoes."

Amazingly, Hershel chuckled. Then he became serious again. "Brazilians are a very proud people. Having an obvious Anglo being the first and only man to dance with the guest of honor was pretty hard to take, and I was truly afraid for your life after the end of the banquet."

"What did you expect me to do?" I asked. "The President of Brazil gave us his blessing, and it was the honored guest's request that I should be her partner. Was I to refuse them both? To have refused would really have upset the applecart and created a far worse situation for me and you and the State Department."

"I know, I know, but it doesn't matter anyway. Her Excellency gave the necessary gesture and resolved the situation with considerable grace and firmness, and so now you are undoubtedly out of harm's way – probably the safest man in Brazil!"

"What did she do?" I asked, remembering only the warmth of our farewell that could surely not have stopped a gunman's bullet.

With considerable relish, my guardian said, "What saved your goose, Peter, was her farewell kiss on both cheeks, signifying to all the guests gathered here that she is your protector. This means you have nothing more to fear. Brazilians value honor above all. Incidentally, thank you for presenting me to her. She was not at all what I expected, and she was very knowledgeable about America, didn't you think?"

"I was amazed."

"But I still don't understand the reason for her wanting you to be at the dinner. Do you?"

I knew, but I could not tell Hershel. It was too complicated, and he wouldn't have understood it anyway. So we let it rest and never spoke about it again.

Sadly, not too long after that, President Getulio Vargas committed suicide in his Catete, finally overwhelmed by the runaway inflation that was undermining the country's stability and the international markets, not to mention putting the exchange rate for the cruzeiro in serious jeopardy. Plus, after he had been in office as President for some twenty years, and had, against great odds, brought his country into the twentieth century, this dangerous collapse of the Brazilian economy was the final blow to an old and beloved man who was too tired and sick to cherish his life any more.

I wept for him, as did all of Brazil. Within a matter of a few years, I wept also for Evita Perón and the shirtless ones she left behind, when she died of ovarian cancer at the age of thirty-one.

In different ways, I loved them both.

The Great Event and After

I was doing my best, but there were so many details and such pressures, and I was so ignorant about the business of setting up this tremendous event, that I felt truly overwhelmed. Although certain things that were essential to the creation of such a spectacle had fallen neatly into place, I was well aware that I was having a lot of luck and that it probably wouldn't last. What I needed was a specialist in the art of creating such ventures, and, through a fortuitous appointment at my barber's, I found him sitting in the chair next to me. This gentleman had just returned from California, where he had set up a very similar enterprise. He was now free!

I immediately called Ademar, who was out canvassing votes in Belem. Though the price of our specialist seemed high, we agreed to his terms. After I showed him what I had done so far, he congratulated me, and said that, for someone with no previous experience, I would have made him a treasured assistant. High praise, indeed.

Lordy, lordy, was I ever relieved! I felt like I had been reborn.

Among the many achievements that our specialist put into effect was to dispense with the boxing-ring idea and have a considerably larger platform built: a round platform, high enough for all to see the biggest political names that wished to be seen, basking in Ademar's celebrity. Many of them had been wavering as to which presidential candidate to support, but they were now convinced that Ademar was the man to win.

A neat twist to the round platform that our specialist contrived was the addition of a powerful engine underneath it, which had an independent top floor. There would be a backup engine for emergencies, in order to move the platform slowly around, so that the thousands of spectators could see and hear those in the spotlight every four minutes, the time of one complete circle, giving each of them one whole minute of direct viewing and hearing.

In addition, there would be two helicopter pads to bring the politicians to the platform over the heads of the crowds, should their route be blocked. One pad would be next to the road leading up to the field where this event was occurring, with its own private parking lot, while the other would be at the foot of the stairs leading up to the platform. A steel fence would separate the pads from the public, with the state police responsible for both of them and for providing public protection.

An enormous area of the fazenda had been reserved for parking the hundreds of buses that had already made reservations for space. They would be coming from all over the state of São Paulo, with a huge influx from many other states arriving by bus, car, motorbike, and even private airplane. To that end, an airfield with a wind-directional sail was already in place, along with a temporary gasoline station for the planes. All of this effort was being carried out for the sole purpose of making it possible for everyone, whoever they were, or from wherever they came, to jump on Ademar's bandwagon.

Neusa, thank goodness, would be here for the occasion, and to my and Ademar's delight, she had volunteered to be presented to the crowd as a surprise guest just prior to his speech. This was a master-stroke, for which Ademar was vastly grateful. He insisted that she fly with him on his private plane to the great event. They would then be driven to their host's elegant home on the fazenda, where they would eat and rest; finally, at seven-fifteen p.m., Ademar would take one of the helicopters to the platform to greet those of his political guests who had already arrived, leaving Neusa with their host until the other helicopter came for her shortly before he would make the speech of his life.

I had arranged for two well-known Brazilian bands, playing only Brazilian or South American music, to perform interchangeably throughout the afternoon, with regular fifteen-minute breaks between their forty-minute performances. At seven p.m. they were to depart, allowing the crowd suspense factor to build up to when Ademar himself would appear to make his speech at eight sharp.

On the round platform where the politicians were stationed, food and drink were available. They were encouraged to take turns addressing the crowd over the loudspeakers during the fifteen-minute breaks between band performances. Chairs were provided on the platform, and there were toilets in the engine room beneath; these were approached down a stairway that moved with the platform, but not disturbing anything else in the basement. At night, everything was lighted by huge generators. Our specialist was really earning his keep, and running up enormous bills, but for a good cause.

Neusa and I, now that I was out from under the pressure cooker and she was home for a while, could make up for some of the time we had lost while she was away. We particularly enjoyed wonderful weekends at a charming hotel in Guaraja, off Santos, that was pure heaven – so relaxing, and so peaceful. It was always our favorite getaway from São Paulo, because it was reasonably accessible and particularly attentive to all our needs. Now that I think about it, I don't remember any other hotels there, anyway.

When the day of the event dawned, thank goodness the weatherman's prophecy was fulfilled: The humidity was at a surprisingly low reading, and there were plenty of non-rainy clouds to shade us from the sun. With a twelve-mile-an-hour breeze capable of stirring the air around us, it was weather worthy of the day. I was told later that buses and cars had been pouring in from all points of the compass from four in the morning, all anxious to secure their parking space. Because the state police had surmised that this might happen, the first shift was fortunately already in place by three a.m.

Neusa and I spent the morning together, and after lunch I went to the office at Ademar's headquarters to write checks for our superlative ringmaster. I was also charged with providing a bag of money for the workers, few of whom had bank accounts. The workers were listed in several grades; since there were quite a few of them, it took me almost until the evening, when Neusa had left to board Ademar's plane, to finish up at the office.

I showered and changed into fresh clothes; since it was a few minutes after six thirty, and it took only forty minutes to get there, I felt reasonably secure about my on-time arrival. Bad idea. All the upper-crust laggards who were Ademar fans had waited for the last minute to make their ride to the fazenda; they were now frantically racing each other in their incredibly elegant automobiles to be there by eight, by which time, as I discovered, too, their lateness would leave them to listen to Ademar's speech along with all the rest of the crowd, whether professors or taxi drivers. The platform, high above the crowd, was only for politicians. Actually, most of the laggards were very nice people, but at least at that time, tardiness appeared to be a virtue.

Because of all these cars on the way to the event, with two accidents holding us up for more than twenty minutes, my chauffeur got me there at ten minutes to eight. He parked beside a police headquarters, just beyond the crowd and some of the concession stands. There was a ladder against a pylon nearby. In order to decide how I was going to get to the platform, or failing that, to the helicopter pad, I climbed to the top, to be met by the most extraordinary sight I think I have ever seen. Many thousands of people were spread out in all directions, seemingly almost to the horizon, while the platform, from where Ademar was supposed to address the crowd, was a tiny dot in the midst of a swirling mass of humanity, amazingly all in good humor, as the curtain was soon to go up on the greatest speech of Ademar's life.

I was utterly stunned. I came back down the ladder and went into the state police headquarters, where I recognized the police captain whom I had met on more than one occasion at events in Ademar's home. Fortunately, he spoke some English. I was slowly explaining my present dilemma of wondering how to get to the helicopter pad in order to reach Ademar and Neusa, when I was transfixed by hearing Ademar's voice bellowing over the loudspeakers, "Peter, where are you? Peter, where are you?" over and over again. Then came Neusa's voice, saying, "Darling, call us, please call us if you are here." The captain pointed to one of three phones and personally dialed the internal phone to the platform. Ademar was quickly brought to the platform's phone; when he knew where I was, he told me to have the captain send a wedge of policemen to get me through to the helicopter on a road other than the one our car was on, but only about a thousand yards farther into the crowd from where I was. But with that mass of people, I couldn't see how it would be possible to get to the helicopter pad without starting a stampede, or worse still, seriously hurting people. I didn't know the São Paulo State Police. They were wonderful, as was the crowd. They had all picked up on my name, and from all over the fazenda, at first softly, and then gradually growing into an enormous, swelling wave, many in unison, thousands upon thousands upon thousands of voices rang it out at the top of their lungs -- Peter! Peter! Peter -- even after the helicopter had landed on the pad by the platform, which was still turning slowly in the late evening breeze.

To hear my name being called at the top of their lungs by a crowd of over sixty-five thousand happy people – they stopped counting after that number, though many more continued to arrive – was the most thrilling and exalting experience of my life. I could understand now what major successful politicians and world leaders, not to mention football stars and movie stars, enjoyed from the adulation of their fans. In my case, this was just a name being tossed in the wind, of no valid consequence to anybody, but it was *my name*. I felt like a child with his first lollipop.

But the show must go on. I was warmly welcomed by Neusa and Ademar, the latter making me feel truly that my cup runneth over, when he exclaimed to Neusa, "I might not be here without Peter's work on my campaign." He then introduced Neusa, and the vast crowd went wild. The Brazilians were great moviegoers, and there were few in that crowd who didn't know of the Hollywood honor that had been bestowed upon their Brazilian-made movie. Even if they couldn't see her, they knew the star was there, on the platform, and that was good enough.

The waves of adulation continued until Neusa began the first sentence of her speech introducing Ademar. In three minutes the crowd had simmered down to almost a stillness. Neusa made a brief but spectacular introduction that roused them up again, until she raised her arm, and a searchlight was turned on her, and she looked like Joan of Arc holding back the enemy. Like a wave receding from the shore, the multitudes in front became silent, and the silence rolled back until only the tinkle of children's voices could be heard under a night laced with stars.

When Ademar came to the microphone, there was one explosion of applause, and then Ademar raised his hand, and the waves of silence extended back into the uttermost edge of that giant configuration of mass humanity.

Ademar was at his best. I had never seen him so poised, so confident, so human. His message brought constant applause and cries of "Ademar! Ademar!"

I and other aides had spent a considerable amount of time crafting his speech, and then having him rehearse it and memorize it. It was a brilliant speech, most of the material having been provided by Ademar himself. It was material with which he was most comfortable, arranged by us to have a surprise attention-getting opening, a reasonably detailed explanation of the plans he wanted to put into effect and how they would better serve people's lives, and a crescendo of a finish. It worked.

Looking back on that day, I can say it really was just about flawless. The applause at the end was like thunder such as I have never heard. It was almost earbusting. It was not only beyond all sound, but you knew the sacrifice that this wonderful coalition had undergone to make it here and would have to endure again to return the way they had come. It was an enormous compliment to Ademar, and on this unique day their sincerity and admiration for him were totally true.

I returned with Neusa in the car I had come in, and we held hands like kids all the way back to our apartment. Ademar had told us he was staying overnight with his friend, the owner of the fazenda, in order to assure him that any destruction of any kind would be corrected or paid for, and also to show his appreciation for his friend's allowing his peaceful and profitable life to be temporarily overwhelmed with enough people to make up a small city.

In spite of the fact that we were all dead tired, that blessed crowd of people, with their extraordinary loyalty and enthusiasm for Ademar and his speech, had left us all in a euphoria of well being. Truth to tell, we didn't go right to sleep. We had better things to do.

Ademar was running ahead and working incredibly hard to keep the momentum going. He was flying from one political rally to the next in his private airplane, being greeted with great fanfare at almost every gathering. Sometimes he even came home in the middle of the week in order to discuss future plans and rest up before going back into the fray over the weekends, when more people were available to participate.

For me in particular, it was a breath of fresh air after the grueling lead-up to the Great Event. Unless Ademar wanted me with him for some reason, Neusa and I were able to relax and enjoy each other in a more leisurely manner, until she got an offer to take the lead in a new movie production that she said "she could taste." In other words, she thought the role suited her to a "T."

The only drawback, and it was a big one, was that the film would be shot far away in some out-of-reach part of the Amazon, where the entire production crew and actors would be housed in tents. Neusa, the director, and the producer would drop anchor in a bungalow on the rim of the area where most of the film would be shot. It was to be produced, directed, and recorded in six to eight weeks; no one would be permitted to leave for even one day – where was there to go, anyway? – unless it was a genuine matter of life or death. Except for bringing in supplies, no one from the outside would be allowed into the film company's province.

Though I would regret very much Neusa's absence for that length of time, it did open up the opportunity of speaking with her regarding the gamble of politics. I told her of Harry Truman's run for the Presidency of the United States of America, when a very large proportion of American citizens gave him no chance at all. And yet, his opponent, Thomas Dewey, did not win the election in spite of being a very popular and admired candidate, who seemed to a lot of people to be a shoo-in. Yet I was not a doubting Thomas at all. As long as Ademar stayed ahead of the field up until the votes were counted, he and I and a few others of our staff were counting on taking over an office inside the Brazilian White House.

But I told Neusa that I was at the same time thinking of returning to the United States and starting a new life there. That was my country, my people, my heritage, and I loved it dearly. If Ademar somehow lost the election, this would be as good a time as any to make that change.

Neusa thought I was crazy, and at times I kind of thought that way myself. In the meantime, members of the British and American colony were lionizing me with lunches and dinners, and introducing me to their friends returning from holidays in England and America as a man soon to be very powerful when Ademar de Barros became President of Brazil. Of course, a few of my friends were sincerely pleased, for my sake alone, that the prize was within Ademar's grasp, for they knew of my efforts to promote him in every way I possibly could. The rest of them just thought I was the one who would open doors and provide connections for their businesses and the sale of their products, with the imprint and support of my Catete office. Whenever they broached that subject, I told them that my area of work would not have anything whatsoever to do with their field of work; they needed, rather, to go to the American Consul's building in São Paulo and ask for the commercial attaché, who would be very pleased to provide them with whatever the Consulate was at liberty to provide. The same advice held for the British equivalent.

During that period, my watch went on the blink, and I took it to a jewelry store. The husband and wife owners restored it in no time, with a one-year warranty to boot. We became friends. They were Jewish, a bit older than I, with two children and three stores, including this one. They were very successful, and also very hardworking. We soon became more than just friends, and I was often invited to their beautiful home in an elegant part of town, equivalent to lower Berkeley Street in London's Mayfair, or Gramercy Square, Gramercy Park, in New York.

My friend had grown up in England and was well educated in private schools. His father had six jewelry stores in four cities. He had served in the British Army during the war, and afterward learned the jewelry business along with his wife under his father's tutelage. His parents had stayed on in England, but finally joined the son and daughter-in-law in their retirement.

My friends had left England for the same reason I had, that is, the grinding incursion into their lives by the tax collectors. This was not the tax collectors' fault, but the government's. Unfortunately it could do no less, or it would have bankrupted the nation.

Weeks passed, with Ademar cruising the states for ever more votes. I kept the pressure on, campaigning both by radio and news media, a vast expense, because it had to cover an enormous territory. But still the big money was coming in to carry the campaign to ever greater heights, and we in his executive suite, focused on this incredible drive for the presidency, were getting light headed and very happy, for the end was in sight. It would not be long now.

Neusa and I had become closer than ever. Because of our urgency and the limited time before she would leave to film in the Amazon, we grew to know each other so much better, finding so many qualities that we had not had the time or the opportunity to reveal until now. It was a glorious time for both of us, and when I finally had to see her off at the São Paulo airport, we both knew that, whatever happened in the future, our regard for each other had grown immeasurably. Come what might, we would always have these last weeks before the filming began, to cherish our memories or, better still, to build upon in the future.

Ademar's São Paulo headquarters was getting almost blasé by now. Ademar, who was pretty winded from all his traveling and speechmaking, was spending less time out in the field, saving his strength for the final two months leading up to the election itself. That would give him two weeks to relax, and an opportunity for me to help him with new speech ammunition.

And then it happened! Candidate Kubitschek had had a rally that very day before a much smaller audience than Ademar's, but in his speech to those attending, including the radio and print media, he declared that the main political plank in his program to gain the presidency would be to move the Brazilian government from Rio de Janeiro to a piece of land supposedly in the general location of the center of Brazil, where a new city would be built. This would open up that underprivileged area by creating a great new center of activity, where all the states would be on an equal footing with their government. This would replace the present arrangement where everybody had to go to Rio de Janeiro with hat in hand, knowing that the government, being in the city of Rio itself, would naturally provide great advantages to the politicians and citizens living there. Furthermore, the name for the new city, the city that the new government itself would eventually occupy, would be Brasilia.

The idea, when Kubitschek's speech was broadcast and hit the newspapers the next day, was at first discredited as a firecracker that didn't explode. But people talked about it, and in no time all the other states realized that, with the government transferred to Brasilia, Rio would no longer be the government's favorite. That is, after decades of taking second best, every state would find the floor level and open. Indeed, with so much available and negotiable as the government took its first steps into what was at present an isolated and barren piece of earth, everyone would have an equal chance. And it was to be named Brasilia: It would belong to everyone!

Hershel Johnson and all the other ambassadors hated the idea. Many thought it was just a quirky presidential contender's crazy dream to upset Ademar's successful campaign, after which the idea would never be carried out. Those who thought like this did not know Mr. Kubitschek, a handsome man with a keen political mind. That's all I can say about him because that's all I know about him, except that he will always be remembered as the founder, creator, and father of Brazil's present capital.

As for me, like most people I knew, I disregarded Kubitschek's speech as not worthy to worry over. I had not realized the resentment to the State of Rio de Janeiro held by practically all the other states.

The bottom had suddenly dropped out of Ademar's bandwagon. I knew that the grand prize had now been turned over to his contender, leaving Janio Quadros, the only other contender, in the dust. For Ademar and his staff, it was a real wallop in the stomach. We all felt sick and dislocated from events, numb and dejected after such a wonderful lead-up almost to the door of the Catete, only to be deprived of the prize by the brilliant move of a clever politician, who knew the time to strike and the weapon with which to do it.

To the victor ever go the spoils.

The New World

I t took two weeks to break down the campaign headquarters and its satellite offices spread throughout Brazil and turn Ademar's political and commercial empire back to normal. He kindly arranged to have Neusa flown back to be with me for three days, during which time the movie she was starring in would shut down for a brief break, while the cameramen were out busily taking background scenery to be incorporated later into her new film.

My beloved Neusa and I knew without saying it that we would probably never see each other again. Though it was heartbreaking beyond measure, deep down I knew that her acting talent would take her into many more successful movies, and that acting was the best and most rewarding accomplishment she could achieve. It was in her blood. She was an artist, and true artists are not like other people. I loved her dearly, and we wished each other well. Our pillows were wet with our tears on the morning she left me forever to return to the Amazon. God, I whispered, take good care of her.

My so-called friends who had been so proud of knowing me and making a great fuss over me, for the most part now turned away when seeing me, whispering among themselves, offering me nary a greeting of consolation.

Among other things, Mother had taught me two particular lessons. One was that, when I grew older, I should cultivate younger friends, or I would end up alone, and alone is not a good thing. The other was to ensure that I had some Jewish friends, for in times of adversity they might well be all I could depend on. Many of the rest of one's so-called friends, she observed, may have used you for their own benefit, and when they find

369

you are of no further use to them, they will drop you with impunity. But not your Jewish friends.

Soon after Kubitschek became the obvious winner, Ademar told me that in South America it is the custom for the losers in a Presidential election to get out of country for a year. He was going to Bolivia, and I was going back to America. He also told me to take all of my money out of my bank or it would be confiscated, at least for a while. He had had his money transferred to a Bolivian bank as soon as he realized his political dam had burst. Fortunately for him, he owned his own bank.

A year later, he returned to São Paulo, where in no time he was elected Mayor. God bless him, too, for he was always a wonderful friend to me. He even sent me out of Brazil on one of his transatlantic commercial planes that ended its flight in Miami.

As it turned out, half my money had already been siphoned out of my account before I stopped the bleeding and took what was left. The manager seemed under considerable stress but assured me that it would all be returned within the year. And so it was.

Incidentally, my godfather, Hershel, leaped into the fray when he realized the situation. In no time at all, my passport and papers were stamped and approved, and on my arrival in Miami, the American Consul met me at Hershel's request. He took me to a fine hotel on Miami Beach, where a room had been reserved for me and where I stayed for some time, enjoying the sun and the sand in a state of complete lethargy. In this utterly relaxed atmosphere, I finally realized how worn out I had become from all the past months of intense excitement and the everlasting nose to the grindstone, except for brief but infrequent reprieves.

Actually, my departure from the São Paulo airport for the US was a family affair – Bart's family affair, because not only Bart but all his family, including his parents, had come to see me off at the airport, along with my two faithful Jewish friends, plus a contingent from Ademar's office. Ademar himself had already said goodbye and flown on to Bolivia.

All of these people seeing me off were subdued and sad. We had been together for the most part during the best of times, and now it was difficult for all of us to part. I was glad when the call came to board the plane; we embraced with tears and anguished hugs and I walked quickly up the steps, waving to my cohort of well-wishers and decent people – my friends. Then I found my seat and, looking out the window, saw them re-entering the airport. Most of them I never saw again.

In 1959, I married Clementine Japour, and Bart and his wife paid us a visit at our Snell Isle home in St. Petersburg, Florida. My wife and I enjoyed their company very much, and we promised each other we would do it again when the opportunity arose. It never did, though we did keep up a correspondence for many years, always including a card at Christmastime.

Clementine Japour was a second-generation American of Lebanese extraction, with a brilliant legal mind, who was the manager of a fine law office in St. Petersburg. I adored her. It was an extraordinarily good marriage, and we had a wonderful life in St. Petersburg. In its own way, it was our Shangri-La. We had forty-four joyful years together until Clementine died in 2003. I will always miss her very much.

When I returned to America from Brazil, I was soon back in the public-relations field, from which I retired when I was sixty-two. My beloved stepfather, John Bigelow Dodge, died in 1961, and my precious mother, Minerva Arrington Dodge, died in 1980.

Life has been very good to me, as have my guardian angels. With few regrets, I end these memoirs, wishing all my blessed readers good health, and hoping that you have enjoyed reading about at least some of the events that I have recorded herein for your entertainment and edification.

Thank you for letting me be your guide.

The Author in 1960

Charles Austin Sherman III has lived a charmed life. As a young man had brushes with history's greatest characters starting with his actress mother and step-father war hero. His personal experiences allow the reader to touch the lives of such famous people as Hemmingway, Churchill, Eva Peron, Wallis Simpson, and Hitler.

Mr. Sherman continues to live a charmed life in Tampa, Florida.

CPSIA information can be obtained at www.ICGtesting.com
Printed in the USA
LVOW082208190412

278290LV00001B/388/P